THE BEST 80
BUSINESS
SCHOOLS

THE PRINCETON REVIEW

THE BEST 80
BUSINESS
SCHOOLS

2000 EDITION

BY NEDDA GILBERT

Random House, Inc.
New York

Princeton Review Publishing, L.L.C.
2315 Broadway
New York, NY 10024
E-mail: comments@review.com

ISSN: 1067-2141
ISBN: 0-375-75463-6

Editors: Gretchen Feder and Susan McCarthy
Production Editor: Julieanna Lambert
Production Coordinator: Scott Harris

Manufactured in the United States of America on partially recycled paper.

9 8 7 6 5 4 3 2 1

2000 Edition

Acknowledgments

This book absolutely would not have been possible without the help of my husband, Paul. With each edition of this guide, his insights and support have been invaluable—this book continues to be as much his as it is mine. That said, I also need to thank my five-year-old daughter, Micaela, and my newest addition, Alexa, for enduring all my time immersed in this project.

The following people were also instrumental in the completion of this book: My father, Dr. Irving Buchen, for his razor's-edge editorial suggestions; David Ro Hall—proofreader; Meher Khambata, who designed this book; Rob Zopf, for his tireless phone interviews with business school administrators; Evan Schnittman, Tom Meltzer, Susan McCarthy, Kristin Waldron, Julieanna Lambert, Iam Williams, Karl Engkvist, Jens Stephan, Gretchen Feder, and Laurie Barnett for putting all the pieces together; Alicia Ernst and John Katzman, for giving me the chance to write this book; and to the folks at Random House, who helped this project reach fruition. Special thanks go to all those section-A mates, HBS-92, who lent a hand and provided valuable feedback. Likewise, I'd like to acknowledge Lea Hallert for her insights on technology and business education.

Thanks are also due to the business school folks who went far out of their way to provide essential information:

Robert J. Alig, Director of Admissions—The Wharton School, MBA Program

Will Makris, Director of Admissions—Babson University

David Irons—University of California, Berkeley

Allan Friedman, Director of Communications—University of Chicago

Carol Swanberg, Director of Admissions and Financial Aid—University of Chicago

Meyer Feldberg, Dean, and Ethan Hanabury, Director of Admissions—Columbia Business School

Skip Horne, Director of Admissions, and Elaine Ruggieri, Director of Public Relations—University of Virginia

Cathy Castillo and her staff at the News and Publications Office—Stanford University

Marie Mookini, Director of Admissions—Stanford University

Contents

Preface

In the late 1980s, The Princeton Review began working with Fortune 500 companies to provide their employees with on-site preparation classes for the GMAT. In the course of our work, it became clear that most of these prospective business school students were lacking critical information about the business school admissions process on which they were about to embark. Over and over, students asked:

- How many times should I take the GMAT?
- If I take it twice, which score will admissions offices count?
- How high does my score need to be?
- What points do I need to make in my essays?
- What if all I've done is work? I don't have any extracurriculars to write about.
- Should I interview?
- How much do my grades count?
- Who should write my recommendation—an immediate boss who knows me well or a senior V.P. who's a power alum of the school?
- When's the best time to send in the application—early or close to the deadline?

These students were confused, with good reason. Unlike high school students—who can turn to guidance counselors and professional advisors for help navigating the undergraduate admissions process—prospective MBAs have almost nowhere to turn for advice on selecting and applying to the right business school. Even the information that is available—mainly guidebooks and magazine rankings—is obscure and contradictory. What, then, is a b-school applicant to do?

READ THIS BOOK

We surveyed 18,500 students, hundreds of admissions officers, and dozens of recruiters and business school grads to bring you the real scoop on b-school.

Want to know what really happens to the applications you toiled, sweated, and bled over? This book gives you an exclusive inside look at the deliberations of top admissions committees—University of Chicago and Babson College—and shows you what committee members are looking for in an applicant. Ever wonder who actually reads your essays? We not only tell you, we show you what they liked about fifteen essays submitted to twelve top schools. This book tells you what admissions officers are looking for in an essay. Marie Mookini, Director of Admissions for Stanford Graduate School of Business, outlines specific advice on how to write an honest and vivid essay. Discover what your life as a business school student will be like, what to talk about in your interviews, when to apply, and more. But, most importantly, this book gives you essential facts, unique insights, and up-to-the-minute information on the nation's top 80 b-schools, so you can make an educated decision about where you should apply.

WHY THESE 80 SCHOOLS?

For several years now, two leading magazines have been telling you who's hot and who's not. They've crunched objective data and subjective ratings into a quantified format to create the perception of precise numerical rankings. But the rankings are as imprecise as they are arbitrary. The weighting of different criteria leads to dramatically different interpretations of a program. While the rankings make news and sell a lot of magazines, in real life, prospective students are equally, if not more, interested in those characteristics that distinguish one school from another. What makes a program tops? To find the answers, we took a more holistic approach and gathered input from a variety of sources.

First on our list was student opinion. Mass-interview style, we surveyed more than 18,500 currently matriculated b-school students. We surveyed hundreds of admissions officers and administrators. In addition, we looked at more traditional measures, including a school's acceptance rate, applicants' GPAs and GMAT scores, placement rate, curriculum, learning environment, and caliber of the student body. As we progressed, we learned that many lesser-known schools belonged in this book because of their regional reputation, star faculty, "bang for the buck," or unique course offerings. Finally, we sought to focus on those schools that are accredited by the International Association for Management Education (referred to as the AACSB because of its previous name, the American Assembly of Collegiate Schools of Business, www.aacsb.edu). Of the more than 800 business programs in the nation, 355 are accredited by AACSB. Almost all of the schools included in this book are accredited by the AACSB with the exception of four schools, three of which are international representatives—Pepperdine University, University of Western Ontario (Canada), INSEAD (France), and London Business School (England). We've included these nonaccredited schools because employers and academics regard them, widely and accurately, as top business schools. We've also added Boston College, University of California—Davis, University of California—Irvine, and University of

South Carolina to this new edition. In a few cases, schools that might have met our criteria for inclusion had to be omitted because they wouldn't allow us to poll their students.

A final note: We've chosen to list schools in our book alphabetically, rather than rank them. We believe our profiles highlight each program's major strengths and weaknesses, as well as capture its distinct personality. The profiles take into account the reputation, prestige, and status of a school without ranking it. The question is, which school is the best for you? We hope this book helps you make the right choice.

GMAT CHANGES

In recent years the GMAT has evolved from a paper-and-pencil exam to a CAT (Computer Adaptive Test). Once entirely multiple-choice, the GMAT now includes two essay questions, collectively known as the AWA (Analytic Writing Assessment). To get the lowdown on the exam, pick up our book *Cracking the GMAT* (with or without CD-ROM), which includes both the latest information available on the GMAT CAT and, of course, our techniques and tips on how to beat the test. If you're an expert at math, but weak in the verbal areas (or vice versa), check out *GMAT Verbal Workout* or *GMAT Math Workout*. They both review the latest info, but focus only on math or verbal techniques. We'd also be happy to tell you about The Princeton Review's intensive six-week GMAT course. You can reach us at 1-800-REVIEW-6 or by e-mail at comments@review.com. Whatever you do, we wish you good luck in b-school and beyond!

Introduction

AT THE TOP B-SCHOOLS, BUSINESS IS BOOMING AND GETTING IN IS GETTING TOUGH

ONCE UPON A BEAR MARKET

The MBA, often perceived as the golden passport to power and wealth, took some hard knocks in the late 1980s. First, there were all those business scandals in the 1980s that made MBAs look smarmy. Then corporate downsizing shrunk middle management (the destination for grads), and job prospects became bleak. To make matters worse, corporate recruiters became critical of MBA programs, claiming that the business education added no measurable value to the skills of those it was graduating. What was an MBA wannabe to do? Many switched to graduate study in areas in which there was renewed interest—teaching, medicine, and public service. Others decided to forgo the degree. The bottom line? By 1992, the number of individuals taking the Graduate Management Admissions Test (GMAT) had dropped 20 percent from its peak level.

B-schools fell on tough times. Even top-tier programs couldn't count on a bottomless cup of applications, much less a high yield of the applicants they accepted. To fill the spots, schools had to work harder. Applicants were aggressively wooed, provided 800 numbers and Saturday interviews, and treated to personal calls from the dean and faculty. Admission into the top schools was still tough, but under these circumstances, getting in was relatively easier.

MBAs: GOLDEN AGAIN

But of course, things change. Enter the late-1990s. A surge in applications, starting salaries, and more job offers and favorable press have made the MBA a winning ticket again. Applications have swung back to levels not seen since the 1980s. At Columbia University, for example, admissions officers are reporting application increases of 100 percent over the last five years. A fixed number of spaces in the top programs means it's even more competitive to get in. The 10 most selective schools accepted only 12 percent of applicants on average in 1998. The top 25 most selective schools accepted just 21 percent on average.

Is the surge in applications limited to the very top schools? No. The Graduate Management Admissions Council reports that in 1997, 80 percent of the 100 schools it surveyed saw an increase in applications, the largest increase in their applicant pool in years. In fact, more than a quarter of the programs saw the number of applications surge 20 percent or more.

"Everyone refers to the mid-1980s as the long-gone heyday for MBAs," says Ethan Hanabury, the former associate director of admissions and administration at Columbia Business School. "But the myth that the MBA is no longer essential has been thoroughly debunked by double-digit increases at the top schools."

Applications at the University of Chicago mirror the trend. For Carol Swanberg, Director of Admissions and Financial Aid at Chicago and newly arrived from the University of Pittsburgh's Katz School, settling in has been a bit like riding a tidal wave: "In just this year alone, we saw an enormous increase in applications, over 28 percent for students who will matriculate in the fall of 1999. We've had increases before, but nothing this dramatic. Our acceptance rate is now probably around 15 percent. Last year, it was 23 percent." Adds Swanberg, "People are valuing the experience of the MBA. What we're seeing in our applications and follow-up letters are candidates mentioning that there are three or so Chicago MBAs that sit next to them, or that they work with. So, there are large numbers of our alumni out there who are having an influence on their peers in terms of what the MBA can do for them."

Robert J. Alig, director of admissions and financial aid for the Wharton MBA Program, concurs, "The MBA Class of 1998 was another record breaker for the Wharton School, a remarkable feat given that last year's applications were up nearly 20 percent over the previous year. The incredible momentum we've seen over the last several years has continued . . . . The competition to date has been incredible, with the average GMAT for admitted students being nearly 680. We're also seeing a higher average undergraduate GPA versus last year's class." Nearly 7,500 students applied for the 750 spots available in Wharton's Class of 1998.

Alig also observes that, "As students have witnessed record numbers of applications over the last few years, they've become more savvy consumers. They've started doing a better job of looking at how they might use some of the objective data of the various rankings to clarify the best fit and where they are going to excel. This is a positive for both students and the programs because more candidates are better equipped to contribute both inside and outside the classroom. A student's self-assessment of his or her fit with our school is a critical component of our evaluation."

MBA MANIA

Gurus point to several factors. First, major curriculum overhauls at the b-schools have helped to produce better-trained, more well-rounded managers. Now that programs are integrating real-life management, leadership, and teamwork projects into class study, business students are graduating with more relevant experiences. Satisfied recruiters say these experiences have expanded the skill set of newly minted MBAs so that they better grasp the complexities of modern business at the beginning of the new millennium.

Second, the longest period of economic expansion on record has made MBAs, once again, critical to the workforce. After jettisoning layers of middle management during the cost-cutting years of the early 1990s, corporate America now finds it often lacks the management depth to pursue growth initiatives. This is particularly true of industries hit hardest by the cost cutting: health care, telecommunications, and financial services. Further, the economy is widely recognized to be evolving toward a "knowledge-based" economy in which managers must be adept at managing ambiguous environments. These are among the skills b-schools have sought to develop in their retooled curriculums. The emerging corporate environment is tailor-made for MBA skills—skills that emphasize strategic insight, analytical thinking, and team building to be used in environments where decisions need to be made quickly without always having all of the necessary information. Strategic decisions are no longer anchored to the annual strategic planning process. In our wired economy, decisions must be made in Internet time. Entirely new business models are emerging. Industries that were once stable are now colliding into one another and converging to pursue of revenue streams from new markets and new technologies.

As corporate America has returned its attention to graduating MBAs, b-schools have transformed their long-neglected placement offices into key components of their programs. From installing state-of-the-art computer databases to hiring more career counselors to giving facilities a decorating makeover, b-schools have made recruiting efforts a priority.

Led by the consulting firms and investment banks, industry flagships are rushing b-schools for the best and the brightest. These days, students at the most prestigious schools are finding themselves with multiple job offers, a robust return on their investment.

DESTINATION: SIX-FIGURE SALARIES AND SIGN-ON BONUSES THAT WIPE OUT STUDENT LOANS

After six years of unprecedented growth, a booming economy seems a sure thing, and MBAs have a rosy future. It's easier to get back into the workforce when the economy is in an upswing. After coming of age during a period of corporate restructurings and layoffs, applicants now consider the MBA insulation from future downsizings. Further, with 40 million BAs out there, the opportunity to differentiate oneself with an MBA, particularly from a top-tier school, is still alluring.

But what's the number one reason for the surge in MBA applications? Why would you want to drop out of the workplace for two years and pay up to $50,000 in tuition? Money. And lots of it. Starting salaries have shot off the scale for freshly minted MBAs from premium schools. In just the last ten years, average compensation packages have increased by a dramatic 30 percent. Students at the best schools can now expect to pocket offers with an average range of $75,000–$150,000.

And for those entering the consulting profession, the rewards can be even higher. According to the Kennedy Information Research Group, average starting salaries in consulting are up 9.4 percent from last year to a high of $139,000. Stanford grads can expect as much as a staggering $165,000 total first year package, evidence of the value recruiters place on elite talent. But there's plenty to go around.

With the fierce demand for MBAs, it's not just show me the money, but throw me the money, and lots of it. Recruiters dangle everything from double-digit sign-on bonuses (*and* end-of-year bonuses) to tuition reimbursement paybacks and generous stock options to get their grad. At the top-tier schools starting compensation packages average $126,000, more than one-and-a-half times what their graduates made before entering the program. In fact, the average starting comp package for the next 15 most selective programs is still more than $100,000. Of course, all of this makes today's newly minted MBAs newly rich. And the return on investment has never been greater.

BUT GETTING IN IS BECOMING EXTREME

What does all this mean? Basically this: If you plan on applying to the most competitive programs this year, brace yourself. Perhaps you were a sure shot in previous years. But this time around, you'll enter a far more competitive pool. You will be competing not only against a reinvigorated group of candidates who were always interested in getting the MBA, but also against applicants who in years past would have been pursuing legal careers. Scared off by the glut of lawyers, lots of aspiring attorneys have reconsidered their career choices; in recent years, the number of people taking the LSAT has actually dropped.

So getting in is tougher than ever. At some of the most popular b-schools they accept as few as 9 percent of applicants. Of course, in a b-school bull market the payoffs are bigger. But if you want to beat the odds, you'll need to develop a solid application strategy and apply to a diverse portfolio of schools.

Alig advises, "I don't think it's effective to apply to ten or so schools. It compromises a student's ability to critically evaluate each program and do a thorough job on each of the applications by spreading him or herself too thin." His advice: "Apply to four or five. Make one or two a long shot. Make another a solid possibility. And another very safe."

"Over the course of this year we've conducted nearly 6,000 interviews of prospective students, including 3,000 on campus," adds Alig. "One of the reasons we've made the decision to interview as many applicants as we can is to give applicants every opportunity to distinguish themselves from the applicant pool—even if their experiences are quite similar to another candidate's. The interview gives us insights into choices they've made, and that automatically sheds light on their individuality. And this is what our applicants are struggling with—a way to truly distinguish themselves. Just listing the data points on their resume doesn't do that."

Perhaps Alig best sums up the scenario for admissions officers at the top schools: "It's become almost a cliché; most students who apply to this program can handle the workload." But the hurdle for successful applicants is higher: "I'm looking for someone who has left an indelible impression on me that he or she will make the business school community stronger by being here."

PROVEN STRATEGIES FOR WINNING ADMISSION

So now you know. Admission to the top programs will require your absolute best shot. Thousands and thousands of prospective MBA candidates spend loads of time and money making sure they select, and are in turn admitted to, the "best" school. Their time and money go toward working in jobs they think will impress a b-school, studying and preparing for the GMAT, writing essays, interviewing, visiting prospective schools, and buying guides like—but not as good as—this one.

This book is your best bet. It takes you into the secret deliberations of the admissions committees at the top schools. You get a firsthand look at who decides your fate. More important, you learn what criteria are used to evaluate applicants. As we found out, things aren't always the way you'd expect them to be. You also get straight talk from admissions officers—what dooms an application and how to ace the interview.

In addition to getting inside information on the application process, you learn when the best time to apply is, how to answer the most commonly asked essay questions, and the key points to make in your essays. There's also loads of information on what you can do before applying to increase your odds of gaining admission.

We also give you the facts—from the most up-to-date information on major curricula changes and placement rates to demographics of the student body—for the seventy-five best b-schools in the country. And we've included enough information about them—which we gathered from admissions officers, administrators, and students—to help you make a smart decision about where to go.

Good luck!

B-school Admission Goes Electronic

Universities were among the first organizations on the Internet and most MBA programs have a lot of useful information online. B-school web sites typically include detailed information about the program, course offerings, housing options, and campus life. If you are at all interested in a school, checking out its web site is a great way to gather more facts.

PRINCETON REVIEW ONLINE

One of the best places to start your search for b-school information on the Internet is at Princeton Review Online—www.review.com/business. There you can access a variety of services to help you learn more about universities and the b-school admissions process.

Find-O-Rama

Our b-school search engine, Find-O-Rama, is the most sophisticated MBA program search tool available on the Internet and is a great companion to this book. To use Find-O-Rama, you first enter as much (or as little) data as you like about your preferences. You can narrow your search by region, average GMAT scores of admitted applicants, and program size and by using the specialized Quality of Life rating and other b-school characteristics that are in our database. The result of the Find-O-Rama search is a list of all the schools that match your needs and links to those b-schools' web sites.

B-school Admissions Discussion

Visitors to our discussion group post messages describing their experiences as they go through the admissions process and get expert advice from Princeton Review moderators. It's the most popular MBA admissions discussion area anywhere on the Net.

Remind-O-Rama

The b-school admissions process is filled with dates and deadlines. Remind-O-Rama can help you keep on schedule by sending you e-mail reminders about the deadlines for everything from your top choice's application deadline to the day you need to buy your boss' birthday present.

THE GMAT

As previously mentioned, the GMAT is now offered only in the computer-adaptive (CAT) format. The test begins with two essay questions, called the Analytical Writing Assessment (AWA). In the past, all essay questions that have appeared on the official GMAT have been drawn from a list of about 150 topics that appear in The Official Guide to the GMAT (ETS). Review that list and you'll have a pretty good idea of what to expect from the AWA. By the way, you will be required to type your essay at the computer.

Next comes a 75-minute math section. The math section includes standard problem-solving questions (e.g., "Train A leaves Baltimore at 6:32 a.m. . . .") and data-sufficiency questions; for these questions you must determine whether you have been given enough information to solve a particular math problem. The good news about data sufficiency is that you don't actually have to solve the problem; the bad news is these questions can be very tricky.

The test ends with a 75-minute verbal section. The verbal section tests reading skills (reading comprehension), grammar (sentence correction), and logic (critical reasoning).

For those unfamiliar with CAT exams, here's a brief overview of how they work: on multiple-choice sections, the computer starts by asking a question of medium difficulty. If you answer it correctly, the computer asks you a question that is slightly more difficult than the previous question. If you answer incorrectly, the computer asks a slightly easier question next. The test continues this way until you have answered enough questions that the computer program can assign you an accurate score, at which point the section ends.

APPLYING TO B-SCHOOL VIA ELECTRONIC APPLICATION

Once you've gathered all the information that you need about the schools and have decided where to apply, you may not need to leave your keyboard. Just a handful of years ago, electronic applications were never going to happen. Today, business schools are scrambling to make electronic versions of their applications available.

There is an excellent package for electronic applications, and we've convinced one company to give you a 10 percent discount on the software because you bought *The Best 80 Business Schools*. (Make sure to mention this book, and don't say we never gave you anything.) The package is called MBA MULTI-App. The software allows you to fill out your applications on-screen, print out exact replicas of the school's applications, and submit them directly to the admissions offices. When you use the program, you only have to enter common information once, saving you time and hassle.

You can sample MBA MULTI-App's HeadStart Edition (which contains the previous year's applications for participating schools) for FREE by installing the CD-ROM included with this book. The HeadStart Edition is a trial software package that allows you to complete 90 percent of your b-school application before the new versions of the applications become available, and then you can transfer this data into MULTI-App's most recent software when it becomes available (usually in early August).

The software is available for Windows computers, versions 3.1 and above. You can download the software for FREE from MULTI-App's website and later purchase your individual PIN number allowing you to print valid copies of the schools' applications. To order the 2000 edition of MBA MULTI-App, call MBA MULTI-App at (800) 516-2227, fax them at (610) 544-9877, submit an order through their secure online order form at www.multi-app.com, or write them at MCS MULTI-App, 740 South Chester Road, Suite D, Swarthmore, PA 19081.

A final note of advice: No matter which form of electronic application you choose, you should still contact the admissions office for an application packet. This guarantees that you will have all the information and materials that you need to put together the strongest candidacy possible. Some, but not all, schools will let you download this information at their web sites; usually, such information is packaged as a .pdf file, which can only be read by a free, downloadable program called Adobe Reader (www.adobe.com/acrobat). Still, despite the increasing online presence of business schools and the convenience of the electronic medium, "snail mail" remains an integral part of the process.

If you have any questions, comments, or suggestions, please e-mail your insights to us at comments@review.com. We appreciate your input and want to make our books as useful to you as they can be.

Part I

ALL ABOUT B-SCHOOL

Picking the Right Business School for You

## Chapter 1

MAKING THE DECISION TO GO

The first step for you may be b-school. Indeed, armed with an MBA you may journey far. But the success of your trip and the direction you take will depend on knowing exactly why you're going to b-school and just what you'll be getting out of it.

The most critical questions you need to ask yourself are the following: Do you really want a career in business? What do you want the MBA to do for you? Are you looking to gain credibility, accelerate your development, or move into a new job or industry? Perhaps you're looking to start your own business, and entrepreneurial study will be important.

Knowing what you want doesn't just affect your decision to go, it also affects your candidacy; admissions committees favor applicants who have clear goals and objectives. Moreover, once at school, students who know what they want make the most of their two years. If you're uncertain about your goals, opportunities for career development—such as networking, mentoring, student clubs, and recruiter events—are squandered.

You also need to find a school that fits your individual needs. Consider the personal and financial costs. This may be the single biggest investment of your life. How much salary will you forego by leaving the workforce? What will the tuition be? How will you pay for it? If you have a family, spouse, or significant other, how will getting your MBA affect them?

If you do have a spouse, you may choose a program that involves partners in campus life. If status is your top priority, you should simply choose the most prestigious school you can get into.

The MBA presents many opportunities, but no guarantees. As with any opportunity, you must make the most of it. Whether you go to a first-tier school or to a part-time program close to home, you'll acquire the skills that can jump start your career. But your success will have more to do with you than with the piece of paper your MBA is printed on.

WHY THE RANKINGS AREN'T A USEFUL GUIDE TO SCHOOL SELECTION

All too many applicants rely on the magazine rankings to decide where to apply. Caught up with winners, losers, and whoever falls in between, their thinking is simply: Can I get into the top five? Top ten? Top fifteen?

But it's a mistake to rely on the rankings. Benjamin Disraeli once said, "There are lies, damn lies, and statistics." Today, he'd probably add b-school rankings. Why? Because statistics rarely show the whole picture. When deciding on the validity of a study, it's wise to consider how the study was conducted and what exactly it was trying to measure.

First, the rankings have made must-read news for several years. Not surprisingly, some of the survey respondents—current b-school students and recent grads—now know there's a game to play. The game is this: Give your own school the highest marks possible. The goal: that coveted number-one spot. Rumor has it that some schools even remind their students of how their responses will affect the stature of their program. This kind of self-interest is known as respondent bias, and the b-school rankings suffer from it in a big way.

The rankings feature easy-to-measure differences such as selectivity, placement success, and proficiency in the basic disciplines. But these rankings don't allow for any intangibles—such as the progressiveness of a program, the school's learning environment, and the happiness of the students.

To create standards by which comparisons can be made, the rankings force an evaluative framework on the programs. But this is like trying to evaluate a collection of paintings—impressionist, modern, classical, and cubist—with the same criteria. Relying on narrow criteria to evaluate subjective components fails to capture the true strengths and weaknesses of each school.

The statistically measurable differences that the magazines base their ratings on are often so marginal as to be insignificant. In other words, it's too close to call the race. Perhaps in some years two schools should be tied for the number-one spot. What would the tie-breaker look like? A rally cry of "We're number one" with the loudest school winning?

A designation as the number-one, number-five, or number-ten school is almost meaningless when you consider that it changes from year to year—and from magazine to magazine. (At least Olympic medalists enjoy a four-year victory lap.)

JUDGING FOR YOURSELF

Depending on what you're looking for, the rankings may tell you something about the b-schools. But it's wise to use them as approximations rather than the declarations of fact they're made out to be.

The rankings don't factor in your values or all of the criteria you need to consider. Is it selectivity? The highest rate of placement? The best starting salary? Surprise! The number-one school is not number one in all these areas. No school is.

The best way to pick a program is to do your homework and find a match. For example, if you have limited experience with numbers, then a program with a heavy quantitative focus may round out your resume. If you want to stay in your home area, then a local school that's highly regarded by the top regional companies may be best for you. If you know that you want to go into a field typified by cutthroat competition, or a field in which status is all-important . . . well, obviously, keep your eyes on those rankings.

You also need to consider your personal style and comfort zone. Suppose you get into a "top-ranked" school, but the workload is destroying your life, or the mentality is predatory. It won't matter how prestigious the program is if you don't make it through. Do you want an intimate and supportive environment or are you happy to blend in with the masses? Different schools will meet these needs. Lecture versus case study, specialization versus broad-based general management curriculum, and heavy finance versus heavy marketing are other kinds of trade-offs.

One last thing to consider is social atmosphere. What is the spirit of the student body? Do students like each other? Are they indifferent? Perhaps a bit hostile? If you go through graduate school in an atmosphere of camaraderie, you'll never forget those two years. But if you go through school in an atmosphere of enmity . . . okay, you'll still remember those two years. It's up to you to decide how you want to remember them.

Remember when you applied to college? You talked to friends, alumni, and teachers. You visited the campus and sat in on classes (or should have). It's not all that different with b-school. Here are some of the things you should check out:

ACADEMICS

- Academic reputation
- International reputation
- Primary teaching methodology
- Renown and availability of professors
- General or specialized curriculum
- Range of school specialties
- Opportunities for global/foreign study
- Emphasis on teamwork
- Fieldwork/student consulting available
- Student support—extra study sessions, accessible faculty, tutoring
- Academic support—libraries, computer facilities, and expertise
- Grading/probation policy
- Workload/hours per week in class
- Class and section size
- Pressure and competition

CAREER

- Summer and full-time job placement (number of companies recruiting on and off campus)
- Placement rate
- Average starting salaries
- Salaries at five-year mark
- Career support—assistance with career planning, resume preparation, interview skills
- Networking with visiting executives

QUALITY OF LIFE

- Location
- Campus
- Orientation
- Range of student clubs/activities
- Diversity of student body
- Housing
- Social life
- Spouse/partner group
- Recreational facilities

EXPENSE

- Tuition
- Books, computer
- Cost of living
- Financial aid

HOW TO USE THIS BOOK

Each of the business schools listed in this book has its own two-page spread. Each spread has six components: two "sidebars" (the narrow columns on the outside of each page that contain statistics) and four profiles on each school (that contain actual student quotes).

Here's what's in each section.

THE SIDEBARS

The sidebars contain various statistics that we gathered either from the questionnaires we sent to the schools or from our own student surveys. Some schools did not provide us information for all categories; in this case the statistic is left out of the sidebar.

OVERVIEW

■ *Type of School*

Whether the school is public or private.

■ *Affiliation*

Any religion with which the school is affiliated.

■ *Environment*

Whether the campus is located in an urban, suburban, or rural setting.

■ *Academic Calendar*

How the school breaks up its academic year (i.e., semesters, trimesters).

■ *Schedule*

Whether the school offers full-time or part-time schedules.

STUDENTS

■ *Enrollment of Parent Institution/Enrollment of Business School*

Total number of students in the entire institution and MBA program.

■ *Percent Men, Percent Women, Percent Out-of-State, Percent Part-Time, Percent Minorities, Percent International Students, Number of Countries Represented, Average Age at Entry, and Average Years Work Experience at Entry.*

The demographic breakdown of last year's entering class.

ACADEMICS

■ *Student/Faculty Ratio, Percent of Female Faculty, Percent of Minority Faculty, Percent of Part-Time Faculty, and Hours of Study Per Day.*

A breakdown of the faculty and the amount of work they pile on.

■ *Specialties*

This tells you what specialized curriculum options are available to allow students to major in or specialize in one or two areas.

■ *Joint Degrees*

Lists any special graduate degrees offered by the school.

■ *Special Programs/Study Abroad Programs*

Lists any exchange, internship, or job programs.

HITS AND MISSES

Summarizes the results of our survey. The lists show what students felt unusually strong about, both positively and negatively, at their schools. Following are the categories:

- Gym—if this appears under the "hits" list, the students at the school love the gym facilities; if it appears under the "misses" list, the students are dissatisfied with the facilities.

- Helping Other Students—if this appears under the "hits" list, the students feel that students are willing to help each other; if it appears under the "misses" list, the students feel that their classmates aren't willing to help each other.

- Accounting Skills—students rated their improvement in the area of accounting. If this listing appears under the "hits" list, the students were happy with the quality of accounting instruction; if it appears under the "misses" list, they were not satisfied.

- Finance Skills—same as above, only for finance skills.

- Marketing Skills—same, only for marketing skills.

- Quantitative Skills—same as above, mutatis mutandis.

- Placement—a rating of the efficiency of the school's job placement office.

- Ethnic and Racial Diversity—students were asked whether their school is ethnically and racially diverse. If it is, this rating appears in the "hits" list; if not, it appears under "misses."

- Classmates Are Smart/Classmates Are Below Average—reveals students' opinions about the intelligence of their classmates.

- Recruiting—rates students' satisfaction with their school's recruiting efforts.

- Social Life—if students have active social lives, this rating appears in the "hits" list; if not, it appears in the "misses" list.

- Diverse Work Experience—this rating appears in the "hits" list if students said their classmates had come from diverse work backgrounds; if it appears in the "misses" list students came mostly from the same type of company.

- Off-campus Housing—students' rating of the quality of off-campus housing.

- On-campus Housing—students' rating of the quality of on-campus housing.

- Library—a rating of the usefulness of the library.

- Location—this is a rating of whether or not students like the town in which their school is located.

- Cozy Student Community/Don't Like Classmates—students were asked whether they liked to hang out with their classmates. If they did, "Cozy student community" appears in the "hits" list; if not, "Don't like classmates" appears in the "misses" list.

- School Clubs—a rating of the breadth and number of extracurricular clubs and organizations on campus.

- Staying in Touch—students were asked whether their classmates were the kind of people they'd want to stay in contact with after business school. If this rating appears in the "hits" list, they did want to stay in touch with their classmates; if it appears in the "misses" list, they felt they wouldn't stay in touch.

PROMINENT ALUMNI

Lists some of the shining MBA stars of the past and what they're doing now.

FINANCIAL FACTS

■ *In-state Tuition, Out-of-state Tuition, Tuition per Credit, Fees, Estimated Cost of Books, Costs of On-campus and Off-campus Housing, Percent of Students Receiving Aid, Percent of First-year Students Receiving Aid, Percent of Aid that Is Merit-based, Percent of Students Receiving Loans, Percent of Students Receiving Paid Internships, Percent of Students Receiving Grants, Average Award Package, Average Grant, and Average Graduation Debt.*

ADMISSIONS

■ *Number of Applicants, Percent of Applicants Accepted, Percent of Applicants Enrolled for Last Year's Entering Class, Average GMAT Score, Minimum TOEFL Score, Average Undergrad GPA, Application Fee, Whether an Early Decision Program Is Available, Early and Regular Application Deadlines and Dates of Notification, Admission Deferment, Transfer Policy, Nonfall Admission, and Whether the Admissions Process Is Need-blind.*

APPLICANTS ALSO LOOK AT

Lists other schools applicants also consider.

EMPLOYMENT PROFILE

■ *Placement Rate, Number of Companies Recruiting On Campus, Percent of Graduates Employed Immediately and Within Six Months of Graduation, Average Starting Salary, and Percent Breakdown According to the Individual Employment Fields Graduates Enter.*

THE PROFILES

Academics

This section describes the academic atmosphere of each school, what the professors are like, where the curriculum is headed, and what students think about the education they are receiving.

Placement and Recruiting

One of the most important issues to MBAs is the quality and efficacy of their school's recruiting and placement offices. This section explains the programs each school offers.

Student/Campus Life

From dating to off-campus housing, this section describes the social atmosphere and quality of life at each campus.

Admissions

This section tells you what aspects of applications are most important to the school's admissions officers. We used the admissions officers' responses to our questionnaire, as well as telephone interviews with many admissions officers, to write this section.

A GLOSSARY OF INSIDER LINGO

You've probably already noticed this, but b-school students, graduates, and professors—like most close-knit, somewhat solipsistic groups—seem to speak their own weird language. With that in mind, here's one last set of tools that will help you on your way through this book and into the business world: a list of MBA jargon (with English translations).

Air Hogs: students who monopolize classroom discussion and who love to hear themselves speak.

Air Time: a precious opportunity—speaking or making comments in class.

Analysis Paralysis: not being able to make a decision because you've gotten lost in the thicket of your own analysis.

Back of the Envelope: an abbreviated analysis of the numbers.

Barriers to Entry: conditions that prevent entry into a particular market.

Beta of a Stock: the inherent volatility of a stock.

Bottleneck: the point in a plant or process that determines or blocks the pace.

Burn Rate: amount of cash a company consumes each day.

Case Cracker: a comment in class that gets to the essence of case.

Case Study Method: popular teaching method that uses real-life business cases for analysis.

Chip Shots: unenlightening comments made during class discussion for the sole purpose of getting credit.

Cold Call: unexpected, often dreaded request by the professor to open a case.

Core Courses: courses in the basic disciplines of business, usually mandatory.

Corner Office: office location that all MBAs aspire to and the exclusive province of partners, managing directors, and senior executives.

Cost-Benefit Analysis: calculating whether something is worth doing on the basis of the real dollar cost versus real dollar benefit. This is often used as a shortcut in analyzing the numbers.

Cycle Time: how fast you can turn something around.

Deliverable: what your end product is.

Finheads: finance heads. See also sharks.

Four Ps: elements of a marketing strategy—Price, Promotion, Place, Product.

Fume Date: date the company will run out of cash reserves.

Functional Areas: the basic disciplines of business.

Globalization: trend of the 1980s and 1990s; expanding the definition of your market to include the challenges of operating in a multicountry, multiconsumer market.

Hard Courses: anything with numbers.

HP12-C: the calculator of choice for number crunching.

I-Bankers: investment banking analysts coming out of the two-year training programs and into b-school.

Incentivize: a bastardized version of the word incentive, used as a verb.

MBA Weenies: students who believe that once they get their MBAs, they'll be masters of the universe.

Net Net: end result.

OOC: out of cash.

Opportunity Costs: the cost of pursuing an opportunity, for example, for b-school, tuition and loss of income for two years.

Out-of-the-Box Thinking: business strategies that challenge conventional business wisdom.

Poets: students with little quantitative skills or experience (numerically challenged).

Power Naps: quick, intense in-class recharge for the continually sleep deprived.

Power Tool: someone who does all the work and sits in the front row of the class with his or her hand up.

Pre-enrollment Courses: commonly known as MBA summer camp—quantitative courses, generally offered in the summer before the first year to get the numerically challenged up to speed.

Pro Forma: financial presentation of hypothetical events; for example, how much new debt would a company require if it grows 10 percent a year?

Quant Jock: a numerical athlete who is happiest crunching numbers.

Quick and Dirty: an abbreviated analysis, often involving numbers.

Run the Numbers: analyze quantitatively.

Sharks: aggressive students who smell blood and move in for the kill.

Shark Comment: comment meant to gore a fellow student in class discussion.

Soft Courses: touchy-feely courses such as human resources and organizational behavior.

Soft Skills: conflict resolution, teamwork, negotiation, oral and written communication.

Slice and Dice: running all kinds of quantitative analyses on a set of numbers.

The Five Forces: Michael Porter's model for analyzing the strategic attractiveness of an industry.

Three Cs: the primary forces—Customer, Competition, Company.

Total Quality Management: the Edward Demming method of management that caught on with the Japanese and is now "hot" in American business—managing the quality of products, service, work, process, people, and objectives.

Valuation: adds up projected future cash flows into current dollars.

Value-Based Decision Making: values and ethics as part of the practice of business.

## Chapter 2

SUSPENDERS AND
POWER BREAKFASTS
What Does an MBA Offer?

NUTS-AND-BOLTS BUSINESS SKILLS

Graduate business schools teach the applied science of business. The best business schools, the ones in this book, combine the latest academic theories with pragmatic concepts, hands-on experience, and real-world solutions.

To equip students with the broad expertise they need to be managers, most business schools start new MBAs off with a set of foundation or "core" courses in what are known as the "functional areas": finance, accounting, management, marketing, operations, and economics. These courses introduce you to the basic vocabulary and concepts of formal business culture. They also develop your practical skills—ones you'll be able to use immediately in your new career.

Your learning occurs on three levels: You become familiar with concepts. For example, in finance you learn that a company's cost of equity is greater than its cost of debt. You acquire tools such as ratio analysis, valuations, and pro formas. Finally, you experience action-based learning by applying your skills and knowledge to case studies, role plays, and business simulations. Over the course of this three-tiered study, you will explore the complete business cycle of many different kinds of organizations.

B-schools also teach the analytical skills used to make complicated business decisions. You learn how to define the critical issues, apply analytical techniques, develop the criteria for decisions, and make decisions after evaluating their impact on other variables.

After two years, you're ready to market a box of cereal. Or prepare a valuation of the cereal company's worth. You'll speak the language of business. You'll know the tools of the trade. Your expertise will extend to many areas and industries. In short, you will have acquired the skills that open doors.

THE FAST TRACK AND BIG BUCKS

Applicants often have big bucks in mind when they decide to go to business school, believing that earning an MBA is equivalent to winning the lottery. At some schools, this is (sort of) the case. The top talent at elite schools are commonly offered salaries in the six-figure range. For example, the median starting package for Stanford's 1998 MBAs at graduation was $139,000; three out of four will earn more than $100,000. Just as impressive is the fact that 99 percent had jobs by graduation day. But this is not an across-the-board experience.

Many factors have an effect on a student's first-job-out-of-school salary. First, there's a correlation between school reputation and average starting salary. The better the school (or the better the current perception of the school), the better the compensation. Second, compensation varies by industry. For example, consulting and investment banking are at the high end of the salary spectrum these days. Some companies in these industries even offer students "sign-on bonuses" and reimbursement of their second-year tuition. By contrast, advertising firms and small businesses offer smaller compensation packages and fewer perks. Third, previous work experience and salary will boost or deflate your perceived value. A clear track record of success before school is likely to secure a bigger package after graduation.

Another common reason for pursuing an MBA is to get on the proverbial "fast track." Many students do find that the degree allows them to leapfrog several notches up the ladder. But the guaranteed fast track is something of an illusion.

B-school students these days are older than they used to be: The average age is twenty-seven, as opposed to twenty-two a couple decades ago. This indicates that students typically spend more time working after college before entering a graduate degree program. Their age, maturity, and previous work experience allow these graduates to move into substantive, responsible positions right after completing their programs. In contrast, twenty years ago a recent MBA's first job out of school was in a management development track, but at a fairly low level in the organization.

All that said, the MBA can lead to accelerated career development. But like your salary, much of this depends on the industry you enter and the program from which you graduated.

DATA ON SALARY EXPECTATIONS

Looking at starting salaries at some of the nation's most selective schools—according to data collected from *Business Week*—is helpful in assessing the value of that school's particular MBA in a given year. As we've said before rankings can be misleading because they don't consider your unique program needs or career prospects. However, as a general guide to the range of starting salaries out there, we think this chart is illustrative.

Report Card for the 25 Most Selective*

	Applicants Accepted	Meridian Pay Pre-MBA	Meridian Pay Post-MBA	% Increase	Grads Earning Over $100,000	Average Job Offers
Stanford, Stanford CA	7%	$55,000	$138,000	+151%	74%	3.6
UC–Berkeley (Haas) , Berkeley CA	11%	$48,000	$117,000	+144%	54%	2.5
Columbia, New York NY	12%	$49,000	$125,000	+155%	76%	3.0
Dartmouth (Tuck), Hanover NH	12%	$50,000	$127,000	+154%	83%	2.7
Pennsylvania (Wharton), Philadelphia PA	13%	$50,000	$125,000	+150%	83%	3.2
Harvard, Boston MA	13%	$60,000	$145,000	+142%	86%	4.0
MIT (Sloan), Cambridge MA	13%	$47,000	$130,000	+177%	74%	3.7
Northwestern (Kellogg), Evanston IL	14%	$46,000	$125,000	+172%	72%	3.4
UCLA (Anderson), Los Angeles CA	14%	$45,000	$115,000	+156%	57%	2.7
Virginia (Darden), Charlottesville VA	15%	$42,000	$115,000	+174%	64%	2.9
Duke (Fuqua), Durham NC	17%	$42,000	$109,000	+160%	50%	3.2
NYU (Stern), New York NY	18%	$40,000	$120,000	+200%	62%	2.7
Maryland (Smith), College Park MO	21%	$35,000	$84,500	+141%	28%	3.2
Michigan, Ann Arbor MI	22%	$44,000	$115,000	+161%	67%	3.5
Texas, Austin TX	23%	$40,000	$97,000	+143%	39%	3.1
Chicago, Chicago IL	24%	$49,000	$120,000	+145%	80%	3.4
UNC (Kenan-Flagler), Chapel Hill NC	24%	$40,000	$107,000	+168%	52%	2.9
Yale, New Haven CT	25%	$35,500	$116,000	+227%	54%	3.1
Purdue (Krannert), W. Lafayette IN	25%	$33,500	$86,500	+158%	23%	4.2
USC (Marshall), Los Angeles CA	26%	$39,000	$93,000	+138%	31%	3.0
Cornell (Johnson), Ithaca NY	28%	$42,000	$115,000	+174%	64%	3.3
Carnegie Mellon, Pittsburgh PA	30%	$43,000	$109,000	+153%	55%	3.7
Washington U. (Olin), St. Louis MO	34%	$32,000	$89,000	+178%	19%	3.4
Indiana, Bloomington IN	40%	$38,500	$92,000	+139%	31%	2.9
Wisconsin, Madison WI	47%	$30,000	$70,000	+133%	11%	3.0
Averages						
Top 10	12%	$49,200	$126,200	+157%	72%	3.22
Top 10-25	27%	$38,900	$101,533	+161%	44%	3.2
Top 25	21%	$43,020	$111,400	+160%	56%	3.2

*Reprinted from the October 19, 1998 issue of *Business Week* by special permission. Copyright 1998 by The McGraw-Hill Companies.

ACCESS TO HUNDREDS OF RECRUITERS, ENTRY TO NEW FIELDS

Applicants tend to place great emphasis on "incoming" and "outgoing" statistics. First they ask, "Will I get in?" Then they ask, "Will I get a job?"

If the first is getting tougher to accomplish, then the second is getting easier. MBAs are in strong demand, thanks in part to the intense interest in hiring from consulting firms and investment banks. Students graduating from the classes of 1998 are awash with three or more job offers. In fact, at some schools, students can count up to ten offers. Consulting firms, which traditionally offer generous packages, are making more offers at higher starting salaries than ever before. Investment banks are upping those offers and providing bigger signing bonuses to compete against the consulting firms' appetite for more bodies. Starting salaries are weighing in at the $120,000+ mark, and that doesn't include the approximate $20,000 plus many newly minted MBAs get as a sign-on bonus. The majority also receive a generous relocation package. Indeed, if you were fortunate enough to have spent the summer in between your first and second year at the consulting company, then you will, in all likelihood, also receive a "rebate" on your tuition. These companies pick up student's second-year tuition bill. The big enchilada, however, goes to those MBA students who worked at the firm before b-school. These lucky capitalists get their whole tuition paid for.

A survey of placement offices reveals that salaries are up, ranging from $73,000–$142,000 for average first-year packages for students from top-flight programs. At the twenty or so most selective schools, the prime hunting grounds for consultants, 30–40 percent of the graduating classes have heard the siren song of big money and signed on the dotted line with the consulting firms.

What will all these talented MBAs be doing? Many of them will be flying around the country to client companies to help them develop growth strategies, implement new information technologies, and develop closer relationships with key suppliers. To institute these changes, companies often require the help of outside consultants. Because of the breadth of companies and industries that MBAs as consultants are exposed to, consulting is seen as "MBA finishing school." Most new MBA hires will stay for only three years before joining the industry as strategic planners and managers.

A RECRUITER SPILLS THE BEANS

Liz Tunkiar
Senior V.P.—Director of Personnel, Ogilvy and Mather

"We've gone back and forth on whether we should hire MBAs. We've finally come to the conclusion that from an account point of view, they fit well into our organization.

Many of our clients have MBAs—Kraft, General Foods, Unilever—so it makes sense that we hire MBAs to work on those businesses. They tend to have instant credibility with the client.

MBAs have an advantage over BAs in that they bring a certain maturity to the account work. They also bring marketing knowledge and problem-solving and analytical skills.

MBAs cost us more. We pay them higher salaries. In return we expect them to understand the business much more quickly than non-MBAs. We also expect them to move quickly up the learning curve and make immediate contributions.

Obviously, this puts them on a faster track."

Where are the remainder of MBAs headed? Wall Street continues to take a chunk of the remaining students. Investment banking, sales and trading, and venture capital offer packages comparable to consulting. Although the pendulum of Wall Street hires has not swung back to its peak in the mid- to late 1980s, nearly 30 percent of Wharton's Class of 1997 headed to the Street. With mergers and acquisitions at historic records, and a continued boom in the bond and equity markets, Wall Street has its doors wide open to MBAs again.

Mainstream industry also wants its share of MBAs. Like Wall Street, years of downsizing have created the need for fresh hires and talent. For many companies, it's cheaper to hire new MBAs through on-campus recruiting than through other means. MBAs are also attractive because they bring fresh, state-of-the-art ideas, are eager to implement them, can tackle the grittier, more complex problems of the modern business world, and, most important, can make immediate contributions. As an MBA might put it, that's a solid return on one's investment.

GETTING A JOB

For most would-be MBAs, b-school represents a fresh beginning—either in their current profession or in an entirely different industry. Whatever promise the degree holds for you, it's wise to question what the return on your investment will be.

As with average starting salary, several factors affect job placement. School reputation and ties to industries and employers are important. At the top programs, the lists of recruiters read like a "Who's Who" of American companies. These schools not only attract the greatest volume of recruiters, but consistently get the attention of those considered blue chip.

Not to be overlooked are lesser-known, regional schools that often have the strongest relationships with local employers and industries. Some b-schools (many of them state universities) are regarded by both academicians and employers as number one in their respective regions. In other words, as far as the local business community is concerned, these programs offer as much prestige and pull as a nationally ranked program.

Student clubs also play a big part in getting a job, because they extend the recruiting efforts at many schools. They host a variety of events that allow you to meet leading business people, so that you can learn about their industries and their specific companies. Most important, these clubs are very effective at bringing in recruiters and other interested parties that do not recruit through traditional mainstream channels. For example, the high-tech, international, and entertainment student clubs provide career opportunities not available through the front door.

Another important factor is the industry you enter. The place to be in the late 1990s is consulting. The appeal is two-fold: First, consulting firms pay the most. Second, they now offer an unbeatable combination of on-the-job training, exposure to strategy (typical for consulting), and more recently, opportunities to be involved in the nitty-gritty of tactical implementation. A hands-on, fix-the-business type of job used to be found only in brand management. But these days, consulting firms are being called on not only to diagnose a client company's ills, but also to administer the medicine as well. Roughly 35–40 percent of top-flight business school grads will go into consulting this year. In fact, at Kellogg, a school renowned for breeding brand managers, 40 percent of its grads will take jobs in consulting, up from 34 percent just a year ago.

Of course, brand management positions in packaged-goods companies such as Procter & Gamble, Church & Dwight (Arm & Hammer), Quaker Oats, and Johnson & Johnson are still appealing; you get to manage a product as though you were a mini-CEO. Also, brand management experience is a real resume builder; becoming a brand manager is the closest thing there is to earning a stripe in the business world. Investment banking, once the place to be, is popular (sky-high salaries are a big draw), but it has been usurped by consulting. An emerging area of demand is for the techno-MBA: people who have information technology skills with more traditional management skills. Companies off the beaten track, such as start-up ventures, offer unique opportunities, but many of them are unknowns. However, numerous schools have developed entrepreneurial programs, so newly credentialed MBAs leave feeling confident that they are better equipped to handle these riskier prospects. Indeed, in the 1990s many more students are interested in these unconventional, high-growth entrepreneurial opportunities.

Your background and experiences also affect your success in securing a position. Important factors are academic specialization (or course of study), academic standing, prior work experience, and intangibles such as your personal fit with the company. These days, what you did before b-school is particularly important; it helps establish credibility and gives you an edge in competing for a position in a specific field. For those using b-school to switch careers to a new industry, it's helpful if something on your resume ties your interest to the new profession. It's smart to secure a summer job in the new area.

Finally, persistence and initiative are critical factors in the job search. Since the beginning of this decade, many fast tracks have been narrowed. Increasingly, even at the best schools, finding a job requires off-campus recruiting efforts and ferreting out the hidden jobs.

FRIENDS WHO ARE GOING PLACES, ALUMNI WHO ARE ALREADY THERE

Most students say that the best part about b-school is meeting classmates with whom they share common goals and interests. Many students claim that the "single greatest resource is each other." Not surprisingly, with so many bright and ambitious people cocooned in one place, b-school can be the time of your life. It presents numerous professional and social opportunities. It can be where you find future customers, business partners, and mentors. It can also be where you establish lifelong friendships. And after graduation, these classmates form an enduring network of contacts and professional assistance.

Alumni are also an important part of the b-school experience. While professors teach business theory and practice, alumni provide insight into the real business world. When you're ready to interview, they can provide advice on how to get hired by the companies recruiting at your school. In some cases, they help secure the interview and shepherd you through the hiring process.

B-schools love to boast about the influence of their alumni network. To be sure, some are very powerful. But this varies from institution to institution. At the very least, alumni will help you get your foot in the door. A resume sent to an alum at a given company, instead of "Sir or Madam" in the personnel department, has a much better chance of being noticed and acted on.

After you graduate, the network continues to grow. Regional alumni clubs and alumni publications keep you plugged in to the network with class notes on who's doing what, where, and with whom.

Throughout your career, an active alumni relations department can give you continued support. Post-MBA executive education series, fund-raising events, and continued job-placement efforts are all resources you can draw on for years to come.

AN INTEL MANAGER (AND RECENT UCLA GRAD) TELLS US HOW HER MBA EDUCATION WIRED HER FOR SUCCESS

AUTHOR'S INTERVIEW WITH LEA HALLERT, PROJECT MANAGER, STRATEGIC MARKETING AT INTEL CORPORATION

Technology more and more defines how we work and how we solve problems. It provides the tools to make better decisions, to comb through and manipulate data, to manage vast amounts of information, and to perform sophisticated analysis. In short, it delivers faster cycle times for analysis and decision making (even improving the quality of those decisions).

Arguably, business school students who know how to effectively use this technology may provide the best value to employers. With that in mind, we identified one program notable for its standard-setting technology and business education curriculum—The Anderson School at UCLA.

For a what-it's-really-like take on the skills and learning acquired at UCLA, we spoke with Lea Hallert, class of 1997, who now works for the Intel Corporation, a world-class technology company.

Gilbert: How has UCLA embedded technology in the learning process?

Hallert: To begin with, every seat at UCLA is wired to the school's ethernet, which of course means local-area network access and Internet access. So no matter where you sit—whether it's in a classroom, in the library, in an office, in a club's office, or in a break-out room (which is really important), you have Internet access.

Gilbert: Wait. What's a break-out room?

Hallert: Well, as you know, most projects at UCLA are done in teams. A break-out room is where you go with your team to do work. It is a like a small conference room, with a table, chairs, white boards, and ethernet connections. This makes it really easy for us to share files and access research all at the same time. But this is the extent to which Anderson went to provide access for students to everything. Every seat, everywhere in the building, is wired.

Gilbert: Including the classrooms that you use to take electives?

Hallert: Absolutely. Each seat is, of course, wired. Also, the front of every classroom at UCLA is wired. There is a giant console that houses a PC with CD-ROM and a VCR. This is connected to a projection system for a large screen (like a huge forward projection TV). This is wired for the network, so of course any material there or on the Internet can be seen at the front of every classroom. Also, you can attach laptops or other PCs to this console, so that you can present directly from your laptop in front of the class. So the professor can show you a presentation, which you could download at any time, and access outside information to enhance the presentation—perhaps downloading the latest 10Q from an Internet web site, to make things a little more interesting.

So, that's the first important thing: all of UCLA is wired. The second is that every student has a laptop. It's part of the requirement. Every student is wired to the network so that in class the professor can say, "Go get this data. We want to play with it now." That's really important for your very basic classes in finance, statistics, and economics. But here's an example why: Econ was one of my more difficult classes. The professor would have these very complex sets of charts and graphs that were embedded in his presentation. But during class, even sometimes before (depending on how up-to-date the professor was), but at least by the time you're in class, you could go to the network, download the presentation, and have it on your machine. So you can watch it in the front of the classroom while he lectures, yet at the same time you have it on your machine with all the embedded graphs at your disposal. You can change them, because the graphs are connected in such a way that they're malleable—so that if you don't understand something like supply and demand, you can make a change and see what happened.

Gilbert: So the UCLA program presupposes a level of competence?

Hallert: Yes, but if you don't have it, the school gives you plenty of time to develop it. The minimum they assume is facility with a spreadsheet. After evaluating you, they might say you are going to have a problem with economics and statistics. There are a whole bunch of classes scheduled outside of school hours to help you with that.

Gilbert: And that's your choice? It's not required, but the wise student says: "I probably need this," and enrolls?

Hallert: Pretty much. But the school does try to give you guidelines about what sort of proficiency that you might want to have. For example, they send out a sample spreadsheet to put together. If you had any trouble with it, they recommended the prep class.

Gilbert: What is the connection between the use of technology in the learning process at UCLA and preparing one to be a good manager in a technology field or other fields like brand management, investment banking, or other typical MBA destinations?

Hallert: Hmmm. That's a really good question. I am not sure that technology helps you be a better manager. The interpersonal skills for any type of manager are pretty inherent; you are not likely to be able to learn them sitting in a classroom. Those that gravitate toward technology already are really interested in playing around with all the things that you can do with it. So they may be operating at such a high level of facility with technology already that they're just pleased to be learning in the language they already speak as opposed to feeling turned on to really cutting-edge tools. It's probably some place in between these extremes. Technology gives you a terrific framework and vocabulary to be a presentable manager. It helps to better frame what is going on for you and a good point of reference from which to develop questions. A program like UCLA will attract more technologically inclined people. Thirty to forty percent of my class already had some familiarity with it. In terms of being a good *manager*, your people skills are clearly a separate and critical issue.

For other professions, technology competence gives you a level of superiority that you don't originally expect to be important. For example, I knew I wanted to do marketing, I was very interested in computers, but I was concerned that because I didn't have a marketing background, I ought to do brand management instead of technology. So I spent my summer (after the first year of business school) working in brand management.

Gilbert: With whom?

Hallert: Nestlé. They're headquartered in California and have a large operation in Cleveland. And I begged them to go to Cleveland.

Gilbert: I wouldn't let too many people know about that. But back to the subject, so you know brand management well?

Hallert: Oh yeah, I think that I know a little bit about it. And because of my familiarity with technology, I was much more sophisticated in terms of being able to do presentations and get data. I had a really easy time with IRI data (store-based consumption data), downloading, and putting it in a format that could be easily digested by the people that needed it. Nestlé asked me to write a case study, so it was easy for me to integrate pictures, logos, and graphs into it. The things that make something look really polished, I could do in a snap.

People who like to mess around with software are always going to do that, I'm not sure that that's specifically from UCLA. But for me, being in an environment like UCLA, you know it's like playing tennis with people who are much better than you are. You can't help but get better, and you don't even realize it. It may not even be your goal. So I was much more comfortable with technology than some of the other people who worked for Nestlé; I just used it more.

Gilbert: I bet they loved you, because brand management doesn't often attract that type of person.

Hallert: No, it really doesn't. It attracts numbers people; so once the numbers are in Excel, brand managers could play around with it a bit. But with sophisticated stuff—they asked me the questions. And then with other work things, I could help, like accessing their e-mail via the network. That was a side benefit from UCLA. I knew how to work my way around a pretty open network.

Gilbert: So having technology integrated into the learning process at UCLA gave you skills that immediately and dramatically affected your capabilities at your job. You then went to Nestlé and demonstrated skills that were superior to your peers in this area.

Hallert: Exactly. And there's no fear.

Gilbert: What do you mean there's no fear?

Hallert: There's no fear. Because at UCLA everybody's working with technology; it's expected of you. It's a tool. Lots of people see technology as an end, instead of a tool. UCLA, by making it so integral to everything you do—all communications are done by e-mail; rarely is anything printed, (well, your diploma is printed)—it just becomes part of how you do things.

Gilbert: If the learning process is somewhat dependent on technology, and technology changes so rapidly, how does that affect the durability of the learning you take from the program?

Hallert: By viewing technology as a tool, and by using it that way, you realize that there are always new tools available. You kind of incorporate the fact that there is always something newer and better around the corner, and that you should be watching for it, so that you could incorporate it into your work process (a Palm Pilot is a good example of a tool that you might look for to incorporate). I have a huge advantage in all of that because I work for a leader in technology. Presentations are actually less sophisticated at Intel than they were at school.

Gilbert: Really? Why?

Hallert: Well it's not as integrated into the culture here; not every person has the same level of skill, and not every room is wired. Something I learned at b-school is that one of the very first things you do in a technology environment is find a guru, a technology guru, like a technology mentor.

Gilbert: In a technology environment, you mean like at Intel? Technology environment applies to what?

Hallert: Well, most companies now are networked. If you don't know how the network is wired, you're left a neophyte for that. So you need help—how to get on the network, how to access other networks, just the basic stuff. For example, when I first started getting files I didn't know what to do with at Intel, I went to my technology friend at Intel; he gave me a program so I could unpack it. That's a key thing I learned at b-school—there's always somebody who knows more than you do. Make friends with them.

Gilbert: How does this technology training make the UCLA graduate, or any student coming from this kind of wired MBA program look different? In other words, who would find these gradates attractive?

Hallert: Well, I think that being immersed . . . they understand how to access resources. Also, technology never works if it is one person, operating alone. It requires many users, many consumers to make innovations useful. The technology and the teamwork that are inherent in the UCLA program are essential for technology to be successfully used in business—that is another advantage that a wired program offers.

Gilbert: Given that this program continues to pioneer the use of technology in business education, what will it look like in five years?

Hallert: It will look different in a couple of ways. When I started, it was very cutting edge: The prof would say download Edgar stuff [the SEC database, open to the public, of annual reports and 10K reports] about a company, say Chevron . . . and that was cool, download all this information about Chevron. No one else was doing this, most students at other business schools would have to haul over to the library and look that stuff up.

In terms of shared technology, we will do much better with videoconferencing and shared speakers across campuses and companies. Imagine Andy Grove speaking to a marketing class about an Intel case at several schools at once, all videoconferenced together! This kind of activity won't be limited to special events, but ingrained in the curriculum.

As far as the big picture, I think b-school students in particular have a responsibility as the next generation of leaders to know what technology looks like whether you are a banker, a brand manager, or a consultant. Technology permeates business—it's a tool, and you shouldn't be afraid of it. You must embrace it.

## Chapter 3

WHAT B-SCHOOL IS REALLY LIKE

THE CHANGING FACE OF BUSINESS

In the previous decade, b-schools were regularly taken to task. An article in *The Chronicle of Higher Education* observed, "Hardly a month passes without a new article in the business press lamenting the narrow, overly quantitative focus of graduate business curricula, the irrelevant research done by business schools' faculty members, and the inability of graduates to grapple successfully with the nation's economic problems. Reporters gleefully interview unemployed graduates of business schools and pump corporate executives for unflattering comments about their employees with master's degrees in business administration."

Things have certainly changed. B-schools are responding to past criticisms by carving out new images for themselves. Many programs, for example, have sprouted social consciences. The 1990s MBA student hardly resembles the Gordon Gekko stereotype (remember that evil arbitrager from the movie *Wall Street*?) of the 1980s. Gone is the tolerance for avaricious, self-important MBAs. B-schools are recruiting students with broader, more humanitarian outlooks—students interested in contributing as much as in profit-taking. And, importantly, schools are trying to break down the rich white male stronghold on the business world by actively recruiting women and minorities.

Schools are also training students differently, both in content and in style. There's a move toward the medical school model of education—learning by doing. Business "residencies," product "laboratories," and fieldwork augment classroom instruction with real-world experiences. Schools are placing greater emphasis on public service and citizenship. Professional ethics classes are now mandatory in many schools. Outward Bound–style orientations and leadership programs are in vogue. Interpersonal communication skills, such as negotiation, conflict resolution, and team playing, have moved to the forefront. In short, the "bottom line" is no longer the bottom line.

Much has been made in recent years about the rise of a global economy. To make sure MBAs have the skills necessary to be effective in this economy, leading business programs have developed courses on global business operations and international economics. To teach sensitive leadership in an increasingly multicultural work force, they've enhanced offerings on cultural diversity and human resources.

One other change is worth noting. The reason that the average age of the business school student has steadily increased to the current high of twenty-seven is that b-schools have sought older students to satisfy the new demands of the marketplace. Recruiters want graduates with more than a degree; they want the skills that come with maturity, and the maturity that comes with several years of work experience.

AN ACADEMIC PERSPECTIVE

The objective of all MBA programs is to prepare students for a professional career in business. One business school puts it this way:

Graduates should be all of the following:

1. Able to think and reason independently, creatively, and analytically

2. Skilled in the use of quantitative techniques

3. Literate in the use of software applications as management tools

4. Knowledgeable about the world's management issues and problems

5. Willing to work in and successfully cope with conditions of uncertainty, risk, and change

6. Astute decision makers

7. Ethically and socially responsible

Sound like a tall order? Possibly. But this level of expectation is what business school is all about.

Nearly all MBA programs feature a core curriculum that focuses students on the major disciplines of business: finance, management, accounting, marketing, manufacturing, decision sciences, economics, and organizational behavior.

Unless your school allows you to place out of them, these courses are mandatory. Core courses provide broad functional knowledge in one discipline. For example, a core marketing course covers pricing, segmentation, communications, product-line planning, and implementation. Electives provide a narrow focus that deepens the area of study. For example, a marketing elective might be entirely devoted to pricing.

Students sometimes question the need for such a comprehensive core program. But the functional areas of a real business are not parallel lines. All departments of a business affect each other every day. For example, an MBA in a manufacturing job might be asked by a financial controller why the company's product has become unprofitable to produce. Without an understanding of how product costs are accounted for, this MBA wouldn't know how to respond to a critical and legitimate request.

At most schools, the first term or year is devoted to a rigid core curriculum. Some schools allow first-years to take core courses side by side with electives. Still others have come up with an entirely new way of covering the basics, integrating the core courses into one cross-functional learning experience, which may also include sessions on 1990s topics such as globalization, ethics, and managing diversity. Half-year to year-long courses are team-taught by professors who see you through all the disciplines.

TEACHING METHODOLOGY

Business schools employ two basic teaching methods: case study and lecture. Usually, they employ some combination of the two. The most popular is the case study approach. Students are presented with either real or hypothetical business scenarios and are asked to analyze them. This method provides concrete situations (rather than abstractions) that require mastery of a wide range of skills. Students often find case studies exciting because they can engage in spirited discussions about possible solutions to given business problems and because they get an opportunity to apply newly acquired business knowledge.

The other teaching method used by b-schools is lecturing in which—you guessed it—the professor speaks to the class and the class listens. The efficacy of the lecture method depends entirely on the professor. If the professor is compelling, you'll probably get a lot out of the class. If the professor is boring, you probably won't listen. Which isn't necessarily a big deal, since many professors make their class notes available on computer disc or in the library.

THE CLASSROOM EXPERIENCE

Professors teaching case methodology often begin class with a "cold call." A randomly selected student opens the class with an analysis of the case and makes recommendations for solutions. The cold call forces you to be prepared and to think on your feet.

No doubt, a cold call can be intimidating. But unlike law school, b-school professors don't use the Socratic method to torture you, testing your thinking with a pounding cross-examination. They're training managers, not trial lawyers. At worst, particularly if you're unprepared, a professor will abruptly dismiss your contributions.

Alternatively, professors ask for a volunteer to open a case, particularly someone who has had real industry experience with the issues. After the opening, the discussion is broadened to include the whole class. Everyone tries to get in a good comment, particularly if class participation counts heavily toward the grade. "Chip shots"—unenlightened, just-say-anything-to-get-credit comments—are common. So are "air hogs," students who go on and on because they like nothing more than to hear themselves pontificate.

Depending on the school, sometimes class discussions degenerate into wars of ego rather than ideas. But for the most part, debates are kept constructive and civilized. Students are competitive, but not offensively so, and learn to make their points succinctly and persuasively.

YOUR FIRST YEAR

The first six months of b-school can be daunting. You're unfamiliar with the subjects. There's a tremendous amount of work to do. And when you least have the skills to do so, there's pressure to stay with the pack. All of this produces anxiety and a tendency to overprepare. Eventually, students learn shortcuts and settle into a routine, but until then much of the first year is just plain tough. The programs usually pack more learning into the first term than they do into each of the remaining terms. For the schools to teach the core curriculum (which accounts for as much as 70 percent of learning) in a limited time, an intensive pace is considered necessary. Much of the second year will be spent on gaining proficiency in your area of expertise and on searching for a job.

The good news is that the schools recognize how tough the first year can be. During the early part of the program, they anchor students socially by placing them in small sections, sometimes called "cohorts." You take many or all of your classes with your section-mates. Sectioning encourages the formation of personal and working relationships and can help make a large program feel like a school within a school.

Because so much has to be accomplished in so little time, getting an MBA is like living in fast-forward. This is especially true of the job search. No sooner are you in the program than recruiters for summer jobs show up, which tends to divert students from their studies. First-years aggressively pursue summer positions, which are linked with the promise of a permanent job offer if the summer goes well. At some schools the recruiting period begins as early as October, at others in January or February.

YOUR SECOND YEAR

Relax, the second year is easier. By now, students know what's important and what's not. Second-years work more efficiently than first-years. Academic anxiety is no longer a factor. Having mastered the broad-based core curriculum, students now enjoy taking electives and developing an area of specialization.

Anxiety in the second year has more to do with the arduous task of finding a job. For some lucky students, a summer position has yielded a full-time offer. But even those students often go through the whole recruiting grind anyway, because they don't want to cut off any opportunities prematurely.

Most MBAs leave school with a full-time offer. Sometimes it's their only offer. Sometimes it's not their dream job. Which may be why most grads change jobs after just two years.

One University of Chicago Business School student summed up the whole two-year academic/recruiting process like this: "The first-year students collapse in the winter quarter because of on-campus recruiting. The second-years collapse academically in the first quarter of their second year because it's so competitive to get a good job. And when a second-year does get a job, he or she forgets about class entirely. That's why pass/fail was invented."

Females at my school were well-represented. But in terms of minority ethnic groups—Black and Hispanic, and that applies to myself—these were underrepresented. I could count on my two hands how many minorities were in that program. This is not an indictment of the school, it's just that as a minority, you have to be comfortable with the numbers.

There's a lot of press out there that says the MBA is not the golden ticket it's cracked up to be. But it does make you more competitive. I remember interviewing for a job in one of the other IBM offices. I had just started the MBA program again, and this manager said, 'It's really good you're doing that. All the other people who work for me have MBAs. Every one of them.' So I can see the degree helping with my short- and long-term career goals.

The MBA gave me credibility. It helped me understand my customers' needs better. Business school changes HOW you think about a problem. And I've made better business decisions because of that."

Female MBA, Graduate School of Business, Claremont College, 1991 Manager, IBM

LIFE OUTSIDE OF CLASS

Business school is more than academics and a big-bucks job. A spirited student community provides ample opportunities for social interaction, extracurricular activity, and career development.

Much of campus life revolves around student-run clubs. There are groups for just about every career interest and social need—from "MBAs for a Greener America" to the "Small Business Club." There's even a group for significant others on most campuses. The clubs are a great way to meet classmates with similar interests and to get in on the social scene. They might have a reputation for throwing the best black-tie balls, pizza-and-keg events, and professional mixers. During orientation week, these clubs aggressively market themselves to first-years.

Various socially responsible projects are also popular on campus. An emphasis on volunteer work is part of the overall trend toward good citizenship. Perhaps to counter the greed of the 1980s, "giving back" is the b-school style of the moment. There is usually a wide range of options—from tutoring in an inner-city school to working in a soup kitchen to renovating public buildings.

Still another way to get involved is to work on a school committee. Here you might serve on a task force designed to improve student quality of life. Or you might work in the admissions office and interview prospective students.

For those with more creative urges there are always the old standbys: extracurriculars such as the school paper, yearbook, or school play. At some schools, the latter takes the form of the b-school follies and is a highlight of the year. Like the student clubs, these are a great way to get to know your fellow students.

Finally, you can play on intramural sports teams or attend the numerous informal get-togethers, dinner parties, and group trips. There are also plenty of regularly scheduled pub nights, just in case you thought your beer-guzzling days were over.

Most former MBA students say that going to b-school was the best decision they ever made. That's primarily because of nonacademic experiences. Make the most of your classes, but take the time to get involved and enjoy yourself.

A DAY IN THE LIFE OF A STUDENT

Male MBA, First Year

Kenan-Flagler Business School, The University of North Carolina at Chapel Hill

7:00 am:	Review notes for my first class.
7:30 am:	Eat some high-energy cereal; read *The Wall Street Journal*—professors like to discuss news items that relate to the class topics.
8:00 am:	Read review for quantitative methods exam; do practice problems; reread case on control systems for organizational behavior class.
9:00 am:	Arrive at school. Go to "reading room" to hang out with everyone. Check student mailbox for invitations to recruiter events.
9:30 am:	Integrative Management Class: guest speaker from case-study discusses how the company approached problems.
10:45 am:	Hang out.
11:00 am:	Organizational Behavior Class: Get in a couple of good comments; debate the effectiveness of a management decision with another student in class.
12:15 pm:	Grab some lunch and sit with friends. Talk about the lousy cafeteria food and who's dating whom.
1:00 pm:	Go back to reading room to review for 2:00 class.
2:00 pm:	Microeconomics Class: Listen to lecture on monopolistic competition.
3:15 pm:	Arrive at home, change into work-out clothes. Go running, lift weights—relax.
6:00 pm:	Eat dinner; watch the news. Read the next day's case.
7:30 pm:	Head back to campus for study group.
7:45 pm:	Discuss cases, help each other with homework problems on interpreting regression statistics; discuss how to account for capital leases versus operating leases.
10:00 pm:	Back at home. Review more cases; read next class assignment in textbook; work on problem set.
Midnight:	Sports on ESPN 'til I fall asleep. Boardroom dreams.

Female MBA, Second Year

The Fuqua School of Business, Duke University

6:45 am:	Get dressed, listen to CNN, and pick up *The Wall Street Journal* on way to school.
8:00 am:	Arrive at school. Bargaining and Negotiations class. Perform role play on conflict resolution.
10:15 am:	Hang out—grab a bagel.
10:30 am:	Intermediate Accounting Class—discussion on cash flow statements—nothing exciting.
12:45 pm:	Arrive at admissions office to review resume of applicant to b-school.
1:00 pm:	Conduct interview of applicant.
1:45 pm:	Write evaluation of candidate. Hand in to admissions secretary.
2:00 pm:	Attend quality advisory board meeting—discuss creation of corporate survey.
3:30 pm:	Competitive Strategy class. Lecture on barriers to entry.
5:45 pm:	Attend recruiter event. Tell the recruiter how interested I am in the industry (I know nothing about it).
7:45 pm:	Over to the health club for aerobics.
8:45 pm:	Drive home, eat dinner, and finally read *The Wall Street Journal*—of course, it's not news by now.
9:30 pm:	Study class notes; prepare next day's case.
11:45 pm:	Quality phone time with my boyfriend.
12:30 am:	Boardroom dreams.

## Chapter 4

MONEY MATTERS

How to Finance B-School and Calculate the Return on this Investment

THE BOTTOM LINE*

Paying for business school is not an expense that most people are prepared to incur without some help. The good news is that getting an MBA takes just two years (and maybe less), after which you can expect your income to increase, perhaps dramatically. The bad news is that there is less in the way of "gift aid," such as scholarships and grants, for business school than there is for law or medical school. You'll likely be forced to take out loans to pay your way. But, after all, what's one more loan? Especially one as valuable as an investment in your future. So relax and get comfortable with debt; it's a concept you'll have to become familiar with when you're running a large corporation. Anyway, it's only money, and you can't take it with you. Figure out what business school will cost you, using the Return on Investment worksheet on page 41, then figure out your rate of return on investment. Feel better? Good.

*Much of this article was reprinted with permission from *Time/The Princeton Review's The Best Graduate School for You*, 1998 edition.

HOW DO I FUND MY MBA?

The vast majority of b-school students finance their education through some combination of the following:

- Federally insured loans. The Perkins loan is available for students who show exceptional "need," as determined by your business school's financial aid office. The Stafford loan is the most popular method of financing an education, and is available to most students. The government makes each of these loans very attractive to students through its subsidy of the programs. (Your tax dollars are working for you, after all!)

- Private lenders. Many lenders (not just banks!) have developed specialized programs for people who want to borrow for b-school. Be careful of guarantee and insurance fees, though, since they can add dramatically to the cost of borrowing.

- Grants and scholarships. There are fewer of these for business school than for law, medical, or graduate school, so you'll have to dig hard to find one for which you qualify. We've listed some at the end of the chapter, but also consult any organizations you belong to and your business school for more sources.

- Educational reimbursement from your company. Every company will handle this slightly differently, but obviously if you can get your company to pick up part (or all) of the cost of your education, you'll help yourself tremendously. And you may be able to take advantage of this once you complete your MBA as well. In today's heated job market, some companies are even offering newly minted MBAs signing bonuses that cover the previous year's tuition.

- Gifts. If you can get your family or some benefactor to help you out, consider yourself one of the lucky ones.

APPLYING FOR FINANCIAL AID

To become eligible for any financial aid at all, you will need to fill out the Free Application for Federal Student Aid (FAFSA). The application can be submitted any time after January 1 in the year that you will enter graduate school and is typically due shortly thereafter. You can get a copy of the form from a school's financial aid office or download a copy from the U.S. Department of Education (DOE) web site at www.fafsa.ed.gov.

You can also download FAFSA Express software and complete the form electronically. FAFSA Express runs only on a PC with Windows and can be transmitted directly to the Department of Education via modem. An electronic data exchange between your computer and the DOE computers ensures quick receipt of your official Expected Family Contribution. The software also speeds up the application process by automatically checking electronic FAFSA data.

Many schools also require you to fill out their own financial aid forms. Make sure you check with the schools to which you are applying to find out exactly what forms they require and their deadlines for submission. Also, these deadlines may vary by school, so be sure to double check and get the paperwork in on time!

WHAT LOANS ARE AVAILABLE?

Sometime in 1998 Congress is expected to vote to determine the rate students will pay for loans; call 888/888-3469 to get the most up-to-date information on loans. There are several sources of loans for students attending business school. The most common are ones you may be familiar with from your undergraduate years.

Stafford Loans

These are very low-interest loans guaranteed by the federal government. Unfortunately, you can't just decide to take out a Stafford Loan. You must file the FAFSA form to qualify for this loan. The interest rate on Stafford Loans is variable but capped at 8.25 percent. The current limit for graduate students is $18,500 a year total for both subsidized and unsubsidized Stafford Loans, of which $10,000 must be unsubsidized. The total aggregate amount you can borrow through the Stafford program, including loans from undergraduate school, is $138,500—only $65,500 of which can be subsidized.

If you receive a subsidized Stafford Loan, you pay no interest when you are in school (the government "subsidizes" it) or for the first six months after you graduate, and you can take up to ten years to repay the money. For an unsubsidized Stafford Loan, you'll be charged interest while you are in school, but you don't have to start repaying principal until you've been out of school for six months.

All Stafford Loans are subject to an origination fee of up to 4 percent (1 percent of that is usually the guarantee fee). Although the origination fee has to be paid up front, it is deducted from the loan amount and does not come out of pocket. In actual dollars, the amount isn't incredibly onerous: 4 percent of $2,500 is $100. Depending on the school, you either borrow directly from the school or from a bank.

Subsidized Stafford Loans are awarded only as part of the aid packages created by colleges and are based on need; unsubsidized Stafford Loans aren't based on need. For more information on the Stafford and other federal student loan programs, call 888/888-3469 or visit web sites from the DOE (www.ed.gov/prog_info/SFA/StudentGuide) and The Princeton Review (www.review.com).

Perkins Loans

These are loans made by colleges with money provided by the federal government. The interest rate is quite low—currently 5 percent. Students can borrow up to $5,000 each year. As with the Stafford Loans, interest payments are picked up by the government during school, and repayment doesn't begin until after graduation.

Perkins Loans are awarded only as part of an aid package and are based solely on need. Financial aid officers have the only say in deciding which students qualify for these loans. You should never turn down a Perkins Loan.

Grants from Clubs and Organizations

Clubs, alumni groups, and civic organizations provide scholarship money for graduate students, although not as much as for undergraduate students. These awards are usually small, so don't waste a lot of time scouring the countryside for a few hundred dollars, but be aware of opportunities in your own backyard. If your local hospital offers scholarship money to former candy stripers and that was your childhood summer job, you may be in luck. You should also be aware that many companies offer scholarships in addition to their tuition reimbursement programs. Although an outside scholarship will help, it won't lower your Expected Family Contribution. You must divulge to the colleges the amount of outside aid you are receiving, and it will be counted against money the college would have given you.

Commercial Loans

Banks and other lenders lend money. That's their job. If you have to go this route, though, you leave the world of below-market interest rates, sometimes paying as much as 19 percent, much higher than the rates offered on federal loans. The terms are also different: in many cases, payment cannot be deferred until after graduation. Before borrowing, check to see if a local lender offers a rate reduction to students who attend a school in its state. See the chart on the next page for a listing of some of the organizations that offer popular loans to business school students:

Each of these loans should be used in addition to either Stafford or Perkins loans or both, whenever possible. Because the loans are unsecured, they generally will charge significant guarantee and insurance fees. Shop aggressively to avoid paying too much.

Lender	Loan Amount Range	Interest Rates	Guarantee and other Fees	Repayment
The Education Resources Institute (TERI) PEP Program www.teri.org	$500–$15,000 annually on own good credit (up to cost of education)	Prime Rate	10% guarantee fee on own signature, 6% with creditworthy cosigner	Repayment can begin six months after you leave school. Repayment can be up to 25 years.
The Access Group Business Access Loan 800/282-1550	From $500 up to the cost of education. Maximum total education debt, including all undergraduate and graduate debt, is $120,000.	Based on the 91-day Treasury Bill. Rate equals T-bill +3.25% before repayment and T-bill +3.4% during repayment	At disbursement, a first guarantee fee is charged. At repayment, a second guarantee fee of 2.0% is charged.	Defer interest until repayment begins, which may be 9 months after you leave school. Repayment period can be up to 20 years.
Citibank MBA Assist Loan 800/692-8200	$500–$15,000 annually.	91-day T-bill +3.40% during school and +4.25% during repayment	At disbursement, a guarantee fee of 8.5% is charged if there is no cosigner or 6% with a cosigner.	Defer interest until repayment begins, which may be 6 months after you leave school. Repayment period can be up to 15 years.
Nellie Mae MBA-Excel Loan 800/9-TUITION	$2,000–$10,000	Prime Rate +0.5% during the first year and Prime + 1% during subsequent years.	At disbursement, guarantee fee is 9% without a cosigner or 7% with one.	Defer interest until repayment begins, which may be 6 months after you leave school. Repayment period can be up to 20 years.
Sallie Mae MBALOANS 800/239-4211	From $500 up to the cost of education, minus other financial aid. May have to apply for federal student aid before being approved for these loans.	91-day T-bill +3.25% during school and T-bill +3.40% during repayment.	At disbursement, guarantee fee of 7.5% is charged. An additional fee of 2.5% is charged at repayment, unless there is a cosigner.	Defer interest until repayment begins, which can be up to 6 months after you leave school. Repayment period can be up to 15 years.

Students and their families may also decide to investigate financing options other than those targeted at the educational market. These can turn into very expensive propositions, so be careful. They include personal lines of credit from your bank, credit cards, loans from your retirement fund or insurance plan, and personal loans from relatives. Personal lines of credit are usually comparable to those charged by credit cards. Another last-resort option is to find a credit card that's trying to attract customers with a low introductory rate and to put your expenses on that. The rates, which can be as low as 6 percent, typically last six months to a year, so pay off as much as you can in that time to save money.

Funding your b-school education may require some fancy financial moves, but it's good preparation for the real world. After all, there's hardly an investment banking, sales, or economics job that doesn't require restructuring debt. Start learning at the company that matters most: You, Inc.

Scholarship	Award	Deadline	Contact	Requirements
Karla Scherer Foundation Scholarship for Women	Varies; renewable	MARCH 1	737 N. Michigan Ave Suite 2330 Chicago, IL 60611 312/943-9191	Female students in finance or economics entering corporate business in the private sector. Need-based.
Donald W. Fogarty International Student Paper	Up to $1,700	MAY 15	APICS 500 W. Annandale Rd. Falls Church, VA 22046-4274 800/444-2742	Business administration and management students. Essay required on topic relevant to resource management.
National Urban League Scholarship Program for Minority Students	$10,000	APRIL 15	6030 Wilshire Blvd., Suite 302 Los Angeles, CA 90036 213/299-9660	Minority students in engineering, sales, marketing, manufacturing, finance, or business administration.
The Consortium for Graduate Study in Management	Full tuition and fees	JAN. 15	200 South Hanley Rd. Suite 1102 St. Louis, MO 63105 314/935-5614	African, Hispanic, and Native American students who are U.S. citizens and have a bachelor's degree.

THE TRUE COSTS AND REWARDS OF BUSINESS SCHOOL

Business school offers the opportunity to improve your current job status or satisfaction level, increase your earning power, or even step into a new career. But the price is high. In dollars and time. The financial price in the beginning is even higher. Will you ever recoup the money? To estimate the financial payoffs of business school, fill out this worksheet created by Jens Stephan, a University of Cincinnati business school professor. "Going to graduate school can be viewed as a classical financial investment decision," says Stephan. "Estimate your return on graduate school, as you would with any investment."

Use Part One to find out what b-school will cost in tuition and lost income. Turn to the profile (A–Z beginning on page 153) for a school you are considering and under Financial Facts you will find the tuition costs for line 2. Part Two will help you figure out how much more—percentage-wise—you will earn in the long run by getting your MBA. Use the Starting Salaries chart to estimate what you may earn your first year out of school. But don't limit yourself to the jobs we list. If you have another job in mind, plug in that starting salary to figure out your return on investment.

Starting Salaries	
consulting	85,000
corporate finance	71,000
investment banking	70,000
marketing/ brand management	69,000

RETURN ON INVESTMENT

Part One:
INVESTMENT IN GRADUATE EDUCATION

1. Fill in your current salary. If you are not working, estimate what you would earn based on your education and prior work experience. This is your opportunity cost of going to graduate school to earn an MBA degree.

2. Fill in the annual tuition plus any fees less any aid you will not have to repay.

3. Divide line 2 by .65 to determine the pretax earnings required to pay tuition and fees.

4. Add lines 1 and 3 for your annual investment.

5. Multiply line 4 by the length of the program in years. This represents your total investment in an MBA degree: the opportunity cost (lost earnings) and the out-of-pocket cost (net tuition and fees).

Part Two:
RATE OF RETURN ON INVESTMENT

6. Find the job you expect to obtain after graduation. Enter the starting salary (see starting salaries chart).

7. Subtract line 1 from line 6. This is the expected salary increase resulting form the MBA degree.

8. Find the intersection of your expected salary increase (line 7) and your total investment (line 5) in table A (one-year MBA programs) or Table B (two-year MBA programs). This is an estimate of your annualized percent return on investment in graduate school over a ten-year period measured from the start of your MBA program.

You can also estimate the payback period. Divide your total investment (line 5) by the expected salary increase (line 7), and add the length of the program in years (either one or two). This represents the number of years, from the start of the program, required to recoup your investment in the MBA degree. For example, if your total investment is $100,000 and your expected salary increase is $30,000, then your payback period for a two-year MBA program is 5.33 years ($100,000/$30,000 + 2 years).

TABLE A One-Year MBA Programs				
Salary Increase	Total Investment			
	50,000	75,000	100,000	125,000
10,000	9%	−2%	−8%	−13%
20,000	35%	19%	9%	3%
30,000	58%	35%	23%	15%
40,000	79%	50%	35%	25%
50,000	99%	65%	47%	35%

TABLE B Two-Year MBA Programs							
Salary Increase	Total Investment						
	50,000	75,000	100,000	125,000	150,000	175,000	200,000
10,000	5%	−5%	−12%	−16%	−19%	−22%	−24%
20,000	27%	13%	5%	−1%	−5%	−9%	−12%
30,000	44%	27%	17%	10%	5%	1%	−3%
40,000	58%	38%	27%	19%	13%	8%	5%
50,000	71%	49%	36%	27%	20%	15%	11%

Part II

HOW TO GET IN

## Chapter 5

PREPARING TO BE A SUCCESSFUL APPLICANT

GET GOOD GRADES

If you're still in school, work on getting good grades. A high GPA says you've got not only brains, but discipline. It shows the admissions committee you have what you need to make it through the program. If you're applying directly from college or have limited job experience, your grades will matter even more. The admissions committee has little else on which to evaluate you.

It's especially important that you do well in courses such as economics, statistics, and calculus. Success in these courses is more meaningful than your success in classes like "Monday Night at the Movies" film appreciation. Of course, English is also important; b-schools want students who communicate well.

STRENGTHEN MATH SKILLS

Number-crunching is an inescapable part of b-school. Take an accounting or statistics course for credit at a local college or b-school. If you have a liberal arts background, did poorly in math, or got a low GMAT math score, this is especially important. Getting a decent grade will go a long way toward convincing the admissions committee you can manage the quantitative challenges of the program.

WORK FOR A FEW YEARS—BUT NOT TOO MANY

Business schools favor applicants who have worked full-time for several years. There are three primary reasons for this: 1) With experience comes maturity; 2) you're more likely to know what you want out of the program; 3) your experience enables you to bring real-work perspectives to the classroom. Since business school is designed for you to learn from your classmates, each student's contribution is important.

How many years of work experience should you have? From two to five seems to be the preferred amount, although there is no magic number. The rationale is that at two years you've worked enough to be able to make a solid contribution. Beyond four or five, you may be too advanced in your career to appreciate the program fully.

If your grades are weak, consider working at least three years before applying. The more professional success you have, the greater the likelihood the admissions committee will overlook your GPA.

LET YOUR JOB WORK FOR YOU

Many companies encourage employees to go to b-school. Some of these companies have close ties to a favored b-school and produce well-qualified applicants. If their employees are going to the kinds of schools you want to get into, these may be smart places to work.

Other companies, such as investment banks, feature training programs, at the end of which trainees go to b-school or leave the company. These programs hire undergraduates right out of school. They're known for producing solid, highly skilled applicants. Moreover, they're full of well-connected alumni who may write influential letters of recommendation.

Happily, the opposite tactic—working in an industry that generates few applicants—can be equally effective. Admissions officers look for students from underrepresented professions. Applicants from biotechnology, health care, not-for-profit, and even the Peace Corps are viewed favorably.

One way to set yourself apart is to have had two entirely different professional experiences before business school. For example, if you worked in finance, your next job might be in a different field, like marketing. Supplementing quantitative work with qualitative experiences demonstrates versatility.

Finally, what you do on your job is important. Seek out opportunities to distinguish yourself. Even if your responsibilities are limited, exceed the expectations of the position. B-schools are looking for leaders.

MARCH FROM THE MILITARY

A surprising number of b-school students hail from the military (although the armed forces probably had commanders in mind, not CEOs, when they designed their regimen).

Military officers know how to be managers because they've held command positions. And they know how to lead a team under the most difficult of circumstances.

Because most have traveled all over the world, they also know how to work with people from different cultures. As a result, they're ideally suited to learn alongside students with diverse backgrounds and perspectives. B-schools with a global focus are particularly attracted to such experience.

The decision to enlist in the military is a very personal one. However, if you've thought of joining those few good men and women, this may be as effective a means of preparing for b-school as more traditional avenues.

CHECK OUT THOSE ESSAY QUESTIONS NOW

You're worried you don't have interesting stories to tell. Or you just don't know what to write. What do you do?

Ideally, several months before your application is due, you should read the essay questions and begin to think about your answers. Could you describe an ethical dilemma at work? Are you involved in anything outside the office (or classroom)? If not, now is the time to do something about it. While this may seem contrived, it's preferable to sitting down to write the application and finding you have to scrape for or, worse, manufacture situations.

Use the essay questions as a framework for your personal and professional activities. Look back over your business calendar, and see if you can find some meaty experiences for the essays in your work life. Keep your eyes open for a situation that involves questionable ethics. And if all you do is work, work, work, get involved in activities that round out your background. In other words, get a life.

Get involved in community-based activities. Some possibilities are being a big brother/big sister, tutoring in a literacy program, or initiating a recycling project. Demonstrating a concern for others looks good to admissions committees, and hey, it's good for your soul, too.

It's also important to seek out leadership experiences. B-schools are looking for individuals who can manage groups. Volunteer to chair a professional committee or run for an office in a club.

It's a wide-open world; you can pick from any number of activities. The bottom line is this: The extracurriculars you select can show that you are mature, multifaceted, and appealing.

We don't mean to sound cynical. Obviously, the best applications do nothing more than describe your true, heartfelt interests and show off your sparkling personality. We're not suggesting you try to guess which activity will win the hearts of admissions directors and then mold yourself accordingly. Instead, think of projects and activities you care about, that maybe you haven't gotten around to acting on, and act on them now!

PICK YOUR RECOMMENDERS CAREFULLY

By the time you apply to business school, you shouldn't have to scramble for recommendations. Like the material for your essays, sources for recommendations should be considered long before the application is due.

How do you get great recommendations? Obviously, good work is a prerequisite. Whom you ask is equally important. Bosses who know you well will recommend you on both a personal and professional level. They can provide specific examples of your accomplishments, skills, and character. Additionally, they can convey a high level of interest in your candidacy.

There's also the issue of trust. B-school recommendations are made in confidence; you probably won't see what's been written about you. Choose someone you can trust to deliver the kind of recommendation that will push you over the top. A casual acquaintance may fail you by writing an adequate, yet mostly humdrum letter.

Cultivate relationships that yield glowing recommendations. Former and current professors, employers, clients, and managers are all good choices. An equally impressive recommendation can come from someone who has observed you in a worthwhile extracurricular activity.

Left to their own devices, recommenders may create a portrait that leaves out your best features. You need to prep them on what to write. Remind them of those projects or activities in which you achieved some success. You might also discuss the total picture of yourself you're trying to create. The recommendation should reinforce what you're saying about yourself in your essays.

About "Big Shot" recommendations: Don't bother. Getting some professional golfer who's a friend of your dad's to write you a recommendation will do you no good if he doesn't know you very well, even if he is President of the Universe. Don't try to fudge your application—let people who really know you and your work tell the honest, believable, and impressive truth.

PREPARE FOR THE GRADUATE MANAGEMENT
ADMISSION TEST (GMAT)

Most b-schools require you to take the GMAT. The GMAT is now a three-and-a-half-hour computer adaptive test (CAT) with multiple-choice math and verbal sections. It also features an analytical writing assessment section, which is comprised of two essays on business-related topics. It's the kind of test you hate to take and schools love to require.

Why is the GMAT required? B-schools believe it measures your verbal and quantitative skills and predicts success in the MBA program. Some think this is a bunch of hooey, but most schools weigh your GMAT scores heavily in the admissions decision. If nothing else, it gives the school a quantitative tool to compare you with other applicants.

Most people feel they have no control over the GMAT. They dread it as the potential bomb in their application. But you have more control than you think. You can take a test-preparation course to review the math and verbal material, learn test-taking strategies, and build your confidence. Test-prep courses can be highly effective. The Princeton Review offers what we think is the best GMAT course available. Another option is to take a look at our book *Cracking the GMAT CAT*, which reviews all the subjects and covers all the tips you would learn in one of our courses.

How many times should you take the GMAT? More than once, if you didn't ace it on the first try. But watch out: Multiple scores that fall in the same range make you look unprepared. Don't take the test more than once if you don't expect a decent increase, and don't even think of taking it the first time without serious preparation. Two tries is best. Three, if there were unusual circumstances or if you really need another shot at it. If you take it more than three times, the admissions committee will think you have an unhealthy obsession with filling in dots. A final note: If you submit more than one score, most schools will take the highest.

If you don't have math courses on your college transcript or numbers-oriented work experience, it's especially important to get a solid score on the quantitative section. There's a lot of math between you and the MBA.

## Chapter 6

ADMISSIONS

HOW THE ADMISSIONS CRITERIA ARE WEIGHTED

Admissions requirements vary from institution to institution. Most rely on the following criteria (not necessarily in this order): GMAT score, college GPA, work experience, essays, letters of recommendation, interviews, and extracurriculars, of which the first four are the most heavily weighted. The more competitive the school, the less room there is for weakness in any one of these areas.

Most applicants suspect that the GMAT score or GPA pushes their application into one of three piles: "yes," "no," or "maybe." But that's not the way it is. Unless one or more of your numbers is so low it forces a rejection, the piles are "looks good," "looks bad," "hmmm, interesting," and all variations of "maybe." In b-school admissions, the whole is greater than the sum of the parts. Each of the numbers has an effect but doesn't provide the total picture.

What's fair about the system is that you can compensate for problem areas. Even if you have a low GMAT score, a high GPA, evidence of quantitative work experience, or the completion of an accounting or statistics course will provide a strong counterbalance.

As we've said, no one single thing counts more than everything else. Your scores, work experience, and essays should give the admissions committee a clear idea of your capabilities, interests, and accomplishments. Any particular weakness can be overcome by a particular strength in another area—so make sure you emphasize whatever strengths you have, and don't take them for granted.

THE GMAT AND GPA

The GMAT score and GPA are used in two ways. First, they're used as "success indicators" for the academic work. In other words, if admitted, will you have the brain power and discipline to make it through the program? Second, they're used to comparing applicants with the larger pool. In particular, the top schools like applicant pools with high scores. They think that having an incoming class with high scores and grade profiles is an indicator of their program's prestige and selectivity.

Some schools look more closely at junior and senior year grades than the overall GPA. Most consider the academic reputation of your college and the difficulty of your curriculum. A transcript loaded with courses like "Environmental Appreciation" and "The Child in You" isn't valued as highly as one with a more substantive agenda.

WORK EXPERIENCE

B-schools pay particularly close attention to your work history. It provides tangible evidence of your performance in the business world thus far and hints at your potential. This helps b-schools determine whether you're going to turn out to be the kind of graduate they'll be proud to have as an alum. Your work experience reveals whether you've progressed enough (or too far) to benefit from a b-school education. It is also telling of the industry perspective you'll bring to the program.

Five elements are considered. First, the stature of your company: Does it have a good reputation? Does it produce well-qualified applicants?

Second, diversity of work experience. Have you done something extraordinary like starting your own business or inventing a new software program? Or maybe you've lucked out to work in an industry that is underrepresented at the prospective school?

Third, your advancement: Did you progress steadily to ever more responsible positions, or did you just tread water? Do your salary increases prove that you are a strong performer? Did you put in your time at each job, or just jump from company to company?

Fourth, your professional and interpersonal skills: Did you get along well with others? Work as part of a team? Do your recommenders see you as future manager material?

Fifth (and this is critical), your leadership potential: Did you excel in your positions, go beyond the job descriptions, save the day, lead a team?

THE ESSAYS

Admissions committees consider the essays the clincher, the swing vote on the "admit/deny" issue. Essays offer the most substance about who you really are. The GMAT and GPA reveal little about you, only that you won't crash and burn. Your work history provides a record of performance and justifies your stated desire to study business. But the essays tie all the pieces of the application together and create a summary of your experiences, skills, background, and beliefs.

The essays do more than give answers to questions. They create thumbnail psychological profiles. Depending on how you answer a question or what you present, you reveal yourself in any number of ways—creative, witty, open-minded, articulate, mature—to name a few. Likewise, your essay can reveal a negative side, such as arrogance, sloppiness, or an inability to think and write clearly.

THE RECOMMENDATIONS

Admissions committees expect recommendations to support and reinforce the rest of the application. They act as a sort of reality check. When the information from your recommender doesn't match up with the information you've provided, it looks bad.

Great recommendations are rarely enough to save a weak application from doom. But they might push a borderline case over to the "admit" pile.

Mediocre recommendations are potentially harmful: An application that is strong in all other areas now has an inconsistency that's hard to ignore.

Bad recommendations—meaning that negative information is provided—cast doubt on the picture you've created. In some cases they invalidate your claims. This can mean the end for your application. Again, be careful whom you ask for recommendations.

THE INTERVIEW

Like the recommendations, the interview is used to reinforce the total picture. But it is also used to fill in the blanks, particularly in borderline cases.

Not all b-schools attach equal value to the interview. For some, it's an essential screening tool. For others, it's used to evaluate those hovering in the purgatory between accept and reject. Still others strongly encourage, but do not require, the interview. Some schools make it simply informative. If you can't schedule an on-campus interview, the admissions office may find an alum to meet with you in your hometown.

If an interview is offered, take it. In person, you may be an entirely more compelling candidate. You can further address weaknesses or bring dull essays to life. Most important, you can display the kinds of qualities—enthusiasm, sense of humor, maturity—that often fill in the blanks and sway a decision.

Our strongest advice: act quickly to schedule your interviews. Admissions officers lack the staffing to interview every candidate who walks through their doors. So interview slots go faster than tickets to the Final Four. Grab a slot early by phoning the schools in September. You don't want your application decision delayed by several months (and placed in a more competitive round) because your interview was scheduled late in the filing period. Worse, you don't want to hear that your opportunity for face-to-face selling and convincing is gone, because all time slots are booked.

A great interview can tip the scale in the "admit" direction. How do you know if it was great? You were calm and focused. You expressed yourself and your ideas clearly. Your interviewer invited you to go rock climbing with him next weekend. (Okay, let's just say you developed a solid personal rapport with the interviewer.)

A mediocre interview may not have much impact, unless your application is hanging on by a thread. In such a case, the person you're talking to (harsh as it may seem) is probably looking for a reason not to admit you, rather than a reason to let you in. If you feel your application may be in that hazy, marginal area, try to be extra-inspired in your interview.

Did you greet your interviewer by saying, "Gee, are all admissions officers as pretty as you?" Did you show up wearing a Karl Marx T-shirt? Did you bring your mother with you? If so, it's probably safe to say you had a poor interview. A poor interview can doom even a straight-A, high-GMAT, strong-work-history candidate. Use good taste, refrain from belching, avoid insulting the interviewer's tie, and you'll probably be okay.

B-school interviews with alumni and admissions officers rarely follow a set formula. The focus can range from specific questions about your job responsibilities to broad discussions of life. Approach the interview as an enjoyable conversation, not as a question-and-answer ordeal that you're just trying to get through. You can talk about your hobbies or recent cross-country trip. This doesn't mean that it won't feel like a job interview. It just means you're being sized up as a person and future professional in all your dimensions. Try to be your witty, charming, natural self.

Students, faculty, admissions personnel, and alumni conduct interviews. Don't dismiss students as the lightweights; they follow a tight script and report back to the committee. However, because they're inexperienced beyond the script, their interviews are most likely to be duds. You may have to work harder to get your points across.

Prepare for the interview in several ways: Expect to discuss many things about yourself. Be ready to go into greater depth than you did in your essays (but don't assume the interviewer has read them). Put together two or three points about yourself that you want the interviewer to remember you by. Go in with examples, or even a portfolio of your work, to showcase your achievements. Practice speaking about your accomplishments without a lot of "I did this; I did that." Finally, be prepared to give a strong and convincing answer to the interviewer's inevitable question, "Why here?"

HOW TO BLOW THE INTERVIEW

1. Wear casual clothes.

This is an automatic ding. Wearing anything but professional attire suggests you don't know or don't want to play by the rules of the game.

2. Bring your mom or dad. Or talk about them.

Business schools value maturity. If Mom or Dad takes you to the interview, or your answer to the question "Why an MBA," begins with "Dad always told me . . . ," the interviewer is going to wonder how ready you are for the adult world of b-school.

3. Talk about high school.

Again, they'll question your maturity. Stories about high school, and even college, suggest you haven't moved on to more mature, new experiences.

Exceptions: Explaining a unique situation or a low GPA.

4. Show up late.

This is another automatic ding at some schools. Short of a real catastrophe, you won't be excused.

5. Say something off the wall or inappropriate.

No doubt, the conversation can get casual, and you may start to let your guard down. But certain things are still off-limits: profanity, ethnic jokes, allusions to sex, your romantic life, and anything else that might signal to the interviewer that the cheese fell off your cracker.

6. Forget to write a thank-you note to your interviewer.

Sending a thank-you note means you know how to operate in the business world, and it goes a long way toward convincing the interviewer you belong there.

MAKING THE ROUNDS: WHEN TO APPLY

You worked like a dog on your application—is there anything else you can do to increase your odds of getting accepted? Perhaps. The filing period ranges anywhere from six to eight months. Therefore, the timing of your application can make a difference. Although there are no guarantees, the earlier you apply, the better your chances. Here's why:

First, there's plenty of space available early on. As the application deadline nears, spaces fill up. The majority of applicants don't apply until the later months because of procrastination or unavoidable delays. As the deadline draws close, the greatest number of applicants compete for the fewest number of spaces.

Second, in the beginning, admissions officers have little clue about how selective they can be. They haven't reviewed enough applications to determine the competitiveness of the pool. An early application may be judged more on its own merit than how it stacks up against others. This is in your favor if the pool turns out to be unusually competitive. Above all, admissions officers like to lock their classes in early; they can't be certain they'll get their normal supply of applicants. Admissions decisions may be more generous at this time.

Third, by getting your application in early you're showing a strong interest. The admissions committee is likely to view you as someone keen on going to their school.

To be sure, some admissions officers report that the first batch of applications tend to be from candidates with strong qualifications, confident of acceptance. In this case, you might not be the very first one on line; but closer to the front is still better than lost in the heap of last-minute hopefuls.

Of course, if applications are down that year at all b-schools or—thanks to the latest drop in its ranking—at the one to which you are applying, then filing later means you can benefit from admissions officers desperately filling spaces. But this is risky business, especially since the rankings don't come out until the spring.

Conversely, if the school to which you are applying was recently ranked number one or two, applying early may make only a marginal difference. Swings in the rankings from year to year send school applications soaring and sagging. From beginning to end, a newly crowned number-one or two school will be flooded with applications. Regardless, do not put in your application until you are satisfied that it is the best you can make it. Once a school has passed on your application, it will not reconsider you until the following year.

ROUNDS AND ROLLING ADMISSIONS

Applications are processed in one of two ways: rounds admissions or rolling admissions. With rounds, the filing period is divided into three to four timed cycles. Applications are batched into the round in which they are received and reviewed competitively with others in that grouping. A typical round might go from February 15th to March 15th.

With rolling admissions, applications are reviewed on an ongoing basis as they are received. The response time for a rolling admissions decision is usually quicker than a decision with rounds. And with rolling admissions, when all the spaces are full, admissions stop.

QUOTAS, RECRUITMENT, AND DIVERSITY

B-schools don't have to operate under quotas—governmental or otherwise. However, they probably try harder than most corporations to recruit diverse groups of people. Just as the modern business world has become global and multicultural, so too have b-schools. They must not only teach diversity in the classroom but also make it a reality in their campus population and, if possible, faculty.

Schools that have a diverse student body tend to be proud of it. They tout their success in profiles that demographically slice and dice the previous year's class by sex, race, and geographic and international residency. Prospective students can review this data and compare the diversity of the schools they've applied to.

But such diversity doesn't come naturally from the demographics of the applicant pool. Admissions committees have to work hard at it. While they don't have quotas per se, they do target groups for admission, most notably women and minorities. In some cases, enrollment is encouraged with generous financial aid packages and scholarships.

But those targeted for admission are not limited to women and minorities. The committees seek demographic balance in many areas. Have they admitted enough foreign students, marketing strategists, and liberal arts majors? Are different parts of the country represented?

Only toward the end of the admissions filing period do shortages in different categories emerge. Although you can't predict, women and minorities are almost always on the short list. But here's some good news. According to the Graduate Management Admissions Council, in the 1996–97 academic year, 30 percent of the schools they surveyed said minorities made up 30–39 percent of their applicant pool. Happily, roughly 20 percent of the schools also reported increases in the number of women's applications.

WHO ARE THOSE ADMISSIONS OFFICERS?

ONE SCHOOL'S COMMITTEE REVEALED

Just who are those nameless, faceless people who pore over thousands of applications and determine the future of budding CEOs like you?

Most applicants picture a committee of white male MBAs in blue suits and power ties. But that's not the whole picture. Although many admissions officers do hold MBAs, they represent a wider slice of the demographic spectrum than do the b-school classes they admit. There are more women. More studied liberal arts and worked in fields such as human resources and teaching. In short, they're not necessarily what you'd expect; they're more diverse.

But as diverse as they are in background, they share a certain perspective: They believe that qualities, such as drive and discipline, rather than skills, such as financial analysis, are the true and enduring engines of success. In other words, at least as much value is placed on who you are as on your accomplishments.

Why does knowing this help you? Because in writing your application you need to consider your audience. Admissions officers aren't necessarily the people you thought they were. Moreover, they don't necessarily share your love of business. Their role in the business world is different from yours: They sustain the profession by launching inductees, while you actually practice business. Many officers, even some with MBAs, have limited business experience.

Remember, they're not only admissions officers, they're daughters, sons, mothers, fathers, and grandparents too—in other words, regular people. Would you write the same kind of essay for them that you would for your boss? The essays for b-school should be a combination of the two: strong on substance and heavy on personality.

Here's who reads your application at the University of Chicago Graduate School of Business (GSB):

THE DIRECTOR OF ADMISSIONS
Gender: Female
Race/Ethnicity: White
Age: Mid 30s
Marital/Family: Single
College Major: Information Science
Graduate Degree: MBA
First Job out of Graduate School: Systems Analyst

"After reading many applications over the years, it's pretty easy to tell when someone is trying to tell us what they think we want to hear. I can tell you that it is never what we want to hear. I'm more compelled by an application that conveys an honest picture of the individual behind all of the paper. If an applicant really understood how much every application looks the same—not in format, but content—they would think twice about how they prepare their applications."

ADMISSIONS OFFICER
Gender: Female
Race/Ethnicity: White
Age: Early 30s
Marital/Family: Single
College Major: English/Sociology
Graduate Degree: MS in Education
First Job out of Graduate School: Graduate Admissions Counselor

"Most candidates who apply to top b-schools self-select...they already know they've got the academic profile and quality of work experience we're seeking. That makes our job incredibly difficult because we could easily admit 75 percent (or more!) of those

who apply simply because they are qualified to be here. That's why qualifications alone are not enough. I look for evidence of well-roundedness, curiosity, self-assessment, and personal responsibility. Tell me who you are, what inspires you, what you're passionate about…that's what gets my attention."

ADMISSIONS OFFICER
Gender: Female
Race/Ethnicity: African American
Age: Late 20s
Marital/Family: Married/Mother
College Major: English
First Job out of School: Project Assistant with an entertainment marketing firm

"When I evaluate applications, I look well beyond academic performance and professional experience. While these areas are important, many, if not most, applicants have phenomenal qualifications in the aforementioned areas. Therefore, I have to discern the better of the best through other areas. Two major concerns are extracurricular/ community service activities and the desire for Chicago. I more or less look for characteristics that show a commitment to others and solid team player skills during and since college. I desire to see evidence of research conducted on the program and /or possible reasons why the city of Chicago is an ideal place of residence for the next two years. Whereas the program may be attractive, you need to feel comfortable with your surroundings. I want to know how Chicago will add more definition to the applicant's life, both professionally and personally. While an MBA will add value to your professional development, it also plays an integral role in enriching your life personally."

ADMISSIONS OFFICER
Gender: Male
Race/Ethnicity: White
Age: "Very" early 40s
Marital/Family: Married/Father of one son
College Major: Business Administration
Graduate Degree: MBA
First Job out of Graduate School: Marketing Administrator for an adult undergraduate program; adjunct professor of undergraduate and graduate marketing/management courses.

"When people ask me why I'm in admissions, my first response is that I really enjoy working with prospective candidates and current students alike. Also, with almost seven years of teaching experience at the graduate and undergraduate level, I've found that it's just not the numbers (GMAT/GPA) that contribute to a student's success. A person can be absolutely brilliant; however, if they can't 'personalize' the message they're sending, whether it's to other students/professors or future clients/business colleagues, ultimately, they won't be able to achieve their full potential."

ADMISSIONS OFFICER
Gender: Male
Race/Ethnicity: African American
Age: Early 40s
Marital/Family: Single
College Major: Bachelor of Fine Arts
First Job out of School: Development Office

"I guess I'm considered the tough guy when reviewing applications or interviewing. I'm interested in just the facts. I do enjoy reading the applications. The information that's provided is sometimes very revealing and many comments tend to be pretty funny. It's nice to see a sense of humor during such an intense procedure. Interviewing is what I like best. Eye contact, body language, and the lively exchange of conversation provide the edge I need when I make a decision."

DEAN'S STUDENT ADMISSIONS COMMITTEE MEMBER
Gender: Female
Race/Ethnicity: White
Nationality: Canadian
Age: Late 20s
Marital/Family: Married
College Major: Economics
Graduate Degree: Law and MA (Econ), MBA
First Job out of Graduate School: Law Clerk to federal judge (1 year), M and A Attorney (2 years)

"I decided to get involved in the admissions process because I thought it was important to give something back to the GSB community. When I review an application, I of course look at such factors as employment experience, academic record and GMAT scores; but, at least as important are articulate and thoughtful responses to the essay questions and a reasoned explanation as to why an MBA from Chicago is important to the applicant. At the end of the day, I try to review the application as a whole and determine whether the applicant is someone I would want as a classmate."

DEAN'S STUDENT ADMISSIONS COMMITTEE MEMBER

Gender: Male
Race/Ethnicity: White
Age: 30
Marital/Family: Single
College Major: English Literature
Graduate Degree: MS in Accounting
First Job out of Graduate School: Accountant, Real Estate Investments, Equity Research

"As a student I have a vested interest in the process. I'm looking for peers, not GMAT scores. Tell me who you are, not merely what you have done. A common fatal flaw is to recycle the 'why school X' essay: it's amazing how many people haven't even read the school's literature. Don't regurgitate facts I already know about the school, tell me why they're important to you. If you used to be a forest ranger and want to get into venture capital that's great as long as you can spell out why, not merely listing facts. Never decline an interview; you'll appear antisocial. Even if you can't get an alumni interview, make that the school's problem, not yours. With the ratio of applications to slots, you have to stand out somehow. Sending seven letters of recommendation, ignoring the essay lengths and abusing the optional essay to repeat information are all bad ways of standing out. I'm looking for classmates, not padded statistics; tell me what makes you tick and where a GSB MBA fits in that picture."

DEAN'S STUDENT ADMISSIONS COMMITTEE MEMBER

Gender: Male
Race/Ethnicity: African American
Age: Late 20s
Marital/Family: Married/Father
College Major: Accounting
Graduate Degree: MBA

"Reading an application should be a personal experience, in that the person reading your essays should have a good picture of who you are professionally and personally when they are finished. The feedback from the interviewer only serves to validate what I will have already learned from a set of strong essays. I look for sincerity and clarity. Sincerity in that it is obvious when people are trying to say 'all the right things,' or have skimmed the brochure and stuck in a couple of blurbs. I want to see people who have given our program some serious thought, and I want to know why they think this place would be a good fit for them. By clarity I mean clearly defined goals that are the product of introspection and maturity."

UNIVERSITY OF CHICAGO GRADUATE SCHOOL OF BUSINESS — ADMISSIONS PROCESS

The University of Chicago Graduate School of Business (GSB) uses an admissions process in which three members of the Admissions Committee read each application before a final decision is made—reviewing and taking into account every piece of information that is supplied in the application, including, if conducted, an interview. Below is an outline of the process that this committee takes to find qualified and dynamic individuals to admit to their program.

Interviews are optional for the Chicago application process. The admissions committee does, however, strongly recommend that applicants use the opportunity to set themselves apart and to make an impression on staff, students, or alumni interviewers. If an interview cannot be scheduled, they will waive the interview. When an interview is waived it is marked in the applicant's file so that all readers see that the applicant attempted to schedule an interview. If, in the admissions process, it is felt that an interview is necessary, they will notify the applicant. Once an interview is conducted, the interviewer provides the admissions office with feedback and a recommendation to either "admit," "deny," or "wait list" the applicant.

The first reader is a member of the Dean's Student Admissions Committee (DSAC, pronounced dee-sak). DSAC members are a group of about 175 first- and second-year MBA students who assist in the admissions process. DSAC first-year students assist with reading applications, and DSAC second-year students assist with on-campus interviewing. When a first reader has reviewed all of the materials in an application she will make a recommendation to either "admit," "deny," or "wait list" the applicant.

The second reader is a member of the full-time staff. He, too, will review all of the materials in an application with the exception of the first reader recommendation. He will make his own recommendation to either "admit," "deny," or "wait list" the applicant.

The last reader and final decision is made by the Director of Admissions, who takes into account all of the materials in the application as well as the recommendations of the first and second readers and, if conducted, the interviewer's recommendation.

What are all these people looking for in an application? An applicant's academic preparation is of particular importance. How applicants performed throughout their undergraduate academic career, how they fared among their peers, and particularly the rigor of their program are all elements considered. To a lesser extent, the GMAT is used as a predictor of success.

Beyond academic matters, they consider the personal characteristics and professional accomplishments of applicants. The Chicago admissions committee seeks students with records of distinguished leadership in work, school, and community activities, and who possess outstanding communication and interpersonal skills. They also seek a practical, realistic sense of value of the Chicago MBA in light of the applicant's career aspirations.

According to the school, there is not one particular area that is weighted more than another to secure admission. They say that most of the applicants are very qualified individuals, which presents the committee with some very difficult decisions. The Admissions Committee is responsible for selecting the most dynamic group from the applicant pool to ensure what they call "the tradition of excellence at the GSB."

A DIRECTOR OF ADMISSIONS TELLS US ABOUT THE ADMISSIONS PROCESS

AUTHOR'S INTERVIEW WITH CAROL SWANBERG, DIRECTOR OF ADMISSIONS AND FINANCIAL AID, UNIVERSITY OF CHICAGO GRADUATE SCHOOL OF BUSINESS

Gilbert: Carol, it must be exciting to have just become Director of Admissions at Chicago, one of the most selective and sought after programs in the country. That being said, with your depth of business school experience, we thought our readers would be particularly interested in your thinking as it relates to admissions today. Has the weighting of admissions criteria changed in the last five years? In what way?

Swanberg: Chicago doesn't weight any of the criteria in an application. We want to look at the whole picture of the applicant. We want to select people who we think will fit in well and be part of the GSB community. I haven't seen any admissions criteria change, but I have seen a change in the applicant pool. I think more and more people are really doing some research and they are choosing to apply to schools that are more aligned to their needs. Of course, when the applicant pool is more aligned with the program, it makes our job of selecting candidates even more difficult.

Gilbert: To the extent that an applicant's employer is unknown to your committee, how does an applicant demonstrate that his or her skills and background are as rigorous as one coming from a more well-known firm? What would be your issues? How could a candidate address them?

Swanberg: An applicant should convey what it is they have accomplished. I'm less concerned with how familiar we are with a specific employer than with the tangible skills that are learned on the job and what kinds of accomplishments have been made. There are quite a few smaller, lesser-known firms that really give their employees a lot of authority and many different kinds of experiences. We are much more interested in the takeaways. Have they learned how to work in a team? What kind of responsibility level do they have? Have they made some progression in their level of responsibility? How has the experience prepared the individual to be a better manager? Does the experience have relevance to future goals and aspirations?

Gilbert: What can a wait-listed applicant do to enhance his or her standing on the waitlist?

Swanberg: A wait-listed candidate can call our office for wait-list counseling. (We do get a lot of requests for feedback and it can take up to five working days for one of our admissions officers to contact the applicant.) Our admissions officer will discuss with the candidate the strengths and weaknesses of his or her application, and any questions that we need to have answered. The admissions officer will make recommendations on how the applicant should respond and what it is we're seeking. I can also tell you that the worst thing that a wait-listed applicant could do is nothing. If there is no response from applicants we tend to feel that maybe they are not really interested in the GSB. Also by not responding, it usually means that we're not getting information or questions answered that we were seeking in the first place.

Gilbert: What are the best explanations and worst explanations for low GMAT essay scores?

Swanberg: I don't know if there is a "best" explanation for a lower GMAT score. I believe that most people can answer a good portion of the test questions—if they had no time pressure and they didn't psyche themselves out. I think that an applicant should be honest in what they found to be difficult with the exam, and prove that those difficulties will not be a problem in the classroom. The worst explanation is "I just don't do well on these kinds of tests," then taking the exam only once, and never explaining how they prepared for it. To me, this always seems like a write-off by the applicant.

Gilbert: What are the most commonly avoidable mistakes in how candidates present themselves?

Swanberg: The biggest mistake people make is not following the directions in the application. I think that applicants should put themselves in the shoes of an admissions officer. Address questions that you know we're going to ask and address areas in the application that are weak. Also realize, with so many applicants, that there are things that we just don't have time to review and are unnecessary such as including books, publications, thesis and dissertation papers, and audio and video tapes. It's better to leave them out and just describe them and explain why it is important to mention them. The other big mistake people make is that they try to tell us what they think we want to hear in their essays. Applicants should really approach essays by first looking into themselves and really asking some honest questions, then writing their essays. One of the things I see a lot is when applicants say that earning an MBA is "the next logical step" in their career without ever explaining why. In my experience, life and careers don't necessarily have logical steps: they are what you make of them.

Gilbert: To what extent are extracurriculars, such as community service involvement, still important?

Swanberg: Here at Chicago, they are very, very important. But only if they're genuine. If someone is involved in different extracurriculars outside of when they attended undergraduate school, we feel that they will be involved in some of the many student and community groups that are part of the GSB. We also feel that that type of person is more likely to stay involved and to give something back to the school upon graduation—by being involved in GSB activities and volunteering to attend receptions, interview candidates, be a contact for current students, etc. We're very suspicious of applicants who join a community service or other group just prior to applying for graduate school. It just doesn't seem sincere.

Gilbert: What advantages does a foreign applicant have? How can they best leverage themselves?

Swanberg: An international applicant has the same chances as anyone else who applies to the GSB. Something that international applicants need to be aware of is that many state in their essays that their contribution to the class is that they are international. Most international students as well as domestic students have lived and/or traveled extensively. Many applicants are multicultural. What international students really need to do is to explain what kind of things they can contribute based on their experience and culture as it compares to other internationals and to U.S. students.

WHO DO YOU THINK READS YOUR ESSAYS?

Now that you know who those admissions officers are, here's the next surprise. Many top b-schools farm out the essays to paid readers. Why would the schools use readers instead of trained admissions officers to evaluate the essays? The answer is volume. As the number of applications to top b-schools has soared, it has become cost-effective to hire part-timers to do the most time-intensive work. Admissions officers are then free to make the higher-level admissions decisions.

Most applicants aren't pleased to know that an admissions officer isn't the one reading the essay they worked on for two weeks. But admissions committees couldn't be more pleased. Now instead of an enormous pile of unread essays—some terrific, some not—they have a pile that's been evaluated. Moreover, they point out, the essays are now read in greater depth than before.

But what you need to know is this: How do readers affect the admissions decision?

At most schools readers make general recommendations, then pass them on to other members of the committee for other opinions. They don't have the authority to make a final judgment. They're trained to evaluate essays in the same way admissions officers do—writing style, content, message, etc. More than one staff member usually reads them, often a combination of reader and admissions officer, so a reader's opinion is not the only one. Also, readers don't examine or have input into the evaluation of the applicant's total candidacy.

INSIDE BABSON COLLEGE'S ADMISSIONS DEPARTMENT

WHAT REALLY HAPPENS TO YOUR APPLICATION

Are specific weights or scores assigned to each component of the application?

Do admissions committees get together and read applications at one big table—or do they take them home and cover them with coffee stains?

How many people read your essays? How do they decide whether they're good or terrible? Is there is a system for standardizing the reading of the essays? Are they graded? Do they disagree? How are disagreements resolved?

Who are the surprise admits, the surprise rejects? Why are some students put on the wait list? What can be done to pull them off?

These are just a few of the questions surrounding an admissions process that often operates with the concealment strategies of the CIA. But all is not lost. The Babson Graduate School of Business agreed to open its files for our review. And while this is only one school's admissions process, you can certainly draw some interesting conclusions. Here's a flow chart of their process:

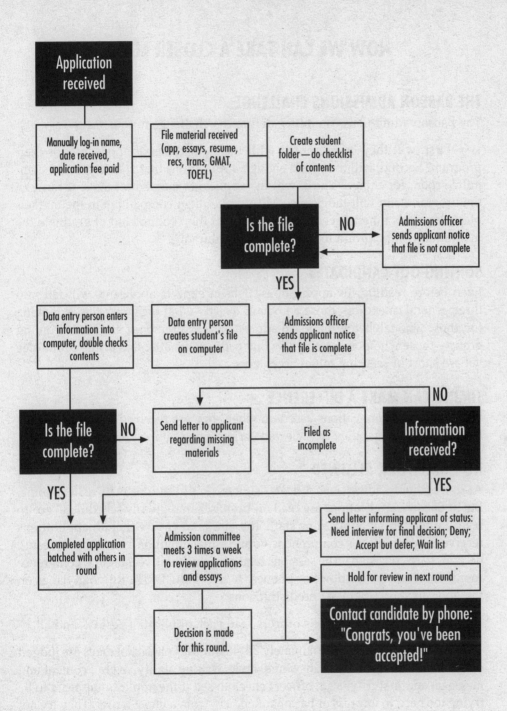

Application received

Manually log-in name, date received, application fee paid

File material received (app, essays, resume, recs, trans, GMAT, TOEFL)

Create student folder — do checklist of contents

Is the file complete?

NO → Admissions officer sends applicant notice that file is not complete

YES

Data entry person enters information into computer, double checks contents

Data entry person creates student's file on computer

Admissions officer sends applicant notice that file is complete

Is the file complete?

NO → Send letter to applicant regarding missing materials

Filed as incomplete

Information received?

NO

YES

YES

Completed application batched with others in round

Admission committee meets 3 times a week to review applications and essays

Send letter informing applicant of status: Need interview for final decision; Deny; Accept but defer; Wait list

Hold for review in next round

Decision is made for this round.

Contact candidate by phone: "Congrats, you've been accepted!"

NOW WE CAN TAKE A CLOSER LOOK

THE BABSON ADMISSIONS CHALLENGE

The Babson admissions committee defines its challenge in four ways:

First, will they be presented with the right types of applicants for their program? Second, will they yield enough applications that year to give the committee room for choice? Third, will the applicants they admit make it through the program, and will the Babson MBA make them competitive in the marketplace when it's time to get a job? Fourth, will they be the kind of graduate the institution will be proud to have among its alumni?

SORTING OUT CANDIDATES

Even before reading the applications, Babson expects applicants will fall into three general categories: those who have exactly what the institution is looking for, those who fall below standard admissions requirements, and the intriguing group—those who possess qualities that capture the attention of the committee yet are short of securing initial acceptance.

TIMING CAN MAKE A DIFFERENCE

Babson batches applications based on when they are received. Early applicants have the advantage; they're reviewed earlier when more spots are available.

NO HOMEWORK ALLOWED

At some schools, admissions officers "sign out" applications to be read at home. But at Babson, applications are read on-premises in regularly scheduled "group reads" attended by admissions staff. The aim is to ensure that all applications receive the committee's comprehensive and equal attention and that, as a result, decisions are consistent. The sessions take place in a long rectangular conference room. There are no windows or phones. A "DO NOT DISTURB" sign hangs on the door. In short, there are no distractions.

At least three admissions officers read each application, essays and all.

An officer spends approximately 30–45 minutes on each. Essays are judged on how well the question is answered, style, writing ability, overall content and message, and maturity; also, officers check to see if the applicant appears to be trying too hard to impress or has obtained help from a ghost writer. They try not to form opinions on the views expressed in the essay. Because the committee shares the same standards of evaluation, these assessments are qualitative. Essays are not subjected to an internal grading system or checklist of criteria.

DECISIONS, DECISIONS, DECISIONS

Occasionally there is disagreement about a particular essay. But since the admissions decision is based on the entire package, agreement on one essay is not as important as agreement on the overall candidacy of the applicant. When the committee doesn't agree on this, a lengthy discussion about the applicant takes place. If a consensus isn't reached, one of two steps is taken. Either the application is placed into a pile of "re-reviews" to be read again against each other at a later date (up to two weeks) or, depending on the problem area, the applicant is asked to have an additional interview with a dean or faculty member, do some extra coursework, or retake the GMAT. Applicants in the latter category may be put on conditional admit or wait lists. If they satisfy the additional requirements and a place is available, they're in.

After the "group read" and review session, the three admissions officers are joined by the remaining admissions staff for a presentation of the applicant's candidacy.

CASE STUDIES

Here are the dossiers of four hopeful applicants to Babson, and the admissions committee's evaluations:

> **Applicant I** is an undergraduate finance major from the University of Connecticut. She has a B grade point average and scored in the high 500s on the GMAT. Her work experience is substantive: five years, including two spent in the Peace Corps. The essays are descriptive and full of enthusiasm for her Peace Corps experience. The admissions committee learned she was up against major odds trying to secure loans from various funding sources for native African businesspeople.

The committee used the interview with this applicant to obtain further insight into why she chose to go into the Peace Corps rather than pursue her original career. A small but important point the applicant had overlooked—what had motivated her decision? In the interview, the admissions officer found her poised, well prepared, and able to articulate why she wanted the MBA. Her clarification of her job experience helped the committee better understand why she made the career decision she made.

Decision: *Admit*

Applicant II is a pharmaceutical salesman for a major international firm. His GMAT score is borderline, his GPA from a small liberal arts school in Maine is a low B. In reviewing his file, however, the committee found that he played a star position on his college's varsity hockey team and held a leadership position in student government. This helped explain and balance his marginal grades.

This applicant requested an interview early in the admissions process (this showed initiative even though interviews are required). He communicated clear expectations of the degree and what he wanted to accomplish. His essays also reflected a concise and persuasive presentation of his ideas. The letters of recommendation strongly supported his candidacy. His successes at work (many of them involving quantitative skill) also gave weight to his future business potential.

Decision: *Admit*

Applicant III is an art major from the Art Institute in Chicago. In addition to her current position as a marketing assistant at a special-events planning company, she has been recognized as one of the most creative students in the school and won the opportunity to present her work in the gallery at the museum. The committee felt a gallery show in such a prominent institute is a great accomplishment, particularly for a recent undergraduate.

This applicant took a "risky" approach to the essays, disclosing very personal information about emotional challenges she faced as a young adult. The essays were forthright, strong, and well structured. Most compelling was that her art exhibit was a pictorial essay of young women experiencing the same emotional challenges. The committee saw this as evidence that she had moved beyond the limitations of her emotional issues.

The greatest concern for this applicant was whether she would be able to manage the quantitative demands of the program. She performed poorly on the math section of the GMAT. Her undergraduate coursework and limited work history provide no evidence of quantitative experience. For her benefit and the benefit of her classmates, she needs to bolster her skills before she can begin.

Decision: *Denied. Needs to retake the GMAT, take quantitative courses, and reapply.*

Applicant IV is a Venezuelan banker, one of many applying to the
school because of its program's ties to Latin America.

This applicant was visiting Boston on a business trip and thought she
would use the opportunity to come in for an interview before she applied. She
was outstanding interpersonally. Her application later revealed an undergraduate GPA of a B+, eight years of work experience, and a mid-400 GMAT score. She
has progressed in her job from being an economist with a bank to a senior loan
officer—a nice progression. But her low GMATs blocked a clear "accept." Moreover, the committee needed to balance the number of students so there was not
a predominant presence in any class from any one country.

Decision: *Hold her application for review in the next round and within the Latin
American pool of candidates; ask her to retake the GMAT.*

## Chapter 7

The Right Stuff

CREATING PERFECTION TAKES TIME

No one ever said it was going to be easy. Depending on where you're applying and how prolific a writer you are, a b-school application will take anywhere from 50 to 100 hours to complete. Sound excessive? Go ahead and try it. You'll probably scrap and rewrite an essay many times over. It takes time for thoughts to gestate. Indeed, it might feel like a fine wine ages faster than it takes you to write an essay.

This chapter should speed the process along. It deciphers some of the most commonly asked essay questions. It also provides you with a list of the mistakes applicants make most often.

ESSAY ADVICE FROM AN EXPERT

Before we move on to the nuts and bolts of essay writing, Marie Mookini, Director of Admissions, Stanford Graduate School of Business, offers step-by-step advice on how to write a good essay.

MARIE MOOKINI, DIRECTOR OF ADMISSIONS
STANFORD GRADUATE SCHOOL OF BUSINESS

For most applicants to MBA programs it is the essays that seem to create the greatest anxiety. This is ironic since, in fact, the essay is the one part of the process over which you have the most control. Your essays are—no more and no less—stories about you. Your primary responsibility in the application process is to tell that story, and to tell it in a natural and descriptive way. Everyone loves to read and listen to stories. The ones that are most memorable and compelling are not the dramatic, bare-all essays, but rather those that are honest and full of vivid examples.

Think of your essays as the centerpiece of your application. This is your opportunity to begin shaping the admission committee's impression of who you are—by sharing your core values and your interests and describing how you make sense of the world around you. Admissions committees are as interested in who you are as in what you have accomplished, because in assembling a community of students they wish to achieve a richness and diversity of backgrounds and perspectives.

Ask a group of admissions officers for the one piece of advice they would give applicants and nine out of ten will say without sarcasm: "answer the question that is asked." While the temptation is great to submit cut-and-paste essays, it simply is not a good idea. Admissions staffs make it their business to know what their competitors are asking.

Because the admission rates at the top business schools tend to be very low, candidates wishing to gain entrance into these programs must try to present as many strengths in as many different areas as possible. That means a strong academic profile is a must, along with glowing letters of reference from employers who can testify to significant workplace contributions, and yes, well-crafted essays.

Applicants will find an abundance of self-help books that highlight sample essays of successful applicants. While these publications serve a useful purpose in providing applicants with a range of possibilities, what might be more helpful is the following step-by-step guide on preparing the essay:

Step One: Read the school's literature. Get a feel for the culture of the school based on what is said and how the school is described. What does the school consider to be its most important attributes? What is the school most proud of?

Step Two: Read the essay questions. There should be some symmetry between the content and tone of the questions and what the school is all about. If there is little that resonates between you and the school, chances are that it will be a very uncomfortable and awkward exercise for you to prepare answers to that school's essay questions.

Step Three: Start jotting down your responses to the questions that are asked. Persuasive responses are ones that include specific anecdotes, and highly descriptive prose. The admissions staff spend a lot of time crafting the questions to elicit the types of information they find valuable in assessing the fit of a candidate with their programs. They are interested in what you say, as well as how successful you are in communicating.

Step Four: By "descriptive prose" I do not mean gimmicks such as videotapes in lieu of essays: essays posing as interviews with you in the year 2020 (unless the question specifically asks for this) or screenplays featuring you. Your time is better spent giving details of your role and impact in situations. These specific examples will make you come alive in the readers' minds because they will be able to visualize you and your behavior in that particular situation. The bulk of your time preparing your essays should be spent talking with friends and colleagues and asking their help to recall those specific situations where you demonstrated a quality or behavior that is illustrative of the essay question.

Step Five: One of the most common mistakes by applicants is that they try hard to sell themselves to the committee instead of thoughtfully and candidly describing themselves. Instead of saying, "I have leadership skills that will enable me to start a company," describe the time you used your leadership skills toward a favorable outcome. Let the admissions committee extrapolate from your story that you have leadership skills, rather than boast about it.

Step Six: Give your essays to a friend or someone who knows you well. Ask that friend one simple question, "Is the real me coming through?" Asking you to reformat your wonderfully rich three-dimensional life into two dimensions means that something is bound to get lost in the translation. Having another pair of eyes to give you feedback on tone and content can be useful. For example, one reader might tell you that your lighthearted side did not come through since your essays seemed cold and sterile, in which case you might want to revisit some of the essays to add an appropriate touch of humor, levity, or anecdotes that reveal your personality. Or perhaps you failed to mention a favorite hobby that your friends say defines your personality.

Step Seven: Even though a well-conceived essay is important to your candidacy, keep in mind that the admissions committee does look to other sources to corroborate their impressions of you. For example, many schools conduct interviews to complement their paper assessments. Letters of reference should also be viewed as complementary and supplementary information. Carefully choosing people who will be enthusiastic cheerleaders and knowledgeable enough to describe your wonderful personal qualities and professional accomplishments is another key success factor. Do not underestimate the power of a set of references.

COMMON ESSAY QUESTIONS

WHAT THEY'RE REALLY ASKING

Each school has its own set of essay questions. Although posed differently, all search for the same insights. Here's a list of commonly asked questions and what's behind them.

1. Theme: Career Goals and the MBA

> Describe your specific career aspirations. How will your goals be furthered by an MBA degree and by our MBA program in particular?

> How do you feel the X school MBA degree can help you attain your specific career and personal goals for the five years after you graduate?

> Discuss your career progression to date. What factors have influenced your decision to seek a general management education? Based on what you know about yourself at this time, how do you envision your career progressing after receiving the MBA degree? Please state your professional goals, and describe your plan to achieve them.

Translation:

What do I want to be when I grow up, and how will the MBA get me there?

This may be the most important essay question. It lays out the reasons why you should be given one of the cherished spots in the program. Even if your post-MBA future is tough to envision, this question must be answered.

A good way to frame this essay is to discuss how the MBA makes sense in light of your background, skills, and achievements to date. Why do you need this degree? Why now? One common reason is being stymied in your work by a lack of skills that can be gained in their program. Or you may want to use the MBA as a bridge to the next step. For example, an actress wants an MBA to prepare for a career in theater management. The more specific, the better.

It may be easier to provide specifics by breaking your plans into short-term and long-term objectives.

Don't be afraid to present modest goals. If you're in accounting and want to stay there, say so. Deepening your expertise and broadening your perspective are solid reasons for pursuing the degree. On the other hand, feel free to indicate you'll use the MBA to change careers; 70 percent of all students at b-school are there to do just that.

If you aspire to lofty goals, like becoming a CEO or starting your own company, be especially careful that you detail a sensible, pragmatic plan. You need to show you're realistic. No one zooms to the top. Break your progress into steps.

Finally, this essay question asks how a particular program supports your goals. Admissions committees want to know why you've selected their school. That means you not only have to know, but also show, what's special about their program and how that relates specifically to your career aspirations.

(Hint: Many admissions officers say they can tell how much someone wants to go to their school by how well their essays are tailored to the offerings in their program.)

2. Theme: Extracurriculars and Social Interaction: Our Nonwork Side

What do you do for fun?

What are your principal interests outside of your job or school?

What leisure and/or community activities do you particularly enjoy? Please describe their importance in your life.

Translation:

Would we like to have you over for dinner? Do you know how to make friends? What are your special talents—the b-school Follies needs help. Are you well balanced, or are you going to freak out when you get here?

B-school is not just about business, case studies, and careers. The best programs buzz with the energy of a student body that is talented and creative and that has personality. You won't be spending all your time in the library.

Are you interesting? Would you contribute to the school's vitality? Are you the kind of person other MBAs would be happy to meet? Describe activities you're involved in that might add something to the b-school community.

Are you sociable? B-school is a very social experience. Much of the work is done in groups. Weekends are full of social gatherings. Will you participate? Initiate? Get along with others? Communicate that people, not just your job, are an important part of your life.

Can you perform at a high level without being a nerd?

B-school can be tough. It's important to know when to walk away and find some fun. Do you know how to play as hard as you work?

How well rounded are you? Business leaders have wide-angle perspectives; they take in the whole picture. How deep or broad are your interests?

(A warning: Don't just list what you've done. Explain how what you've done has made you unique.)

3. Theme: The Personal Statement

Does this application provide the opportunity to present the real you?

The admissions committee would welcome any additional comments you may wish to provide in support of your application.

What question should we have asked you?

Translation:

What did we miss? Appeal to us in any way you want; this is your last chance. Be real.

If you have an experience or personal cause that says something interesting about you, and it hasn't found a place in any other essay, this is the time to stick it in. Keep in mind that you are hoping to present yourself as unique—so show some passion!

4. Theme: Whom You Most Admire

If you were able to choose one person from the business world, past or present, to be your personal professor throughout the MBA program, who would this person be and why?

Describe the characteristics of an exceptional manager, using an example of someone whom you have observed or with whom you have worked. Illustrate how his or her management style has influenced you.

Translation:

What are your values? What character traits do you admire?

This is the curve-ball question. The committee isn't looking to evaluate your judgment in selecting some famous, powerful person in your firm or in the world. What they're really after, which you reveal in your selection of the person, is the qualities, attributes, and strengths you value in others, as well as in yourself. Some important qualities to address: Drive, discipline, vision, ethics, and leadership. As always, provide specific examples, and avoid choosing anyone too obvious.

Since the person you select is not as important as what you say about him or her, your choices can be more humble. You might write about a current boss, business associate, or friend. Bad choices are your mother or father.

If you like, it's perfectly fine to go for a famous figure. Indeed, there may be someone whose career and style you're passionate about. Make sure your essay explains why you find this person so compelling.

5. Theme: Teamwork—How Do You Work with Others in a Group Setting?

At X School, a team, which consists of approximately five first-year students, is often assigned group projects and class presentations. Imagine that, one year from now, your team has a marketing class assignment due at 9:00 am on Monday morning. It is now 10:00 pm on Sunday night; time is short, tension builds, and your team has reached an impasse. What role would you take in such a situation? How would you enable the team to meet your deadline? [Note: The specific nature of the assignment is not as important here as the team dynamic.] Feel free to draw on previous experiences, if applicable, in order to illustrate your approach.

Translation:

We need cooperative, one-for-all and all-for-one students here. Are you cut out to be one, or are you a take-over type who has all the answers? Are you likely to help everyone get along and arrive at solutions? (We like those kinds of students). Can you lead others to order and synergy? (We especially like leaders). Or do you retreat or become a follower?

This too is a curveball question. But you can't afford to get it wrong. After the career goals question, it probably ranks as the most critical essay you write. Here the committee isn't looking to see how you save the team (so put yourself on ego-alert as you sit down to write this one). They want to see how you can create an environment in which everyone contributes so the sum is greater than its parts. Bottom line—the admissions committee is looking to see whether you have "emotional intelligence." Understand that schools today believe that emotional intelligence, the ability to navigate emotion-laden situations, is as important as strategic and analytical skills. This question is intended to illustrate this particular type of intelligence.

Expect to shift gears with this essay. Almost the entire application process thus far has asked you to showcase *me-me-me*. Now the focus of your story needs to be on the *we* and how you made the *we* happen.

As you write your essay, consider that when you get to school, some team members will be from different countries where cultural attitudes play into team dynamics. Your sensitivity to these cultural differences, as well as to personality types, will go a long way toward demonstrating your emotional intelligence. For example, a team member hailing from a certain culture may withhold an opinion in an attempt to foster consensus. How can you help this person make a contribution? Likewise, consider differences among team members in terms of their academic and professional strengths. If the assignment is heavy on numbers, finance students may dominate teammates from softer sciences. How can you ensure that everyone feels valued? Teams are inspired to success when everyone is motivated and taking ownership within a context of respect.

Remember: the team in this particular essay is at an impasse, as most teams are at some point and time. Write about how you unjammed the jam. Ideas: a change of scene, food, twenty push-ups, a quick round-the-room confessional about why you came to b-school. Introducing some *process* is also useful: ground rules such as voting, speaking times, a division of labor and a timeline, all create a method out of the madness. Perhaps you encourage members to adopt roles—business or otherwise. Hint: the leader or CEO in this case might be your most soft-spoken team member. Whatever you do in this essay, be careful not to present yourself as the one who single handedly gets the team dynamic going.

6. Theme: Diversity and What Makes You Unique

Our Business School is a diverse environment. How will your experiences contribute to this?

During your years of study in the X program, you will be part of a diverse multicultural, multiethnic community within both the Business School and the larger university. What rewards and challenges do you anticipate in this environment, and how do you expect this experience to prepare you for a culturally diverse business world?

Translation:

What about you is different in terms of your background, your experience, or your cultural or geographic heritage? Can we count on your unique voice and perspective in our wide-ranging classroom discussions? How will you support the diverse, cultural climate we are fostering here?

This essay gets at two concerns for the admissions committee: 1) how will you enrich the student body at this school and 2) what is your attitude toward others' diverse backgrounds? Today's business leaders must be able to make decisions in situations that cut across geographic and cultural boundaries. If your essay reveals that you have dinosaur-era, only-white-males-rule thinking, you're going to close the door on your candidacy.

So what if you are a white male? Or you have no immediate point of distinction? Maybe a grandparent or relative is an immigrant to this country and you can discuss the impact of his or her values on your life. Perhaps you are the first individual in your family to attend college or to attend graduate school. What does that mean to you? Perhaps you are involved in a meaningful or unusual extracurricular activity. How has this changed your perspective? Perhaps you did a business deal with a foreign country—what did you observe about that culture, and how did it affect your decisions?

Whatever you write about need not be dramatic—maybe you take art classes, coach a little league team, or race a motorcycle. Sound goofy? It's all in the framing. Racing a motorcycle might be about the physical and mental stamina, the ability to take risk, the commitment to learning something new.

This question can be relatively easy to answer if, of course, you have diversity or some unique element in your background. If you don't have something obvious, then you're going to have to dig about a bit and find something you can amplify to suggest you bring a unique voice to the school.

7. Theme: Your Greatest Personal Achievement/Accomplishment

Describe a personal achievement that has had a significant impact on your life. In addition to recounting this achievement, please analyze how the event has changed your understanding of yourself and how you perceive the world around you.

In reviewing the last five years, describe one or two accomplishments in which you demonstrated leadership.

Translation:

Do you know what an achievement is? Have you done anything remarkable? What made it remarkable to you? Bonus points if you showed leadership or inspired others in some way.

This is one of those maddening essay questions. On the one hand, b-schools seek out applicants whose average age is 27 (a relatively young age to have achieved much of anything) yet on the other hand, the schools want to know what miracles you've performed. Don't pull your hair out yet. There is a way out. Like all the others, this essay is just one more prove-to-us-you-have-some-character hoop you'll have to jump through. It's less about the achievement and more about who you are and how you see yourself.

Again, this question can be easy to answer if you have some clear accomplishment or event in your background. But if you're like the rest of us—you guessed it—you'll have to rely on framing.

Let's cover bad essay topics for achievements. Getting straight A's in college is not an achievement because every one else at b-school has probably done the same. Surviving a divorce or breakup is a bad accomplishment topic. Personal stories are acceptable—but one taboo area is romance and marriage. If this is all you can come up with, you're going to look like you're as deep as a donut.

The accomplishment you choose might show some of the following qualities: character, sacrifice, humility, dedication, high-personal stakes, perseverance over obstacles, insight, and learning. You need not have published a business article or won an award to answer this question. *This essay is not about excellence of outcome, but what it took for you to reach some personal worthy objective.* Maybe you didn't lead a sports team to a victory. The victory may be just that you made it onto the team.

8. Theme: Failure/ What Mistakes Have You Made?

Discuss a nonacademic personal failure. In what way were you disappointed in yourself? What did you learn from the experience?

Translation:

Can you admit to a genuine failure? Do you have enough self-awareness to know what one is real? Can you learn from your mistakes? Do they lead to greater maturity and self-awareness? Do you take accountability when the fault is yours?

Many applicants make the mistake of answering this question with a failure that is really a positive, "I'm a perfectionist and so therefore I was too demanding on a friend when she was in a crisis." Or, they never really answer the question, fearful that any admission of failure will throw their whole candidacy into jeopardy. The truth is, if you don't answer this question with a genuine failure or mistake, one that the committee will recognize as authentic, you may have jinxed your application.

In this essay you want to write about a failure that had some high stakes for you. Demonstrate what you learned from your mistake and how it matured you. What's the relevance to b-school here? Your ability to be honest, take account-ability, and face your failures head on reflects what kinds of decisions and judg-ments you will make as a business professional.

Can't think of a time you failed? Discuss the essay question with a friend or family member. An outsider's perspective may jar your memory. Remember, if your whole application has been about work, work, work, this is a great place to convince the committee you're a real person.

MUST-FOLLOW CHECKLIST FOR THE ESSAYS

- Communicate that you're a proactive, can-do sort of person. Leaders take initiative and aren't thwarted by roadblocks.

- Put yourself on ego alert; stress what makes you unique, not what makes you great. You want admissions officers to respect and like you.

- Position yourself as a stand-out from the crowd; empha-size your distinctiveness.

- Make sure your leadership qualities really come through. Admissions officers want to hear about skills that enabled you to rally folks around your solution.

- Communicate specific reasons why you're a "fit" for a school (but avoid pompous, fluff statements such as "I am the ideal or perfect candidate for your program").

- Use your gender, ethnicity, minority, or foreign back-ground—but only if it has affected your outlook or experiences.

- Bring passion to your writing—admissions officers want to know what you're really excited about.

- Avoid too many sentences that begin with "I." Use ex-amples and anecdotes instead.

- Play up an unorthodox path to b-school. Admissions officers appreciate risk-takers. But be convincing about your ability to handle the program, especially quantitative skills that schools can take for granted in applicants in finance.

STRAIGHT TALK FROM ADMISSIONS OFFICERS: FIFTEEN SURE-FIRE WAYS TO TORPEDO YOUR APPLICATION

1. Write about the high school glory days.

Unless you're right out of college, or you've got a great story to tell, resist using your high-school experiences for the essays. What does it say about your maturity if all you can talk about is being editor of the yearbook or captain of the varsity team?

2. Submit essays that don't answer the questions.

An essay that does no more than restate your resume frustrates the admissions committees. After reading 5,000 applications, they get irritated to see another long-winded evasive one.

Don't lose focus. Make sure your stories answer the question.

3. Fill essays with industry jargon and detail.

Many essays are burdened by business-speak and unnecessary detail. This clutters your story. Construct your essays with only enough detail about your job to frame your story and make your point. After that, put the emphasis on yourself—what you've accomplished and why you were successful.

4. Write about a failure that's too personal or inconsequential.

Refrain from using breakups, divorces, and other romantic calamities as examples of failures. What may work on a confessional talk show is too personal for a b-school essay.

Also, don't relate a "failure" like getting one "C" in college (out of an otherwise straight "A" average). It calls your perspective into question. Talk about a failure that matured your judgment or changed your outlook.

5. Reveal half-baked reasons for wanting the MBA.

Admissions officers favor applicants who have well-defined goals. Because the school's reputation is tied to the performance of its graduates, those who know what they want are a safer investment.

If b-school is just a pit stop on the great journey of life, admissions committees would prefer you make it elsewhere. However unsure you are about your future, it's critical that you demonstrate that you have a plan.

6. Exceed the recommended word limits.

Poundage is not the measure of value here. Exceeding the recommended word limit suggests you don't know how to follow directions, operate within constraints, organize your thoughts, or all of the above.

Get to the crux of your story and make your points. You'll find the word limits adequate.

7. Submit an application full of typos and grammatical errors.

How you present yourself on the application is as important as what you present. Although typos don't necessarily knock you out of the running, they suggest a sloppy attitude. Poor grammar is also a problem. It distracts from the clean lines of your story and advertises poor writing skills.

Present your application professionally—neatly typed and proofed for typos and grammar. And forget gimmicks like a videotape. This isn't *America's Funniest Home Videos*.

8. Send one school an essay intended for another—or forget to change the school name when using the same essay for several applications.

Double check before you send anything out. Admissions committees are (understandably) insulted when they see another school's name or forms.

9. Make whiny excuses for everything.

Admissions committees have heard it all—illness, marital difficulties, learning disabilities, test anxiety, bad grades, pink slips, putting oneself through school—anything and everything that has ever happened to anybody. Admissions officers have lived through these things, too. No one expects you to sail through life unscathed. What they do expect is that you own up to your shortcomings.

Avoid trite, predictable explanations. If your undergraduate experience was one long party, be honest. Discuss who you were then, and who you've become today. Write confidently about your weaknesses and mistakes. Whatever the problem, it's important you show you can recover and move on.

10. Make the wrong choice of recommenders.

A top-notch application can be doomed by second-rate recommendations. This can happen because you misjudged the recommendors' estimation of you or you failed to give them direction and focus.

As we've said, recommendations from political figures, your uncle's CEO golfing buddy, and others with lifestyles of the rich and famous don't impress (and sometimes annoy) admissions folk—unless such recommenders really know you or built the school's library.

11. Let the recommender miss the deadline.

Make sure you give the person writing your recommendation plenty of lead time to write and send in their recommendation. Even with advance notice, a well-meaning but forgetful person can drop the ball.

It's your job to remind them of the deadlines. Do what you have to do to make sure they get there on time.

12. Be impersonal in the personal statement.

Each school has its own version of the "Use this space to tell us anything else about yourself" personal statement question. Yet many applicants avoid the word "personal" like the plague. Instead of talking about how putting themselves through school lowered their GPA, they talk about the rising cost of tuition in America.

The personal statement is your chance to make yourself different from the other applicants, further show a personal side, or explain a problem. Take a chance and be genuine; admissions officers prefer sincerity to a song and dance.

13. Make too many generalizations.

Many applicants approach the essays as though they were writing a newspaper editorial. They make policy statements and deliver platitudes about life without giving any supporting examples from their own experiences.

Granted, these may be the kind of hot-air essays that the application appears to ask for, and probably deserves. But admissions officers dislike essays that don't say anything. An essay full of generalizations is a giveaway that you don't have anything to say, don't know what to say, or just don't know how to say whatever it is you want to say.

14. Neglect to communicate that you've researched the program and that you belong there.

B-schools take enormous pride in their programs. The rankings make them even more conscious of their academic turf and differences. While all promise an MBA, they don't all deliver it the same way. The schools have unique offerings and specialties.

Applicants need to convince the committee that the school's programs meet their needs. It's not good enough to declare prestige as the primary reason for selecting a school (even though this is the basis for many applicants' choice).

15. Fail to be courteous to employees in the admissions office.

No doubt, many admissions offices operate with the efficiency of sludge. But no matter what the problem, you need to keep your frustration in check.

If you become a pest or complainer, this may become part of your applicant profile. An offended office worker may share his or her ill feelings about you with the boss—that admissions officer you've been trying so hard to impress.

## Chapter 8

ESSAYS THAT WORK

Writing Your Way into Business School

CASE EXAMPLES:
ADMISSIONS OFFICERS CRITIQUE WINNING ESSAYS

To show you how some applicants have answered the essay questions, we asked the b-schools for samples of "winning" essays. To show you what worked, we also asked the admissions officers to provide a critique.

As you read through the essays, keep in mind that each was but one of several submitted by an applicant for admission. Moreover, they were part of a package that included other important components. One essay alone did not "win" admission.

One other reminder. The purpose of including essays in this book is to give you a nudge in the right direction, not to provide you with a script or template for your own work. It would be a mistake to use them this way.

Obviously, this collection is by no means all-encompassing. There are thousands of winning essays out there; we just couldn't include them all.

A final note: Because Harvard features a whopping ten-essay application, we especially wanted it in this section. Harvard declined our request. So to access what apparently is guarded as closely as FBI files, we contacted the students and grads directly. To our delight, everyone was eager to supply an essay. We selected those we believe the admissions officers would also have considered "winning."

BOSTON UNIVERSITY

Essay #1:

Imagine a straight line of infinite length, stretching out of sight in two directions. Assuming the line represents time, one can stand at any present moment and simultaneously look back at past experience and project one's sight into the future.

The time line is an assumption that makes planning possible. Though it may someday be proven a false, or at least incomplete, model, it can be useful for both personal and professional planning. For this essay, I'll limit myself to the latter.

Where I Stand

Looking back at what I've done and ahead to what I'd like to do, I can find great sense in beginning a graduate management program.

I have: a foundation of experience in the administration of educational and cultural institutes. Past jobs have ranged from directing a college admissions office to promoting an opera company, to managing a modern dance company, to running a day care center, to editing a weekly newspaper.

I have: an understanding of how groups function, what makes an organization healthy, and various ways people can organize to accomplish a goal. This has come from work experience as well as graduate study in organization theory and design at Harvard and at M.I.T.

I have: dreams and plans for a range of jobs and enterprises that extend ahead through my life.

From Here to There

Among many goals, I would like to direct a major cultural institution. I would also like to head a major educational institution, run a major foundation, and start and run my own cultural or educational organization—not necessarily all at the same time.

To achieve the above, there are skills and arenas of knowledge and experience that I'd like to have in my grasp. Some of these are presently out of reach, others are at my fingertips, but none are firmly in hand.

Financial management is, for me, perhaps the largest arena of knowledge in which I want, but do not have, agility. A course of study that refreshes my quantitative skills and teaches me principles of economics, fiscal planning, and other financial management skills would be very useful.

Another such arena includes management information systems and computer programming. I presently work on word processing equipment with comfort and joy. I hope, with time and guidance, to do the same with other systems at an even deeper level.

I would also like more personal contact with professional peers, particularly in the Boston and New England region. The public management program appears to offer that.

Some of my more obvious strengths and weaknesses should be evident from the above. I have confidence in myself. I have a great deal of curiosity. I generate ideas and develop interests, and can usually turn these into realistic, well-organized, and flexible plans. These I consider my strengths.

I can also stretch myself too thin, which can be a problem. Though I realize taking on the new demands some letting go of the old, I also believe experience increases capacity. There seems to me a need for more trained generalists to protect against overspecialization and fragmentation.

One great tool for that kind of protection is humor. My own sense of the comic can be quite dry and subtle, or broad and bizarre. Regardless of the form in which it spills out, it provides me perspective, balance, and spontaneity.

Cooperation, too, is a central motivation for me, and I am glad to see it stressed in the public management literature.

Arrivals

To accept two accomplishments and to label these significant runs counter to my way of assessing substance. I try to resist measuring my achievement by individual moments of arrival. Still, when pressed, I can come up with a few.

Performing professional theater at the age of 17 is an accomplishment that seems more significant now than it did at the time. Being appointed a college admissions director at 23 seems similarly significant. Both provided a sense of competence at a young age, and both provided peer experience with people older and more experienced than myself.

Doing well in a graduate program at Harvard feels notable in that the school was an environment very different from any in which I had worked before. The program became a test of adaptability as well as intellect. Other accomplishments might include a few backpacking ventures taken in severe conditions, some of which became life threatening. These provided dramatic tests of my reserves, and gave me confidence in my capacity for survival.

Less dramatic, and not quite finished, is a quilting project that I have worked on for more than six years. I have just completed the top sheet, a mutipieced pattern in fabric. Still ahead is the quilting process itself, stitching the top sheet to a sturdy backing, with a layer of batting between the two. When done, the quilt takes on an identity far greater than the sum of its many parts.

The work on this piece has been a teacher of patience and harmony. The quilt, with its assortment of shapes and fabric, can serve as a model for the organization for one's life and the people and activities in it.

Now, imagine a fine thread of infinite length weaving in and out of all those pieces.

CRITIQUE

Admissions officers review several hundreds or thousands of applications each year. Due to this high volume, any given applicant should formulate a creative approach in composing the essay to attract attention to its quality and content. Unfortunately, many applicants write essays that are similar to a detailed resume or a cover letter. This not only discourages a thorough review but also eliminates the opportunity for the individual to express his or her own uniqueness. The admissions officers are also usually interested in how an applicant responds to a specific question, rather than to a general statement.

This essay creatively suggests the applicant's general outlook on his life, what he hopes to achieve, and how he will do it. He does not go into great detail about any of these issues but allows what he does say to have a powerful impact. Reading this essay gives the evaluator the opportunity to get to know the values as well as interests and accomplishments the candidate has. This is particularly helpful when applying to a school that does not have evaluative interviews as part of the application process.

The essay is also brief and concise and makes an effort to link all the topics mentioned in the essay to create a well-defined image. The use of subtitles introduces the outline and scope of the essay.

BRIGHAM YOUNG UNIVERSITY

Essay #1

Donald J. Buehner

MBA Admissions Committee
640 TNRB
Brigham Young University
Provo, UT 84602

Dear Members of the BYU MBA Admissions Committee:

In response to your request, I am writing to inform you of my intentions for this coming year as well as to describe my employment experience acquired during the past year.

I plan to attend the MBA program commencing in September 1991. You should have already received my Bishops Form.

During the past year I have had extensive international and national work experience. In February of 1990 I was promoted by Franklin International Institute Inc. to assist in opening a European Distribution Center in England. My specific assignment was to establish and manage the order entry and customer service departments as well as to hire and train British employees in the various operational functions. Inclusive with this training assignment was to implement the corporate values, philosophies, and quality, and to instill in our employees the high standards of excellence and consumer satisfaction for which the Franklin International Institute strives. During my six-month assignment, I worked under pressured time constraints.

The international exposure in Europe during historic times as Britain and the other eleven continental countries prepare for the economic union in 1992 was extremely beneficial for me. Combined with my work experience in Japan and my mission to South Africa, as well as my ability to speak Japanese, Dutch, and Afrikaans, working in the British Isles increased my confidence and desire to pursue a career in international business.

My next promotion came in September last year, which was to help open and manage the first Franklin Day Planner Retail center to be situated in a mall. This opportunity is providing me with more valuable experience in hiring, training, and management skills, as well as useful retail understanding including sales, stock control, and profit and loss flows. Working with the extremely qualified and professional upper management of Franklin International has been valuable in shaping my career goals.

Regarding my decision to defer attendance at Brigham Young for one year, I believe Dr. Peter Clarke's counsel that additional exposure in the workforce would only enhance my graduate experience was wise advice. I feel better prepared to both learn from and be a progressive participant in the Master of Business Administration program at Brigham Young University. I request admittance for the fall of 1991.

Essay #2

Dean of Business School
Brigham Young University
Provo, UT 84601

Dear Sir:

In preparation for a career as an International Businessman, I am seeking entrance into the graduate program at Brigham Young University. This letter will provide the requested information regarding my wish to study at BYU.

My family experience has significantly influenced my preparation for a career in business administration. As the youngest of six children I have shared family responsibilities of managing our 48-acre farm. Because my father worked full-time, my brothers and I learned at a young age to operate a farm. At fourteen, being the only son left at home, I learned to creatively utilize my resources and to seek expert advice from local farmers in managing the farm. I learned other important business principles, such as hard work, commitment, and honesty. I also learned frugality by saving a portion of my earnings in order to attend University and in addition, support myself for two years as a voluntary missionary in South Africa.

I have actively sought for balance by being involved in school plays, learning to play the trumpet and guitar, and to sing. I have sought excellence in athletics: baseball, football, track and field, and swimming. I was actively involved in scouting and obtained the Eagle Scout award and the Order of the Arrow, an award earned through leadership, service, and courage. Such activities taught me self-discipline and team unity.

At sixteen, I was selected to go for one year as a High School Rotary International Exchange student to South Africa. My responsibility was to represent America while there, and then upon returning home, to be an ambassador for South Africa to enhance world peace and understanding. In this effort, I made presentations about America to business clubs, high schools, and social groups. I also became immersed in South African culture by learning to speak Afrikaans, play their sports, enjoy their food, and listen carefully to their interesting and unique perspectives. From this experience in such a diverse land, I learned to respect foreign cultures, and I feel I developed a special talent to communicate with and relate to a wide variety of people.

As a missionary to South Africa, I served as a district and Zone leader, and Assistant to the President. As an Assistant, I became responsible for the mission's 52-car fleet, the supply and distribution of mission products, and the transportation arrangements for more than 130 missionaries. Working both in an intimate and business level in a foreign country was exciting and challenging. On my mission I decided I could best serve my fellow men as an international businessman. This decision was based on my passion for South Africa and my ability to relate with and influence a variety of people for good.

During the summer of my sophomore year at Brigham University, I decided to enhance my international marketability by going to Japan and learning Japanese. After arriving in Japan, I negotiated to establish and to teach an English program to an expanding Japanese company. Through this experience, I became excited and confident in my ability to learn languages, and to conduct business in foreign cultures by being understanding and alert to their traditions and values.

One of my major accomplishments has been financing and completing a college education. In this pursuit, I demonstrated creativity in my capacity to see business opportunities and make them profitable. For example, I installed security door-viewers in apartment complexes in exchange for rent by discovering existing trends of vacancy of various apartments, as well as installing door-viewers in a cost-effective manner. While working ten to thirty hours a week, I maintained an average of fifteen credit hours, I achieved an overall 3.61 GPA with a 3.74 GPA in my major. I feel this reflects my commitment to achieving excellence under challenging situations.

In addition to the university curriculum I have had a valuable experience in the work field. As a salesman for an insulation company in San Francisco, I succeeded at and learned to love honest sales by being competent in my service and by discovering the true needs of the people. My marketing experience as a sales rotator for Karl Lagerfeld products in Utah included direct selling as well as overseeing advertising displays in department stores such as Nordstrom's.

As a full-time employee of Franklin International, I have demonstrated total commitment. I have also sought creative ways to better the company through my organizational behavior training at BYU. Recently, I helped restructure the leadership responsibilities in my department in order for more on-going training and less busywork. As a result of the confidence of my superiors, I have been offered positions of trust and leadership. In March until August, I will be establishing the customer service/order entry department for our company in England. My responsibilities will include hiring, training, and managing a British team of fifteen employees.

I am extremely enthusiastic about the future of international business administration. I believe there are major breakthroughs yet to be made in the field. After completing an MBA, I hope to gain practical experience and exposure with a major international business firm. Eventually, I intend to establish resorts, clinics, and camps in which to motivate and train people of all cultures. To incorporate values and thought patterns conducive to healthier, happier, and more productive lifestyles. Such training would include a physical appreciation of body and environment, as well as a spiritual appreciation of fundamental values such as honesty and integrity. I envision training focused at salvaging youth from drug abuse and inspiring them to become producers. I believe this personal passion can best be accomplished as a professional and competent businessman.

I want to attend the graduate program at BYU for many reasons. I understand the working relationship between local corporations and the business school is conducive to consistent business exposure and experience combined with serious academic study. I desire a top-quality accredited program that incorporates high moral values as part of the curriculum. I am also impressed with the close working association with professors and students at the Business School. I look forward to a challenging and stimulating relationship with professors and peers and feel my unique exposure to business in South Africa, Japan, England, and America will allow me to contribute interesting insight and comparisons.

Thank you for your consideration.

CRITIQUE

Don's letter of intent gives us a picture of a well-rounded human being. He talks about his preparation in terms of his work experience as a youth as well as an adult, his high school activities in music, sports, and travel, his community experience in scouting and service to his church, as well as his academic preparation.

International Experience: Since 85 percent of our students speak second languages and 35 percent speak a third, we are interested in international experiences that enrich the class. Don mentions four experiences of significance.

The first was his high school exchange student experience in South Africa. He not only explains how he presented information about America to business clubs and social groups, he also talks about what he has learned individually in playing South African sports, learning Afrikaans, and relating to people of different cultures.

The second experience was Don's voluntary mission for the Church of the Jesus Christ of Latter-day Saints to South Africa. The admissions committee is well aware of the growth and maturity that occurs on a mission, but Don chose to elaborate by explaining his specific responsibilities as a leader and manager for the mission's fleet of cars.

The third was a choice Don made as a college student to learn Japanese and Japanese ways. He explains his work with a Japanese company in helping to expand their English program.

The fourth experience was Don's assignment in England to open a new branch of the Franklin International (now Franklin Quest) office.

Work Experience: Don shows valuable work experience from his youth. He supports his assertion that he learned how to work early with specifics about being in charge of a farm at fourteen because his brothers had grown up, looking to neighboring farmers for advice, and saving his earnings for his own future plans.

Don financed his own college education. He mentions creative part-time work—installing door-viewers.

After college Don gained marketing and sales experience with some well-known companies before he joined Franklin International and was promoted to management positions.

Leadership: Evidence of Don's leadership skills is shown in his experience as district and Zone leader and eventually Assistant to the President on his church mission in South Africa.

Future Plans: Don has some definite ideas about what he would like to do in international business administration. He presents his plan to establish resorts and camps to train people. This information gives the admissions committee some idea about whether our program can contribute to what he has in mind.

Good Writing Skills: Don's writing indicates an ability to express himself well and reflect on his undergraduate preparation. He frames his letter in the first paragraph by telling us what the letter is about and he concludes in the final paragraph by pulling together the reasons the Marriot School of Management is attractive to him. This indicates he has done his homework to find out what our program is about. Within the framing are clear paragraphs explaining Don's experiences that make him a viable candidate.

What the Student Brings to the Class: Don shows he has something to contribute to his peers. He shows diversity in his experiences, a teachableness, some definite goals, and an ability to work hard. His international experiences show an ability to cooperate and get along with people and demonstrate good problem-solving skills.

This area is very important. The Admissions Committee works at building a class with diversity in backgrounds and educational experiences that will enrich and contribute to the whole class.

UNIVERSITY OF CALIFORNIA—BERKELEY

Question #1: *What seminal influences, broadly defined, have especially contributed to your personal development? What correlation, if any, has your personal development to your professional goals? In your response to this question, please do not discuss the influence of members of your immediate family, athletic endeavors, or professional experiences.*

Essay #1:

Bangkok, Vientiane, Malaysia, Singapore, Tokyo, Washington D.C., Manhattan, Boston, Camden, and San Francisco are the places where I have grown up. My father was a diplomat, my mother a teacher, and I am the youngest of four children. Together, my family moved every two or three years to a new city. Growing up was an adventure: as children, my brothers, sister, and I did not choose to move so frequently, but we became accustomed to it. We learned to assimilate quickly, make new friends, adjust to unfamiliar customs, even speak foreign languages.

The diverse cultural experiences that are part of my childhood have shaped the way I think about the world and my purpose in it. Living abroad cultivated my curiosity in politics and international relations, and moving frequently developed my interpersonal skills and created a strong personal motivation to make the best of a new situation.

Living abroad and moving frequently influenced who I am today, yet they are facts about my life that I have had little control over. When I think about who I am today, I focus on the choices I have made, the actions I have taken, and the guidance I have received from relatives and friends through various struggles. One choice I made stands out as an important influence because it resulted in challenges that stretched me in new directions and dramatically changed my perspective.

*   *   *   *

Following High School graduation, I worked as a roustabout out on an offshore oil rig in the Gulf of Mexico, 125 miles off the coast of Louisiana. For graduation, my family had pitched in for a round-trip plane ticket to Europe. I had been preparing for a trip across the continent when my oldest brother called about a job opportunity on an oil rig. I opted for the job because it was both an adventure and an opportunity to earn a lot of money for college (my savings amounted to one year at Harvard).

Within a week I was on a helicopter heading for Block 352, an oil field leased from the government by Chevron. I had several lasting impressions of the experience. The first is primarily sensory as I recall the physical conditions under which we lived and worked. The incessant noise of power generators and welding machines hummed in our ears day and night. Every species of dirt and grime thrived on the rig. The platform was characterized by its oppressive heat, magnified by the flames from the acetylene torches and welding rods and by the exhaust from the welding machines. The only activity we looked forward to was mealtime in an air-conditioned bunkhouse.

The work was dangerous, and if it were not for luck and the other hands who kept a close eye on me, I certainly would have been injured. That summer seven people died on Block 352, four in a helicopter accident, two in a crane accident; the seventh was a close friend of mine. At twenty-one, Eric was the closest person to my age. When I first started, he and I worked closely together and he explained everything he knew about work on the rig. Eric was related in one way or another to many of the people in our crew, and as Eric's friend, I became one of the clan. Most of the elder clans looked out for me as they did for Eric.

One day Eric was hurrying around a corner when he tripped on the extra slack of his torch line and he fell through a hole he had just cut in the deck. He fell 200 plus feet, hit the structure before landing, and drowned, taken swiftly under either by the current or the barracuda that circle below waiting for kitchen trash.

The lawyers and the search party came and went, and work began as usual the next morning. I was struck by two reactions to Eric's death. The first was the other hands barely spoke of it. It was as though the danger of the job was something they had all accepted and put behind them so they could carry on. I will never know if I could have helped Eric if I were there, but I still wonder why it wasn't me. The other response was an unusual step taken by the foreman that morning: someone still needed to descend through the hole that Eric had fallen through and climb out to the very end of the structure to attach a cable. Without a word, our foreman joined us, climbed through the hole, attached the cable, and was back before we realized the spell was broken. His action made me realize that to earn respect as a leader, never ask another person to attempt what you might not try yourself.

Another lasting impression I have of work on the rig, in direct contrast to the harsh conditions, is the strong personal relationships that made the experience memorable. The men I worked with from 5:00 a.m. to 10:00 p.m. were an extraordinary crew, all Cajuns from southern Louisiana, all hard working, all part of a team. On my first day, one of the hands later told me, they thought I was an engineer because I came dressed with new Chevron hard-hat, clean Levi's, and a clean T-shirt. Far from an engineer, I was worse than a 'worm' (someone new on the rig) because I had no training. As a young kid from Maine who did not know how to cut, weld, fit, grind, or stack steel pipe, I had a lot of ground to cover. The interests that had been a strong part of my identity in high school: student athlete, leader, etc. were suddenly irrelevant. Where I had come from and where I was going at the end of the summer had no bearing in the context of working offshore. All that mattered was what I could accomplish that summer. The way to join this crew was straightforward: work hard, learn quickly, and interact during mealtime.

Initially I was a "rigger," someone who supports welders by hauling steel and creating safe, makeshift platforms for welders to stand on as they weld. Early in the summer I asked our foreman, Henry Calais, if I could learn to weld. I did not know about the months of training it takes to become a certified pipe welder, but Henry was kind and offered instead to have me work with Charlie Reitenger as his assistant. Charlie was the crew's "fitter" and, after Henry, was the most experienced person on the platform. A fitter measures and cuts pipe to length so that when the ends of two sections meet, they are adjacent, plumb, and square.

Charlie never wore a shirt, just a jeans jacket with cut-off sleeves. Charlie was an intense man with a subtle sense of humor; on the morning of our first day working together, immediately after a healthy breakfast (at an unhealthy 5:00 a.m.) Charlie opened his first can of Skoal Long cut, pinched a lip full of tobacco, and then offered me a can. We were hanging mid-air, about 200 feet above the water, and descending rapidly toward the workboat below as the crane operator lowered us. I smiled declining: "Thanks, no, maybe after a second cup of coffee." This exchange became a morning routine with us.

Charlie and I did not start off with a lot in common. I was not sure how to create a common ground between us, but I began by showing interest in what he had to teach me. For the first week I hauled steel all over the platform for Charlie to measure and cut. Over time Charlie taught me everything there is to know about cutting and fitting pipe, and I, in turn, taught him some of the basic concepts of trigonometry. I was less successful with physics. One day I was trying to calculate how high we were above the water by dropping a welding rod and counting how many seconds it took to hit the water. For a moment Charlie thought I was an idiot. He argued that my methodology was flawed because a heavier object would fall faster.

I tried to explain that gravity exerts the same force on all objects, but as our discussion progressed other hands took an interest, and Charlie prevailed by the sheer weight of popular opinion. Galileo would have been empathetic; we eventually conducted an experiment from the heliport, which is the highest level on the rig. We dropped several objects of varying mass before the debate was finally resolved and a basic law of physics restored. It was quite a revelation, and I was surprised by how it consumed the conversation that evening, interrupting the usual ribald dinner talk.

The summer spent offshore was unique preparation for college and for life. I still have not taken a summer off to travel in Europe, but I have never regretted passing up that opportunity to work on the oil rig. The experience exposed me to the human drama of a working class that I had not had contact with. The extreme working conditions and contact with a much older group of peers accelerated a period of growth and maturity for me. Working on the rig gave me an opportunity to reexamine what I wanted to accomplish in college and who I wanted to become. When the summer was over I felt like a completely changed person. In the helicopter heading back to Morgan City, Louisiana, I realized how fortunate I was to have the opportunity to go to college.

CRITIQUE

In reviewing Haas's MBA application essays, the admissions committee places considerable weight on intellectual performance and potential; a sense of purposiveness; evidence of ethical character; and skill in the development, organization, and presentation of thoughts and ideas. We seek candidates who demonstrated initiative, creativity, thoughtfulness, receptiveness, and resourcefulness in the conduct of their personal and professional lives. We look for individuals who can provide a satisfactory account of who they are, what they have accomplished in the context of their own experiences and opportunities, and what they intend to accomplish during graduate school and beyond. Most compelling are those candidates whose reflections on their experiences and on their record of accomplishments, however defined, suggest an adaptability to make significant contributions to their class and to the Haas School.

The previous essay ostensibly describes a summer job following graduation from high school. Although the nature of the job may be unusual by MBA-application standards, it is not merely the novelty or drama of the situation that makes this essay successful. Its principal strengths are the degree of thought and writing skill the author exhibits in this composition. The essay is compelling because the author imparts a deep insight, wry humor, and a seemly modest ability to work successfully with people of widely different backgrounds, education, and cultures to the mutual benefit of all concerned. It is exceptional because while the author suggests that he was the principal beneficiary of that summer job on the oil rig in the Gulf, it is clear that his account is as instructive to the reader as his participation was to his colleagues.

CASE WESTERN RESERVE UNIVERSITY

Question #1: *Describe the most difficult personal or professional challenge that you have faced in the past five years. What did you learn from that experience?*

Essay #1:

In 1990, I formed my own company, Asian Profiles, Inc., to conduct research on the automotive industry, focusing primarily on East Asian markets. The compiled research is stored in a computer database system which allows me to analyze the data and forecast future automotive trends. Through the evaluation of automotive markets, I am able to construct "profiles" of East Asian nations and determine their relative potential as manufacturing sites and/or consumer markets for American automobile manufacturers and suppliers. My position as a research consultant and president of the company has given me the opportunity to test my professional and personal strengths as well as verify my leadership abilities.

Asian Profiles, Inc., has created a multitude of professional challenges for me. Running a small business of any kind requires a great deal of resourcefulness and ingenuity. When I started my business, my company had a database system with zero information. Four of the major management decisions I was confronted with at the time were: assessing the type of information my clients required, determining the availability of such information, selecting appropriate sources for the information, and choosing the methods for retrieving such information. I take pleasure in the fact that my company now has an extensive operating database. However, I am still faced with the above management decisions in addition to the daily challenge of determining the speed at which I need to retrieve information, and the price I am willing to pay for it. I have to constantly ask myself, "Is there a better, quicker, more cost-effective way to find this information?" Often the answer is yes, and I have found that local resources can offer more practical means of information retrieval than other sophisticated sources such as computer network systems and expensive publications. Ultimately, though, I have come to realize that people are the most valuable resource in the business. Since incorporating my company, I have carefully developed useful contacts whom I can call upon for professional advice. (To date) my company has enjoyed great success primarily because I have learned when to seek advice, when to give it, and when to solve a problem on my own. During this period I have learned that networking is an important part of any successful business career.

Being self-employed is a true test of one's personal character. When I first made the decision to go into business for myself, many questions ran through my mind. I wondered where I was going to find reliable data, how I was going to compile it, and when I would find time to learn new computer programs. One thing I never questioned, though, was whether I was capable of attaining my goals. From the outset I understood that being self-employed would require incredible self-discipline and emotional maturity. Because I did not have the years of work experience behind me, I have had to learn to rely on my own judgment. For example, soon after incorporating Asian Profiles, Inc., I was faced with the challenge of negotiating business contracts, setting up the company's finances, and deciding which computer system to purchase. With advice from experts and personal research, I found that lack of experience did not have to be a stumbling block to success but, rather, was a challenge to overcome. As company president, I have had to become my own supervisor and supporter, which has been the most challenging aspect of the position. Employing a healthy level of self-judgment has allowed me to improve my job performance by acknowledging and working with my strengths and weaknesses.

In addition to the professional challenges Asian Profiles, Inc., has created for me, it has also given me the opportunity to test my leadership abilities. Although I perform all the research and manage the company myself, I am fortunate to have the support of two secretaries. Being a manager has been a novel and rewarding experience for me. I have learned that in any working relationship, being a good manager is more about leading people and less about being a boss. I have worked hard to establish a consistent and professional management style for dealing with my clients and employees. With the personal and professional responsibilities required of a small business manager, I have had the opportunity to realistically assess my leadership capabilities. I am confident that I do possess leadership potential, but I recognize the need for expanded experience and new challenges. Asian Profiles, Inc., has fostered in me a tremendous amount of self-reliance and business know-how which I will continue to draw upon in my future endeavors.

CRITIQUE

We gave this essay high marks on the following dimensions:

Style: Well-constructed essay; gave succinct but sufficient background information about the experience, then described the challenge, how she met the challenge, and what she learned. Tone of the essay was honest and eminently readable.

Content: Situation was unique and interesting to the reader. Descriptions provided specifics, which made the challenge more believable. Cause and effect between the situation and the learning process were made clear.

Reader would have liked to have seen reference to any measurable success resulting from meeting the challenge and learning from the experience.

DARTMOUTH

Question #1: *Discuss your career progression to date. What factors have influenced your decision to seek a general management education? Based on what you know about yourself at this time, how do you envision your career progressing after receiving the MBA degree? Please state your professional goals, and describe your plans to achieve them.*

Essay #1:

As a senior, my initial goal was to gain a thorough education in finance, which I could then apply in a field related to my personal interest in the outdoors. The most efficient way to achieve this education was as an analyst at a major investment bank. Most of the available positions were in New York. Although I was offered an analyst position there, I realized that I was unwilling to sacrifice my personal interest in order to move into the city. Instead I headed West and dedicated a year of fulfillment of these interests before beginning my professional career.

I spent the summer and fall as a professional river guide on the Snake River in Wyoming. Guiding more than 2,000 people in class IV white water rafting and fly-fishing trips taught me to interact comfortably with clients and to effectively promote myself and my abilities. I often draw upon these marketing skills in my current career when soliciting new clients. I then spent the following winter and spring in California managing a cross-country ski touring center. In this position, I gained valuable experience managing people and an appreciation for the numerous responsibilities of running a business, regardless of its size and purpose. More importantly, both experiences instilled within me an appreciation for our natural environment and an obligation to help preserve it.

Shortly thereafter, I began my professional career at Drexel Burnham Lambert in San Francisco. I was one of the first junior members to join its innovative debt restructuring group. The culture was highly entrepreneurial. Since we were the first group on Wall Street to enter the debt restructuring field, we had no standard operating procedures to rely on and therefore created our own. Our success has been a function of our creativity in developing innovative restructuring techniques as well as our cooperative group dynamics. All members of the team are encouraged to contribute to the creative process, regardless of their position. I performed well in this environment and was rewarded with a promotion from analyst to associate, a position usually reserved for MBA graduates. As the business flourished and the group expanded, I had the opportunity to train and manage several second- and third-year associates who were new to the group and therefore junior to me in experience. When Drexel entered bankruptcy, I was the only one out of ten junior members invited to join the senior group in their move to another investment bank, Smith Barney. Our group's continued success at Smith Barney has allowed me to further expand my responsibilities. We recently closed the largest public debt restructuring ever completed, which resulted in the sale of one of America's oldest and largest publishing companies. In this transaction I led our team of associates and analysts from Smith Barney and two other investment banks representing the buyer in a comprehensive financial review and valuation of our client. In collaborating with senior team members, I presented these analyses to our client's Board of Directors, who relied upon them in determining the viability of the offer.

In the last four and a half years, I have gained a solid background in finance, experience in line management, and strong negotiating skills by executing numerous transactions in a wide variety of industries. Clearly, I have surpassed the original goal I set out as a senior in college. I now plan to pursue other professional goals that I have developed during my tenure at Drexel and Smith Barney.

My next professional goal is to combine my desire to run my own business with my passion for mountaineering, as a manufacturer of outdoor recreational equipment. Mountaineering has advanced at such a rapid pace that athletes in several technique disciplines have exceeded the limits of the equipment available to them. Modern technologies have only been applied to improve the equipment in such recently popular areas as technical rock climbing where sufficient demand has justified the cost of implementation. My focus would be on product development through technology-based innovation in other areas of mountaineering that are gaining popularity, such as back-country skiing. I believe that the increased costs of such technology can be offset by more efficient production management. For example, back-country ski boots are still made of leather, which freezes when wet and must be hand-stitched. A lightweight plastic boot with a removable synthetic liner, however, would not only improve performance but reduce production costs as well through automation of the manufacturing process. I plan to enter the outdoor recreational equipment market with lines through a) additional technological innovations, b) joint ventures with or acquisitions of other specialty manufacturers, and c) leveraging my brand recognition to promote related clothing and accessories which typically yield a higher profit margin.

Clearly, my goal is not to run a Fortune 500 company. I believe the future of American manufacturing lies in small, highly specialized companies that can not only quickly respond to technological change but also help direct the public's shifting values regarding our natural environment. To create this type of enterprise, I plan to assemble a small team of individuals with diverse skills but common interests. The structure of this enterprise will combine the many positive organizational aspects of my current organization. I will create a "meritocracy" in which personal and professional growth will be rewarded with increased responsibility. All members of the team will be encouraged to contribute to the creative process regardless of their position. Compensation will be based strictly on performance rather than tenure, so that all members who share the responsibilities may also share the profits. Personal profit, however, will not be the sole motivation. The team will also be motivated by a common interest in environmental protection.

My mentor in the outdoor is Yvon Chouinard, founder of Patagonia, a leading manufacturer of outdoor equipment and clothing. Through product innovation he has advanced the sport of mountaineering and achieved a position at the forefront of the outdoor industry. As an industry leader, he has become a vocal proponent of "sustainable development," which encourages managers to balance economic growth with environmental concerns. I agree with his thesis that our country's current business practices are generally not sustainable. In the past several years, I have witnessed the effects of irresponsible growth at Drexel and many of its clients that I helped restructure. Currently we are all witnessing the effects of irresponsible growth on our natural environment. Through the success of my own company, I could fulfill the obligation to the environment I developed years ago as a river guide. As an industry leader, I would be in a position to promote responsible and sustainable growth at all levels—by example within my own organization and industry, by communication with other industry leaders, and by volunteering my time and skills to increase public awareness of the need to protect the wilderness areas on which my industry and interests depend.

I understand that, in order to pursue my entrepreneurial interest in manufacturing, I will need the skills to manage across an entire organization, from finance and production to sales and marketing. I have developed strong financial skills and gained experience in line management in my current career. An MBA education is clearly not a perfect substitute for experience, but I believe it will provide me with the framework necessary for effective decision-making in these areas. An MBA program would also allow me to further research my business ideas through the experience of my peers, independent study, and related summer employment. Education and experience may not change my goals, but they may well change the means by which I achieve them. Finally, since I will not be able to create this organization alone, I look forward to the opportunity to meet other individuals who share my interests in entrepreneurship, manufacturing, and sustainable development.

CRITIQUE

The admissions essay is a critical component in an application to the Amos Tuck School's MBA program. Throughout the process of reviewing an application, which includes careful reading of essays, the admissions committee will seek compelling reasons to admit the applicant. Although writing an excellent essay will not guarantee an applicant admission into Tuck, submitting a poorly organized or badly written essay as part of an otherwise good application will significantly reduce his or her chances for acceptance.

In addition to meeting our more immediate and obvious expectations of a well-organized, articulate presentation of his candidacy, the applicant who wrote our example essay offers (1) compelling reasons for the admissions committee to accept him and (2) convincing evidence that he would both thrive in, and contribute to, the academic and social environment at Tuck. In evaluating any essay, however, keep in mind that we judge neither the experiences nor the goals an applicant presents. Instead, we judge (1) how well the applicant presents these experiences and goals, (2) how well the applicant's accomplishments support his long-term goals, and (3) how the applicant's rationale for wanting an MBA fits into his or her overall career plan.

There are a number of indicators throughout the example essay that the writer possesses attributes that Tuck seeks: (1) the types of experiences and interests that demonstrate sufficient intellectual preparation for a rigorous curriculum of professional study, (2) a high motivational level for achievement, (3) a creative approach to problem solving, (4) a blend of leadership skills to successfully manage multiple aspects of an organization, (5) the interpersonal skills needed to work successfully with diverse groups of people, and (6) an appreciation of a need to balance one's professional and personal lives.

The applicant demonstrates these attributes in describing his career progress, relating each stage to long-term goals. He explains why general management training, central to Tuck's educational mission, is essential for implementing the next stage of his plan toward reaching those goals. The applicant knows what he wants—skills to manage an R&D-based manufacturing operation in close proximity to the great outdoors—and has a clear-cut idea of how to get it. In his essay, he indicates that he made a steady progression of conscious choices that supported his long-term goals by strategically identifying: (1) Where to live and work (on a river in Wyoming, near a ski area in California, then in a major financial center in California), (2) What types of industries were most valuable to gain experience in for his personal and professional interests (an outdoor excursion outfit, a customer-service oriented sports operation, an investment banking firm), (3) What roles would prove useful for the future (leader of white-water rafting trips, general management of a cross-country ski touring center, a member of a team in an investment bank's new debt-restructuring group), and (4) What issues to monitor (the environmental consequences of commercial land development, growth pattern of technological innovations in the sports-equipment industry, how manufacturing factors into the overall national economy).

The applicant asserts that he is management material and backs up this assertion in describing how his superiors at Drexel Burnham Lambert promoted him to a level of responsibility normally reserved for MBAs. He also demonstrates familiarity with current consequences of a slow economy by showing successful adjustment to a new position in another company after his own employer went bankrupt. This flexibility, along with his varied experiences, will enable him to offer an interesting perspective in class discussions.

In conclusion, this particular applicant's attitude, experience, goals, and interests all provided a close match with what Tuck seeks in prospective MBAs. The admissions committee was confident that his interests and abilities provided a close fit with our requirements and that he would be happy in the type of environment that Tuck offers: a rural, residential lifestyle; small classes emphasizing cooperative, highly interactive group learning; a close-knit and cohesive community that welcomes people from diverse backgrounds; and the ability to take full advantage of the career placement services and connections one would expect from an Ivy League business school.

HARVARD

Question #1: *Discuss a change you would make in your work environment and how you would implement that change.*

Essay #1:

The Gillette Personal Care Division is in financial difficulty having severely missed its profit objectives in the last half of 1989. The Division responded to its profitability problems by giving the sales force a more aggressive sales quota. To control escalating costs, the corporate Controller took over P&L responsibility from the divisional marketing department.

I feel the above divisional and corporate responses to raising profitability were ill-considered and create new problems. First, the way in which a Sales Representative will respond to an aggressive new sales quota can, ironically, exacerbate the profitability problem. To achieve the aggressive new sales quota, the sales force will push high-volume brands (i.e. White Rain) that contribute little to profit. This short-term volume increase comes at the expense of the field's promoting and building smaller, high margin brands.

Second, the Controller cut out advertising and field discretionary funds, showing his insensitivity to market considerations and trade issues; an immediate spike in profits comes at the expense of future consumer pickup.

The change I propose to make is to make the field more responsible for Divisional profitability. This can be done by giving the Sales Reps new Business Development Funds and more profit "accountability." With the funds, the Reps would be better able to respond to opportunities to develop and build the brands.

However, "accountability" would present implementation problems. How do you define and enforce accountability? The field cannot control many of the variables that impact on profitability: production costs, advertising commitments, price increases, and the size of trade allowances. Nor can the field break out different regions on a P&L basis. Because developing and maintaining some accounts will be more expensive than others. It might cost more to develop more promising markets where P&G, for example, is also trying to make inroads.

The best solution for field profit accountability is a dual quota system: by sales and by brand. A brand quota would force the Rep to promote a more profitable mix of product regardless of whether he understood the profitability concerns. With the Business Development Fund, he would be able to build the profitable brands emphasized in the new brand quota.

These funds would encourage the Rep to be much more entrepreneurial. The rep could design trade push and consumer pull programs that best suit his territory. Sales Planning would represent the interests of the sales force in determining fair brand quotas with the marketing department. Ultimately, this change would help balance Divisional and corporate needs. With the Business Development funds, Reps would better be able to respond to local opportunities. With brand quotas, Corporate could better control product profit mix.

The downside is that the trade will come to expect these additional allowances and give little incremental promotional support. Further, career Reps might not adapt well to the new entrepreneurial demands and may develop ineffective programs. While the immediate solution would be to give the Business Development funds to the Reps who could use the funds most effectively, this would create resentment. The longer-term solution is to recruit and build a sales force of entrepreneurial Reps who could run their own "franchises."

Question #2: *Describe your avocations and hobbies.*

Essay #2:

My most passionate nonacademic pursuit is athletics. I have learned invaluable lessons through playing on the Harvard Varsity Water-polo and Squash teams. As goalie in the Water-polo team, I learned the importance of teamwork. During a fast-paced game, a goalie must be able to quickly identify potential problems and solve them in an effective manner. Collective responsibility is integral to teamwork. One cannot lay the blame on another player without jeopardizing team unity.

Squash taught me that progress can only be achieved through diligence and patience. Hitting a small black ball thousands of times for hundreds of hours in a small room can be perceived as a meaningless pursuit—or a disciplined process of developing precision and control. There are no shortcuts to improvement in the game of squash.

I have found these valuable lessons of teamwork and discipline to be easily transferable to other areas. Working with others in a competitive and tense environment can only be successfully achieved through proper teamwork. The discipline that I developed on the squash court has (similarly) enabled me to focus in other pursuits with equal determination.

Question #3: *Describe your most substantial accomplishments, and explain why you view them as such.*

Essay #3

1) Last spring I exported nearly $100,000 worth of exercise equipment to Japan. This shipment saved my company more than $250,000, due to the price discrepancies between the United States and Japan. I was solely responsible for selecting the equipment, negotiating the price, arranging the insurance, and packing and shipping the equipment to Japan. The first step of the process of selecting the equipment and the company involved inspecting manufacturing facilities based in California, Maryland, Texas, Vermont, and Colorado. I researched the legitimacy of the companies by calling their previous clients, checking credit records, and calling the Better Business Bureau. After exporting the equipment to Japan, I flew to Japan to facilitate the import process. This involved meeting with Japanese customs, as well as assisting in the domestic transportation and installation of the equipment.

I consider this a major accomplishment for three reasons. Firstly, I was solely responsible for the entire project. Secondly, it was a complicated process that involved many unrelated details. Finally, and not least of all, the fact that it was successful also contributes to my sense of pride.

2) When the Japanese company opened its third health club in Japan in July, 1988, it was a great sense of personal satisfaction. Two summers ago, I participated in the planning and design of this club. I saw many of my substantive recommendations implemented, including the installation of a racquetball court system that has movable glass walls to allow squash, racquetball, basketball, and volleyball to be played on the same court. My idea more effectively utilizes very limited and costly space and also provides greater recreational variety for the users. I have previously discussed my export deal that provided more than half of the equipment for the club, which was another source of personal satisfaction. In addition to helping design the club, I was actively involved in sales and marketing. I also conducted club tours for prospective members, and designed a new marketing strategy targeting foreigners living in the area. My combined efforts resulted in more than 150 new members.

These accomplishments demonstrate my ability to work successfully in a large group setting as well as in an entirely different language and culture. In addition to the satisfaction of seeing my design recommendations actually implemented, I also enjoyed the challenges of sales and marketing.

3) I am currently co-teaching a Harvard college freshman seminar focusing on the economic development of Japan with Professor X. As a teacher, I had to design a reading list that would provide sufficient information without overwhelming the freshmen who have had no background on the topic. A reading list has to have an overall argument with weekly topics to provide specific examples. Teaching in a seminar format presents a tremendous intellectual challenge of stimulating and guiding discussion. I try to give only directive or stimulative comments rather than to lecture. In this manner students will ask questions and I will try to steer the discussion so that the student is able to answer his or her own question.

Teaching the seminar represents the cumulative total of my academic career. My studies have largely revolved around Japanese economics and Japanese history. In addition, my practical experience of working in a Japanese company in Japan complements my academic understanding and has further enhanced my abilities as a teacher.

UNIVERSITY OF MARYLAND

Essay #1:

My multi-page application answered the question, "Who am I?" Now it is the time to answer another one—"Why am I here, in the pool of applicants to the Maryland MBA program?" That's a question many people have asked me.

My friends' confusion is understandable. Why would a graduate student who enjoys doing research and teaching, with an expertise in a politically important part of the world and who allegedly would be able to get full funding in any school if he chose to go all the way to the Ph.D. in political science, want to change his career to take an unknown road in business? Quite a legitimate question. Let me explain why I chose to apply to the Maryland MBA Program and not to do something else; first revisit my life history.

In 1990 I joined the analytical division of a trading firm in Moscow—International Secondary Resources Exchange. I discovered consulting as a career and developed an interest in assessment of market potential, including a degree of political risk. At the time, Russia and other former communist countries were opening their markets and it was fascinating, but also very important to try to predict how promising the Russian market was. So I decided to get my masters in political science in order to be able to competently assess such important categories for estimating market potential as government capacity, public administration competence, political risk (legal and other obstacles to foreign investment), entrepreneurial culture, and economic training of the population.

Still working on projects with the exchange, I started a graduate program with concentration in international relations, comparative politics (Europe), and economics. It has been an important part of my education, given the importance of the political situation and, therefore, political forecasting for the business future of the former communist world.

My education now has to enter its most critical stage—actual study of business. This would let me have a deep understanding, as I hope, of financial and other market structures, competitiveness, and other factors that a consultant needs to take into account when recommending whether to conduct business in a foreign country.

Taking advantage of my bi-cultural background, long study of international relations and foreign languages, and business experience, I plan to pursue a career as an international business consultant. The

UMCP certainly has a focus on global business. I am attracted by the Center for International Business Education and Research—I work for CIBER at the University of Utah and my colleagues spoke highly of the Maryland Program. At the same time the School offers a strong general management program—something I need, coming from a country with no free market traditions.

These are the "career" reasons to apply to Maryland. But there is also a "character" reason. It is critically important for me to be challenged. Only when sufficiently challenged, can I work at full capacity and deliver results. Without doubt, Maryland provides enough challenge, without mentioning that an application process itself is very stimulating.

Business schools' quality criteria are no secret. From these I pay special attention to location. The Washington-Baltimore metropolitan area is a perfect location for somebody interested in an international business career. It is also the place to be for a person, who, coming from Utah, is just hungry for student body diversity and culture attractions. I visited the area on two occasions during my first year in this country and just fell in love with the place.

Add to these advantages a critical one for me—generous financial aid options. Unfortunately, without financial aid, I will not be able to attend school.

The Program's diverse environment is of special importance for me. I appreciate diversity and I think I could add something myself to the already culturally rich Maryland MBA Program—after two years in the United States I am a walking example of cultural interaction. I picked up a lot of American practices, keeping at the same time some of my old ones. I do not protest anymore when my friends take me out to dinner around my birthday, but on my birthday itself, I, as the Russian tradition goes, have them over for dinner. I try not to go with the flow and never say "how are you?" when I do not care and "nice to meet you" when I do not mean it, but sometimes I am supposed to say these meaningless phrases. I still pass with my face, rather than my back, to people sitting in a theater. I use Kleenex tissues, but still have a handkerchief in my pocket just in case. I kept my main dining habit—never putting down a knife when having salad and a main course. I changed, on the other hand the way I approach desert [sic], when I dine by myself; I still eat it with a spoon, as the Russians do. And I drink both hot tea and coke.

From my Russian background I keep moral integrity, industriousness, strong attachment to my family, self-reliance, cooperative spirit, sense of humor, strong interest in spending time with children, and my three other hobbies—movies, soccer, and travel. My American present made me friendly, punctual, conscientious, self-disciplined, law-abiding, determined to help people who are less lucky than I am (first of all, my fellow Russians), and two more past-times—basketball and hiking. I hope that a person combined with two cultures will be a good edition to the School's environment.

I believe that the Maryland MBA Program will provide me with a training I need and enough challenges to launch me into a new intellectual orbit. And, also, it would just be nice to be back East.

CRITIQUE

One important way MBA programs strengthen their international focus is by attracting talented students from different parts of the world. Indeed, a priority of the Maryland Business School is actively to recruit such students, because they increase both the breadth and depth of the school's international perspective.

In addition to fulfilling the basic requirement of every application's essay section—i.e., answer the questions asked (a surprising number of people fail to do this)—"Andrei's" statement also provided the admissions director with a vivid glimpse into his personality. And though English is obviously not his first language, his command of "Americanisms" is impressive and his sense of humor engaging. He comes across as a bright, self-motivated, high-energy individual. Just the type for Maryland.

He also did his homework. For instance, he mentions Maryland's Center for International Business Education and Research and the fact that the university is located in the culturally rich Washington D.C. area. To the admissions director, this means he is serious about his application to the program; that he is not using the shotgun approach in applying to graduate school.

Had he wanted to make an even stronger impression, however, "Andrei" should have asked a native English speaker to read over his essay. One or two native speakers, for that matter. They would have helped him smooth over some of his sentences with proper punctuation and usage. For though his message is clear to the reader, his occasional lapses into fractured English somewhat detract from his many fine qualities.

UNIVERSITY OF MICHIGAN

Question #1: *During your years of study in the Michigan MBA program, you will be part of a diverse multicultural, multi-ethnic community within both the Business School and the larger University. What rewards and challenges do you anticipate in this campus environment, and how do you expect this experience to prepare you for a culturally diverse business world?*

Essay #1:

High return on investment...

One quality I have always admired is independent thinking. I always strive to be different and befriend those who share the same goal. I see conformity as a moral deficiency. "Group think" is the enemy of creativity and innovation. In contrast, diversity in thought is the key to any successful endeavor. I want to be a part of creative concepts proposed from a wide array of sources. These creative concepts can only be reached by assembling individuals with discordant views and from varying backgrounds. For this reason, I find the growing diversity of Michigan's student body to be one of its greatest selling points. I feel that understanding a wide range of views, opinions, and judgments on a variety of subject matter broadens the base of experience from which effective solutions may be derived. Therefore, learning, sharing, and growing within the context of diverse individuals is an avenue for developing a successful manager.

While there will be rewards from this melting pot, there is always the potential for difficulty when assembling people with divergent views and from different cultures. As a member of an international exchange program, in both training and travel, I was able to witness the glaring problems of cultural bias, prejudice, and close-mindedness. One thing I learned through this experience is that nobody is above prejudice of some kind, myself included. Everyone has some innate sense that they are superior to other individuals in some manner. When people feel superior because of their intellect, we call them arrogant. When people feel superior because of their nationality or culture, we call them elitists. And when people feel superior because of their race, we call them racists. The first step in understanding each other is to better understand ourselves and develop an understanding of our own prejudices. This will be the challenge facing every student in the melting pot. For some this challenge will be great and for some it may be overcome easily, but in either case I feel that the rewards from integration of people and ideas provide a great return on the time and energy invested to make it so.

Beyond the hallowed halls...

I expect my time at Michigan to enhance my understanding and appreciation of the benefits of mixing ideas and opinions among people from different backgrounds. The business community I will enter is a global-, multinational-, multicultural-based body. Any business manager willing to shun certain peoples or ideas because they are foreign will be injuring his company. And yet, I have every reason to believe that I will inevitably encounter these types of individuals.

While universities are taking the lead in cultural and ethnic diversification, the business world is somewhat behind. The reasons for this are twofold: those people who are fearful of new ideas tend to fight diversity, while those individuals in favor of diversity often find developing it a daunting task. For this reason, many companies concede to the status quo, to the old way of doing business. Yet there are firms willing to shift paradigms of current thinking. These are the companies that will prosper in the future. The company that takes the initiative to broaden its personnel base will find that any short-term expenses it may incur in this diversification process are easily offset by the long-term benefits of having a dynamic, progressive, and enterprising staff. This is the type of firm I would like to associate with. Just as I expect to do at Michigan, I hope in the business company to be an active part of the melting pot of ideas, developing creative concepts, and forging new paths by engaging divergent viewpoints.

CRITIQUE

Originality, insight, and graceful writing immediately capture the reader of this essay. Tackling the topic directly and substantively, the author effectively relates the subject to past personal experiences and future career aspirations. The writer avoids the platitudes that slide all too easily into application essays. With admirable honesty, he acknowledges the challenges posed by a multicultural environment, admits the prejudices he has felt, and identifies the personal rewards of being part of the Michigan community.

The essay goes beyond any superficial treatment of the issue and reveals how the author thinks. Indeed, the independent thinking admired by the writer emerges from the piece. The reader finds clear evidence of the analytical reasoning skills so critical to success and leadership in management. Finally, the writing style, characterized by flowing, balanced prose and apt word choice, is eloquent. The essay convinces the reader that this is someone whose thinking and ability to convey thoughts will enrich the learning process in and out of the classroom.

UNIVERSITY OF NOTRE DAME

Question #1: *As a Notre Dame student, what contributions would you make to the life of the program, both inside and outside the classroom? How will an MBA from Notre Dame help you achieve your short-term career goals and long-term professional aspirations?*

Essay #1

As a Notre Dame M.B.A. student there are many contributions I will make to enhance the excellence of the program. These contributions include attributes such as professional insight, an inquisitive mind, and innovative ideas along with high moral and ethical standards.

My two years' experience with Sikorsky Aircraft has given me a good understanding of multifunctional disciplines within American aerospace firms. I have grown from these experiences, and I will bring them to the classroom in the form of anecdotes. My job has helped me to gain a good perception of some of the best and worst ways to run a business. These experiences are ones you could never pick up from a textbook, but they will enhance the lessons found in one.

To the classroom I also bring an inquisitive mind. I am never satisfied with the statements of "that's the way it is" or "if it's not broke don't fix it." I feel that if you do not ask why or try to completely appreciate a theory or technique, you may never truly understand it. There is always an alternative to any method or theory, and questioning is a way of developing new understandings.

Outside the classroom I bring innovation. I enjoy adding to the competitiveness of the organization of which I am a part, and I am always willing to try new things. For example, while at Michigan State, I assisted in developing the first annual Materials and Logistics student/faculty retreat. This retreat is now an event supported by both the University and the professional world. In the same respect, as an intern at Sikorsky Aircraft, I worked in our Overhaul and Repair facility (O&R). One of my first observations was that O&R had no definitive way of tracking our suppliers' performance. Every individual department had a different tracking system. I combined the best attributes of each system to form a consolidated tracking run which is now used throughout the entire 600-person facility.

Two other contributions I will bring to Notre Dame cannot be labeled either inside or outside of the classroom because they pertain to both. Number one, I am a good team player. I have a good disposition, which helps me not only get along with many different types of people but to enjoy working with them. Number two, through my business trips and experience of serving on MSU's Anti-Discrimination Judicial Board I have developed a unique appreciation of others' cultures and beliefs. I enjoy learning about other people and what makes them tick.

A Notre Dame M.B.A. will help me obtain my short-term and long-term goals by providing a solid foundation and setting a direction from which I can build. Before choosing the M.B.A. programs to which I would apply, I sat down with a former professor to obtain his insight into this decision. He told me that when choosing an M.B.A. program, I am choosing a label to carry with me throughout my career. This label aligns me with the beliefs and practices of my M.B.A. institution. I chose to apply to Notre Dame because of the school's strong stand on ethics and the international market. At Notre Dame I will be exposed to people not only from the Midwest but from around the world. This will further help me to broaden my horizons and understanding of people.

My long-term professional aspiration is to enter into a field of management consulting. An M.B.A. from Notre Dame in Interdisciplinary Studies will enhance my understanding of all aspects of business. This will contribute significantly to becoming effective in the consulting profession.

In conclusion, as a Notre Dame M.B.A. candidate I will bring a sincere attitude to succeed in the classroom, high ethical standards, and the willingness to go the extra mile. Upon graduation from Notre Dame, I will represent the university as a sign of excellence a Notre Dame M.B.A. portrays in the professional world.

CRITIQUE

We chose Ed's essay because it was clearly and concisely written, using examples from college and career to make his points. For example, he used his experience in O&R at his current employment to highlight his technical and analytical abilities with the establishment of a tracking system now used throughout the facility. He backed up his claim for being innovative by citing his assistance in developing the first faculty and student retreat in his college department.

He dealt with both the short-term and long-term orientation of the program. In seeking advice from his professor, he showed seriousness about making his choice of schools. He wanted an international thrust to his studies and chose Notre Dame because of its reputation in that area as well as its commitment to ethics in business. That fit in nicely with what he learned from his experience on the Anti-Discrimination Judicial Board of his university. And his choice of Interdisciplinary Studies reinforces Notre Dame's focus on preparing students for General Management. Finally, his choice of consulting for a career flows naturally from his prior experiences and his curricular choices.

We like Ed's essay because it was to the point, responded to the essay question, and in a subtle but concrete way "sold" the candidate to the admissions committee. Ed managed to weave in accomplishments on the job with commitments he planned to make to the Notre Dame program. He demonstrated college leadership in a large, public, "anonymous" kind of school in which students often get lost. Based on his experience, his career goals and aspirations appear to be realistic. While he has high ideals, they do not seem to be "pie in the sky" notions, and he displayed a certain kind of maturity and sensitivity that we liked.

STANFORD UNIVERSITY

Question #1: *Tell us about those influences that have significantly shaped who you are today.*

Essay #1:

I am a descendant of a long line of Quaker business people. My family, the Xs , have been Quaker since 1630. The common punch line about this group, at gathering of Friends, is that Quaker business people set out to do good and ended up doing very well. I am just beginning to emerge as a Quaker in business.

Relating to background about my Quaker heritage should help to illustrate how values of the Religious Society of Friends (the official name of "Quakers") have shaped my sense of who I am. Quakers have particular ethics that I try to develop in myself and live out. Quakers believe that there is a God in every person—they often call it the "Inner Light"—and that all people, regardless of rank and position, should be treated with dignity and integrity. This vision has helped me to see the potential in other people, even those who may be difficult to work with. It has also helped me to relate comfortably to people of every rank; in my current job, I enjoy friendships with everyone from secretaries to the president. In addition, a belief in my own Inner Light helped my self-confidence, especially in those situations where intuition must complement facts and objective measures in making decisions.

This faith in the Inner Light has many other implications, of course, but two of the most important ones involve how group decisions should be made, and the equality of women.

As a way of doing business, Quakers believe in consensus decision-making; in fact, they don't believe in hiring or paying ministers. All administration for Quaker Meeting is done by voluntary committees. From participating in consensus decision-making, I have learned to work with diverse groups of people, to negotiate between individual agendas, and to build effective teamwork between people. Consensus decision-making gives everyone a chance to contribute, and helps all members of the group to understand and articulate both the problem and the solution.

Because of the Quaker belief that all people possess an Inner Light, they have traditionally believed in the full equality of men and women. In fact, Quakers held separate business meetings for men and women until about 50 years ago, because it was felt that otherwise women would be overshadowed by the men. This separation allowed Quaker women to develop leadership skills in speaking and administration.

Strong Quaker women like Lucretia Mott, a leader in the movement to abolish slavery, and Elizabeth Cady Stanton, a leader among the suffragettes, were products of this culture.

Several other characteristic Quaker beliefs are placing a high value on simplicity, and on speaking and living the truth. For example, Quakers refuse to swear to anything, even at a trial or for a marriage license, because it implies that at other times one might not tell the truth. Being practical and "grounded" are Quaker values that discourage otherwordly or naive thinking. As a general rule, Quakers don't proselytize or even talk very much about their religion. They believe that their lives should speak of their convictions.

Quaker values can interact with business priorities in many ways, mostly positive, but some potentially negative as well. For example, because Quakers didn't limit their business contacts to the highest social echelon, they found opportunities for more customers and a wider circle of business associates. As Quaker women developed leadership skills, their ingenuity contributed to the success of Quaker businesses. Quaker businesses put a high value on providing products that truly add value for consumers, rather than devising ways to trick them into buying something. In the days before *Consumer Reports*, people saw many advantages to doing business with Quakers, because it was widely known that they wouldn't cheat you. Since Quakers were known to try to seek the truth regardless of the cost to themselves or whether the news was welcome, their word was trusted. Of course, being honest didn't prevent Quakers from being shrewd business people.

But although Quakers tend to be highly ethical, they can also be somewhat naive. Consensus decision-making can be far too slow and unwieldy for some decisions, and it runs a risk that people will feel coerced by the group into settling for less than they want. Rather than making everyone responsible, it can end up making no one responsible. Even people with an Inner Light can behave badly. "Speaking truth to power," to use the common catch-phrase for Quakers, can either increase long-run credibility or can be a cover for venting harsh feelings at inappropriate times.

My mother has told me that she married my father partially because he had been raised Quaker and was comfortable with strong, independent women. During my senior year at college, I was disheartened to find that many men of my own age found me intimidating. It was also a time when my mother was diagnosed with serious and potentially life-threatening breast cancer. Now I'm happily married, and my mother has at least survived the chemotherapy, but I still keep and reread a letter I received from my father that year about the strong women in my family. Here's an excerpt.

"Let's start with this generalization: Highly articulate, handsome, intelligent women are not terribly rare. No doubt you yourself have many friends that would easily fit such categorization. But if you add two further adjectival phrases, then such women are rare indeed. Namely, passionate commitment and courageous. (I'm willing to concede that these may even be redundant... they, in your case, certainly go together.) Obviously these same characteristics are very rare in men too.

"The problem arises primarily for women. These characteristics scare the bejabbers out of others . . . they may be admired by some, vilified by others, and wholly misunderstood by the majority. But even those that admire them generally want to do it at a safe distance. Let's face it—sparks are given off by such people. The prudent man usually decides that the warmth and excitement isn't worth the high risk of being consumed in a conflagration set off by so many sparks.

"You are the fourth in line of such women."

I am enclosing a photocopy of this letter with application (Attachment I) because it illuminates the way Quakers like my father can support and encourage women in leadership. Also, it provides some insight into my family.

Another important influence is my new husband, Timothy. We were married July 6 of this year. Tim is the managing editor of the *Journal of Economic Perspectives*, which is based at Stanford. My husband's background in economics informs and counterbalances my perspectives.

My career has forced me to balance the idealistic qualities of Quakerism with real-life experience, where the rubber meets the road. My first job out of college was as editor and then executive director for a nonprofit foundation called Fellowship in Prayer (FIP), whose purpose was to "encourage the practice of prayer or meditation among people of all faiths." This nonprofit was a rare one; it actually had an endowment that grew from $2.7 to $3.5 million during my three-year tenure. My job was to organize the programs and facilities from complete chaos to something more effective and methodical. I managed the budgets so that operating expenditures came only from the interest on the endowment, not from the capital. I also learned some lessons that went well beyond business. I was sexually harassed by two members of the Board of Trustees, and had to face the problem of other Board members stealing from the endowment.

Perhaps my biggest lesson from Fellowship in Prayer was that systems—the way information is transferred, decisions are made and reporting relationships defined—largely determine the effectiveness of the organization. When I started working there, the organization had no functioning systems in place, and no objectives or strategies beyond the general mission statement quoted a moment ago. I had previously looked on things like standard operating procedures and methods of reporting and accountability as necessary evils. But I found that it's not nearly enough to have an operating budget and some staff. An organization also needs some definite goals, strategies for achieving them, and ways of measuring success. While working at FIP, I came to understand that structure is enabling: without it, people spend too much time wondering what they are supposed to be doing or reinventing the wheel. Now I appreciate the need to organize structures, and the significance when such systems work well.

My position as executive director at FIP forced me to learn a wide range of business skills and responsibilities. I wrote the annual budget and the annual report and oversaw expenditures. I bought a $300,000 property for headquarters of the foundation (previously, it had rented space), arranged for $20,000 of structural repairs and another $20,000 for redecorating and furnishing, and moved the office. I edited the bimonthly magazine for nine months, until I became executive director. I supervised other staff. I tried to create a counterbalance to the power of the Board of Trustees, some of whom had been stealing from the foundation, by recruiting a lawyer with financial expertise to the Board. I also formed an advisory board composed of Christians, Jews, Baha'is, Buddhists, a Mohawk Chief, and others to improve the programs and create a balance of power with the Board of Trustees. Also, this group helped in generating ideas for programs, like lectures and retreats.

I also worked on developing my own speaking and writing skills; I gave lectures, workshops, and retreats myself. I have continued to pursue my interest in designing programs and giving talks that help people deepen their spirituality and fulfill their potential. During the past few years, for example, I have led retreats at the Quaker Center in Ben Lomond, California, and for Faith at Work, a national ecumenical group with which I continue to do volunteer work. With my application, I have enclosed some flyers publicizing these retreats (attachment II). I wrote the ones for Quaker Center.

CRITIQUE

General Guidelines—The strongest essays give us a real sense of who the applicant is. Because we do not offer interviews, this is the applicant's only opportunity to provide insight into who they are; in a way, it is like an interview on paper. But it should be more personal and less resume-like. Ideally, after reading the essay, we should have a good idea of what this person would like to discuss if we (hypothetically) met over coffee. We're looking for who someone is rather than what he or she has done. This is the fundamental distinction we make: We want to get to know the person behind the grades, scores, and job accomplishments— what are his or her passions, values, interests, and goals? We expect applicants to get beyond the standard "I did this; I did that" model to share with us what they care about and what has shaped them. We look for an honest and natural tone, hoping to find essays that are engaging and immediate rather than dry and distant—ideally, a conversation on paper.

For this student, being Quaker has been the most significant influence in her life. She does a good job of focusing deeply on that single influence, extracting specific insight from its effects on her. She ties it in to her values (simplicity, truthful living, living one's convictions), her social/emotional experiences (dating, equality of women), and even her philosophy of business (consensus decision-making, honesty). For her, being Quaker is more than a religious faith; it is a life choice, and by explaining its influences on her she provides insight into who she is and why she developed that way.

This essay is honest and immediate; she opens up about personal matters in a way that allows us to get to know the real her; for example, she shares a personal and emotional letter her father sent her during a difficult time for her family. She has analyzed the positives and negatives that her Quaker upbringing has fostered, further showing intelligent self-analysis and thoughtfulness. Overall, she presents a picture of a smart, committed woman who has thought hard about who she is and is able (and willing) to communicate what she cares about and why.

Toward the end of the essay she shifts from the personal to the professional (from the "who" to the "what"), but does so relatively effectively. We learn how she puts her passions into action, as well as some key lessons she has learned from her initial work experiences. There is a bit too much "I did this; I did that" at the end of the essay; it would have been stronger had she let her resume tell us her accomplishments, focusing here only on personal introspection. However, as a whole the essay is strong because some of that introspection is present, and even the "what" section tells us something about her.

TULANE UNIVERSITY—A.B. FREEMAN SCHOOL OF BUSINESS

Question 1: *Why are you seeking a Tulane MBA at this time? In your answer, please include critical academic and professional experiences that led to your decision, a self-assessment of your suitability for graduate management school, your career goals, and your specific interest in the Freeman School.*

Essay #1:

I am seeking a Tulane MBA because the curriculum and international programs offered by the A.B. Freeman School of Business at Tulane University will expand my knowledge of core business concepts while allowing me to focus on the area in which I plan to make my career: international business. As the national accounts officer at ABC Bank, I serve as the account handling officer for the bank's national and multinational corporate customers, such as General Motors Acceptance Corporation, Anheuser-Busch, and Westinghouse Electric. In working with these firms, both now as an officer and previously as a credit card analyst, I have observed that many of them plan to increase their international presence, especially in Mexico and Europe. My career objective is to work for a multinational firm for several years to gain the experience needed to ultimately establish my own international service-related firm. The knowledge needed and experience offered by the programs at the Freeman School will help me achieve this goal.

After working at ABC Bank for three years, I have decided that I need more academic training in order to pursue a more challenging career. The will and drive to succeed has characterized my tenure at ABC Bank. I attribute my success to two of my personal strengths that will be equally important in future careers: persistence and interpersonal skills.

After graduating from the University of XYZ in August of 1986, my goal was to secure a credit analyst position with ABC Bank. I believed the analyst position would help me build a foundation for making credit decisions as a lender, as well as allow me to study the operations of many industries. Upon applying for the position, however, I was told that no analyst positions were available and that the bank preferred to hire internally for such jobs. With this guideline in mind, I asked for any available job at the bank. I was offered a commercial-vault teller position and accepted it. Although the work of processing commercial deposits for eight hours a day was monotonous, I kept my strategy in mind: perform my teller duties well, be persistent with credit management, and thereby earn the credit analyst job. After nine months in the vault, my determination was rewarded; the credit manager offered me the position that I sought. As an analyst, I was responsible for writing detailed analyses of a firm's operations to assist the commercial lenders with credit decisions. After working only eleven months in the credit area (the normal tenure is eighteen to twenty-four months), I was elected national accounts officer, thus becoming the bank's youngest officer. Although I wrote very good credit reviews, I was not promoted for this reason; there were several other analysts who also wrote good reviews. I was promoted largely because of my strong interpersonal and communications skills, since the National Accounts position requires an officer who can work well with both current and prospective customers. The National Accounts position entails handling the lending and cash management needs of the bank's national customers.

At ABC Bank, I have moved from a teller to an officer position in a short time. I have used my intelligence, persistence, and interpersonal skills to move up rapidly, and now I wish to pursue a more challenging career. I am ready to use my past experience, combined with my strengths that I have discussed above, to obtain a graduate management degree and then excel in the area of international business.

Goal: Career in International Business

I want to build on my three years of banking experience and my travels, literally around the world, in preparation for an international management position either within the United States or abroad. My travels to Australia, Latin America, and South Africa on behalf of my family's cattle ranch first stimulated my interest in international business and trade. This interest has subsequently evolved during my three years in the banking business.

While I was a credit analyst, I learned much more about the international direction in which many firms are increasingly moving. Some of the firms that I reviewed are aggressively pursuing opportunities in Mexico because of their proximity to the border, the probable free trade agreement between the United States and Mexico, and the burgeoning maquiladora industry along the international border. The common denominator among these firms is a desire to take advantage of Mexico's abundance of labor and natural resources. I believe these two resources, coupled with Mexico's progressive government and an increasing interest in Mexico by U.S. business, will provide great opportunity in this emerging area of trade.

In addition, the National Accounts position has afforded me the opportunity to travel nationwide to call on my customers' home offices, and, in the course of conducting the bank's affairs, inquire about each firm's international operations. Although noting the obstacles, political and economic, many customers have eagerly outlined their plans to expand into Latin America, Eastern Europe, and China. They made it clear to me that trends such as the movement toward common markets and the increasing capability of long-distance communication via satellite will further encourage foreign trade. Furthermore, most noted their company's need to employ more personnel in the international area; the general consensus among my contacts is that there will be an increasing demand for international managers in the next decade.

At present, I am undecided as to which path I will choose in international business. Some possibilities that I have considered are finance-related and should capitalize on my lending and cash management experience with a multinational bank. Another option I am considering is to establish a firm that provides translation services to companies wishing to conduct business abroad. As more firms enter the international market, the language barrier could be an obstacle to many U.S. businesses. A translation service would overcome this problem and innovations such as video teleconferencing make this idea quite feasible.

Why a Tulane MBA?

Clearly, there are a number of options available to someone pursuing a career in international business in order to be an effective manager. The Freeman School's curriculum provides the opportunity for me to obtain this knowledge.

The program's first year of required core courses, such as Financial Accounting and Marketing Management, followed by a flexible course scheduled in the second year appeals to my desire to expand my knowledge in the areas of finance and accounting, and then focus on international topics. I also hope to take advantage of the school's international internship program or the study abroad program. It is important that I take advantage of one of these programs, since I believe one should have a sense of culture and economic climate of a region if she or he hopes to conduct business in that area.

Since I will spend almost two years in a master's program and the school I choose could well determine my career options, I have treated the selection of schools to which I will apply with great care. I am quite aware of the Freeman School's outstanding reputation for international studies. Furthermore, since New Orleans is one of the nation's largest ports, I will have the opportunity to obtain first-hand knowledge about international commerce. Finally, several of the school's alumni have highly recommended the Freeman School to me due to its significant global focus.

In summary, the combination of my three years of banking experience, international travels, and completion of the MBA program at

Tulane should prepare me quite well to succeed as an international manager. As you can see, I have demonstrated both motivation and initiative during my tenure at ABC Bank. I realize that my grade point average is below the published median 3.1 for a recently entering class. I attribute my relatively low GPA to lack of career focus and immaturity during my undergraduate years. I want to assert my belief, however, that I have as much character, determination, and will to succeed as any student in the MBA program. I might note that there are several credit analysts who obtained their jobs before I did mainly due to higher GPAs; most of these analysts are still in the credit department writing reviews while I travel nationwide representing the bank. I can successfully complete the MBA program at Tulane and would certainly like the opportunity to do so.

CRITIQUE

Our admissions committee felt that this was an extremely strong essay. Many applications have the tendency to treat this as an open-ended "tell us about yourself" kind of question and write very general essays that elaborate on their backgrounds without providing adequate rationale regarding their suitability for MBA studies, an outline of their of their goals, or how a Freeman MBA can help them attain these goals. Although often cleverly written, such essays do not help the committee in making an admissions decision.

This essay is well structured, well written, and gives us a clear picture of the applicant as an individual who is both motivated and focused. The description of his rapid progression at ABC Bank from commercial vault teller to credit analyst (his initial goal) to national accounts officer clearly shows that the applicant is able to assess his options, set goals and successfully develop and execute a strategy to reach them. These are characteristics we seek in our MBA students. The essay also shows that the applicant has gained important knowledge and insights along the way which have helped him formulate his goals for the future. These goals include a Freeman MBA and a career in international business.

Although this applicant confesses that he is still weighing two options in the area of international business (rather refreshing, since many of the very specific career goals we read about are obviously contrived or not well supported in the essay), he makes a convincing case for his interest in the field. He also explains his interest in the Freeman School well, citing our global focus, locations in one of the nation's largest port cities, and some of our specific international programs. The applicant shows a strong interest in the Freeman MBA program. He has researched the program and has clearly taken the time to speak with alumni.

Finally, the applicant acknowledges a weakness (his GPA), and, without making excuses, emphasizes the characteristics he has which he believes will make him a strong candidate for our program. These characteristics were amply demonstrated throughout the essay, but he does a nice job of summarizing them and "closing the sale" at the end.

UNIVERSITY OF VIRGINIA

Question #1: *What is the most difficult ethical dilemma you have faced in your professional life? Articulate the nature of the difficulty. Upon present reflection, would you have resolved this dilemma in a different manner?*

Essay #1:

Upon graduation from college, my sense of adventure and quest for learning continued when I accepted a nontraditional position with the Bank of Credit and Commerce International (BCCI). I accepted a position with BCCI with the understanding that overseas placements were the requirement, given the bank's limited U.S. presence. BCCI was founded in 1972 by Pakistani financier Agha Hasan Abedi, whose goal was to create the first multinational bank for the Third World. Its shareholders were rich Middle Eastern oil sheiks. Healthy growth fueled by increasing international trade helped BCCI expand to $20 billion in assets that circled the globe in a 70-country branch network.

After completing BCCI's international trade finance training program with distinction at Pace University in New York, I received my first placement in London, England, working as a trainee in bank branch operations and special country-analysis projects. After quickly completing my London assignment in three months, BCCI management promoted me to a marketing role at their main offices in the United Arab Emirates (UAE). The ruling sheiks of each of the emirates were BCCI's major stockholders and had enormous international political and economic clout.

By quickly absorbing the local culture and the basics of the Arabic language, I earned the respect of my peers at the bank and in the local business community. Through my efforts, I marketed and received commitments for trade financing and investing from many multinational businesses operating in the UAE.

It was right after my third month working in the UAE that I was faced with a major ethical dilemma. During my search for new business, I learned from a contact at the government ministry of trade that a European sportswear manufacturer had applied for permission to start up a business in the UAE. (An application to do business is required of all foreigners along with the requirement to find a local partner.) I immediately informed bank management of the prospect and began my research into the company. After an initial meeting with the company in the UAE a few weeks later, I learned that the firm required a $30 million line facility. I requested the necessary financial information from the company and began my analysis of the company to assess its creditworthiness. My recommendation to bank management was not to proceed any further with the company, given its losses over the past three years and very high leverage. The risks posed by the company's profiles were too great.

My manager, who had always valued my credit skills, mysteriously ignored my recommendation and ordered me to negotiate a loan facility with the company. I was puzzled by my manager's actions, especially since he offered no explanation. I structured a smaller facility at a premium interest rate with adequate primary and secondary fallback collateral to protect the bank from any credit risks. After presenting the new proposal to my bank manager, he dismissed it without comment and made the necessary arrangements to grant the company a $30 million unsecured line of credit at an interest rate reserved for the bank's highest creditworthy clients. A new provision was added, though. A finder's fee of one percent of the loan ($300,000) was due. Even though the fee was paid, there existed no mention of it in the loan documents. Through a search of the bank's accounting records, I learned that the fee was transferred out of the UAE to my manager's personal account abroad. I was naive to think that the manager did not have his contacts in the bank who would report my inquiring.

My manager explained that the fee was not to be considered extorted funds, rather it was his finder's fee. Further, he explained that this was a customary practice. In fact, to show good will, he offered to share his fee with me and suggested $50,000. The only stipulation was that I had to keep the matter quiet from "jealous" employees.

My dilemma was whether to accept part of my manager's illegally obtained funds and keep quiet or to report the matter to a higher level of bank management. Being only 23 years of age and in a foreign country 8,000 miles away from home, I was scared. If this was a customary practice and the branch was covering up for him, then my reporting this incident would put my job in jeopardy as well as my life. I was always taught by my family to practice high ethical and moral standards and to obey the law. This was my guiding principle in refusing the illegal funds and notifying the bank's London headquarters of this serious matter. Immediately, I was transferred back to London within 48 hours, and no mention of the incident was ever made to me either in the UAE or in London. My newly assigned job in London was nonmarketing related and consisted of counting checks in a windowless basement room. Even though it felt like BCCI management was punishing me for good ethical conduct, I still believed that my decision was right. I resigned from the bank one month later and returned to the United States, where I obtained a banking job with an organization that, I feel proud to say, has never presented me with a choice of compromising my ethics and moral standards.

If, in the future, I am unfortunately presented with an ethical dilemma of any degree, I feel confident in holding my ethical and moral standards as priority.

CRITIQUE

What makes an application to the Darden School stand out from among the thousands received each year? One important key is well-written essays. As with many business school applications, the essay portion is the applicant's chance to showcase his or her writing talents while at the same time communicating a lot of explicit (and sometimes implicit) information to the admissions committee.

Many b-schools offer the first-year student traditional courses in such functional areas as accounting, marketing, and operations, but Darden was one of the first to include required, graded courses in both communications and ethics. Nowhere at Darden do these two disciplines dovetail more perfectly than in Essay #4 of Darden's application, which asks: "What is the most difficult ethical dilemma you have faced in your professional life? Articulate the nature of the difficulty. Upon present reflection, would you have resolved this dilemma in a different manner?"

While this essay question often prompts the most reflection and introspection on the part of the applicant, it is also often the least understood. The admissions committee is looking not necessarily to judge the nature of the dilemma but rather the candidate's ability to articulate an often personal and complex decision-making process. The key to an effective Essay #4 is in dissecting the terms *ethical* and *dilemma*. Too often, themes reflected in this essay are of a legal nature: Should I disagree with my boss? Should I turn a co-worker in who's stealing office supplies? Should I break the law? And many situations do not accurately present a true dilemma in which there is no clear right or wrong answer but two or more possible solutions, none of which are necessarily better than another.

The essay above serves as an outstanding example by setting the scene, explaining clearly the nature of the dilemma and summing up the candidate's experience in a concise and well-written essay. The admissions committee was particularly impressed by the author's honest approach and engaging writing style. The firm does not have to be well-known, in this case BCCI, nor must the dilemma involve large sums of money or shady characters. Rather, the essay should reflect the candidate's personal and professional commitment to ethics, a commitment that also underlies the foundation of the Darden School.

Part III

THE SCHOOLS

SCHOOLS RATED BY CATEGORY

ABOUT THESE "RANKINGS"

Now before you say, "Hey, wait a minute! I thought this book wasn't going to rank schools," let us explain. Surveying 18,500 business school students is no easy task. In fact, it practically killed several staff members. But among the fruits of our labors—a reward that made our task seem worthwhile—was the fascinating numbers we came up with. We wanted to present those numbers to you in an informative and slightly less-than-serious way. The following rankings cannot and must not be considered objective. These lists are based entirely upon student opinion. So when our list rates a campus location, for example, we didn't use any scientific formula based on cost of living, climate, crime rate, etc. We simply listed the schools at which students raved about the location most, or complained about it most. So focus on the categories that are important to you, and make of these opinions what you will.

And remember, every one of the schools profiled in this book is a top-notch institution.

ACADEMICS

STUDENTS DEVELOP STRONG MARKETING SKILLS

Indiana University
College of William and Mary
University of Massachusetts at Amherst
University of Michigan
Vanderbilt University
University of Southern California
University of Tennessee at Knoxville
The Pennsylvania State University
Texas A&M University
University of North Carolina at Chapel Hill

WEAK MARKETING SKILLS

Tulane University
University of Kentucky
University of Georgia
Southern Methodist University
University of Texas at Arlington
Massachusetts Institute of Technology
University of Denver
Harvard University
University of Alabama
University of Wyoming

FINANCE WHIZZES
(students develop strong finance skills)

University of Rochester
University of Pennsylvania
Columbia University
Indiana University
University of Chicago
Tulane University
Yale University
Carnegie Mellon University
New York University
Massachusetts Institute of Technology

HAVE TROUBLE MAKING CORRECT CHANGE
(weak finance skills)

University of Massachusetts at Amherst
Pepperdine University
Duke University
University of Georgia
University of Kentucky
Syracuse University
University of Texas at Arlington
University of Washington
University of Wisconsin—Madison
University of Alabama

STUDENTS DEVELOP STRONG ACCOUNTING SKILLS

University of California—Irvine
Cornell University
University of Chicago
Indiana University
Dartmouth College
University of Rochester
University of Texas at Austin
Wake Forest University
University of Southern California
University of Alabama

WHAT'S A SPREAD SHEET?

University of Kansas
University of Texas at Arlington
University of Wisconsin—Madison
Duke University
Harvard University
University of Western Ontario
Michigan State University
University of Colorado at Boulder
Loyola University
Syracuse University

STUDENTS DEVELOP STRONG GENERAL MANAGEMENT SKILLS

University of Virginia
Dartmouth College
Harvard University
University of North Carolina at Chapel Hill
Texas A&M University
Georgetown University
Duke University
Yale University
Stanford University
Indiana University

WEAK GENERAL MANAGEMENT SKILLS

University of Texas at Arlington
University of Wisconsin—Madison
University of Chicago
University of Pittsburgh
University of Florida
Syracuse University
University of Washington
Thunderbird
Pepperdine University
University of Massachusetts at Amherst

STUDENTS DEVELOP STRONG OPERATIONS SKILLS

Carnegie Mellon University
Washington University
College of William and Mary
Georgetown University
Purdue University
Georgia Institute of Technology
Indiana University
Vanderbilt University
University of Southern California
Wake Forest University

OPERATIONS NOT A STRONG POINT

University of Wisconsin—Madison
University of Texas at Arlington
CUNY Baruch College
University of Georgia
Syracuse University
Texas Christian University
University of Chicago
University of Massachusetts at Amherst
Michigan State University
Dartmouth College

STUDENTS DEVELOP STRONG TEAMWORK SKILLS

University of Arizona
Texas A&M University
University of Alabama
Dartmouth College
Duke University
Georgetown University
Indiana University
University of North Carolina at Chapel Hill
Northwestern University
Wake Forest University

NOT MUCH TEAMWORK

CUNY Baruch College
University of Texas at Arlington
University of Wyoming
Harvard University
University of Kansas
Syracuse University
University of Kentucky
University of Chicago
Northeastern University
Pepperdine University

STUDENTS DEVELOP STRONG INTERPERSONAL SKILLS

University of Arizona
Dartmouth College
The Pennsylvania State University
Duke University
Indiana University
Texas A&M University
Tulane University
University of Southern California
University of Tennessee at Knoxville
Case Western University

STUDENTS DEVELOP STRONG PRESENTATION SKILLS

The Pennsylvania State University
University of Arizona
Brigham Young University
Dartmouth College
University of Tennessee at Knoxville
Vanderbilt University
Duke University
University of Maryland
Southern Methodist University
Texas A&M University

QUANT JOCKS
(students develop strong quantitative skills)

Carnegie Mellon University
University of Rochester
University of Chicago
Massachusetts Institute of Technology
Columbia University
Indiana University
Yale University
University of Pennsylvania
New York University
University of Maryland

WEAK INTERPERSONAL SKILLS

University of Texas at Arlington
University of Western Ontario
University of Kentucky
Syracuse University
University of Kansas
University of Wyoming
CUNY Baruch College
Harvard University
Northeastern University
University of Massachusetts at Amherst

WEAK PRESENTATION SKILLS

University of Massachusetts at Amherst
Harvard University
University of Kentucky
University of Texas at Arlington
Washington University
University of Kansas
University of Pittsburgh
Columbia University
University of Wyoming
CUNY Baruch College

POETS
(weak quantitative skills)

Harvard University
Boston University
CUNY Baruch College
University of Western Ontario
Syracuse University
University of Texas at Arlington
Claremont Graduate University
Northeastern University
University of Kansas
Northwestern University

COMPUTER GENIUSES
(students comfortable with computers and managing data)

University of California—Irvine
Wake Forest University
Indiana University
University of Iowa
Massachusetts Institute of Technology
University of California—Los Angeles
Carnegie Mellon University
University of Alabama
Columbia University
Dartmouth College

HOW DO I TURN THIS THING ON?
(students uncomfortable with computers)

Harvard University
CUNY Baruch College
University of Texas at Arlington
University of North Carolina at Chapel Hill
University of Western Ontario
Claremont Graduate University
University of Massachusetts at Amherst
Syracuse University
Yale University
Northeastern University

PRESSURE

GOOD SAMARITANS
(noncompetitive students)
Yale University
Stanford University
Northwestern University
University of California—Berkeley
University of Massachusetts at Amherst
Wake Forest University
University of California—Los Angeles
Dartmouth College
Georgetown University
University of Virginia

BACK-STABBERS
(competitive students)
Texas Christian University
University of Western Ontario
Southern Methodist University
Columbia University
University of Alabama
Baylor University
University of Chicago
Carnegie Mellon University
University of Georgia
University of Tennessee at Knoxville

LIGHT WORK LOAD
University of Texas at Arlington
University of Kentucky
Baylor University
CUNY Baruch College
Loyola University
Arizona State University
Stanford University
University of Georgia
Northwestern University
Texas Christian University

UP ALL NIGHT
(heavy work load)
University of Virginia
College of William and Mary
Rice University
University of Southern California
Babson College
The Pennsylvania State University
University of Rochester
Massachusetts Institute of Technology
University of Pittsburgh
University of Tennessee at Knoxville

OVERALL MELLOW
University of California—Berkeley
Yale University
Arizona State University
University of Massachusetts at Amherst
Stanford University
University of Colorado at Boulder
University of Kentucky
University of Texas at Arlington
Duke University
University of Georgia

OVERALL TENSE
University of Virginia
Columbia University
Georgetown University
Indiana University
New York University
University of Western Ontario
Rice University
Brigham Young University
Texas Christian University
University of California—Irvine

SOCIAL LIFE & FELLOW STUDENTS

MULTICULTURAL SMORGASBORD
(ethnic & racial diversity)

Massachusetts Institute of Technology
Case Western Reserve University
Thunderbird
Tulane University
University of Michigan
University of Maryland
Penn State University
Boston University
Carnegie Mellon University
University of Rochester

WHITE BREAD
(ethnic & racial homogenity)

Brigham Young University
University of Alabama
College of William and Mary
Dartmouth College
Wake Forest University
University of Colorado at Boulder
Baylor University
University of Wyoming
Rice University
University of Virginia

STUDENTS ARE EAGER TO HELP OTHERS

University of North Carolina at Chapel Hill
Georgetown University
Dartmouth College
Yale University
Indiana University
Texas A&M University
University of California—Los Angeles
University of California—Berkeley
University of Virginia
University of Michigan

ONLY IF YOU ASK

University of Texas at Arlington
Northeastern University
CUNY Baruch College
University of Connecticut
Harvard University
University of Kansas
Syracuse University
Loyola University
University of Western Ontario
University of Kentucky

TOP OF THE MORNING TO YOU
(students are very friendly)

Indiana University
University of California—Los Angeles
Northwestern University
Dartmouth College
University of North Carolina at Chapel Hill
Georgetown University
Yale University
University of Michigan
Texas A&M University
University of Alabama

DON'T BOTHER ME
(students aren't very friendly)

University of Texas at Arlington
Northeastern University
Harvard University
CUNY Baruch College
Syracuse University
University of Connecticut
Hofstra University
University of Chicago
University of Kansas
University of Kentucky

HERE'S MY CARD
(students will keep in touch)

Harvard University
University of Massachusetts at Amherst
University of North Carolina at Chapel Hill
University of Western Ontario
Claremont Graduate University
Yale University
Georgetown University
Northeastern University
Boston University
University of Kansas

WHAT'S NETWORKING?
(students won't stay in touch)

University of Texas at Arlington
University of Connecticut
Northeastern University
Syracuse University
Hofstra University
University of Kansas
CUNY Baruch College
University of Wyoming
University of Kentucky
University of Pittsburgh

SOCIAL BUTTERFLIES
(active social lives)

Northwestern University
University of California—Los Angeles
Stanford University
Dartmouth College
Columbia University
University of North Carolina at Chapel Hill
University of Colorado at Boulder
University of California—Berkeley
Thunderbird
Tulane University

THE HEART IS A LONELY BROKER
(moribund social lives)

University of Texas at Arlington
CUNY Baruch College
Carnegie Mellon University
University of Kentucky
University of Kansas
University of Rochester
Northeastern University
Hofstra University
University of Virginia
Rice University

SHINY, HAPPY MBAS
(best quality of life)

Vanderbilt University
Yale University
Case Western University
Cornell University
University of Texas at Austin
University of Pennsylvania
Arizona State University
University of California—Berkeley
Washington University
Claremont Graduate University

SCHOOL OF THE LIVING DEAD
(worst quality of life)

University of Connecticut
CUNY Baruch College
Indiana University
Northeastern University
University of Kansas
University of Texas at Arlington
University of Michigan
Syracuse University
Stanford University
Boston University

BEEN THERE, DONE THAT
(students have diverse work experience)

University of California—Berkeley
Yale University
Cornell University
University of California—Los Angeles
Georgetown University
Duke University
Babson College
Northwestern University
University of Western Ontario
University of Michigan

YOU WANT FRIES WITH THAT?
(students' work experience NOT diverse)

Brigham Young University
University of Kansas
University of Alabama
Baylor University
Texas Christian University
University of Wyoming
Texas A&M University
Syracuse University
University of Denver
University of Kentucky

GENIUS FOLK
(students say their classmates are smart)

Massachusetts Institute of Technology
Carnegie Mellon University
Yale University
Stanford University
Dartmouth College
Georgetown University
University of California—Los Angeles
University of California—Berkeley
University of Pennsylvania
University of Maryland

NOT-SO BRIGHT
(students say classmates are not smart)

Northeastern University
CUNY Baruch College
University of Kansas
Syracuse University
University of Texas at Arlington
University of Wyoming
University of Connecticut
University of Wisconsin—Madison
University of Denver
University of Kentucky

FACILITIES

SO MUCH TO DO
(lots of school clubs & activities)
Harvard University
University of Pennsylvania
University of Texas at Austin
Vanderbilt University
Cornell University
Case Western University
University of Western Ontario
University of Virginia
Yale University
University of Washington

BOOOOOORING
(not many school activities)
CUNY Baruch College
Loyola University
University of Texas at Arlington
University of Connecticut
Northeastern University
Claremont Graduate University
Michigan State University
University of Kansas
University of Wyoming
University of Kentucky

SCHOOL TOWN IS PARADISE
University of Washington
University of Texas at Austin
Michigan State University
University of Wisconsin—Madison
Arizona State University
University of Colorado at Boulder
University of Denver
Georgia Institute of Technology
Vanderbilt University
University of Virginia

SCHOOL TOWN A PIT
Thunderbird
University of Connecticut
Yale University
University of Pennsylvania
Rensselaer Polytechnic Institute
University of Notre Dame
Indiana University
Purdue University
Baylor University
Hofstra University

A FIVE-STAR LIBRARY
Vanderbilt University
University of California—Los Angeles
University of Western Ontario
University of California—Berkeley
Wake Forest University
University of Illinois at Urbana-Champaign
University of Notre Dame
Harvard University
Washington University
Stanford University

SOMEONE LOST THE BOOK
University of Kentucky
Georgia Institute of Technology
Ohio State University
Texas Christian University
Michigan State University
New York University
University of Denver
Columbia University
University of Kansas
College of William and Mary

MAXIMUM PUMPITUDE
(gym facilities excellent)

Harvard University
Vanderbilt University
University of Illinois at Urbana-Champaign
Arizona State University
University of Texas at Austin
University of Virginia
University of Western Ontario
University of Colorado at Boulder
University of Wisconsin—Madison
Michigan State University

WIMPY, WIMPY, WIMPY
(like maybe a jump rope or something)

Massachusetts Institute of Technology
University of Pennsylvania
Stanford University
Duke University
Claremont Graduate University
Thunderbird
CUNY Baruch College
University of Chicago
University of Texas at Arlington
Texas Christian University

ON-CAMPUS HOUSING GOOD

Harvard University
University of Western Ontario
University of Notre Dame
University of Illinois at Urbana-Champaign
University of Wyoming
College of William and Mary
University of Rochester
Cornell University
Pepperdine University
Hofstra University

LOUSY

Arizona State University
CUNY Baruch College
Texas Christian University
Duke University
University of North Carolina at Chapel Hill
University of Chicago
Wake Forest University
Carnegie Mellon University
Case Western Reserve University
Georgetown University

PLACEMENT & RECRUITING

RECRUITING
(quality, range, & number of companies recruiting on-campus)

University of Pennsylvania
Stanford University
Massachusetts Institute of Technology
University of California—Los Angeles
University of Chicago
University of Texas at Austin
University of Virginia
University of Western Ontario
Vanderbilt University
Arizona State University

RECRUITING
(not satisfactory)

Northeastern University
University of Kentucky
Hofstra University
University of Massachusetts at Amherst
University of Texas at Arlington
Boston University
Babson College
University of Denver
University of Wyoming
Claremont Graduate University

WE GOT JOBS
(placement office very effective)

University of California—Los Angeles
Stanford University
University of Pennsylvania
Vanderbilt University
Washington University
Pepperdine University
Massachusetts Institute of Technology
University of Maryland
The Pennsylvania State University
University of Pittsburgh

ARE YOU HIRING?
(placement office not so great)

University of Wyoming
University of Massachusetts at Amherst
CUNY Baruch College
Northeastern University
University of Kentucky
University of Georgia
Hofstra University
University of Texas at Arlington
Baylor University
Yale University

## Chapter 10

SCHOOL PROFILES

UNIVERSITY OF ALABAMA
Manderson Graduate School of Business

OVERVIEW

Type of school	public
Affiliation	none
Environment	urban
Academic calendar	semester
Schedule	full-time only

STUDENTS

Enrollment of parent institution	19,000
Enrollment of business school	107
% male/female	70/30
% out-of-state	32
% minorities	8
% international (# of countries represented)	8 (7)
Average age at entry	24
Average years work experience at entry	2

ACADEMICS

Student/faculty ratio	3:1
% female faculty	12
% minority faculty	7
Hours of study per day	4.17

SPECIALTIES
Systems Consulting, Strategic Planning and Implementaion, Strategic Business Management, Marketing

JOINT DEGREES
MBA/JD, 4 years; 3/2 MBA + Undergrad, 5 years

SPECIAL PROGRAMS
The 3-2 Program, Executive MBA Program

STUDY ABROAD PROGRAMS
Belgium—HEC.

SURVEY SAYS...
HITS
Students are happy
Help fellow students

MISSES
Social life

PROMINENT ALUMNI
Thomas Cross, Managing Partner, Price Waterhouse; Samuel A. DiPiazza, Vice Chairman, Coopers & Lybrand; Ron Stewart, Senior Partner, Andersen Consulting

ACADEMICS

According to many of the MBAs at the University of Alabama, the Manderson Graduate School of Business offers an unbeatable combination. A parent institution of 19,000 students means that Manderson is supported by the powerful resources of a major university. An enrollment barely over 100 means that students enjoy a small-school environment within the university setting. And to top it all off, state sponsorship means that a Manderson MBA costs a tiny fraction of an MBA from a private institution, even for out-of-staters.

First-year studies at Manderson are consumed by the core curriculum, presented in lockstep sequence. Core courses cover numerous functional areas, "such as accounting economics, statistics, human resources management, production and operations management, marketing, finance, and management information systems." Professors coordinate instruction of the cores to address themes and case studies presented in other courses; explains one student, "Our professors work closely together to integrate the classes in order to give us the fine points, as well as the overall picture." Second-year students select a concentration in one of the following: systems consulting, strategic planning and implementation, finance/accounting, marketing, banking and financial services, or production/operations management. Students appreciate the fact that "the school is very flexible in what electives you can take. I could take an advertising class in the Communications School to go with my marketing concentration." Another strong point is that "second-year professors are really excellent and care about the students and the program." Assessing the various departments here, students tell us that Manderson boasts "excellent statistics, accounting, MIS (Management Information Systems) faculty. Students also give the administration high marks, reporting that "the MBA office has the best and most helpful people around, any problems or questions are always taken care of right away."

Alabama MBAs appreciate the efforts the school has made to improve the program, including a recent upgrade of facilities. Says one student, "The library system, computer facilities, and classroom multimedia equipment are excellent." While many students feel that "the number of available concentrations needs to be increased," most also recognize the fact that limited choices are part of the trade-off for enjoying such an intimately sized program.

PLACEMENT AND RECRUITING

In response to past complaints, the Alabama Placement Office has worked to improve service to its small MBA student body. Previously, Manderson relied on the university-wide placement office, but in 1997 it added an MBA-specific, full-time Placement Manager to the b-school staff. This move has not only increased recruitment opportunities but also freed up staff to provide more of such services as career counseling and personal coaching for interviews and resume writing. Professors are also helpful in this regard; the placement office reports that "faculty is available and is very involved with students to assist in making the all-important 'foot in the door' introduction relative to career opportunities." So too are Manderson alums; writes one student, "Alumni relations within the companies that come to campus are strong."

Missy Strickland, Coordinator of Graduate Recruiting/Admissions MBA Program
Box 870223 Tuscaloosa, AL 35487-0223
Admissions: 205-348-6517 Fax: 205-348-4504
Email: MBA@cba.ua.edu
Internet: www.cba.ua.edu/~mba

University of Alabama

STUDENT/CAMPUS LIFE

Because of the tiny student body, Manderson students get to know nearly all their classmates during their stay here. Manderson MBAs hold each other in high regard, describing their peers as "a very diverse group with different backgrounds and interests: engineering, liberal arts, business. We blend well together when working on projects and discussing issues because of these differences. The atmosphere is very team based. Everyone looks out for everyone else." The one knock on Manderson students is that they are "inexperienced. UA accepts many people straight from undergrad, which really changes the level of lectures and discussions." Writes another student, "It's a young group that makes up for its lack of experience with intelligence." Most American students come from the region and share "traditional Southern values. They are very conservative." A small group of international students provides most of the ethnic/racial diversity.

The majority of students live off campus in nearby apartments. Parking near campus can be difficult; consider living within walking distance or bringing a bike. Students report that hometown Tuscaloosa "is a fun city. If you like clubs and bars, you have plenty of choices. There are also lots of good restaurants." Tuscaloosa is also home to a number of international corporations, among them Mercedes-Benz, British Steel, and JVC. Manderson students find their workload manageable, leaving sufficient time for leisure activity. Writes one, "Academics are a big part of life here, but the program also stresses professional involvement and extracurricular activities, such as ballroom dancing and the symphony." Agrees another, "Life is great here. If you work, it is a little busy, but we also have fun, especially with stress relief things like intramural sports." Students enjoy a fully equipped, high-tech gym on campus, and many are very enthusiastic about Alabama's intercollegiate sports teams; every football game is a big event, as are meets for the nationally ranked gymnastics team. For those who want to do more than watch football, the MBA Association sponsors a wide range of professional and social events, including MBA Week, which features an intramural sporting competition, a community service activity, a variety of panel discussions and other keynote speakers, and a golf tournament with both MBAs and local business leaders as players.

ADMISSIONS

The admissions office evaluates, with equal weight, the following categories: GPA, GMAT scores, work or other experience, essays, letters of recommendation, extracurricular activities, and a personal interview.

According to the school, "We evaluate applications in a holistic manner. We evaluate applicants' abilities, capabilities, and goals based on all required elements of the application. Each category provides us with various information relative to academic abilities, writing skills, communication skills, and teamwork skills." Decisions are made on a rolling admissions basis during the spring semester. Applicants are typically notified of a decision within four to six weeks after the application has been received.

FINANCIAL FACTS

Tuition (in-/out-of-state)	$2,872/$7,722
Fees (in-/out-of-state)	$1,600/$1,600
Cost of books	$700
Room & board (on-/off-campus)	$4,000/$4,000
% of students receiving aid	39
% first-year students receiving aid	49
% aid that is merit based	100
% of students receiving paid internships	89
Average award package	$7,000
Average grant	$7,000

ADMISSIONS

# of applications received	185
% applicants accepted	39
% acceptees attending	72
Average GMAT (range)	592 (560–620)
Minimum TOEFL	575
Average GPA (range)	3.35 (3.00–3.80)
Application fee (in-/out-of-state)	$25/$25
Early decision program available	No
Regular application deadline	May 15
Regular notification	Rolling
Admission may be deferred?	No
Transfer students accepted?	Yes
Nonfall admission available?	No
Admission process need-blind?	Yes

APPLICANTS ALSO LOOK AT

Vanderbilt University, University of Florida, University of Georgia, Emory University, University of Texas at Austin, University of Tennessee at Knoxville, Tulane University, Wake Forest University

EMPLOYMENT PROFILE

Placement rate (%)	100
# of companies recruiting on campus	170
% of grads employed immediately	81
% grads employed within six months	98
Average starting salary	$50,000

Grads employed by field (avg. salary):

Accounting	7%	$43,500
Consulting	23%	$50,000
Finance	7%	$43,500
General Management	7%	$48,000
Marketing	19%	$44,500
MIS	33%	$51,500
Operations	4%	$48,500

UNIVERSITY OF ARIZONA
Eller Graduate School of Management

ACADEMICS

Students at the Eller Graduate School of Management at the University of Arizona love the fact that their school is an up-and-comer. Writes one, "At Eller you feel like you are part of a new start-up, on the edge of becoming very successful. Everybody is contributing to the ultimate success of the program." Eller has already made a name for itself with its nationally renowned information technology department, which draws substantial financial support from some of America's premier technology companies, including IBM, Apple Computer, and Hewlett Packard. U of A also boasts a "very well respected entrepreneurial program," housed in the Berger Entrepreneurship Program in the Eller Center for the Study of the Private Market Economy. Here students get hands-on experience in workshops and participate in a two-person competitive project. According to our survey, other strong departments at U of A include marketing, finance, and operations. As part of the deal, Arizona MBAs enjoy warm weather, a beautiful campus, and bargain-basement tuition rates.

The U of A offers a basic MBA with an emphasis on quantitative and theoretical skills. Eller does not shunt the importance of communications skills, however; according to school promotional materials, "the Eller School communications component is directly connected to, and completely integrated with, the first-year core courses."

Overall, students agree—an Eller MBA is worth the investment of time and money. "The tuition is dirt cheap, and scholarship money is easy to come by," writes one student. "As a future entrepreneur, why would I spend $20k a year in tuition when that can be my seed capital?" MBAs praised the cohesiveness of the program, but a few critics complain that the program is "over-hyped" and there is too much "work for work's sake." Another mentions that "The MIS department is the focus and other departments tend to be afterthoughts." Others complain that "there is a great emphasis on research rather than experience among the faculty . . . " One dissatisfied student goes so far to lament, "Although MIS professors are well known in their field, they suck as teachers."

PLACEMENT AND RECRUITING

The Eller School Office of Career Development reports that, in addition to scheduling on-campus recruitment, their office coordinates "numerous workshops throughout the year to assist Eller School students in preparing resumes, developing interviewing skills, and conducting a job search campaign." Students give the OCD mixed reviews, complaining that "they need to improve the number and quality of recruiters who come here for marketing and finance." The majority of Eller graduates find work in consulting, finance, and accounting; over three-quarters of their placements are located in the West and Southwest. Top employers of Eller MBAs include Intel, Andersen Consulting, Hewlett-Packard, Ernst and Young, Deloitte & Touche, Tektronix, Wells Fargo, Federal Express, IBM, and American Management Systems.

Susan K. Salinas Wong, Assitant Dean & Director of Admissions
McClelland Hall Rm 210, Box 210108 Tucson, AZ 85711
Admissions: 520-621-3915 Fax: 520-621-2606
Email: ellernet@bpa.arizona.edu
Internet: www.bpa.arizona.edu/ellerschool

University of Arizona

STUDENT/CAMPUS LIFE

Eller MBAs describe their classmates as "team workers" who are "young and energetic, competitive but helpful." Students get along well together, a good thing since the size of the program means that "at Eller, you know everyone." Notes one student: "The small class size allows for a strong sense of community. However, first- and second-year students are clearly delineated." Cooperation abounds. One student writes about his classmates, "If you have a problem with a particular marketing case . . . they will help you out. You have an extra case of beer . . . they will help you out." Reflecting on the fact that 85 percent of Eller's students arrive with work experience, one student writes that "very few students are admitted directly from undergraduate school, which I think is a plus. They are mature, have work experience, and are willing to help." Students feel that their classes would benefit from racial diversity; writes one white student, "There are far too many white students here. The school doesn't give us the social experience to work effectively with minority students." Reflecting this lack of diversity but shrugging it off, a black student tells us: "As an African American student it's been great. I had a few reservations initially, but the eight of us think it's great."

Students here study an average of twenty-five to thirty-five hours a week, and report an intense first-year workload. By the second year, both the workload and pressure lighten up. Still, like other b-school students, many Eller MBAs say they do assignments selectively—skimming and skipping—to manage it all. Classes are small and held Monday through Thursday. No class on Fridays, which are reserved for activities such as on-site business visits and skills workshops.

Social and professional activities are organized by the student-run Master of Business Administration Student Association. Students get most pumped about the gym, which they describe as "amazing." The majority of students live off-campus in surrounding neighborhoods. The U of A campus is beautiful, and outdoor activities are abundant. "There's so much to do," writes one MBA. "Golf, tennis, hiking are all popular pastimes. The study breaks on my mountain bike are quite excellent." Everyone seems to like Tucson. Writes one student, "Tucson is a great place to live as a student. The cost of living is low and it has a laid-back environment." A few hours' drive away—in various directions—are Phoenix, the Grand Canyon, and the beaches of Mexico.

ADMISSIONS

The admissions department considers work experience to be the most important factor, followed by undergraduate coursework, undergraduate GPA, GMAT scores, essays, and recommendations. The admissions office notes, "In general, we look at the 'whole person' and not just isolated components of individual performance such as GMAT or GPA."

FINANCIAL FACTS

Tuition (in-/out-of-state)	$5,259/$12,411
Cost of books	$1,000
Room & board (on-/off-campus)	NR/$5,591
% of students receiving paid internships	90
Average award package	$7,848
Average grant	$4,090

ADMISSIONS

# of applications received	852
% applicants accepted	20
% acceptees attending	54
Average GMAT (range)	637 (550–740)
Minimum TOEFL	600
Average GPA	3.40
Application fee (in-/out-of-state)	$45/$45
Early decision program available	Yes
Early decision deadline	November 1
Early decision notification	December 15
Regular application deadline	March 1
Regular notification	Rolling
Admission may be deferred?	Yes
Maximum length of deferment	1 year
Transfer students accepted?	No
Nonfall admission available?	No
Admission process need-blind?	Yes

APPLICANTS ALSO LOOK AT

University of Texas at Austin, Arizona State University, University of California—Los Angeles, University of Maryland, University of California—Berkeley, Cornell, USC, Stanford University

EMPLOYMENT PROFILE

Placement rate (%)	97
# of companies recruiting on campus	70
% of grads employed immediately	78
% grads employed within six months	98
Average starting salary	$56,800

Grads employed by field (avg. salary):

Accounting	5%	$39,000
Consulting	26%	$55,200
Entrepreneurship	2%	NR
Finance	21%	$63,400
Marketing	17%	$53,300
MIS	23%	$59,000
Operations	5%	$57,850

ARIZONA STATE UNIVERSITY
College of Business

ACADEMICS

Arizona State University understands the virtues of niche marketing. Rather than try to be all things to all MBAs, ASU focuses on creating graduates who excel in a few specific areas. Thus the choices for second-year students, who elsewhere would be free to pursue numerous electives, are limited. As one second-year puts it: "This program is very specialized. There are five tracks: services marketing, finance, supply chain management, and information technology. This program is great if you are looking for in-depth expertise in one of these areas." Students tell us that they like the fact that "the lockstep program focuses students and faculty on specific disciplines." Of the five tracks, students agree that the one offered by the fewest top MBA programs—the supply chain track—is the best. By offering the supply chain major in cooperation with the National Association of Purchasing Management (NAPM), ASU guarantees that its students receive plenty of hands-on experience and graduate with numerous contacts.

Because the ASU College of Business is just one part of a huge university system, MBAs here have ample opportunities to pursue dual degrees. The school offers an MBA/MIM (International Management) degree in conjunction with Thunderbird, an MBA/MS-Information Management degree, an MBA/MS in Economics, and a combined MBA/JD (law degree). Students may also concurrently complete their MBA with master's degrees in Health Sciences Administration, Architecture, or Accountancy. As at most b-schools, first-year at ASU is crammed with core requirements. The school's brochure warns that students "must maintain minimum nonacademic obligations while in the first-year, as the schedule . . . leaves little opportunity for other activities." Students concur, but quickly note that second year isn't nearly as intense.

Professors here receive below-average grades from students, who tell us that "as with all academic institutions, there are great and marginal instructors." Another explains that "some of the faculty for the core courses need improvement. In the school's defense, they realize this and are attempting to correct this." Students are generally more sanguine about the administration, which they describe as "considerate of our feelings and very concerned with the MBA program image, and so take our comments and suggestions seriously." Students also appreciate the "excellent, up-to-date multimedia equipment in all classrooms and computer labs for student and professor use." Although our survey shows that the program does not entirely meet students' academic expectations, it also shows that most consider an ASU MBA a worthwhile degree. Their explanation: "The value of this degree is extremely high given the price. Students leave here well equipped to work with top-level executives as well as loading dock or field representatives."

PLACEMENT AND RECRUITING

ASU students have mixed feelings about the Career Management Office (CMO). Several are very pleased with its work, calling the program "strong." One student reports that "An enormous number of companies recruit here. It has opened many doors of opportunity I never imagined existed." Yet students' overall grades for the office are merely average. The most common complaint is

Judith K. Heilala, Director of Recruiting and Admissions
MBA Program Office, Tempe, AZ 85287-4906
Admissions: 602-965-3332 Fax: 602-965-8569
Email: asu.mba@asu.edu
Internet: www.cob.asu.edu/mba

Arizona State University

that the CMO is less effective in assisting with placements outside of ASU's perceived areas of strength. "Placement for non-supply and information-systems majors needs improvement," writes one student.

Students report a high level of satisfaction with the quality of companies recruiting on-campus, although many feel that not enough of them come to ASU and that companies from outside the Southwestern region are particularly underrepresented. Students who contact alumni when searching for jobs find them to be helpful. In 1997 the demand in the national and international job market for ASU MBAs increased. While maintaining a diverse employer base of technology, consulting, and financial organizations, a significant increase in hiring by computer/electronics manufacturers and consumer products/services firms is particularly noteworthy. Recent top hirers include IBM, Hewlett-Packard, Intel, Honeywell, Frito-Lay, Qualcomm, Deloitte & Touche, Exxon, Lucent Technologies, Pillsbury, and Televerde.

STUDENT/CAMPUS LIFE

Arizona's trimester academic calendar is "very quick," making life for ASU-MBAs a little more hectic than it might otherwise be. Still, students report that "stress levels are low" because "most people are very willing to help you" in this "great teamwork atmosphere." Most students are only mildly competitive, "mature, older, often married, and here to learn." Many students "participate in volunteer or sports activities both on- and off-campus. Although when approached for help most students offer it, the class is divided into regular and somewhat closed social cliques." Although the student body is "very geographically and ethnically diverse," those unaccustomed to the Southwest should be forewarned: as one Easterner remarks, "the students and the general social atmosphere are more conservative than to what I'm accustomed."

First-year students find that their schedule is pretty well defined, as in, "Sleep-class-study but at least one day per week is yours." Free time opens up for second-year students, who enjoy the campus, the city, and the surrounding area. "Very diverse area," comments one student. "You can play golf one day and go skiing the next." Another agrees: "So many things to do within a two-hour drive! Hiking, skiing, pro sports—you name it and Arizona has it!" On-campus facilities—from the computer labs and library to the gym—are universally considered "great." No wonder students tell us that "living in Phoenix is great; it's like going to school in paradise. The campus and the town are basically resorts."

ADMISSIONS

According to the admissions department, your work experience/resume and GMAT score are weighted most heavily. Then, in descending order, your college GPA, "a personal statement reflecting on maturity, strength of purpose, academic potential, and ability to communicate clearly"; letters of recommendation; extracurricular activities; and the interview. Applications are reviewed in rounds. The deadlines for each round are December 15, March 1, and May 1. It is advisable to apply in round one or two. Joint degree programs include: MBA/MIM with Thunderbird and MBA/JD. Scholarships and assistantships are available, including the PepsiCo Minority Scholarship Program.

FINANCIAL FACTS

Tuition (in-/out-of-state)	$2,118/$9,340
Tuition per credit (in-/out-of-state)	$118/NR
Fees (in-/out-of-state)	$3,071/$3,071
Cost of books	$2,000
Room & board (on-/off-campus)	$5,010/$6,950
% of students receiving aid	95
% of students receiving loans	21
% of students receiving paid internships	85
Average award package	$21,000
Average grant	$2,254

ADMISSIONS

# of applications received	1,360
% applicants accepted	41
% acceptees attending	49
Average GMAT (range)	628 (500-750)
Minimum TOEFL	580
Average GPA (range)	3.30 (2.20/4.00)
Application fee (in-/out-of-state)	$45/$45
Early decision program available	Yes
Early decision deadline	December 15
Early decision notification	February 15
Regular application deadline	May 1
Regular notification	Rolling
Admission may be deferred?	Yes
Maximum length of deferment	Once
Transfer students accepted?	No
Nonfall admission available?	Yes
Admission process need-blind?	Yes

APPLICANTS ALSO LOOK AT

University of Texas at Austin, University of Arizona, University of California—Los Angeles, Thunderbird, University of California—Berkeley, Stanford University, University of Washington, University of Colorado at Boulder

EMPLOYMENT PROFILE

Placement rate (%)	97
# of companies recruiting on campus	253
% of grads employed immediately	94
% grads employed within six months	100
Average starting salary	$74,771

Grads employed by field (avg. salary):

Consulting	25%	$77,095
Finance	9%	$70,344
Marketing	20%	$71,662
MIS	12%	$75,491
Operations	25%	$79,585
Other	4%	NR
Venture Capital	8%	$77,100

BABSON COLLEGE
F. W. Olin Graduate School of Business

OVERVIEW

Type of school	private
Affiliation	none
Environment	suburban
Academic calendar	semester
Schedule	full-time/part-time/evening

STUDENTS

Enrollment of parent institution	3,371
Enrollment of business school	1,686
% male/female	68/32
% part-time	73
% minorities	10
% international (# of countries represented)	23 (73)
Average age at entry	28
Average years work experience at entry	5

ACADEMICS

Student/faculty ratio	9:1
% female faculty	32
% minority faculty	9
Hours of study per day	4.88

SPECIALTIES

Strengths of faculty and curriculum in Entrepreneurship, Marketing, Finance, international focus, a fully-integrated, modular first-year curriculum, field-based programs, mentor program, international internships, management consulting programs.

SPECIAL PROGRAMS

International Management Internship Program (IMIP), Management Consulting Field Experience (MCFE), International Study Programs, Business Mentor Program

STUDY ABROAD PROGRAMS

Semester abroad is offered in conjunction with partner schools in Europe and Asia; Cranfield School of Management, Cranfield, England; LÉcole Superieure de Commerce de Paris (ESCP), Paris, France; Instituto de Empresa, Madrid, Spain; Norwegian School of Management (NSM), Sandvika, Norway; Universite de Lausanne, Lausanne, Switzerland; International University of Japan, Niigata, Japan; Universidad Adolfo Ibanez, Vina del Mar, Chile Universidad de San Andres, Victoria, Argentina

SURVEY SAYS...
HITS
Diversity of work experience
Teamwork skills
Profs are great teachers

MISSES
School clubs
Quantitative skills
Gym

ACADEMICS

Although it offers a wide variety of academic options, Babson's MBA program is primarily associated with entrepreneurial studies, a discipline that Babson was among the first in the nation to offer. The school stresses its strength in entrepreneurship in its promotional materials; its slogan is "Entrepreneurial Leadership in a Changing Global Environment," and Babson boasts that the program was ranked number one in the country by both *US News and World Report* and *Success* magazines in 1996. Students agree that the program is top-notch: more than 80 percent of respondents give the entrepreneurship program our highest rating. "Outstanding," is how one student puts it. Students are enthusiastic about course offerings, opportunities for "in-the-field" learning, and the "entrepreneurial incubator space" provided in the newly built Olin Hall, which makes subsidized office space available to student entrepreneurs as well as to recent graduates.

Babson's other strengths lie in management and international business—both areas in which our survey shows not only high satisfaction levels but also improvement in recent years. Students are less satisfied with finance and accounting studies. Students in all departments are pleased with the quality of instruction. Writes one, "Faculty are fabulous. They are tough, fun, and fully committed to students and the program. It really helps the process because they're behind you." Professors are "extremely accessible" and "have extensive professional experience (CEOs, entrepreneurs, etc.). Research is very important, but teaching is tops."

All two-year MBA students (Babson also offers a one-year program and a part-time, evening program) participate in interdisciplinary studies, called "modules," during their first-year. Modules, which are team-taught, cover such subjects as Creative Management in Dynamic Organizations and Designing and Managing the Delivery System. Students respond enthusiastically. Writes one, "First-year integrated curriculum is unbelievable, three professors teaching one class is common and dynamic." One-year MBAs complete modules during a summer session; evening students take traditional courses in lieu of modules. The first-year program also includes a Business Mentor Program, which allows students to work as consultants for companies in the Boston area. The mentor program requires students to assess their assigned company's competitive position in the market and then to work with company executives to evaluate one aspect of the business. A student reports that "the mentor team experience during the first year is a terrific way to integrate the coursework and learn a lot about teamwork." The new Olin Building houses "mentor rooms allocated to teams that are so useful, with phone, voice-mail, computers, etc."

Babson "strongly encourages" students to complete an international concentration, which combines a concentration in finance or marketing with courses in international studies. Students who choose this option must demonstrate proficiency in a second language by graduation.

PLACEMENT AND RECRUITING

All Babson students are required to complete the MBA Career Education curriculum. The curriculum includes a fifteen-hour first-year program called Career Management, which covers the basic skills of self-assessment and presenta-

Rita Edmunds, Director of Admissions
Olin Hall, Babson Park, MA 02457-0310
Admissions: 781-239-5591 Fax: 781-239-4194
Email: mbaadmission@babson.edu
Internet: www.babson.edu/mba/

tion. Babson considers its mentor and internship programs to be important components of its P&R program. As students near graduation they take advantage of Career Search, a computerized database of more than 800,000 employers nationwide, and ACE, an alumni database. Companies that have recruited on campus in the past include SAP, Kellogg, EMC Corporation, Oracle Corporation, Fleet Financial Group, Johnson & Johnson, and A. T. Kearney.

Babson students are very satisfied with their access to internships and mentoring. They are generally pleased with the help they receive from Babson alumni in their job searches. Their satisfaction with the job placement office and with on-campus recruiting is around the national average.

STUDENT/CAMPUS LIFE

Babson MBAs form a close-knit group who think highly of each other. "We're a diverse group of young people with very high aspirations and entrepreneurial goals," writes one student. Another notes that "many are from liberal arts backgrounds; from interesting and diverse backgrounds." Mandatory teamwork forces students to spend a lot of time together, which fortunately they don't mind. In fact, they're very likely to spend their spare time in each other's company. Students report that the on-campus hot spot for group gatherings is "Roger's Pub on Thursday nights. It's lots of fun; a great place to have some beer and blow off some steam." About the only complaint students raise about each other is that "students are primarily from the Northeast or are non-USA. We could use a more diverse mix of American students to match the diversity among the international experience."

Babson's campus is a beautiful 450-acre wooded expanse, "complete with live deer!" Students are very enthusiastic about the "outstanding new building, Olin Hall, that brings all MBA functions within four walls and sits on a beautiful campus. Life is sweet!" Because Boston is only 15 miles away, Babson students also have easy access to the business and cultural advantages of a big city. Still, social life takes a distant back seat to school work at Babson. Says one student, "Babson life is busy—class, class, lunch, class, study group, drinks, sleep. Not much more to say." Explains another, "The workload is very heavy when you include school activities, internships, and job search."

ADMISSIONS

The Babson admissions office ranks your work experience as most important, and then, in descending order, the interview (required), GMAT scores, college GPA, essays, letters of recommendation, and extracurricular activities.

The school writes: "At Babson, we consider each candidate as an individual and look at the entire package, not simply at test scores and GPAs. Accordingly, we require an interview. This personal approach provides both Babson and our candidates an opportunity to determine whether there is a "fit" within the Babson community. We look for goal-oriented individuals with an entrepreneurial spirit, a global mindset, and an ability to grapple with the ambiguities of managing change in a dynamic business world. For the one-year program, applicants must have an undergraduate degree in business administration. Babson batches applications by rounds. There are three rounds for the two-year program and two rounds for the one-year program.

PROMINENT ALUMNI

Neil F. Finnegan, President and CEO, U.S. Trust; Akio Toyoda, Assistant Manager, Domestic Marketing, Toyota Motor Corp.; Rober J. Davis, President and CEO, Lycos, Inc.

FINANCIAL FACTS

Tuition	$22,710
Tuition per credit	$706
Fees	$680
Cost of books	$1,350
Room & board (on-/off-campus)	$10,180/$10,180
% of students receiving aid	67
% first-year students receiving aid	60
% aid that is merit based	48
% of students receiving loans	43
% of students receiving grants	11
Average award package	$15,299
Average grant	$11,303
Average graduation debt	$40,335

ADMISSIONS

# of applications received	871
% applicants accepted	42
% acceptees attending	45
Average GMAT (range)	634 (580–700)
Minimum TOEFL	600
Average GPA (range)	3.10 (2.54–3.60)
Application fee (in-/out-of-state)	$50/$50
Early decision program available	Yes
Regular application deadline	March 1
Regular notification	May 15
Admission may be deferred?	Yes
Maximum length of deferment	1 year
Transfer students accepted?	Yes
Nonfall admission available?	Yes
Admission process need-blind?	Yes

APPLICANTS ALSO LOOK AT

Harvard University, Boston University, Boston College, Columbia, Massachusetts Institute of Technology, New York University, UC — Berkeley, University of Pennsylvania

EMPLOYMENT PROFILE

Placement rate (%)	91
# of companies recruiting on campus	263
% of grads employed immediately	75
% grads employed within six months	95
Average starting salary	$65,487

Grads employed by field (avg. salary):

Consulting	26%	$69,100
Entrepreneurship	16%	$62,770
Finance	23%	$66,100
General Management	9%	$66,700
Marketing	22%	$63,800
MIS	2%	$56,500
Operations	2%	$53,000
Venture Capital	1%	NR

BAYLOR UNIVERSITY
Hankamer School of Business

ACADEMICS

MBAs across the country rarely mention "Christian environment" when listing the assets of their programs, but then again few MBAs attend schools as closely aligned with a church as is the Hankamer School of Business at Baylor University. Baylor guarantees that its Baptist traditions endure, in part by maintaining continuity in its academic community. Not only does the school welcome returning undergraduates but, as one student explains, "Most professors are Baylor alumni. They are dedicated to students and the school."

The Hankamer School reaches out to students who might be passed over by other programs, an aspect appreciated by many who attend the school. The "relatively easy entry requirements" initially attracted one MBA to the school, while another notes that Hankamer is "the only good one-year program I found that did not require work experience." To bring such students up to speed, Hankamer requires a semester-long Integrated Management Seminar (IMS). Non-business degree undergraduates begin their tenure at Hankamer with this intensive review of macroeconomics, microeconomics, accounting, marketing, management, finance, statistics, and information systems. Hankamer nurtures its students, leading one to report that "the school's greatest strength is the close-knit atmosphere and helpful environment. It's a small-school environment. This aids not only in the educational process but in job searches as well."

Those who successfully complete IMS join entering students with undergraduate business degrees in Lockstep One, a semester of required courses in basic business subjects. The following semester, Lockstep Two, involves two required courses, one "restricted elective," (students may choose from among three quantitative courses), and one elective. The Hankamer program concludes with Lockstep Three, during which students may pursue a field of concentration (although they are not required to do so). Lockstep Three also includes a final core course called "Strategic Management and Business Policy."

The students we surveyed tell us that the "greatest strengths of Baylor are its emphasis on team projects, presentation skills, and applicability of coursework to the real world." The faculty "is great. Their availability and openness to one-on-one work helps students. They spend more time with students because this is not a research school." Standout departments include accounting, finance, and management. Marketing, operations, and international business studies receive subpar grades from students. The workload here is described as "moderate." One student tells us, "I study less in graduate school than I did as an undergraduate, and I get out more. My grades are not affected." Classrooms are excellent, other facilities less so, although "a new graduate center and computer lab will be added in the fall [1998], improving crowded facilities."

PLACEMENT AND RECRUITING

Hankamer students give their placement office below-average marks, although they also note that "the school is currently overhauling the placement office, so that it is an area that is improving." Currently, business grads share placement services not only with business undergraduates but also with the rest of Baylor's large undergraduate population. Students give high marks to the quality of companies that recruit on-campus, although they would like to see a wider

Laurie Wilson, Director of Graduate Business Admissions
P.O.Box 98013, Waco, TX 76798
Admissions: 254-710-3718 Fax: 254-710-1066
Email: Laurie-Wilson@baylor.edu
Internet: hsb.baylor.edu/mba

Baylor University

assortment of potential employers represented. Those who responded to our survey are less enthusiastic about Baylor's alumni network; of those who contacted alums during their job searches, more than one-third found them to be of no help.

STUDENT/CAMPUS LIFE

Hankamer graduate students are typically young and eager. Writes one student, "Many are in their early twenties. Very ambitious, talented, and ready to learn." Adds another, "Many students are driven and are hard workers. They force others to go beyond 'normal' levels of performance." Some students, however, complain that "We need to recruit more diverse students, and students with more work experience." Most would agree that the school is "not very ethnically or culturally diverse," although it does attract a sizable international contingent. Nor is it particularly tolerant of eccentricity. One student who doesn't comfortably fit into the 'Baylor bubble' warns: "Baylor attempts to assimilate students and force them to fit the Baylor image. I have experienced a great deal of hostility and resentment due to the fact that I have long hair, wear tie-dyes, and am liberal." For those comfortable within its confines, though, the Baylor community offers "an interesting group of individuals who have high standards. On the whole, an impressive group."

Life at Baylor is "well balanced. The week is spent studying hard, and the weekends are spent relaxing with friends." The atmosphere "is very relaxed, and students and faculty are always helpful and outgoing." Business-related and religious club meetings are augmented by "many outside social activities when students to get to know each other beyond schoolwork." Students also report that "International events are plentiful. Activities, special speakers, and interesting speeches are always available." Although students give the town of Waco middling grades, they do enjoy the fact that they are "close to river, lake, and parks" and live in a "great climate." Many head for Dallas, Houston, or Austin whenever they can make the time.

ADMISSIONS

The admissions office at the Hankamer School of Business MBA program considers applicants' previous academic achievements, GMAT scores, and relevant work experiences. Applicants must have achieved a minimum GPA of 2.7 in undergraduate and, if applicable, postgraduate study. Baylor ignores certain types of courses when determining applicants' GPAs; check with the admissions office for further details. Their academic records should also demonstrate "a scholarly and professional interest considerably above the average." Baylor's promotional material also notes that "Managerial experience, leadership, and other practical experiences are among criteria used in evaluating an applicant's potential for success." International applicants must meet additional language proficiency requirements; applicants to the joint MBA-JD program must take the LSAT as well as the GMAT. Applicants to the accelerated "Lockstep Program" must have received a "B" or better in college-level courses in accounting, economics, finance, statistics, information systems, production management, and marketing. Those failing to meet this requirement must take the one-semester Integrated Management Seminar.

FINANCIAL FACTS

Tuition	$12,500
Tuition per credit	$329
Fees	$500
Cost of books	$1,000
Room & board (on-/off-campus)	$4,800/$4,800
% aid that is merit based	70
% of students receiving paid internships	27

ADMISSIONS

# of applications received	163
% applicants accepted	67
% acceptees attending	59
Average GMAT (range)	584 (460–750)
Minimum TOEFL	600
Average GPA	3.09
Application fee (in-/out-of-state)	$25/$25
Early decision program available	No
Early decision deadline	Admitted on rolling basis
Early decision notification	Admitted on rolling basis
Regular application deadline	July 1
Admission may be deferred?	Yes
Maximum length of deferment	1 year
Transfer students accepted?	Yes
Nonfall admission available?	Yes
Admission process need-blind?	Yes

APPLICANTS ALSO LOOK AT

Texas A&M University, University of Texas at Austin, Southern Methodist University, University of Texas at Arlington, Rice University, Texas Christian University, Tulane, Notre Dame

EMPLOYMENT PROFILE

Placement rate (%)	98
# of companies recruiting on campus	50
% of grads employed immediately	90
% grads employed within six months	95
Average starting salary	$42,800

Grads employed by field (avg. salary):

Accounting	41%	$40,000
Consulting	13%	$49,000
Entrepreneurship	2%	NR
Finance	16%	$40,000
Human Resources	5%	$40,000
MIS	8%	$60,000
Other	15%	$48,000

BOSTON COLLEGE

The Graduate School of the Wallace E. Carroll School of Management

OVERVIEW

Type of school	private
Affiliation	Jesuit (Roman Catholic)
Academic calendar	semester
Environment	suburban

STUDENTS

Enrollment of parent institution	14,696
Enrollment of business school	750
% male/female	65/35
% part-time	73
% minorities	9
% international (# of countries represented)	33 (NR)
Average age at entry	27
Average years work experience at entry	4

ACADEMICS

Student/faculty ratio	8:1
% female faculty	24
% minority faculty	6

SPECIALTIES

Finance, Information Technology, Global Management, Consulting. Strengths: Blend of theory and practice; exposure to entrepreneurs and venture capitalists; consulting experience with industry clients; broad range of international opportunities; state of the art concentrations including techno-MBA options

JOINT DEGREES

MBA/MSF, 24 months; MBA/JD, 48 months; MBA/MSW, 36 months; MBA/MSN, 36–48 months; MBA/MS Biology, Geology, Geophysics, 36 months; MBA/MA Math, Slavic Studies, Russian, Linguistics, Political Science, French Studies, Hispanic Studies, and Italian Studies, 36 months

SPECIAL PROGRAMS

Boston College MBA Program offers a dual degree program with the Robert E. Schuman University in Strasbourg, France. Students earn both an MBA and the Diplome degree.

STUDY ABROAD PROGRAMS

France—ESC Brest, ESC Bordeaux and ESC Clermont; Ireland—Smurfit Graduate School of Business, University College Dublin; Spain—ESADE in Barcelona; Mexico—ITESM in Monterrey; The Netherlands—MSM in Maastricht; China—Beijing International Management Center, China's Peking University

SURVEY SAYS...

HITS
Students are happy
Teamwork skills

ACADEMICS

According to administrators at Boston College, what sets an MBA from the Boston College Graduate School of Management apart from other MBAs is "a unique combination of classroom and real-world learning." The latter is accomplished largely through a first-year, second-semester consulting project involving a local business. This project, the centerpiece of Boston College's first-year curriculum, culminates in a two-day competition during which student consulting teams present their work to faculty and industry judges.

The first-year curriculum at BC is distinctive in other ways as well. The program is divided into core courses and "Management Practice" courses. The former provide instruction in such foundation basics as economics, management, accounting, marketing, and statistics. The latter focus on integrating foundation skills through case study and hands-on projects: the above-mentioned consulting project, for example, constitutes the second of BC's four Management Practice sequences. First-year students at Boston College are also offered a little more curricular leeway than their counterparts at other programs, as the curriculum allows for two electives (which Boston College recommends students use as a stepping stone toward summer internships). Students enjoy the "spirited class discussions and debates" of their first-year classes.

Boston College has only two required courses—the third and fourth sequences of Management Practice—in the second year. The remaining eighteen credits of the second year are devoted to major study and electives. These electives are offered in the evening; notes one student, "By having evening and late afternoon classes, the second year enables students to easily manage the workload, get involved in outside activities, and even work part-time." Students speak highly of the finance, accounting, information technology, and management departments. Professors receive mixed reviews. Writes one student, "Many of the professors are very intelligent, but don't teach very well. Reminds me of the working world." Another observes that there are "a few excellent professors, but many, though qualified, are disorganized." Opinion on the administration is similarly equivocal. One student notes that "The administration is receptive to student input regarding teaching quality and has taken actions to remedy the negatives," but several others complain, "the administration needs to run more efficiently—a common problem at large institutions. It appears that the left hand often does not know what the right hand is doing." Still, students feel that theirs is a program on the rise. As one MBA puts it, "The school has made many improvements since I started—computer labs expanded, career services greatly improved, and overall operations are stronger."

PLACEMENT AND RECRUITING

Students regard the alumni network at Boston College (more than 100,000 strong) and, more importantly, The Graduate School of Management (more than 5,000 alums) as one of their program's great assets. Alumni connections are particularly helpful in Massachusetts, where more than half of Boston College MBAs lands their first post-MBA jobs. Financial services, consulting, investment banking, and commercial banking snap up the lion's share of Boston College's graduates.

Director of Admissions
Fulton Hall 315, Chestnut Hill, MA 02467-3808
Admissions: 617-552-3920 Fax: 617-552-8078
Email: bcmba@bc.edu
Internet: www.bc.edu/mba

The Graduate School of Management's Career Services office maintains resume books, hosts an on-campus career fair in early October, and participates in an area MBA Career Consortium in February. Students tell us that "Career Services made changes recently. It has improved but only time will tell if recent changes will be successful."

STUDENT/CAMPUS LIFE

Full-time, first-year MBA students at Boston College are typically "competitive but friendly to one another. Our class is very close—there are only 100 students in it—and tends to do things as a group. There are quite a few JD/MBA students in our class as well as previous bankers. As a whole, it's a group that's very strong in quantitative skills." Students enjoy the diversity "in age, ethnicity, and type of work experience" among their peers, but although "there is a significant international population," there isn't much interaction between them and the domestic students." The higher percentage of second-year students who opt to work part-time strains class unity: explained one student, "In the full-time program, second-year students don't see much of each other. There's little camaraderie there." Competitiveness and the absence of a communal sense fuel some resentment among students; writes one, "There is definitely an elite group of students in the eyes of the administration. In such a small program, this is very visible."

BC's proximity to Boston—the school is located in Chestnut Hill, a nearby suburb—translates into a "very fun social life." The city is easily accessible by car or mass transit and offers a cornucopia of shopping, cultural, and business-related opportunities. On campus there are "plenty of extracurricular activities, such as intramural sports, and weekend social gatherings are big. Definitely a great experience." Students participate in numerous clubs. Many perform community service; writes one, "The school challenges students to get involved in giving back to the community. The Kids On Campus program is an excellent opportunity for students to share their education with local disadvantaged grade school children." Boston College also encourages its MBAs to establish contacts with students at other schools; reports one student, "This school has supported club events for us to network with fellow MBAs across the nation. Examples: Yale MBA Soccer Tournament, Asia Business Conference, Cyberposium@HBS."

ADMISSIONS

According to the admissions office your career plans, work experience, GMAT scores, and the interview are considered most important; then, in descending order, undergraduate GPA, letters of recommendation, and essays. The admissions offices notes a "match between applicant's interests and the school's core competencies" is another big factor that influences admission.

PROMINENT ALUMNI

Charles Babin, Principal, State Street Global Advisors; Diane Capstaff, Executive Vice President, John Hancock Mutual Life Insurance Co.; Francis Doyle, Vice Chairman, PriceWaterhouseCoopers

FINANCIAL FACTS

Tuition	$23,188
Tuition per credit	$748
Fees	$100
Cost of books	$1,500
Room & board (on-/off-campus)	$13,295/NR
% of students receiving paid internships	90
Average grant	$13,330

ADMISSIONS

# of applications received	646
% applicants accepted	43
% acceptees attending	35
Average GMAT (range)	622 (590–670)
Minimum TOEFL	600
Average GPA (range)	3.10 (2.28–3.38)
Application fee (in-/out-of-state)	$45/$45
Early decision program available	Yes
Early decision deadline	December 1
Early decision notification	January 31
Regular application deadline	April 1
Regular notification	6 weeks
Admission may be deferred?	Yes
Maximum length of deferment	2 years
Transfer students accepted?	Yes
Nonfall admission available?	Yes
Admission process need-blind?	Yes

APPLICANTS ALSO LOOK AT

Boston University, New York University, Cornell Univesity, Babson College, Harvard, University of Maryland, Georgetown University, Columbia University

EMPLOYMENT PROFILE

Placement rate (%)	100
# of companies recruiting on campus	100
% of grads employed immediately	41
% grads employed within six months	99
Average starting salary	$67,943

Grads employed by field (avg. salary):

Consulting	21%	$66,139
Finance	34%	$67,745
Human Resources	3%	
General Management	9%	$59,111
Marketing	27%	$73,689
Operations	3%	
Other	4%	

BOSTON UNIVERSITY
School of Management

ACADEMICS

Boston University's commitment to upgrading its MBA program—best exemplified by a state-of-the-art facility opened in January 1997—has students cheering that "the school is on a very positive path." The "shiny new building puts all business services in one place and provides good high-tech resources." But BU has revamped more than its physical appearance: In the past several years, the school has switched over to a more deeply integrated curriculum, emphasizing "total quality management." Writes one student, "The program is beautifully organized; an almost flawless cross-functional pedagogical approach."

BU structures its MBA program to "concentrate on process instead of function," teaching management as "a system—a horizontal continuum of interdependent departments or functions." The idea is to create students who are "cross-trained" in accounting, finance, marketing, and operations, and who know how to borrow from one discipline to supplement another. This structure stresses teamwork and team teaching over individual achievement, and practical, hands-on education over theory. Professors even assist this approach because the "vast majority of [them] came to BU to teach, not just to conduct research." By and large, professors are "extremely helpful, open for discussion, [and] enthusiastic," although a few were singled out as "arrogant." As for the administration, students note that "it does its best to meet student needs," but warn that "it takes time to navigate the rigid administration structure. To get something done, you need to campaign and sell it."

The third-largest private university in the United States and one of the country's largest MBA programs, Boston University has the resources to offer a wide variety of SPECIALTIES and dual degrees. Students single out dual degree offerings in both Health Care Management and Public and Non-Profit Management as prime reasons for choosing BU. The Finance Department, the Entrepreneurship Program, and the dual offering of a MS/Management of Information Systems also receive their plaudits. But students here also have their complaints. They give mediocre marks to their instruction in marketing, operations, and computer skills. Also, despite the new building and its expanded resources, students continue to tell us that "we need more computers!" and that the "library facilities need to be expanded."

PLACEMENT AND RECRUITING

BU recently created a new placement facility dedicated exclusively to MBAs in an effort to upgrade its career services. So far, student assessments of the Feld Career Center are only middling: nearly half our respondents rate the career center "okay" or worse (however, 9 percent give it an "excellent" grade). Students concede that "the Career Center has come a long way but," they add, "still needs more work." The main focus of the center is its interactive software recruiting program, called "1st Place!" The Feld Center collects resumes of all students, then uses "1st Place!" to match students with prospective employers. A full-time staff of ten also helps students scout potential internships and jobs, compose resumes, and prepare for interviews.

The greatest number of student complaints about the Feld Center concern the number and quality of on-campus recruiters. "The school needs to attract the

Peter Kelly, Director
595 Commonwealth Avenue, Boston, MA 02215
Admissions: 617-353-2670 Fax: 617-353-7368
Email: MBA@bu.edu
Internet: management.bu.edu

Boston University

more exclusive companies to campus," writes one second-year student. "Alumni make it easy to interview with top firms, but I would like to see more on campus." According to the school, during the 1997–98 recruiting season, they achieved a 37 percent increase of on-campus recruiting visits, and means salaries were up by nearly 10 percent.

STUDENT/CAMPUS LIFE

BU attempts to make its large MBA student body feel a little smaller by breaking its incoming classes into cohorts of roughly fifty students. Each cohort stays intact throughout the first semester, completing core courses together. The system works: students report that their classmates are friendly, helpful, and strongly motivated but not "cutthroat." Says one student, "The first-year cohort program gives us a group of peers that not only are our competitors but our friends." Another agrees: "There is a very supportive atmosphere among the student community, where students share information and take the time with others who may be falling behind." Students regard their groups as diverse, primarily because of the pronounced presence of international students. Warns an African American student, "There are lots of international students, but few African Americans."

Students at BU work hard, although most students report that the workload here is manageable. Writes one first-year student, "It's hard work but very fun. My cohort (fifty strong) is extremely close. We spend a lot of time with each other outside of class." Adds another student, "The intense workload is broken up by numerous opportunities to recreate and be social." Those opportunities include student-managed clubs and events ("Students are active in creating extracurricular activity. The Council is active in social activities"), as well as frequent forays away from the campus, which is adjacent to Boston's historic Back Bay district. Fenway Park is just a stone's throw away, the symphony hall isn't much further, and the rest of this "great city" is easily accessible by car or public transportation. Students stay on campus to enjoy the BU Pub (where they can often share a drink with professors), a new MBA-only lounge named, creatively enough, "The Lounge," and intramural sports. Golf and tennis are very popular, as are volleyball matches against nearby MIT and b-school rival Wharton.

ADMISSIONS

The admissions selection process places equal importance on all credentials: essays, college GPA, GMAT score, work experience, letters of recommendation. Interviews are encouraged, but not required. Advises the school, "Work experience is strongly preferred. BU is interested in attracting a high level of diversity in the classroom in work experience, ethnicity, nationality, and gender." Decisions are made on a rolling basis beginning in January for the September cycle (full- and part-time). Applicants are advised to apply early and are notified of a decision within four to six weeks of receipt of the completed application. Students may defer admission up to one year. Scholarships are awarded on the basis of academic merit.

FINANCIAL FACTS

Tuition	$22,830
Tuition per credit	$713
Fees	$268
Cost of books	$1,200
Room & board (on-/off-campus)	NR/$9,130
% of students receiving aid	60
% first-year students receiving aid	60
% aid that is merit based	100
% of students receiving loans	50
% of students receiving grants	20
Average award package	$29,900
Average grant	$11,400
Average graduation debt	$37,000

ADMISSIONS

# of applications received	1,166
% applicants accepted	50
% acceptees attending	43
Average GMAT (range)	608 (580–640)
Minimum TOEFL	600
Average GPA (range)	3.20 (2.90–3.40)
Application fee (in-/out-of-state)	$50/$50
Early decision program available	No
Regular application deadline	April 15
Regular notification	Rolling
Admission may be deferred?	Yes
Maximum length of deferment	1 year
Transfer students accepted?	Yes
Nonfall admission available?	Yes
Admission process need-blind?	Yes

APPLICANTS ALSO LOOK AT

Babson College, New York University, Harvard University, Northeastern University, Columbia University, Georgetown University, Boston College, George Washington University

EMPLOYMENT PROFILE

Placement rate (%)	81
# of companies recruiting on campus	135
% of grads employed immediately	85
% grads employed within six months	94
Average starting salary	$62,363

Grads employed by field (avg. salary):

Accounting	8%	$57,923
Consulting	27%	$66,514
Finance	20%	$57,923
General Management	11%	$59,495
Human Resources	1%	$62,250
Marketing	13%	$64,854
MIS	6%	$62,545
Operations	3%	$55,500
Other	11%	NR
Strategic Planning	1%	NR

BRIGHAM YOUNG UNIVERSITY
Marriott School

OVERVIEW

Type of school	private
Affiliation	Latter-day Saints
Environment	urban
Academic calendar	2 semester
Schedule	full-time only

STUDENTS

Enrollment of parent institution	33,490
Enrollment of business school	271
% male/female	79/21
% minorities	6
% international (# of countries represented)	18 (22)
Average age at entry	26
Average years work experience at entry	5

ACADEMICS

Student/faculty ratio	4:1
% female faculty	12
Hours of study per day	4.13

SPECIALTIES
Entrepreneurship, Corp. Finance, Investment Mgmt., Mgmt. of Financial Institutions, Marketing Mgmt., Info. Systems, Organizational Behavior, Strategic Mgmt., Production & Operations Mgmt., Quantitative Methods, International Business, Accounting, White-Collar Fraud

JOINT DEGREES
MBA/JD, 4 years; MBA/MS, IPD Program with Engineering Department, 5 semesters; MBA/MA International Relations, 2 years

SPECIAL PROGRAMS
The Executive Lecture Series, Entrepreneurship Lecture Series, International Business Series, Computer Summer Prep, 8 Business Language Programs, Computer Business Simulation, Field Study Program, Faculty Hosted International Business Study in Asia and Latin America

STUDY ABROAD PROGRAMS

SURVEY SAYS...
HITS
Classmates are smart
Cozy student community

MISSES
Campus is ugly
Impossible to get into a course

PROMINENT ALUMNI
Robert E. Parsons, Jr., Executive Vice President and CFO, Host Marriott; Nolan D. Archibald, Chairman, President and CEO, Black and Decker Co.; William P. Benac, Group Executive and Corporate Treasurer, EDS; Kevin Rollins, Vice Chairman, Dell

ACADEMICS

As the official school of the Church of Latter-day Saints (more commonly known as the Mormons), Brigham Young University shoulders the responsibility of conforming church ideology and ethics to some fairly secular academic disciplines. According to the largely Mormon student body at BYU's Marriott School of Management, the business school here meets that challenge admirably. Explains one student, "The university and b-school are remarkably strong in moral responsibility and honor code. This is where the competitive advantage of the school is."

Marriott offers five different graduate degrees: a traditional MBA and a distinct master's degree in the following: accounting, public administration, organizational behavior, and information systems management. With the exception of accounting students, all Marriott grad students, regardless of their intended degree, enter in the fall and undergo a lockstep first-year core curriculum. First-year core requirements consist of eighteen courses; in almost all of the core courses, several professors share the podium, team-teaching cases from a cross-functional perspective. This approach doesn't please everyone; griped one student, "[There is an] overemphasis on case method. I feel I'm not getting the practical skills that will be valuable in the short-term." Students note that "School is very challenging and fast-paced. First semester is packed with many group assignments. The second semester has allowed me to take two electives and do more work on my own time." One benefit of all the group assignments, according to several students, is that "you make a lot of good friends."

During their second year, Marriott students must complete three required courses (one in ethics, another in business policy, and a management seminar) but are otherwise free to pursue electives and develop specializations. Students agree that finance and accounting are the strongest areas at Marriott; writes one student, "Classes that are not finance- or accounting-related are too general. The school needs help to develop the marketing, human resources, and operations curriculum." Many Marriott courses incorporate issues of international import, an area in which most Marriott students are comfortable: many Mormons serve as missionaries in foreign nations. Accordingly, many here are fluent in two or three languages and can speak knowledgeably about foreign cultures and intercultural communication.

Marriott students give their professors mixed grades. Some praise the faculty, telling us that "professors are very willing to consider student input when teaching" and that "most professors here have a healthy sense of how their course relates to the 'big picture.'" Other students, however, warn that "We have some stellar names who are total lemons in terms of teaching." Students appreciate the fact that "the administration is making great strides to improve the school"

PLACEMENT AND RECRUITING

Students at the Marriott School have access both to the MBA program's Career Services office and to the larger university's placement center. The CS office also maintains a graduate resume book and a web-based job and application bulletin board. The Marriott School participates in the West Coast MBA Consortium. Students report that "the Career Placement Center needs to be more effective at

Merlene Reeder, Program Administrator
640 Tanner Building, Provo, UT 84602
Admissions: 801-378-3500 Fax: 801-378-4808
Email: mba@byu.edu
Internet: msm.byu.edu/program/grad/mba

Brigham Young University

bringing companies to campus that students are interested in" and also warn that "for students struggling to find an internship, the schools' career services isn't the best source."

Given the close-knit Mormon community worldwide, it should come as no surprise that placement opportunities here are greatly enhanced by alumni relations. An alumni-student mentoring program allows students to make connections with former Marriott School students. Although students report mixed feelings about the effectiveness of the Career Services office, they have nothing but good to say about the benefits of their alumni contacts. Says one, "The alumni network is one of BYU's great strengths."

STUDENT/CAMPUS LIFE

Students report that Marriott "is very Mormon, but non-Mormons do well here, too." Several students took exception to Marriott's reputed homogeneity, telling us that "the student body here is diverse in ways other than race. We have different experiences that mold together due to some similarities." Writes another MBA, "Students do have different backgrounds. They are especially unique in that most speak another language, having lived in other countries." Among the upsides of a nearly all-Mormon campus is that "people here look clean, neat, and decent. I feel safe on campus." Another is that "students are very service-oriented" and "very friendly. My group first semester, first year," writes one student, "was incredible. We still go to lunch once a week and are helping each other find jobs."

Extracurricular activities here are devoted to church, family life, informal get-togethers, and outdoor activities in the nearby mountains. The MBA Association sponsors many events, including community service projects such as reading to the blind and helping foreign students with English. There's even a vice-president for community service. The Latter-day Saint community is divided into "wards" of 100 or so families who meet for worship services and plan social activities. Nonchurch members are welcome to attend. There's also an active "Spouse Association" that organizes dinners and outings. Between school, family, and church responsibilities, "students are very occupied with studies and juggling other areas of their lives. We connect when it comes to school and enjoy the company." Students enjoy Provo, where "The weather is mild and the cost of living is low."

ADMISSIONS

According to the admissions office, your GMAT score is considered most important. After that, in descending order, your college GPA, letter of intent, letters of recommendation, language spoken, work experience, and leadership activities are considered. Writes the school, "Though we look carefully at GMAT and GPA qualifications, we also look at the person behind the numbers. The letter of intent and letters of recommendation are valuable resources in getting acquainted with the person. Because of the international emphasis in our MBA program, we look favorably at applicants who speak a second and third language. As a result we encourage any undergraduate major except business, and we also encourage some work experience."

FINANCIAL FACTS

Tuition (in-/out-of-state)	$5,330/$8,000
Tuition per credit (in-/out-of-state)	$296/$444
Fees (in-/out-of-state)	$50/$50
Cost of books	$1,000
Room & board (on-/off-campus)	$4,600/$4,600
% of students receiving aid	72
% first-year students receiving aid	39
% of students receiving loans	72
% of students receiving grants	34
% of students receiving paid internships	97
Average grant	$4,000

ADMISSIONS

# of applications received	497
% applicants accepted	44
% acceptees attending	60
Average GMAT (range)	634 (600–670)
Minimum TOEFL	570
Average GPA (range)	3.52 (3.30–3.77)
Application fee (in-/out-of-state)	$30/$30
Early decision program available	Yes
Early decision deadline	January 15
Early decision notification	February 28
Regular application deadline	March 1
Regular notification	Rolling
Admission may be deferred?	Yes
Maximum length of deferment	2 years
Transfer students accepted?	Yes
Nonfall admission available?	No
Admission process need-blind?	Yes

APPLICANTS ALSO LOOK AT

University of California — Los Angeles, Arizona State University, Wharton, Stanford, University of Washington, University of Texas at Austin, Indiana, Harvard University

EMPLOYMENT PROFILE

Placement rate (%)	100
# of companies recruiting on campus	221
% of grads employed immediately	77
% grads employed within six months	98
Average starting salary	$58,282

Grads employed by field (avg. salary):

Consulting	11%	$62,950
Finance	36%	$59,219
General Management	11%	$53,745
Human Resources	3%	$43,000
Marketing	19%	$55,424
MIS	3%	$61,600
Operations	9%	$67,588
Other	8%	$42,667

UNIVERSITY OF CALIFORNIA — BERKELEY
Haas School of Business

OVERVIEW
Type of school	public
Affiliation	none
Environment	urban
Academic calendar	semester
Schedule	full-time and evening (part-time)

STUDENTS
Enrollment of parent institution	29,000
Enrollment of business school	477
% male/female	65/35
% out-of-state	102
% minorities	24
% international (# of countries represented)	36 (39)
Average age at entry	28
Average years work experience at entry	5

ACADEMICS
Student/faculty ratio	5:1
% female faculty	14
% minority faculty	10
Hours of study per day	4.14

SPECIALTIES
Entrepreneurship, International Business, Management of Technology, Finance, Marketing, Real Estate, Health Care Management, Organizational Behavior, Corporate Strategy

JOINT DEGREES
Concurrent degree programs in Law, Public Health, Asian Studies, and International and Area Studies, JD/MBA, MBA/MA in Asian Studies, MBA/MPH, MBA/MIAS

SPECIAL PROGRAMS
Entrepreneurship, International Management, Management of Technology, and Health Care

STUDY ABROAD PROGRAMS
Twelve countries in Europe, Asia, Latin America, United Kingdom, Netherlands, Belgium, France, Italy, Spain, Austria Switzerland, Brazil, Mexico, Hong Kong, and Japan

SURVEY SAYS...
HITS
Diversity of work experience
Can't wait to network
Library

MISSES
Safety
On-campus housing
MIS/operations

PROMINENT ALUMNI
Alex Mandl, CEO and President, AT&T Communications Services; Paul Hazen, Chairman and CEO, Wells Fargo Bank; Robert A. Lutz, President, Chrysler Motors

ACADEMICS

Haas students appreciate the diversity their MBA program provides. When asked to name the field of study that attracted them to Berkeley, students reel off a virtual laundry list of subjects. Some come for the nationally renowned Real Estate Development program, administered in conjunction with the Department of City and Regional Planning and the Fisher Center for Real Estate and Urban Politics. Others cite the certificate program in technology offered by Haas and Berkeley's School of Engineering. Still others appreciate the availability of numerous courses in public and nonprofit management. Haas's entrepreneurship program is also well regarded. For those willing to exert the herculean effort necessary, Haas also offers a joint JD/MBA, an MBA/MA in Asian Studies, a combined MBA/Masters in Public Health Services Management, and an MBA/MIAS (International Studies).

Such diversity is one of the benefits a program at a large university can provide. Typically at large schools the downside is that students feel lost in the enormity of their program, ignored by professors, administrators, and even fellow classmates. Not so at Haas, however. Professors here receive high marks for being "very accessible and helpful. They use a lot of cross-referencing to integrate concepts taught in other disciplines (i.e., finance will refer to an economic theory)." One student notes, "I knew the professors at Berkeley would be top-notch, but I didn't realize how personable they would be. I talk to my professors outside of class all the time." Administrators are "extremely responsive" and "put a lot of energy into protecting us from the UC bureaucracy."

Like most b-schools, Haas fills its first year with requirements, allowing students only a single elective. Students appreciate the integrated core: "Some of the top faculty teach the core, which dramatically impacts the quality of the first-year experience. Core courses are very well integrated, ensuring one receives each component as part of the big picture." Courses are "challenging and demanding without being too high pressure. Emphasis is on learning, not grades." One respondent concludes, "My only complaint is that the outside world does not know the quality of education and students at Haas."

PLACEMENT AND RECRUITING

Berkeley MBAs give the school high marks for attracting top-notch recruiters to campus. In fact, the career center boasts that they offer "strong recruiting opportunities in a full range of career options, from investment banking and management consulting to high tech and entertainment start-ups, and everything in between." Students are also enthusiastic about the number and quality of opportunities for off-campus projects and internships. However, they give the Chetkovich Career Center only average grades for overall effectiveness. It should be noted, though, that our survey shows an upward trend at Haas; this year's respondents gave career services higher marks than did students in our previous surveys.

Haas reports that the top recruiters of recent MBAs are A.T. Kearney, Andersen Consulting, Charles Schwab, Citibank, Hewlett-Packard, Intel, McKinsey and Company, Mitchell Madison Group, Price Waterhouse, Silicon Graphics, and Sun Microsystems.

MBA Admissions, Admissions Advisor
440 Student Services Building, Berkeley, CA 94720-1902
Admissions: 510-642-1405 Fax: 510-643-6659
Email: mbaadms@haas.berkeley.edu
Internet: www.haas.berkeley.edu

University of California—Berkeley

STUDENT/CAMPUS LIFE

One word pops up over and over when Haas students describe each other: smart. Writes one, "Smart! I have learned as much from my peers as I have from the coursework." Adds another, "Great, smart people. We have a strong international presence." One student notes, "I expected Berkeley to attract people with a wide variety of backgrounds, but I've been amazed by how interesting those backgrounds are. Everyone has great stories to tell." The international influence of the large foreign student body is supplemented by the many American students who have spent time overseas, and as one student informed us, "a lot of students have international experience." Although students report that the program is ethnically and racially diverse, some worry that "Prop 209 [a law banning racial preferences at California state universities] has hurt our recruiting of African Americans and other U.S. minorities and may really impact on diversity in the future." The typical Haas MBA "works hard in class and on academics but is also very focused on extracurricular and community initiatives."

Quality of life at Haas recently received a major upgrade through the auspices of a new $55 million three-building mini-campus. Students report that "the new Haas building at Berkeley is great. Not only does it have impressive architecture and design, but it is equipped with all the latest in computer hardware." Students here work hard but enjoy a relaxed, noncompetitive atmosphere. And, they manage to find time for extracurriculars. Writes one, "This school is fun! Social life is an integral part of the Haas experience, which means not only a good time while you're here, but also a great network when you graduate." The school and student organizations provide "at least one or two organized social events per week. The number and diversity of quality activities is amazing. It would be impossible to do everything that you wanted to do." Students enjoy outdoor activities such as "rock-climbing, skiing, and mountain biking." And then, of course, there's Berkeley and nearby San Francisco, both of which students love. The "location is superb. The San Francisco Bay Area cannot be topped for climate and lifestyle. It reminds you that there is more to life than work." Near campus students find "excellent food: organic, bread, new restaurants" as well as convenient shopping and a number of pubs, any one of which might serve as "Bar of the Week," a Wednesday tradition at Haas.

ADMISSIONS

The admissions office reports that it accepts applications during one long "continuous cycle" that goes from November to March. Students are notified of a decision generally within six weeks of a file's completion, except for the final deadline. Haas rarely grants deferments. According to Berkeley, "The admissions committee reviews files and makes decisions continuously. Applicants who apply in one of the earlier rounds have a stronger chance of being admitted." The Haas School is also a member of the Consortium for Graduate Study in Management, which offers scholarships to talented minority students. The following criteria are considered in descending order of importance: the essays, college GPA or academic record, GMAT score, work experience, letters of recommendation, extracurricular activities, and the interview.

FINANCIAL FACTS

Tuition (in-/out-of-state)	$10,395/$19,379
Cost of books	$1,300
Room & board (on-/off-campus)	$12,022/$12,022
% of students receiving aid	45
% first-year students receiving aid	45
% of students receiving loans	38
% of students receiving grants	38
% of students receiving paid internships	91
Average award package	$20,000
Average grant	$11,320
Average graduation debt	$15,335

ADMISSIONS

# of applications received	4,162
% applicants accepted	11
% acceptees attending	52
Average GMAT (range)	674 (640–710)
Minimum TOEFL	570
Average GPA (range)	3.50 (3.23–3.66)
Application fee (in-/out-of-state)	$40/$40
Early decision program available	Yes
Early decision deadline	November 20
Early decision notification	January 1
Regular application deadline	March 1
Regular notification	June 1
Admission may be deferred?	No
Transfer students accepted?	No
Nonfall admission available?	No
Admission process need-blind?	Yes

APPLICANTS ALSO LOOK AT

Stanford University, University of California—Los Angeles, Northwestern University, University of Pennsylvania, Harvard University, Massachusetts Institute of Technology, Columbia University, University of Chicago

EMPLOYMENT PROFILE

Placement rate (%)	100
# of companies recruiting on campus	165
% of grads employed immediately	90
% grads employed within six months	99
Average starting salary	$77,797

Grads employed by field (avg. salary):

Consulting	35%	$89,002
Entrepreneurship	3%	NR
Finance	28%	$74,583
General Management	3%	$74,750
Marketing	18%	$76,500
Operations	1%	$70,625
Other	7%	$76,000
Strategic Planning	3%	$76,000

UNIVERSITY OF CALIFORNIA — DAVIS
Graduate School of Management

ACADEMICS

In recent years, the University of California at Davis' Graduate School of Management has worked its way into the upper echelon of public MBA programs. It had done so through its unique combination of small classes and an unusual amount of flexibility "that gives students opportunities to design their own MBA curriculum to suit their special interests and talents." Of the former asset, one Davis MBA tells us that "Small size is the great strength of the GSM. It allows great interactivity among students and between students and instructors." Of the latter, students "enjoy the fact that we have the flexibility to create our own curriculum" and "appreciate the additional opportunities linked to the program." Student satisfaction levels here are high due to the widely held perception that "the school goes out of its way to make the program personable and responsive."

Program flexibility is an attribute of second-year studies at Davis; first year is entirely given over to twelve core curriculum courses that "focus on all the basic management disciplines . . . and provide a strong base for later advanced work in specialized areas and concentrations." Students give the core mixed grades, with some complaining that "First-year courses could use some work. They aren't very interesting." Several students express the hope that Davis will some day allow students with business experience the opportunity to place out of core studies. The core continues into second year with a single capstone course in the winter quarter; the course, entitled Management Policy and Strategy, places students in consulting teams and assigns them projects with area businesses. Second-year students must also complete eleven electives. They may concentrate in one of ten "standing concentrations," opt for a general management degree without concentration, or design their own concentrations. Students tell us that "the school has many concentrations, but finance gets almost all the attention." While "marketing is getting much stronger with many more offerings," "MIS and operations are a weak component of our education." Students also feel that "a more international focus in the classroom would be good."

Davis MBAs are confident that both the quality of the school and the value of their degree will appreciate in years to come, in part because "over the last few years the school has attracted very good new professors. They will set their marks in the years to come." Students give the faculty mixed grades. Some respondents reported that "The professors are very helpful and open to meeting with students. They seem dedicated to making the school better." Others, however, cautioned that "A few of the gem profs are extremely high caliber and very concerned with students' understanding [of] the material. Unfortunately, not all profs are so involved."

PLACEMENT AND RECRUITING

Davis placement services suffer from a malady common to many small MBA programs: the reluctance of many recruiters to visit campuses at which multiple hires are unlikely. Explains one Davis MBA, "We have a small student body. While this has its benefits (small class size, close student relationships), there is a downside: it is difficult to get some employers who want exposure to many students at once."

Donald Blodger, Assistant Dean, Admissions and Student Services
One Shields Avenue Davis, CA 95616
Admissions: 530- 752-7658 Fax: 530-752-2924
Email: gsm@ucdavis.edu
Internet: www.gsm.ucdavis.edu

University of California—Davis

Some very good companies recruit—such as Intel and HP—but not very many recruit out of the area, they are mostly local." Confirming this assessment are the Career Service Center's report that, in a recent year more than half its placements were made in Sacramento; the Bay area accounted for another one-third of Davis MBA employers. Students note that "The alumni work hard to assist in the job search."

STUDENT/CAMPUS LIFE

According to those we surveyed, Davis' small student body is "surprisingly intellectual and competitive. We like to engage professors and other students in discourse." While anxious to succeed, Davis MBAs are also "very helpful, cooperative. It's a competitive environment, but students are competitive with themselves, not with each other." Most students arrive with three or more years of work experience; one MBA estimates, "The average age here is 27 to 28 years old. The average amount of work experience is between four and five years." Peers "bring a lot of skills with them, and also knowledgeable points of view." Students applaud the fact that "about 40 percent of us are women," but also pointed out that the student body is "a tad too local."

A small town located just 12 miles east of Sacramento, Davis offers the comforts of small-town living with the amenities of city life only a short drive away. Students call Davis a "great town to go to school in if you want a break from city life." Writes one, "The pace here is leisurely. There are few distractions in town." Davis is an "ecologically aware and socially innovative" town where students are often "active in [the] community." Says one student, "The town and the small size of the program allow for a very friendly and comfortable atmosphere. In addition, such activities as skiing, the arts (via San Francisco, about 70 miles away), and biking are very accessible." In fact, according to one student, "Davis is the biking capital of the United States. A lot of us bike or walk to school." Students also happily report that "food on campus is good and there are several restaurants within walking distance."

The Graduate School of Management is housed in a small building on the east end of the Davis campus; students report that "The MBA program is very well integrated into the life of the university. Social life and balance are encouraged." Students complain that GSM's computer resources could stand improvement but are otherwise happy with both the facilities and the culture of the school. Notes one student, "I'm a single mom with two kids. The atmosphere here for me is superb. I'm very involved, including with student government, and my fellow students couldn't be more supportive."

ADMISSIONS

According to the admissions office the following are the most important aspects of admission: GMAT scores and work experience top the list, followed by undergraduate GPA, the interview, and essays. The school also looks for "motivation and leadership potential" among prospective MBAs.

FINANCIAL FACTS

Tuition (in-/out-of-state)	$10,468/$19,852
Cost of books	$973
Room & board (on-/off-campus)	$8,997/$8,997
% of students receiving aid	71
% first-year students receiving aid	80
% of students receiving paid internships	85
Average award package	$16,500
Average grant	$5,979

ADMISSIONS

# of applications received	386
% applicants accepted	30
% acceptees attending	53
Average GMAT (range)	663 (620–720)
Minimum TOEFL	600
Average GPA (range)	3.20 (2.60–3.70)
Application fee (in-/out-of-state)	$40/$40
Early decision program available	Yes
Early decision deadline	February 1
Early decision notification	March 31
Regular application deadline	April 1
Regular notification	June 30
Admission may be deferred?	Yes
Maximum length of deferment	1 year
Transfer students accepted?	No
Nonfall admission available?	No
Admission process need-blind?	Yes

APPLICANTS ALSO LOOK AT

Univeirsity of California—Berkeley, Georgetown Unversity, Univeristy of California—Los Angeles, Univeirsity of Michigan, University of Southern California, Columbia University

EMPLOYMENT PROFILE

Placement rate (%)	100
% of grads employed immediately	90
% grads employed within six months	100
Average starting salary	$61,000

Grads employed by field (avg. salary):

Consulting	21%	$60,000
Finance	28%	$65,000
General Management	16%	$61,000
Marketing	16%	$58,000
Management Information Services	12%	$57,000
Operations	7%	$52,000

UNIVERSITY OF CALIFORNIA — IRVINE
Graduate School of Management

OVERVIEW
Type of school	public
Affiliation	none
Academic calendar	quarters
Environment	suburban

STUDENTS
Enrollment of parent institution	17,788
Enrollment of business school	562
% male/female	73/27
% part-time	55
% minorities	3
% international (# of countries represented)	25 (47)
Average age at entry	28
Average years work experience at entry	5

ACADEMICS
Student/faculty ratio	10:1
% female faculty	24
% minority faculty	13

SPECIALTIES
General management curriculum with particular strength in areas of Information Technology for Management, Marketing, Health Care Management, Information Systems, and Finance

JOINT DEGREES
MD/MBA, 6 years

SPECIAL PROGRAMS
Center for Leadership Development, which includes the Corporate Partners Mentoring Program Executive Speaker Series, and Professional Development Workshops.

STUDY ABROAD PROGRAMS
France, Belgium, China, Hungary, Austria, Mexico, Hong Kong, Finland, and Italy

SURVEY SAYS...
HITS
Students are happy
Diversity of work experience
Computer skills

MISSES
MIS/Operations
Impossible to get into courses

ACADEMICS

The Graduate School of Management at the University of California at Irvine has risen through the ranks to contender status with its dual focus on international business and information technology. A willingness to innovate, strength in select niche programs, and state-school tuition levels have also contributed to making the GSM a favorite among those seeking MBAs in the area.

The GSM takes the direct approach in integrating IT throughout its MBA program. All students receive high-end notebook computers and extensive computer training. E-mail, on-line collaboration tools, and the school's intranet are all incorporated into the curriculum. Students appreciate Irvine's efforts to remain on the cutting edge, praising the "young, innovative program. There's nothing set in stone." Writes one student, "The new dean has a great vision and is making many beneficial improvements on a regular basis." Even more important to the students is that ideas for improvements don't always originate with the administration; says one MBA, "The faculty and administration are very open to student feedback on various issues. This goes a long way toward improving student morale and expectations as well as helping the school provide a better program."

The UCI curriculum begins with a "residential course" called Management of Complex Organizations. Residentials require students to leave campus—this class is held in a hotel nearby—"to allow you to focus on the subject matter without any outside distractions and also allows you to work closely with your fellow classmates." The core curriculum consists of twelve classes, taken in a prescribed order. Core classes entail frequent group projects "to create a mutually supportive and cooperative learning environment, as well as to promote a sense of identity and unity among students." Irvine also requires study in international business, either through an elective or through participation in an exchange program. Second-year students take eleven electives in such functional areas as accounting, business strategy, information systems, and public policy. Writes one second-year student, "Overall, this place is excellent. We need more electives in marketing and entrepreneurial studies, but this is hard at such a small school." Students speak highly of Irvine's unique Health Care Management program, which is highlighted by the annual Health Care Forecast Conference, held on campus.

Irvine students are "very pleased with the quality of instruction, especially since professors teach all the courses instead of TAs like at other schools." Writes one student, "The professors here are always available and willing to help!! They all ask for course feedback throughout the quarter to ensure class is meeting our needs and expectations." In addition to the faculty, "We have a lot of industry professionals come to speak to us. They are better than tenured faculty in terms of relating to real-life situations." Sums up one happy MBA, "There is no question that this school is one of the best and getting better."

PLACEMENT AND RECRUITING

UCI maintains an MBA-dedicated Career Service Office to handle placement and recruiting services for its students. The CSO invites employers to recruit on the UCI campus and to take advantage of the school's video teleconferencing

Barbara A. Nelles, Director of Admissions and Marketing
202 GSM, Irvine, CA 92697-3125
Admissions: 949-824-4622 Fax: 949-824-2235
Email: gsm-mba@uci.edu
Internet: www.gsm.uci.edu

University of California—Irvine

facility to conduct interviews. An Internet-based job board and resume books, both in hard copy and Web-based formats, are also included among the CSO's services. UCI supplements CSO efforts by participating in the West Coast MBA Consortium and the International West Coast Recruiting Forum, both held in January. Students in our survey tell us that "we need better on-campus recruiting. Right now it's mostly consulting and IT-related jobs."

STUDENT/CAMPUS LIFE

Students find the workload at UC Irvine heavy but bearable; the workload is intensified by the school's quarterly academic schedule, which makes it seem as though an exam is never too far off. "It's busy, but I feel my time here is well spent," writes one student. After class, students are active in a number of clubs. Reports one, "Great clubs! Toast Masters, IT Consulting, etc. The clubs bring several big speakers to campus each semester." Says another, "Student clubs are important; however, studying and group work come first." School life "encourages networking through such activities as weekly Happy Hours." The school also works hard to serve its married students, who "represent a large percentage of the overall class. This year we have begun a 'Joint Venture' club for students and spouses, which has been terrific."

All this on-campus activity is well and good, since "Irvine is suburbia at its foremost," leaving "not much to do in the area of campus other than study." Located midway between Los Angeles and San Diego, Irvine does facilitate business opportunities for those interested in the region's growing Pacific Rim trade. Located near the ocean and the mountains, Irvine is also hospitable to those interested in the outdoors. The Irvine campus, spread out across 1,500 acres of heavily wooded foothills, is home to more than 18,000 students. UC Irvine boasts all the amenities of a modern university, including numerous exercise facilities.

Students tell us that they are "impressed with the level of intelligence and degree of commitment among students. A strong sense of camaraderie exists, particularly among first-year students." The diversity of their work and educational experiences means that "students have different strengths and use them to help each other. They all come from such diverse occupations that I learn from my peers' experiences as well as from my professors." They are also "very go-getting, with a strong drive to grow and build the school's reputation along with their own." International students arrive from 47 different countries.

ADMISSIONS

According to the admissions office the following are requirements and considered important for acceptance to the MBA program: GMAT score, undergraduate GPA, letters of recommendation, and essays. Work experience, extracurricular activities, and an interview are factored into the decision but not necessary for consideration. Transfer students may apply and be admitted; however, UC Irvine will not accept transfer units other than from within the UC school system.

FINANCIAL FACTS

Tuition (in-/out-of-state)	$11,368/$21,172
Cost of books	$4,448
Room & board (on-/off-campus)	$7,300/$8,757
% of students receiving aid	75
% first-year students receiving aid	65
% aid that is merit based	23
% of students receiving paid internships	94
Average award package	$16,000
Average grant	$5,500

ADMISSIONS

# of applications received	823
% applicants accepted	27
% acceptees attending	57
Average GMAT (range)	652 (600–700)
Minimum TOEFL	600
Average GPA (range)	3.30 (2.83–3.70)
Application fee (in-/out-of-state)	$40/$40
Early decision program available	Yes
Early decision deadline	December 14; January 25
Early decision notification	January 14; February 19
Regular application deadline	May 1
Regular notification	June 1
Admission may be deferred?	No
Transfer students accepted?	Yes
Nonfall admission available?	No
Admission process need-blind?	Yes

APPLICANTS ALSO LOOK AT

University of California—Berkeley, University of California—Los Angelas, University of Southern California

EMPLOYMENT PROFILE

Placement rate (%)	100
# of companies recruiting on campus	80
% of grads employed immediately	76
% grads employed within six months	100
Average starting salary	$73,000

Grads employed by field (avg. salary):

Accounting	5%	$40,000
Consulting	37%	$79,496
Finance	24%	$64,664
General Management	6%	$80,000
Marketing	13%	$66,208
Management Information Systems	4%	$106,200
Operations	2%	$73,000
Other	9%	$60,000

UNIVERSITY OF CALIFORNIA — LOS ANGELES
The Anderson School at UCLA

OVERVIEW

Type of school	public
Affiliation	none
Environment	urban
Academic calendar	quarters
Schedule	full-time/part time

STUDENTS

Enrollment of parent institution	35,796
Enrollment of business school	1,046
% male/female	71/29
% out-of-state	52
% part-time	38
% minorities	20
% international (# of countries represented)	25 (45)
Average age at entry	28
Average years work experience at entry	4.5

ACADEMICS

Student/faculty ratio	60:1
% female faculty	16
% minority faculty	11
Hours of study per day	4.56

SPECIALTIES
Finance, Marketing, Operations and Technology Management, Entrepreneurship

JOINT DEGREES
MBA/JD; MBA/MD; MBA/MA Latin American Studies; MBA/MA Urban Planning; MBA/MLS; MBA/MN; MBA/MPH; MBA/MS Computer Science

SPECIAL PROGRAMS
International Business, Education & Research, Operations and Technology Management, Digital Media, Corporate Renewal, Health Care Management, Public Policy, Real Estate, Entrepreneurial Studies

STUDY ABROAD PROGRAMS
Philippines, Australia, Argentina, Hong Kong, Denmark, France, Netherlands, Peru, Spain, Venezuela, Mexico, Japan, Germany, England, Norway, Chile, Italy, Switzerland, Belgium, South Africa, Austria, Sweden, and New Zealand

SURVEY SAYS...

HITS
Social life
Placement
Cozy student community

MISSES
Safety
On-campus housing
Gym

ACADEMICS

Although most business schools offer study options in entrepreneurship, few go to the extent pursued by UCLA, where more than two-thirds of MBAs take one or more entrepreneurship electives. The Anderson entrepreneurship program gives MBAs a chance to study under top-ranked professors with such improbable names as "Wild Bill" Cockrum and "Big Al" Osborne. Entrepreneurial studies at UCLA emphasize a combination of in-class study and extracurricular field work, much of which is coordinated through the school managed Price Center or the student run Entrepreneur Association. Students searching for start-up businesses to manage may find one through the UCLA Ventures Program, which teams MBAs with UCLA researchers that have a potentially profitable idea but who lack the will or know-how to start a business. Finally, for the top rung of entrepreneurial students there's The Executive Committee on Campus (TEC), which provides two dozen MBAs with mentors from among the area's leading entrepreneurs and CEOs.

Entrepreneurship is not the alpha and omega of an Anderson education, however. Students here praise the Finance and Marketing departments (both of which received very good marks from more than three-quarters of our respondents). In all departments, the case-study method, as opposed to straight lecture and notes, is the preferred method of teaching. Professors receive above-average grades, and students appreciate the fact that "profs have worked together to effectively integrate the core disciplines," although some complain that core profs are "hit or miss." The administration is also highly regarded, particularly because it is "very responsive to student issues, concerns, and suggestions." Students warn, however, that MBAs here encounter "annoying lines, forms, and assemblies, like at any big school." Perhaps most impressive is the new b-school facility, which "is beautiful and technologically very advanced, with network/Internet ports at every seat." Adds another, "Professors and administration take heavy advantage of the easy access to such up-to-the-minute communication vehicles as a school-wide network, the web, and email." Overall, most would agree that Anderson provides an "excellent overall academic experience. Many of my professors have businesses or have had a prominent career in the business world, which enables a great learning experience. Everything is applicable!"

PLACEMENT AND RECRUITING

Anderson's MBA Career Management Center boasts that it was "recently ranked the number one MBA career center in the country by corporate recruiters (*Business Week*). We achieved this noteworthy ranking because of the quality and professionalism of the recruiting service and product (students) we deliver to employers. We are extremely customer-service oriented and work closely with employers to ensure a great environment in which to recruit our students." Students wholeheartedly endorse the CMC's self-assessment: more than half give the service our highest rating. "The Career Center is excellent and very professional," writes one student. Another says, "The Career Center is the best resource of its kind I have ever seen." Video conferencing, resumes on the web, job listings on the web, and on-campus interviews all serve to make "access to students as easy as possible." As if these assets don't give Anderson students

Linda Baldwin, Director of Admissions
110 Westwood Plaza, Box 951481, Los Angeles, CA 90095-1481
Admissions: 310-825-6944 Fax: 310-825-8582
Email: mba.admissions@anderson.ucla.edu
Internet: www.anderson.ucla.edu

University of California—Los Angeles

enough of an advantage, UCLA also benefits from a "California location that attracts both students and employers from the high-tech market." The only complaint: "Anderson is still building the powerful alumni network that would make it the perfect b-school."

Employers recruiting the greatest number of UCLA grads include A.T. Kearney, Andersen Consulting Strategic Services, Avery Dennison, Bank of America, Clorox, Coopers & Lybrand, Deloitte & Touche, Ernst & Young, General Mills, Hewlett-Packard, Intel, J.P. Morgan, McKinsey & Co., Merrill Lynch, Nestle, Netscape Communications, Pittiglio Rabin Todd & McGrath, Price Waterhouse, Salomon Brothers, San Francisco Consulting Group, and Towers Perrin.

STUDENT/CAMPUS LIFE

Anderson students are "cooperative, laid back, and noncompetitive." Reports another, "The environment here is very collegial. At no other school would classmates email their entire class their class outlines!" Students here are "leaders, whether it's socially, academically, or with student government, which plays a very active role at Anderson. They're very active and entrepreneurial, they run almost all the clubs and events." Clubs are, by all accounts, an "excellent resource." Events include "weekly beer busts and over-the-top international night (really an international boozefest)." Students also participate in such student-run clubs as the Anderson Golf and Country Club and the MBA Students for the Environment.

Beyond the school is Los Angeles, where "the quality of life is unsurpassed, especially if you like the outdoors. We make sure we work hard enough so we can enjoy the beaches, sun, and nightlife." Students take advantage of the city's many bars, restaurants, and clubs, often in the company of other MBAs. Second-year students, reports one respondent, "move to the beach. You just can't beat living on the beach with an ocean view." "Life here is good!" adds another. UCLA sits next door to Westwood Village, a bastion of trendy shops and restaurants. Students also live off-campus in nearby Brentwood and Santa Monica, or farther away in Hermosa and Long Beach. No matter where they end up, "everyday is nonstop. There are always tons of activities to choose from. Plenty of social events. Plus, unbeatable location and weather."

ADMISSIONS

Writes the admissions office, "The Anderson School admission policy emphasizes academic ability, leadership, and work experience. The Admissions Committee evaluates applicants' prospects as effective managers and their projected ability to succeed in and profit from the MBA program. Committee members carefully consider biographical and academic background information, GMAT and TOEFL (for most international applicants) scores, achievements, distinctions, awards and honors, employment history, letters of recommendation, and college and community involvement, especially where candidates have served in a leadership capacity."

FINANCIAL FACTS

Tuition & Fees (in-/out-of-state)	$11,019/$20,703
Cost of books	$1,793
Room & board (on-/off-campus)	$6,490/$8,801
% of students receiving aid	70
% first-year students receiving aid	65
% aid that is merit based	15
% of students receiving loans	70
% of students receiving grants	60
% of students receiving paid internships	15
Average award package	$26,200
Average grant	$6,000
Average graduation debt	$45,000

ADMISSIONS

# of applications received	4,366
% applicants accepted	15
% acceptees attending	50
Average GMAT (range)	683 (630–730)
Minimum TOEFL	600
Average GPA (range)	3.50 (3.20–3.80)
Application fee (in-/out-of-state)	$125/$125
Early decision program available	Yes
Early decision deadline	November 19
Early decision notification	January
Regular application deadline	April
Regular notification	June
Admission may be deferred?	No
Transfer students accepted?	No
Nonfall admission available?	Yes
Admission process need-blind?	Yes

APPLICANTS ALSO LOOK AT

Stanford University, University of California—Berkeley, Northwestern University, University of Pennsylvania, Harvard University, University of Southern California University of Michigan Business School, Columbia University

EMPLOYMENT PROFILE

Placement rate (%)	100
# of companies recruiting on campus	198
% of grads employed immediately	98
% grads employed within six months	100
Average starting salary	$77,700

Grads employed by field (avg. salary):

Consulting	27%	$88,000
Finance	33%	$76,200
General Management	3%	$76,700
Marketing	22%	$70,000
Strategic Planning	2%	$73,300
Venture Capital	2%	$91,700

CARNEGIE MELLON UNIVERSITY
Graduate School of Industrial Administration

ACADEMICS

Science and technology have always been among the chief focuses at Carnegie Mellon, and so too are they the essential elements of a business education at the university's Graduate School of Industrial Administration. Graduates here don't earn the Master's of Business Administration (MBA), but rather the Master's of Science in Industrial Administration (MSIA), a departure from the norm that speaks volumes about GSIA's approach to business education. And for those worried about this degree's unusual distinction, don't panic; GSIA is fully accredited by the American Association of Collegiate Schools of Business and highly regarded in the business community.

Innovation has long been a hallmark of GSIA. The school led the way in the educational use of computer simulations with its Management Game, which requires student teams to direct finance, marketing, production, and research for a computer-generated company. Once exclusively the province of GSIA, the Management Game is now an international contest, with student groups in Japan, Mexico, and Sweden competing with GSIA students. More recently the school introduced FAST (which stands for Financial Analysis and Security Trading), a trading simulation for finance students that has also generated mirror programs across the globe. As one student explains, "When I talk with friends at other b-schools, I always find GSIA is in the forefront of teaching techniques." Raves another, "Our projects are real-world oriented. When you get out of here no task is too complicated, intense, or daunting if you've already survived Management Game."

First-year students at GSIA begin with foundation courses in economics, behavioral sciences, and quantitative methods. They proceed quickly to marketing, finance, production, accounting, and strategy; GSIA's eight-week mini-semester schedule keeps courses moving along at a brisk pace. Writes one student, "The first two mini-semesters were overwhelming, a real shock to the system. But, my survival has made me stronger!" Students choose five electives during the spring semester "to develop some depth in a functional area before starting a summer internship." Second-year students participate in the Management Game and pursue elective study in such areas as finance, MIS, production and operations, and entrepreneurship. Throughout the program students "work a lot in teams. Your teamwork skills and time management skills will improve tremendously while you're here." Students describe their professors as "very motivated teachers. They treat us as peers and offer help whenever needed." Most agree that "Professors are extremely accessible and generous with their time" and appreciate the fact that "All courses are taught by recognized leaders."

PLACEMENT AND RECRUITING

GSIA notes that its Career Opportunities Center (COC) "works directly with students to assist them in developing career plans, seeking summer internships, and conducting searches for permanent employment opportunities." GSIA grads do very well in the marketplace, but student satisfaction with the COC is only middling; there is a pervasive sense among students that "Companies are attracted to the quality of the school, but they're not here because of COC's efforts." Students report that alumni are extremely helpful with job searches.

Laurie Stewart, Director of Admissions
Frew & Tech Streets, Pittsburgh, PA 15213
Admissions: 412-268-2272 Fax: 412-268-4209
Email: gsia-admissions@andrew.cru.edu
Internet: www.gsia.cmu.edu

Carnegie Mellon University

STUDENT/CAMPUS LIFE

GSIA's student body is dominated by "lots of engineers with quantitative skills." According to their classmates, they are "analytical and quantitative yet comfortable with qualitative issues" and "extremely diverse but a bit on the boring side. They need help with their social skills, especially in terms of networking." A large portion of the student body is made up of foreign nationals. Writes one student, "Our student body is forty percent international. Our 'International Week' was like a multimedia tour of the world." Is there anything missing here? Our respondents tell us that there are "only a few Wall Street types" in the bunch.

First-year students report a killer workload, which is "murderous on nonmath, nonengineering students. Many barely get by." The pressure is compounded by the acceleration of the mini-semester schedule and up-all-night, number-crunching assignments. Fortunately, many courses are structured around team projects, allowing students to seek help from their study groups. Students agree that there is "an incredible amount of work to do, and thus no private life." Still, most find the experience tolerable. As one student explains, "I know this sounds contradictory, but it's a comfortable atmosphere in a high-stress environment. People work hard, but it's very congenial."

Campus events center on the volunteer GSIA social committee, which organizes picnics, holiday parties, boat cruises, and talent shows. There are "regular social events twice a week. There are also occasionally weekend events." Students share "beers on Friday after class, and 'Bar Crawl' on Tuesday nights. We have a good social scene." The socially responsible can "give back" to the community through the I Have A Dream tutor program. CMU's campus is located in the Oakland section of Pittsburgh, a relaxed, safe, "college town" area set in a tree-lined, residential neighborhood. Students describe the campus as "petite but elegant." New additions recently doubled the physical size of the b-school. MBAs told us the "new building and facilities are super" though the library is still sub-par. Because on-campus housing is not available, many students live in the nearby communities of Shadyside, Oakland, and Squirrel Hill, which are among Pittsburgh's trendiest. As for the city of Pittsburgh, well, it's better than you think. Consistently rated one of America's most livable cities, it's clean, modern, and teeming with cultural events.

ADMISSIONS

According to the admissions office, the following criteria are equally weighed: essays, college GPA, letters of recommendation, extracurricular activities, work experience, interview (required), and GMAT score. Notes the school, "When we evaluate an application, we try to understand that person as an individual. For example, we examine the entire academic record: grade trends, the major, the school extracurriculars, and part-time work, if any." Applications are batched in rounds. The admissions office suggests applying in round two.

FINANCIAL FACTS

Tuition	$25,000
Fees	$130
Cost of books	$3,000
Room & board (on-/off-campus)	NR/$9,600
% of students receiving aid	59
% first-year students receiving aid	62
% aid that is merit based	12
% of students receiving loans	46
% of students receiving grants	50
Average award package	$18,200
Average grant	$7,100
Average graduation debt	$22,000

ADMISSIONS

# of applications received	1,415
% applicants accepted	30
% acceptees attending	58
Average GMAT (range)	640 (620–690)
Average GPA (range)	3.20 (2.85–3.50)
Application fee (in-/out-of-state)	$60/$60
Early decision program available	Yes
Early decision deadline	November 15
Early decision notification	December 15
Regular application deadline	March 15
Regular notification	April 15
Admission may be deferred?	Yes
Maximum length of deferment	2 years
Transfer students accepted?	No
Nonfall admission available?	Yes
Admission process need-blind?	Yes

APPLICANTS ALSO LOOK AT

Massachusetts Institute of Technology, University of Pennsylvania, Northwestern University, University of Michigan Business School, University of Chicago, New York University, Stanford University, Duke University

EMPLOYMENT PROFILE

Placement rate (%)	97
# of companies recruiting on campus	245
% of grads employed immediately	93
% grads employed within six months	98
Average starting salary	$77,081

Grads employed by field (avg. salary):

Accounting	1%	$68,100
Consulting	31%	$87,690
Finance	42%	$71,865
General Management	4%	$62,420
Human Resources	0%	NR
Marketing	9%	$72,776
MIS	3%	$77,299
Operations	5%	$72,233
Strategic Planning	4%	$74,125

CASE WESTERN RESERVE UNIVERSITY
Weatherhead School of Management

OVERVIEW

Type of school	private
Affiliation	none
Environment	urban
Academic calendar	semester
Schedule	full-time/part-time/evening

STUDENTS

Enrollment of parent institution	9,800
Enrollment of business school	1,139
% male/female	64/36
% out-of-state	21
% part-time	58
% minorities	12
% international (# of countries represented)	41 (51)
Average age at entry	28
Average years work experience at entry	6

ACADEMICS

Student/faculty ratio	12:1
% female faculty	18
% minority faculty	1
Hours of study per day	4.54

SPECIALTIES

Marketing, Finance, MIS, Entrepreneurship, Nonprofit Management, Health Care Management, Operations Management, Organizational Behavior

JOINT DEGREES

MBA/JD, 4 yrs; MD/MBA, 5 yrs.; MSN/MBA, 2.5 yrs.; MSMS/MBA, 2.5 yrs.; MNO/JD, 4 yrs.; MNO/MA, 2.5 yrs.; MNO/MSSA, 2.5 yrs.; MBA/MIM, 2.5 yrs.

SPECIAL PROGRAMS

The Weatherhead Mentor Program, International Exchange Programs; International Institutes; Community Service Certificate; Public Policy Certificate; Health Systems Management Certificate; Nonprofit Management Certificate

STUDY ABROAD PROGRAMS

Programs with twenty countries.

SURVEY SAYS...

HITS
Ethnic and racial diversity
Off-campus housing
Students are happy

MISSES
On-campus housing
Computer skills
Quantitative skills

PROMINENT ALUMNI

John G. Breen, Chairman & CEO, Sherwin-Williams Co.; Robert W. Gillespie, Jr., Chairman, President & CEO, KeyCorp; Joseph A Sabatini, Managing Director, J.P. Morgan & Co.

ACADEMICS

The Weatherhead School of Management seeks to separate itself from the MBA pack through its openness to innovation. As one student puts it, "The outstanding aspect of this school is its flexibility. Staff and faculty are open to new course ideas and curriculum enhancements." Since entirely revamping its MBA program in 1990, Weatherhead has continually sought to upgrade, integrate, and expand its program on a regular basis.

The Weatherhead curriculum, designed to impose continuity on the two-year MBA program, uses several required programs to achieve this goal. First is the Management Assessment and Development (MAD) program, a two-year strand that forces students to assess their strengths and weaknesses, then design curricula that will bolster their marketability. The program, which is overseen by mentors, faculty advisors, and "facilitators," requires MAD groups to meet periodically throughout their Weatherhead tenure to assess their progress and reconsider career goals. Students approve of the program. One explains that "the management assessment/competency program, required of all students, is a great idea." The school also encourages students to consider choosing their electives in thematically linked clusters, such as The Global Manager, Leadership and Ethics in Management, and Technology Issues and the Manager.

The first-year courseload at Weatherhead is dictated entirely by core requirements. Eight core courses and the Strategic Issues and Applications (SIA) program, which spans the entire year, are integrated to create the first-year curriculum. SIA places students in management teams, then—as a group—they must walk through their paces with a series of increasingly difficult case studies that ultimately culminates in a class-wide competition. "Classes for first-years are very team-oriented. We work in groups of four to eight people on class projects. The students are constantly on the move from classes to meetings to studying to sleep." Writes one student, "You'll be up to your ears in group projects with students from many other countries. Very challenging, but rewarding."

Weatherhead students report that they are generally satisfied with the faculty. As one explains, "The quality of professors is quite variable. Most are good but some are bad. The problem is that in core courses you cannot select the professor you want." Profs receive high marks for being "totally accessible. They give us their home phone numbers and invite us to call until midnight." Our survey shows a high level of satisfaction with "small class sizes" and the "innovative" administration. Students are particularly approving of finance, accounting, and management courses, and several single out the availability of a specialized degree in nonprofit management as their reason for choosing Weatherhead.

Christine Grill, Interim Director of Marketing and Admissions
10900 Euclid Avenue, Cleveland, OH 44106-7235
Admissions: 216-368-2030 Fax: 216-368-5548
Email: wsommba@pyrite.cwru.edu
Internet: http://weatherhead.cwru.edu

Case Western Reserve University

PLACEMENT AND RECRUITING

In 1998, students had the oppurtunity to meet with 115 companies that recruited Weatherhead MBAs. Eighty-four percent of the class of 1998 had jobs at graduation, 27 percent in finance, and another 36 percent headed into consulting. Major recruiters included: Ernst & Young, A.T. Kearney, Citibank, General Electric, SAP America and Oracle. The average starting salary was $64,300. Students can participate in the career day and several national and international consortiums, as well as meeting companies coming on campus.

STUDENT/CAMPUS LIFE

The Weatherhead student body boasts a large international contingent. One student writes approvingly that, "because of the high number of international students, our diversity makes for an interesting learning and recreational environment." Students think highly of their classmates, giving them good marks for in-class contributions, cooperation in team projects, and overall friendliness. One respondent is pleased that "Unlike undergrad, where you choose to define yourself by your friends, Weatherhead students seek to surround themselves with people who may be different and challenging to them." Students are deeply involved in clubs, on-campus activities, and community service. Writes one student: "Very strong student association, very strong office of student life. Lots of multicultural activities, lots of clubs. If you have an interest that isn't covered by a club, you can simply start one up. Too much choice, really. Too many options, too little time." Students are happy at Weatherhead.

Case's campus is a hotbed of extracurricular activity. One student reports that there are "lots of outside activities like Casino Night and the softball tournament with the faculty. Every week there's something going on, from an International Festival for a whole week to a Speaker's Corner. Students congregate at one of two "meeting places, the atrium and the computer lab" to plan study groups and the evening's social events. Students have mixed feelings about Cleveland. Although some feel the city has "a lot to offer," others say, "Cleveland is not the best city in the world," but add, "that's good because people concentrate more on studying rather than on other activities."

ADMISSIONS

According to the admissions office, your work experience is most important and then, in descending order, college GPA, the interview, GMAT scores, essays, letters of recommendation, and extracurricular activities. Personal interviews are recommended for admission. Students are notified of a decision four weeks after filing an application. Decisions are made on a rolling admissions basis.

FINANCIAL FACTS

Tuition	$21,650
Tuition per credit	$902
Cost of books	$2,600
Room & board (on-/off-campus)	$8,400/$10,225
% of students receiving aid	74
% first-year students receiving aid	76
% aid that is merit based	35
% of students receiving loans	85
% of students receiving grants	27
% of students receiving paid internships	7
Average award package	$24,000
Average grant	$13,500
Average graduation debt	$18,500

ADMISSIONS

# of applications received	1,115
% applicants accepted	40
% acceptees attending	45
Average GMAT (range)	614 (490–730)
Minimum TOEFL	590
Average GPA (range)	3.20 (2.78–3.50)
Application fee (in-/out-of-state)	$50/$50
Early decision program available	Yes
Early decision deadline	March 15
Early decision notification	April 15
Regular application deadline	April 15
Regular notification	Rolling
Admission may be deferred?	No
Transfer students accepted?	Yes
Nonfall admission available?	Yes
Admission process need-blind?	Yes

APPLICANTS ALSO LOOK AT

Northwestern University, University of Michigan Business School, Ohio State University, Washington University, University of Chicago, Duke University, Emory University, Vanderbilt University

EMPLOYMENT PROFILE

Placement rate (%)	98
# of companies recruiting on campus	115
% of grads employed immediately	84
% grads employed within six months	98
Average starting salary	$64,300

Grads employed by field (avg. salary):

Consulting	36%	$70,200
Finance	27%	$68,200
General Management	7%	$59,300
Human Resources	1%	$59,600
Marketing	11%	$64,800
MIS	9%	$61,400
Operations	9%	$66,100

UNIVERSITY OF CHICAGO
Graduate School of Business

ACADEMICS

The University of Chicago has a lot to boast about. For starters, it's the first b-school whose faculty has included five Nobel laureates. Merton Miller, winner of the 1990 Nobel Prize in Economics, and Robert Fogel, winner of the same in 1993, currently teach in Chicago's MBA program. It's also the first to publish a scholarly business journal and to initiate a Ph.D. program. But the nation's second-oldest b-school hasn't chosen to rest on its laurels. As one student put it, "This school is continuously trying to improve itself. There are so many innovative opportunities here." Chief among them is LEAD, a mandatory leadership program that students—not faculty—run each year. Another first for Chicago: Among b-schools, LEAD pioneered the emphasis on leadership, interpersonal and multicultural programs, and learning by doing. Unsurprisingly, Chicago students give themselves high marks for their interpersonal skills (unique to a "quant" school) and tell us minorities and women are more than comfortable here. Students declare the curriculum "the single most flexible around." Beyond the required LEAD program, students can pick and choose from a variety of courses to satisfy Chicago's core requirements, and students aren't required to repeat work they have mastered elsewhere. "There's no hand holding here, and there's a lot of freedom," commented one student, "which is great for students who know what they want." The newest addition to Chicago is the International MBA, which, according to the school, "builds truly global management skills by giving people substantial knowledge of the culture and language of a foreign country." Students can also participate in Chicago's Laboratory in New Product and Strategy Development, acting as consultants to major corporations.

Chicago is best known for its economics and finance departments and is considered "numbers-heavy." But a majority of Chicago MBAs told us "it's much more than a quant school." Though students rate their quant and finance skills as excellent, they also consider themselves to have strong accounting, teamwork, and communication skills. "The excellent academics at Chicago have given me all the tools I need for the business world," wrote one MBA. They also feel terrific about Chicago's faculty, whom they consider passionate, accessible teachers. "Where else can you take classes with Nobel Prize winners both current and future!" exclaimed one student. Another MBA declared, "I would pit my instructors against any other faculty in the nation, bar none." Chicago administration has responded to some prior student complaints about facilities and administration. They recently completed an extensive renovation on classrooms and student areas and have announced plans to construct a new student building. The MBA program recently added some new administrative positions to provide a higher level of service to students. One complaint we did hear from students is about the inordinate focus on the job search. "It begins on Day Number 1," griped one student, "classes just come second."

Don Martin, Director of Admissions and Financial Aid
6030 S. Ellis Avenue, Chicago, IL 60637
Admissions: 773-702-7369 Fax: 773-702-9085
Email: NR
Internet: gsbwww.uchicago.edu

University of Chicago

PLACEMENT AND RECRUITING

Chicago MBAs say that they are satisfied with their career placement office, though several agreed "more West Coast contacts" would be nice. In 1997, over 900 companies recruited on campus for both summer internships and full-time positions. Ninety-eight percent of the second-year class had a job by graduation. Top employers of Chicago MBAs are McKinsey and Co., Andersen Consulting, Goldman Sachs, Lehman Brothers, Deloitte & Touche Consulting, and A.T. Kearney.

STUDENT/CAMPUS LIFE

Students ranked their workload at Chicago as substantial. As one student put it, "If you want to party your way to an MBA, forget it." Much of the pressure results from trying to juggle a job search with academics. Classes tend to be large, and the majority of students work in study groups. MBAs described their classmates as "involved students who expect great work from each other." One student wrote, "Anality is rampant, but we're smart, successful, and on the cutting edge!" Another MBA boldly predicted, "We will be the CEOs, CFOs, partners, and managing directors of the future!" Though the student body is professionally diverse, a few students complained about their narrow focus. One MBA wrote, "The students here are not intellectually diverse; they do not explore and utilize the other facilities here. As a result, an MBA degree becomes shamefully one-dimensional, as does one's conversation. It's business, business, business!"

The school sits on a beautiful campus in the Hyde Park section of Chicago. Known as the "South Side," it's not centrally located, so many students live on the North Side and commute. Some lament the lack of a sense of "community," but students tell us there is a "great transportation system" which provides "easy access to the Chicago downtown and the fantastic lakefront." Hyde Park used to have a reputation for being dangerous, but we were told that "school buses run until one in the morning around Hyde Park areas, which are heavily patrolled. Emergency phones are almost everywhere." As for the social scene, it's teeming with activity. There are plenty of planned activities, both professional and social. And students report that "there are surprising amounts of weekly social events that are low-key and cool to hang at." Although students report active social lives, this doesn't include dating. But the group thing works. Chicago MBAs say they'll be buddies with their classmates long after they graduate.

ADMISSIONS

According to the admissions office, your GMAT scores, work experience, essays, college GPA, letters of recommendation, and extracurricular activities are all considered equally. The interview is strongly recommended, but not required. Notes the school, "All of the above are considered equally. We have no cutoffs on GPA or GMAT scores." Applicants are notified of a decision following each of three rounds: December 1, January 16, and March 15.

FINANCIAL FACTS

Tuition	$26,200
Tuition per credit	$2,620
Fees	$84
Cost of books	$1,350
Room & board (on-/off-campus)	$10,210/$10,210
% of students receiving aid	75
% first-year students receiving aid	75
% aid that is merit based	100
% of students receiving loans	65
% of students receiving grants	9
% of students receiving paid internships	98
Average award package	$45,000
Average grant	$10,000
Average graduation debt	$60,000

ADMISSIONS

# of applications received	3,311
% applicants accepted	23
% acceptees attending	61
Average GMAT (range)	695 (570–790)
Minimum TOEFL	600
Average GPA (range)	3.38 (2.10–4.00)
Application fee (in-/out-of-state)	$125/$125
Early decision program available	No
Regular application deadline	March 15
Regular notification	May 20
Admission may be deferred?	Yes
Maximum length of deferment	1 year
Transfer students accepted?	No
Nonfall admission available?	No
Admission process need-blind?	Yes

APPLICANTS ALSO LOOK AT

Northwestern University, University of Pennsylvania, Stanford University, Harvard University, Columbia University, Massachusetts Institute of Technology, Dartmouth College

EMPLOYMENT PROFILE

Placement rate (%)	99
# of companies recruiting on campus	992
% of grads employed immediately	98
% grads employed within six months	99
Average starting salary	$80,092

Grads employed by field (avg. salary):

Accounting	1%	$81,250
Consulting	35%	$90,995
Finance	48%	$74,514
General Management	3%	$78,107
Marketing	8%	$70,227
Other	4%	$80,278
Strategic Planning	1%	$87,000

CLAREMONT GRADUATE UNIVERSITY
The Peter F. Drucker Graduate School of Management

OVERVIEW

Type of school	private
Affiliation	none
Environment	suburban
Academic calendar	semester
Schedule	full-time/part-time/evening

STUDENTS

Enrollment of parent institution	2,177
Enrollment of business school	200
% male/female	60/40
% out-of-state	47
% part-time	26
% minorities	23
% international (# of countries represented)	20 (26)
Average age at entry	28
Average years work experience at entry	5.5

ACADEMICS

Student/faculty ratio	6:1
% female faculty	29
% minority faculty	5
Hours of study per day	3.88

SPECIALTIES
Strengths of faculty and curriculum in Strategic Management, Leadership/Ethics, Cost Management, Marketing

JOINT DEGREES
Dual-degree programs in Economics, Education, Information Science, Psychology, and Public Policy, and by special arrangement in other disciplines.

SPECIAL PROGRAMS
Strategic Management; International Fellows Certificate Program in Advanced English and Cultural Proficiency for Management

STUDY ABROAD PROGRAMS
France, Groupe ESC Toulouse

SURVEY SAYS...
HITS
Small classes
Profs are great teachers
General management

MISSES
Gym
Quantitative skills
School clubs

PROMINENT ALUMNI
Dr. Robin Cooper, Consultant and Professor of Cost Management; Peter F. Drucker, Author and Teacher; Dr. Peter Farquhar, Consultant and Professor of Marketing

ACADEMICS

The primary drawing card of the Peter F. Drucker Graduate Management Center at Claremont Graduate University is the school's namesake, Peter Drucker. At no other school have so many students named a single professor as the reason for choosing the MBA program. Drucker, for those who don't know, literally wrote the book on modern management practices. *The Practice of Management* was the first book to recognize management as a distinct and important business skill. Drucker has since written numerous other books on management, entrepreneurship, economic history, and Japanese painting (!). Drucker was also a columnist for the *Wall Street Journal* for more than twenty years. Students happily report that Drucker, born in 1909, still teaches well and often. Writes one, "Professor Drucker is very accessible and enjoys spending time socially and academically with us. A family atmosphere is fostered here."

Drucker, however, is not the only "name" professor here. Students also drop the names Robin Cooper, an originator of activity-based accounting, and Jim Meyers, both of whom "consult extensively and bring real-world knowledge into the classroom." Writes a student, "If you plan carefully, you can assemble a schedule of world-class professors. This is unusual in a school with part-time students." Students tell us that teachers are not only famous but capable as well: "The teaching style is the school's greatest strength. Super-high emphasis on hands-on learning." Another student adds, "Teachers are enthusiastic and concerned with ensuring [that] students understand subject matter." Small classes and numerous opportunities "to build dual-degree combinations" enhance the learning experience here even further.

The Drucker school offers both a traditional MBA, which they call the "Early Career MBA," and an Executive Management Program geared toward mid- and senior-level executives. The coexistence of these programs allows for numerous mentoring opportunities, a definite plus for those pursuing the early career option. Both programs stress "leadership and strategy training," with an emphasis on management technique. Students praise the school for its instruction in marketing and international business, and also report "dramatic improvements in operations." In all areas, students appreciate a "progressive style of education" that "encourages us to do 'out-of-the-box' thinking and support it," as well as a "good balance between business skills and ethics." Students are also pleased that "the new administration is significantly improving the program." Among those improvements are new, state-of-the-art classroom and computer lab facilities for the Drucker School.

PLACEMENT AND RECRUITING

Drucker MBAs currently share career services with students from CGU's five other graduate departments. The Office of Career Services and Corporate Relations (OCSCR) provides one-on-one counseling, resume assistance, electronic and hard-copy job postings, a career resources library, and a number of workshops in career skills management. The office also coordinates on- and off-campus recruiting and alumni relations. Among the top companies recruiting recent Drucker grads are Avery Dennison, FHP, Andersen Consulting, Deloitte & Touche, and PepsiCo.

Jack H. Day III, Admissions Counselor
1021 North Dartmouth Avenue, Claremont, CA 91711
Admissions: 909-607-7811 Fax: 909-607-9104
Email: drucker@CGU.edu
Internet: www.cgu.edu/drucker

Claremont Graduate University

The task of OCSCR is made somewhat easier by the fact that a substantial number of Drucker MBAs are part-timers holding jobs they wish to keep. Even so, students give the service only average grades, telling us that there is a "need for a greater number of recruiters and/or opportunities for best jobs." One student reports hopefully that "Career Services needs improvement. This will improve soon, as the majority of students become full-time."

STUDENT/CAMPUS LIFE

Although the balance is shifting from part-time to full-time students, Drucker's student body still consists of a large part-time contingent. Students consider their group a "diverse mix that includes a former Navy pilot who flew in the Antarctic, a Northwestern grad trying to break into singing, and a Bank of China investment banker who managed bond issues." There is a large contingent of foreign nationals at Drucker. The American minority population here, however, is slight. Students "vary greatly in experience, level of social interaction, and ability to contribute to class," but the best among them are "collaborative, intelligent, and team-oriented . . . very motivated and always coming out with initiatives that contribute to the well-being of the academic community and the local community." One student tells us that his "classmates are likely to pose useful challenges in the classroom."

As at most schools with large part-time populations, Drucker's extracurricular world is subdued. Students don't mind much, explaining that "Life here is very peaceful, but if you want excitement, you can take a short drive to downtown, the beach, or Santa Monica. The atmosphere is very conducive to learning." Another student notes that "In the two years I have been here, the social life has improved dramatically, as has student involvement." All students join the Graduate Management Association, which sponsors both career-related events (such as corporate speakers), and social events like the annual spring formal and the occasional barbecue. Claremont's setting, not far from the picturesque San Gabriel Mountains, is breathtaking, and the southern California climate is conducive to all sorts of outdoor activities. About the only gripe students voice about life here is that the "gym facilities and on-campus housing could stand some improvement."

ADMISSIONS

According to the admissions office, college GPA and work experience are considered most important. Then, in descending order of importance, GMAT score, letters of recommendation and essays, interview, and extracurricular activities. Adds the school, "Extracurriculars and work experience are not required, but are considered. Interviews are recommended." Admissions decisions are made on a rolling basis. Students may defer admission for up to one year.

FINANCIAL FACTS

Tuition	$23,543
Fees	$130
Cost of books	$1,008
Room & board (on-/off-campus)	$12,024/$15,000
% of students receiving aid	74
% first-year students receiving aid	72
% aid that is merit based	85
% of students receiving loans	28
% of students receiving paid internships	48
Average award package	$23,000
Average grant	$5,000

ADMISSIONS

# of applications received	301
% applicants accepted	54
% acceptees attending	63
Average GMAT	573
Average GPA	3.13
Application fee (in-/out-of-state)	$40/$40
Early decision program available	Yes
Early decision deadline	Rolling
Early decision notification	within 30 days
Regular application deadline	Rolling
Regular notification	Rolling
Admission may be deferred?	Yes
Maximum length of deferment	1 year
Transfer students accepted?	Yes
Nonfall admission available?	Yes
Admission process need-blind?	Yes

APPLICANTS ALSO LOOK AT

University of California—Los Angeles, University of Southern California, Stanford University, University of California—Berkeley, Dartmouth College, Boston University, New York University, University of Texas at Austin

EMPLOYMENT PROFILE

% of grads employed immediately	74
% grads employed within six months	94
Average starting salary	$57,593

Grads employed by field (avg. salary):
Consulting	25%	NR
Finance	40%	NR
Marketing	30%	NR
Operations	5%	NR

UNIVERSITY OF COLORADO AT BOULDER
Graduate School of Business Administration

OVERVIEW

Type of school	public
Affiliation	none
Environment	urban
Academic calendar	semester
Schedule	full-time/part-time

STUDENTS

Enrollment of parent institution	25,000
Enrollment of business school	316
% male/female	71/29
% out-of-state	45
% part-time	47
% minorities	9
% international (# of countries represented)	12 (11)
Average age at entry	28
Average years work experience at entry	5

ACADEMICS

Student/faculty ratio	25:1
% female faculty	17
% minority faculty	9
Hours of study per day	4.34

SPECIALTIES

Strengths of faculty and curriculum in Technology/ Innovation Management, Finance, Marketing, Entrepreneurship. Emphasis in curriculum placed on real-world, hands-on learning through individual and group projects with local and national companies.

JOINT DEGREES

JD/MBA, 4 years full-time; MBA/MS in Telecommunications, 5–6 semesters full-time

SPECIAL PROGRAMS

Summer course held in London studies international finance and economics of the European community.

STUDY ABROAD PROGRAMS

SURVEY SAYS...
HITS
Social life
Cozy student community
Boulder

MISSES
Profs not great teachers
MIS/operations
School clubs

PROMINENT ALUMNI

G. Chris Andersen, Paine Webber, Inc.; Marcia Pryde, A.T. Kearney, Inc.; William W. Reynolds, Owner and President, W.W. Reynolds Companies; Jerry McMorris, CEO, Nations Way Transport Services and President, Colorado Rockies

ACADEMICS

The Graduate School of Business Administration at Boulder boasts a surprising number of strong offerings for a program of its size. More intriguing still, Colorado's strengths lie in such off-the-beaten-path disciplines as entrepreneurship, telecommunications, and real estate. And although a Boulder MBA is expensive for out-of-state students, native Coloradans can enjoy this unexpected bounty at a bargain-basement price.

Our survey shows a number of Colorado students reporting that "our entrepreneurship is the best in the nation." Offered jointly with the College of Engineering, Boulder's Center for Entrepreneurship emphasizes internships, field projects, and mentoring in its efforts to create tomorrow's venture capitalists. A joint MBA/MS in Telecommunications, also offered in conjunction with the engineering school, benefits from the fact that major telecommunications companies US West and TCI are located in the region. Similarly, Technology and Innovation Management majors profit from "one of the largest clusters of technology firms in the United States" located right in Colorado. Students praise the Real Estate Center for "the fabulous support they give. Great for networking and internships, as well as mentors." Students are less upbeat about Colorado's Accounting, Operations, and Marketing departments, giving all below average marks.

Colorado professors "are a mixed bag." When it comes to teaching skills, "approximately half are excellent, the other half are subpar." Students agree that professors try hard to make themselves accessible to students; writes one, "Professors are willing to go out of their way to help students achieve their academic and career goals." The administration "is great—both administration and faculty have an open-door policy and are willing to listen to students' issues/ concerns." First-year foundation classes, organized in a "lockstep system," are "great and let you know right off the bat that this program is very well run." On the downside, students complain that "the library could stand to be updated a little" and also feel that "a dedicated MBA computer lab would be useful. The current labs, while technologically excellent, are commonly overrun with undergrads."

PLACEMENT AND RECRUITING

University of Colorado at Boulder established an MBA Career Placement Office (CPO) recently; previously the MBA program had relied on a career services office serving the entire university community. Colorado's CPO offers "a variety of services to MBA students including career management workshops, professional development seminars, and job-development outreach and hosts a variety of networking opportunities with top regional employers throughout the year." Just fewer than 100 companies recruited on campus in the last year, and many more participated in an on-campus career fair. CU also participates in the Rocky Mountain MBA Consortium. The CPO reports, "Strong ties with the host of emerging and dynamic growth companies in the Boulder/Denver area also help to promote a supply of high-quality internships and job opportunities."

Dina Maestas, Admissions Coordinator
Campus Box 419 Boulder, CO 80309-0419
Admissions: 303-492-8397 Fax: 303-492-1727
Email: busgrad@colorado.EDU
Internet: http://bus.colorado.edu

Students have mixed feelings about the Colorado CPO. On one hand, respondents give it only average grades. On the other hand, the current survey shows considerable improvement from previous years' results. Furthermore, some students are extremely enthusiastic about the service. One writes, "The MBA-specific career placement office works its butt off to match students with desirable companies. The Center for Entrepreneurship is able to find internships in Denver/ Boulder because of its strong ties to the community."

STUDENT/CAMPUS LIFE

With small minority and international populations, Colorado's students tend toward a certain sameness. The vast majority of students here are white males from reasonably affluent backgrounds. Sums up one first-year, "students here are like anywhere else: good and bad. Most are intelligent, many are shallow and cliquish. Most are materialistic and a bit spoiled. Some are egotistical and antagonistic. Others are very nice people, supportive and respectful." Warns another, "some are lacking in social skills. Almost none lack in business skills, however, and the majority of students are great, friendly, and knowledgeable." The mountain setting attracts a "few token shiny-happy skiers," writes one student, "but the vast majority are dedicated and intelligent."

"If you enjoy balancing social life with a solid academic life," notes one student, "Boulder offers the perfect mix." Our survey shows that most MBAs at Boulder spend a manageable twenty-five hours a week studying. Participation in campus clubs and organizations is also high, and the university's many high-profile intercollegiate sporting events are popular among MBAs. Colorado students "value sports and leisure time. Most are athletic and love sports. People appreciate the quality of life here," which includes "many opportunities for socializing" and a "relaxed, friendly atmosphere." Boulder is "beautiful and fun" but also a "fast-growing city that's much too expensive." One student writes, approvingly, "being in a small city gives you the advantage of concentrating on your work," while many others laud the accessibility of "fabulous snow skiing." Denver is less than an hour's drive from campus, and students make the trip whenever they yearn for big-city amenities.

ADMISSIONS

According to the admissions office, the entire application is evaluated with special consideration given to GMAT score, work experience, and college GPA. Essays, letters of recommendation, and extracurricular activities are also reviewed. The MBA program has three rounds of admission for its full-time program. Applicants are encouraged to apply early.

FINANCIAL FACTS

Tuition (in-/out-of-state)	$3,758/$15,156
Fees (in-/out-of-state)	$361/$361
Cost of books	$750
Room & board (on-/off-campus)	$5,288/$10,000
% aid that is merit based	32
% of students receiving loans	65
% of students receiving grants	25
% of students receiving paid internships	95
Average grant	$1,750
Average graduation debt	$20,000

ADMISSIONS

# of applications received	384
% applicants accepted	51
% acceptees attending	44
Average GMAT (range)	624 (590–660)
Minimum TOEFL	500
Average GPA (range)	3.21 (2.95–3.51)
Application fee (in-/out-of-state)	$40/NR
Early decision program available	Yes
Early decision deadline	December 15
Early decision notification	February 15
Regular application deadline	February 15
Regular notification	April 15
Admission may be deferred?	Yes
Transfer students accepted?	No
Nonfall admission available?	No
Admission process need-blind?	Yes

APPLICANTS ALSO LOOK AT

University of Texas at Austin, University of Denver, University of Washington, University of Arizona, University of California—Berkeley, Arizona State University, University of Michigan Business School, Northwestern University

EMPLOYMENT PROFILE

Placement rate (%)	98
# of companies recruiting on campus	146
% of grads employed immediately	68
% grads employed within six months	98
Average starting salary	$59,514

Grads employed by field (avg. salary):

Consulting	22%	$64,833
Entrepreneurship	5%	$60,000
Finance	31%	$63,500
Human Resources	2%	$52,500
Marketing	31%	$51,200
MIS	2%	$55,000
Operations	2%	$75,000
Other	5%	$59,250

COLUMBIA UNIVERSITY
Columbia Business School

OVERVIEW

Type of school	private
Affiliation	none
Environment	urban
Academic calendar	terms
Schedule	full-time only

STUDENTS

Enrollment of parent institution	21,545
Enrollment of business school	1,373
% male/female	63/37
% minorities	20
% international (# of countries represented)	28 (60)
Average age at entry	27
Average years work experience at entry	4

ACADEMICS

Student/faculty ratio	7:1
% female faculty	18
Hours of study per day	4.24

SPECIALTIES

Accounting, Business Law and Taxation; Finance and Economics; Management; Management Science; and Marketing. In addition, specialized programs — such as the Entrepreneurship; Media, Entertainment and Communications; Public and Nonprofit Management; and Real Estate Programs — provide an opportunity to focus on cutting-edge issues.

JOINT DEGREES

MBA/MS Industrial Engineering; MBA/MS Social Work; MBA/MS Urban Planning; MBA/EdD Education Administration; MBA/MS Journalism; MBA/MS Mining Engineering; MBA/MS Nursing; MBA/MS Operations Research; MBA/EdD Higher Education; MBA/Master of Public Health; MBA/ Master of International Affairs; MBA/Juris Doctor; MBA/BA or BS General Studies; MBA/MD Medicine; MBA/DDS Dental Surgery

SPECIAL PROGRAMS

The Executive MBA

STUDY ABROAD PROGRAMS

Australia, Austria, Belgium, Brazil, China, Finland, France, Germany, Israel, Italy, Mexico, Netherlands, Phillipines, Singapore, Spain, Sweden, Switzerland, and United Kingdom

SURVEY SAYS...

HITS
Quality of recruiting
Finance

MISSES
Campus is ugly
Impossible to get into classes

ACADEMICS

Columbia Business School boasts a world-class faculty, state-of-the-art facilities, and a balanced integrated curriculum. One more aspect which gives it a major advantage over most other MBA programs. That advantage, of course, is its location in New York City, one of America's premier business centers and perhaps the finance capital of the world. But Columbia also brings all of the above-mentioned assets to the table, thereby offering a formidable university-city tandem. As one student puts it, "Columbia mirrors its city host—a beautifully mixed elixir of personality and ambition."

Finance is still the powerhouse department at Columbia—"It's a great school for finance-oriented careers!" bragged a typical MBA—although students also commend the "very challenging classes in entrepreneurship and management of organizations." Others praise the "unique concentration in entertainment and media," while many voice approval for the "strong international emphasis" in their courses. Some students, however, still complain that "some nontraditional areas—nonprofit, for example—need improvement," while others point out that Columbia is "still weak in some nonfinance areas, but constantly making improvements."

First-year studies at Columbia are entirely devoted to the "well-integrated" core curriculum, which focuses on four themes: globalization, total quality management, ethics, and human resource management. Each group of entering students—Columbia admits two groups, one in September and one in January—is divided into "clusters" of approximately sixty students who take all core courses together. During their second year, Columbia MBAs may choose a field of concentration (although they are not required to do so). Eleven areas of concentration are available, with some departments offering areas of subconcentration; finance majors, for example, have the option of concentrating in corporate financial management, futures markets analysis, investment management, or real estate finance. Students may also develop their own areas of subconcentration in conjunction with the many other leading academic departments within the university.

Students give their professors mixed grades, noting that "we have some excellent professors but we also have some poor professors" and that "professors in general are more research- than teaching-focused, but you learn who's good." Several students, however, volunteered that "most of the professors will go out of their way to help students out. They make themselves accessible outside the classroom." Another points out that "the New York City location means excellent adjunct professors who are current leaders in their fields."

PLACEMENT AND RECRUITING

Columbia Business School maintains one of the strongest worldwide recruiting programs, consistently ranking among the top-five favorite hunting grounds of corporate recruiters and, increasingly, for entrepreneurial start-up companies. The school's location and relationships with global firms and industry leaders create unique opportunities for students. Explains one student, "Due to the fact that so many class projects involve major companies and respected CEOs, quality interaction is a given. Access to high-powered, successful businesspeople is

Linda B. Meehan, Assistant Dean and Executive Director of Admission and
Financial Aid
105 Uris Hall, New York, NY 10027
Admissions: 212-854-1961 Fax: 212-662-6754
Email: gohermes@claven.gsb.columbia.edu
Internet: www.columbia.edu/cu/business/

Columbia University

not a problem." Many students take advantage of networking opportunities through Columbia's strong base of more than ninety international alumni clubs, as well as the more than 10,000 alumni who live in and around New York. Writes one student, "There are so many alums on the 'Street' [quotes added]. They are very receptive to phone calls asking for advice or for finding potential connections. Networking is so easy due to the attention given Columbia education and the location of the school." More than half of all MBAs wind up with jobs in finance, naturally skewing the focus of CU's placement office. Complains one nonfinance major, "Get off the finance horse! We need to send more people to places other than investment banks."

STUDENT/CAMPUS LIFE

Columbia is by no means a cookie-cutter institution. In describing their classmates, Columbia MBAs report that "The diversity is great. Everyone has an interesting background and is going places." Writes another student, "They are all different from me—perhaps the greatest thing about 'em." The high-pressure program leaves them "Focused, slightly stressed, but definitely not competitive with each other in a negative way." Most arrive with "impressive prior experience." Sums up one student, "They're awesome! They're fun, interesting, highly motivated individuals who truly care about the school, the student body, and the community."

Columbia's heavy workload means that life in b-school "is hectic and the days are long—often 9 a.m. to 8 p.m. You spend a lot of time (several hours per day) working in groups. It is rewarding, though." New York City adds to the pressure-cooker environment; explains one student, "The pace is hectic since we are in Manhattan. The sense of overload provided by the city permeates the school and little is done by the school to provide a more manageable environment." New York, however, also contributes numerous positives in the areas of both business and pleasure. As one student notes, "The Metropolitan Opera, Carnegie Hall, the Garden, and Broadway shows are all a 15–20 minute subway ride away! Wall Street is also easily accessible." On campus "There are organizations for everyone: community service, follies, yearbook, happy hours, study tours abroad, the Management Consulting Association, etc." The Distinguished Leader Lecture Series "brings so many heavy hitters to campus; I have learned more, I think, about the real world through these speakers than I have in the classroom." At least one student feels that Columbia is "the best school for women. There is a very strong Columbia Women in Business organization."

ADMISSIONS

Applicants are evaluated in three categories: professional promise, personal characteristics, and academic credentials. The Admissions Committee looks for well-rounded people from diverse economic, social, ethnic, geographic, and professional backgrounds. Ideal applicants have demonstrated leadership, have the ability to work as members of teams, are active in the community, and can contribute to the academic experience of their peers. Requirements include: minimum two years' work experience, GMAT, bachelor's degree, essays, letters of recommendation, and TOEFL for international students whose native language is not English.

PROMINENT ALUMNI

Warren Buffett, Chairman, Berkshire Hathaway Inc.; Henry Kravis, Founding Partner, Kohlberg Kravis Roberts & Company; Rochelle Lazarus, CEO, Ogilvy & Mather Worldwide

FINANCIAL FACTS

Tuition	$26,520
Fees	$1,250
Cost of books	$1,030
Room & board (on-/off-campus)	$9,918/$9,918
% of students receiving aid	70
% aid that is merit based	6
% of students receiving loans	65
% of students receiving grants	35
Average award package	$39,000
Average grant	$4,900

ADMISSIONS

# of applications received	5,719
% applicants accepted	12
% acceptees attending	74
Average GMAT	680
Minimum TOEFL	610
Average GPA	3.45
Application fee (in-/out-of-state)	$160/$160
Early decision program available	Yes
Early decision deadline	October 15
Early decision notification	Rolling
Regular application deadline	April 20
Regular notification	Rolling
Admission may be deferred?	Yes
Maximum length of deferment	Case-by-case basis
Transfer students accepted?	No
Nonfall admission available?	Yes
Admission process need-blind?	Yes

APPLICANTS ALSO LOOK AT

Harvard University, University of Pennsylvania, Stanford University, Duke University

EMPLOYMENT PROFILE

Placement rate (%)		98
% of grads employed immediately		98
Average starting salary		$132,000

Grads employed by field (avg. salary):

Accounting	2%	$127,500
Consulting	23%	$137,000
Finance	53%	$136,500
General Management	2%	$102,500
Marketing	8%	$97,500
MIS	2%	$133,000
Operations	1%	$120,000
Other	4%	$136,000
Strategic Planning	2%	$136,000
Venture Capital	3%	$139,000

UNIVERSITY OF CONNECTICUT
School of Business Administration

OVERVIEW

Type of school	public
Affiliation	none
Environment	suburban
Academic calendar	semester

STUDENTS

Enrollment of parent institution	22,979
Enrollment of business school	1,006
% male/female	58/42
% out-of-state	1
% part-time	89
% minorities	7
% international (# of countries represented)	32 (14)
Average age at entry	28
Average years work experience at entry	5

ACADEMICS

Student/faculty ratio	40:1
% female faculty	18
% minority faculty	12
Hours of study per day	4.01

SPECIALTIES

Strong in Information Technology, Finance, Accounting and Health Systems. Curriculum emphasizes new technology and globalization as themes that cut across all disciplines. One of a handful of programs, worldwide, that requires a laptop computer as a "tool of the trade."

JOINT DEGREES

JD/MBA; MD/MBA; MSW/MBA; MBA/MA International Studies, 2.5 years

SPECIAL PROGRAMS

Wolff Program in Entrepreneurial, Health Care Management, Advanced Business Certificate, Business Plan Competition, Mentor Program

STUDY ABROAD PROGRAMS

Maastricht, Netherlands; EM Lyon, France; IELS Strasbourg, France; Stuttgart, Germany; Laval University, Canada; Concordia University, Canada

SURVEY SAYS...
HITS
Alumni helpful in job search
Study groups
Star faculty

MISSES
Campus is ugly
School clubs
Unfriendly students

PROMINENT ALUMNI

Denis J. Nayden, President, G.E. Capital; Denis M. McCarthy, Chairman and President and CEO, Fidelity Management Trust Co.

ACADEMICS

A reasonable tuition and strength in a variety of areas are what attract MBAs to the University of Connecticut's School of Business Administration. Students tout the "very good quantitative concentrations," especially UConn's "excellent accounting program," which is one of only three AACSB-accredited accounting programs in the region, as well as the strong marketing, finance, and real estate departments. All students here must follow a tightly prescribed first-year curriculum that allows no electives. Among the required courses is one covering international business, a nice complement to the multinational flavor of UConn's MBA student body. Enthuses one student, "I participated in one group that had one person from Uganda, three people from Taiwan, and one from India." Second year is devoted to students' areas of concentration, although students must also complete two seminars (one in leadership, the other in planning); students may opt to begin second-year studies during the summer following first year, which allows them to graduate in sixteen months. For some, the curriculum at UConn is too rigid: complains one student, "Too many required courses, preventing us from focusing on any single subject. Also, the courses start out at a high level. This is a bad school if you have no business background." On the other hand, "Teamwork and group activities, as well as presentation skills, are promoted throughout the program and in all classes." During the second year, this takes the form of a consulting project. As one student explains, "The consulting project that we do in the second year with the Connecticut Small Business Association is very important. We help small Connecticut companies achieve growth." Still, some students resent all the enforced teamwork; notes one, "Group work is too big a part of our program. It allows those who do less to do better and penalizes those who do well on their own." Professors here receive respectable marks from their students. "We have very strong, well-respected professors with excellent teaching methods," writes one; another points out that "the professors in management, operations, and finance are particularly strong." Several students, however, feel that "sometimes it seems as if professors do not communicate with each other at all, piling the work up in two- to three-week periods with tests and reports." The administration receives student accolades for "constantly seeking ways to improve the lives of students." Students also applaud the high quality of the business libraries and the "high-tech classrooms," an asset that will only improve when UConn builds its new MBA building (see "Student Campus Life," opposite, for more details).

PLACEMENT AND RECRUITING

Students are satisfied with the efforts UConn's MBA Program Placement Center makes to place them with area businesses, particularly in the areas of accounting and finance. Writes one student, "The school's connections with local alumni and [the] business community are excellent. The mentor program is very helpful and the mentors are quite responsive." However, students also report that "The school's business connections, unfortunately, are limited to the northeast region. The school is not so well recognized outside the region. We need to increase the number of students here; that might help."

Richard N. Dino, Associate Dean and Director
368 Fairfield Road, U-41MBA Storrs, CT 06269
Admissions: 860-486-2872 Fax: 860-486-5222
Email: NR
Internet: www.sba.uconn.edu

University of Connecticut

UConn placement efforts begin during first year, with seminars and one-on-one coaching in such areas as resume building, interviewing, and salary negotiation. Between the first and second years, summer internships—both at home and abroad—are widely available. Efforts step up during the second year, during which the student-run Graduate Business Association coordinates Career Interview Conferences and the Executive Speaker Series, which brings leading execs to the campus to offer career advice and to press the flesh.

STUDENT/CAMPUS LIFE

Students report that "minority/ethnic representation is very high" at UConn, mostly because of the "tremendous number of international students. They make up about half the student body. The majority of [the foreign nationals], unfortunately, do not seem comfortable sharing ideas and experiences." Nearly three-quarters of UConn MBAs arrive with previous work experience; about one-quarter are Connecticut natives. In assessing their classmates, several students admit "there is a significant variance among the students. Some of the students are extremely intelligent and motivated and could be in a top-ten program. However, there are others who do not belong in any MBA program."

Storrs, UConn's hometown, receives mixed reviews from MBAs. Some see the quiet, low-key setting it provides as the perfect counterbalance to the pressures of the academic program. "It's rural and quaint, and in an excellent location, because it is between New York and Boston," writes one student. "A beautiful area, very safe," adds another. Others, however, find the peace and quiet a little too peaceful. Warns one student, "There is no life on campus. The town offers very little to do." This dearth of activity is compounded by the fact that "the campus and campus life are geared toward undergrads" and that the UConn MBA program is "commuter oriented. Not much happening on weekends." Among positives, students tell us that "The Graduate Business Association and the dedicated MBA Lounge improve campus life." The GBA serves as the hub of MBA extracurricular life, providing "opportunities for networking with business professionals as well as socializing with fellow students." Students also love UConn's intercollegiate athletics ("all our teams are contenders," brags one) and the "excellent athletic recreation facility on campus." A new MBA building has encountered some delays, but construction should be underway by the start of the 1999–2000 academic year.

ADMISSIONS

According to the admissions office, the following three criteria are considered most important and are weighted equally: your GMAT score, work experience, and college GPA. Then come your essays, letters of recommendation, and extracurriculars. Writes the school, "We do not use cutoffs for GMAT scores or GPA. Evidence of high promise in one area can offset average accomplishment in another." Admissions decisions are made on a rolling basis throughout the year. There are no deadlines until the class has filled up or April 1. Students typically receive a decision within one month of completion of their file. They may defer admission for up to 11 months, depending on the circumstances.

FINANCIAL FACTS

Tuition (in-/out-of-state)	$5,118/$13,298
Fees (in-/out-of-state)	$948/$948
Cost of books	$10,471
Room & board (on-/off-campus)	$7,126/$7,494
% first-year students receiving aid	11

ADMISSIONS

# of applications received	252
% applicants accepted	49
% acceptees attending	37
Average GMAT (range)	601 (530–640)
Minimum TOEFL	550
Average GPA (range)	3.30 (3.00–3.60)
Application fee (in-/out-of-state)	$40/$45
Early decision program available	No
Regular application deadline	April 1
Admission may be deferred?	Yes
Maximum length of deferment	11 months
Transfer students accepted?	Yes
Nonfall admission available?	No
Admission process need-blind?	Yes

APPLICANTS ALSO LOOK AT

New York University, Boston University, University of Massachusetts, University of Maryland, Penn State University, University of Texas at Austin, Yale University, Columbia University

EMPLOYMENT PROFILE

Placement rate (%)	96
# of companies recruiting on campus	48
% of grads employed immediately	80
% grads employed within six months	96
Average starting salary	$52,600

Grads employed by field (avg. salary):

Accounting	7%	$44,600
Consulting	22%	$52,300
Entrepreneurship	2%	NR
Finance	24%	$49,000
Human Resources	8%	$56,000
Marketing	17%	$46,700
MIS	9%	$53,600
Operations	7%	$53,100
Other	3%	$46,900
Strategic Planning	2%	NR

CORNELL UNIVERSITY
Johnson Graduate School of Management

OVERVIEW

Type of school	private
Affiliation	none
Environment	rural
Academic calendar	semester
Schedule	full-time only

STUDENTS

Enrollment of parent institution	20,000
Enrollment of business school	576
% male/female	73/27
% minorities	7
% international (# of countries represented)	32 (40)
Average age at entry	29
Average years work experience at entry	5

ACADEMICS

Student/faculty ratio	9:1
Hours of study per day	4.71

SPECIALTIES
Strengths of faculty and curriculum in the flexibility of the academic program, access to the rich resources of Cornell U, collaborative community with easy access to faculty members.

JOINT DEGREES
MILR/MBA; MBA/MEng, 5 semesters; MBA/MA Asian Studies, 6–7 semesters; JD/MBA, 4 years

SPECIAL PROGRAMS
Immersion Learning, Twelve-Month Option for scientists and engineers, Park Leadership Fellows Program, Parker Center for Investment Research, Center for Leadership in Dynamic Organizations

STUDY ABROAD PROGRAMS
18 institutions with which the school partners

SURVEY SAYS...
HITS
Easy to get into courses
Students are happy

PROMINENT ALUMNI
Kenneth Derr, CEO, Chevron; Lou Noto, CEO, Mobil; Charles Knight, Chairman and CEO, Emerson Electric; Michael Durham, CEO, Sabre Technology Group; David Duffield, CEO, People Soft; Martin Grass, CEO, Rite-Aid; James Hausleim, Chairman, Sunglass Hut; Irene Rosenfeld, CEO, Kraft Canada.

ACADEMICS

Students at Cornell University's Johnson Graduate School of Management say that their school is the complete package: great curriculum, superior teachers, a supportive administration, and grade-A facilities. With assets like these, it's no wonder that so many students are willing to make the two-year commitment to live in a remote part of upstate New York.

Several unique offerings distinguish the Johnson MBA program. First is a twelve-month MBA option, available to students with advanced degrees in science or engineering. Twelve-month MBAs take an abbreviated core curriculum. Immersion learning in brand management, investment banking, managerial finance, and manufacturing is another unusual feature of the program. Leadership skills classes, experiential workshops led by trainers from GE, McKinsey & Company, Sprint, and other companies, are another distinctive feature of the Johnson MBA. Finally there is the Park Leadership Fellows program, which supplies thirty full-tuition, two-year fellowships and an enhanced leadership development curriculum to entering students who are U.S. citizens and who have a high level of academic achievement, have demonstrated exceptional leadership skills, strong professional accomplishments, and a commitment to community service.

Students appreciate the flexible academic curriculum at Johnson, which provides the "freedom to make your own curriculum." Johnson not only allows students some choices within the core but also provides the opportunity for two electives during first-year studies. Notes one student, "Selecting classes every semester is like attending a mile-long buffet table." Second-year studies are devoted to electives. Students are encouraged to choose courses offered elsewhere within the university to tailor their education toward their goals. Students speak particularly highly of Johnson's marketing program; entrepreneurial studies also garner praise.

Students are uniform in their acclaim for professors, telling us that "the faculty are warm (take students to lunch, play sports) and proactive (revise curriculum based on students' requests)." Students are similarly sanguine about the administration. Writes one MBA, "Professors and administration act with students' interests in mind. There is a strong partnership there." To top it all off, Cornell has recently renovated Sage Hall, the b-school facility. This nineteenth-century landmark has been brought up to twenty-first-century standards. The new "management education environment" boasts 1,400 network ports, real-time data feeds, videoconferencing, advanced visualization capabilities, multimedia production facilities, and technology-enhanced classrooms.

PLACEMENT AND RECRUITING

Cornell's Career Services Office (CSO) received mixed reviews from students in the past, but by all accounts the service has improved in recent years. Writes one student, "Many new companies are recruiting on campus," confirming similar claims made by the school itself. Still, other students feel that "recruiting is still too centered in the Northeast. We need more national recruiters." Cornell has worked hard to improve recruiting in both technology and strategy consulting, in which the CSO has previously been viewed as weak. The school believes that

Nathalie Grinblatt, Director of Admissions
111 Sarge Hall, Ithaca, NY 14853
Admissions: 607-255-4526 Fax: 607-255-0065
Email: mba@cornell.edu
Internet: www.johnson.cornell.edu

Cornell University

the recent addition of the Parker Center for Investment Research to the Johnson School will improve graduates' prospects in the world of finance.

A number of student-run activities supplement the CSO's efforts: "The Consulting Symposium, Week on Wall Street, and the Marketing Symposium are all great recruiting events," according to one student. Johnson alumni, more than 8,000 strong, are also reportedly very helpful to students in their job searches.

STUDENT/CAMPUS LIFE

Cornell's reputation for collaboration is well earned; Johnson MBAs speak just as highly of their classmates as they do of the professors, administrators, and curriculum. Writes one, "The students are a huge plus. They're the type of people who are great to work with on projects, then go have a drink with." These are companionable folks; as one put it, "We're like a big family outside of class." An MBA tells us this illuminating story: "One student missed two weeks of class due to a family crisis and a fellow student took it upon himself to videotape all the classes and mail them to her so she wouldn't fall too far behind. This is typical of the close-knit, caring atmosphere." Perhaps it takes an extra-special student to attend b-school so far outside a major business center. Students certainly think so; as one explains, "This is a true community where people have made a conscious decision to relocate to Ithaca."

By forgoing an urban setting, Cornell students get to enjoy a beautiful campus in the quaint, if sometimes too wintry, town of Ithaca, New York. The university community supports "clusters of bars and ethnic restaurants" in town. According to our respondents, Cornell is "a perfect place for married students." Said one MBA, "The Joint Ventures Club (for spouses and significant others) is a life-saver. It gives my wife and kids a support system and alleviates any guilt I feel when I put in long hours at the library. I think they are having more fun at Cornell than I am." Extracurricular activities abound. "Golf and hockey are the big sports—about fifty men and fifty women are involved in the school's three hockey teams." An unusual attraction is the Frozen Assets Hockey Team, an all-female group of MBAs who compete against Dartmouth's Tuck School in an annual tournament. Students happily report that there is "lots of socializing because the workload is reasonable" and describe the overall atmosphere as "very collegiate with all the clubs, winter formal, spring formal, school-sponsored coffee breaks, happy hours, and Thursday bowling outings."

ADMISSIONS

The admissions office considers, in no particular order, the type of undergrad institution attended, your GMAT scores, work experience, essays, academic record, letters of recommendation, and extracurricular activities. Admissions recommends at least three years work experience prior to application; five years is average. Adds the school, "As we put together a diverse class—one in which students can expect to learn as much from their peers as from the faculty—we look for strong leadership skills, maturity and initiative, demonstrated achievement, and the potential for career success." The school has three decision deadlines; notification occurs within eight to ten weeks of the deadline.

FINANCIAL FACTS

Tuition	$24,400
Cost of books	$890
Room & board	$7,400
% of students receiving aid	55
% aid that is merit based	27
% of students receiving loans	55
% of students receiving grants	27
Average award package	$22,969
Average grant	$17,588
Average graduation debt	$47,639

ADMISSIONS

# of applications received	3,034
% applicants accepted	18
% acceptees attending	56
Average GMAT	678
Minimum TOEFL	600
Average GPA	3.47
Application fee (in-/out-of-state)	$150/$150
Early decision program available	No
Regular application deadline	March 15
Final notification	Approx. 8–10 weeks after deadline
Transfer students accepted?	No
Admission process need-blind?	Yes

APPLICANTS ALSO LOOK AT

University of Pennsylvania, Dartmouth College, New York University, Duke University, Northwestern University, Stanford University, Columbia University, University of Chicago

EMPLOYMENT PROFILE

Placement rate (%)	97
# of companies recruiting on campus	262
% of grads employed immediately	92
% grads employed within six months	97
Average starting salary	$76,000

Grads employed by field (avg. salary):

Consulting	23%	$85,100
Finance	21%	$72,200
General Management	6%	$76,000
Human Resources	3%	$64,800
Marketing	18%	$69,300
MIS	2%	$73,500
Operations	1%	$72,100
Strategic Planning	3%	$78,400
Investment Banking	21%	$76,000
Other	3%	$77,200

CUNY BARUCH COLLEGE
Zicklin School of Business

OVERVIEW

Type of school	public
Affiliation	none
Environment	urban
Academic calendar	semester
Schedule	full-time/part-time/evening

STUDENTS

Enrollment of parent institution	15,091
Enrollment of business school	1,501
% male/female	57/43
% out-of-state	26
% part-time	59
% minorities	17
% international (# of countries represented)	26 (65)
Average age at entry	28
Average years work experience at entry	5

ACADEMICS

Student/faculty ratio	40:1
% female faculty	16
Hours of study per day	3.26

SPECIALTIES
Research-oriented faculty; many faculty consult; many major options available with numerous courses in each major

JOINT DEGREES
JD/MBA, 122 credits

SPECIAL PROGRAMS
Full-time MBA program, executive MBA, executive MS in finance

STUDY ABROAD PROGRAMS
France, Germany

SURVEY SAYS...
HITS
Star faculty
Ethnic and racial diversity
Library

MISSES
Gym
School clubs
Unfriendly students

PROMINENT ALUMNI
Abraham Beame, former Mayor of New York City; Dov Schlein, President and CEO, Republic National Bank of New York; Bernard Schwartz, Chairman, Loral Corp.

ACADEMICS

The Baruch School of Business has recently changed its name to the Zicklin School of Business. Larry Zicklin, a 1957 graduate, donated $18 million to the school in May of 1998—one of the ten largest gifts ever to a business school. The contribution is earmarked for transforming Baruch from a predominantly part-time MBA program (many of its students work, taking classes at night) into a world-class, full-time program. According to Dean Sidney Lirtzman, the gift "comes at a critical moment in our history, as the faculty restructures the school to create a great national full-time MBA program of such excellence that it will establish our ranking within the top twenty-five business schools in the United States." What the future holds for Baruch/Zicklin, then, is a question to be answered gradually over the next several years, as the City University of New York administration determines exactly how this money will be spent.

In the immediate future, Baruch should continue to serve a majority of part-timers in search of an affordable MBA. Cost, in fact, is the reason most respondents give for choosing Baruch. The accounting department, generally considered Baruch's strongest, runs a close second. Writes one student, "Baruch is THE place to get your CPA in New York." Students also give the finance classes high marks, but are less sanguine about marketing, operations, and communications courses. In most departments, professors are "great, very dedicated, but a few rotten apples are always present." As at many government-controlled schools, the administration at Baruch is mired in red tape. "A bureaucratic nightmare," is how one student puts it. Another simply states, "I can't believe how inefficient the administrative staff here is. They are horrible!" A former undergraduate and current MBA, while not exactly contradicting his colleagues, notes hopefully that the administration "has improved a lot since I graduated from undergraduate six years ago." Chief among students' complaints is the difficulty of enrolling in popular courses. Many students report that "building facilities are currently poor," but add, "that will change with the new fourteen-story building that is under construction." The facility is slated to open in 2000.

Core courses constitute the first half of a Baruch MBA; the second half entails coursework covering students' chosen area of specialization. A select group of full-time MBAs participate in the Jack Nash Honors program. The Nash program places students in their own cohort of Baruch MBAs for coursework and gives them access to program-specific research projects (that include a $5,000 stipend). Nash students have their own faculty advisor, their own meeting area (the MBA Honors Center), and study in new multimedia classrooms. Participants regard the program as one of Baruch's major drawing points.

PLACEMENT AND RECRUITING

Baruch recently opened an Office of Graduate Career Services (GCS), dedicated exclusively to the placing of MBA and MS students. The GCS office offers both students and corporate clients individualized attention by identifying and helping to clarify needs, and by matching student prospects to hiring criteria. So far,

Michael Wynne, Director of Graduate Admissions
17 Lexington Avenue, Box H-0880, New York, NY 10010
Admissions: 212-802-2330 Fax: 212-802-2335
Email: graduate_admissions@baruch.cuny.edu
Internet: bus.baruch.cuny.edu

CUNY Baruch College

however, students have not noticed an improvement over the old career services office, which served both the graduate and undergraduate populations. More than half of Baruch's MBAs give the service average or below-average grades. Satisfaction levels with both the placement office and with on-campus recruiting here are among the lowest in our survey.

Among those hiring Baruch MBAs in recent history have been: Deloitte & Touche, Andersen Consulting, Coopers & Lybrand, Republic National Bank, Smith Barney, Reuters, Toys 'R Us, and KPMG Peat Marwick.

STUDENT/CAMPUS LIFE

The Baruch MBA enrollment is one of the largest in the country. The size of the program and the school's location combine to create a student body that is "diverse and interesting," and one that provides valuable insights to class discussion. Students "run the gamut from a cellular biologist to an actor, twenty-one to thirty-nine years old. A great group for any class discussion." Notes another student, "we are a potpourri of different cultures, but we all get along very well." Class unity is diminished by the size of the student body, however, since students are less likely to see the same faces in each class than they would be at a smaller school. Also, many students continue to work while attending Baruch. Explains one student, "The location of Baruch in New York City and the convenience it offers working students is probably the reason there is less camaraderie." As a result, Baruch students are less likely to become involved in school clubs and activities than are their counterparts in other MBA programs. This lack of class unity doesn't bother most Baruch students. As one puts it, "Baruch . . . doesn't strive to be anything else because the city can provide the rest of the equation." Students appreciate the school's excellent new library.

By far the biggest quality-of-life issue at Baruch is New York City itself. The effect of Baruch's urban setting is magnified by the fact that "there really is no campus. It's eight buildings scattered across the East Side." The city has its advocates among students. As one puts it, "New York is the greatest city in the U.S. Lots to do. The financial heart of the world." Another agrees that "New York City is the place to be if you're a b-school student. I can literally walk to Wall Street every day to get a whiff of the financial goings-on." The city also has its downsides, of course: the dearth of affordable housing, the noise, the occasional rudeness of its residents, and a public transportation system that is efficient but intimidating to many out-of-towners. Baruch is located near a beautiful park, but don't get your hopes up: Gramercy Park is the last private park in New York City. Only those who live on its perimeter are given the key necessary to enter it.

ADMISSIONS

According to the admissions board, your college GPA and GMAT scores are considered most important. After that the board considers, in descending order, your essays, letters of recommendation, and work experience. TOEFL and TWE are required for students with degrees from non-English speaking countries. Students may defer admission for up to one year.

FINANCIAL FACTS

Tuition (in-/out-of-state)	$4,350/$7,600
Tuition per credit (in-/out-of-state)	$185/$320
Fees (in-/out-of-state)	$33/$33
Cost of books	$550
Room & board (on-/off-campus)	NR/$5,678
% of students receiving aid	16
% first-year students receiving aid	15
% aid that is merit based	30
% of students receiving loans	43
% of students receiving grants	8
% of students receiving paid internships	10
Average grant	$10,000
Average graduation debt	$10,500

ADMISSIONS

# of applications received	1,443
% applicants accepted	55
% acceptees attending	51
Average GMAT	570
Minimum TOEFL	570
Average GPA	3.20
Application fee (in-/out-of-state)	$40/$40
Early decision program available	No
Regular application deadline	April 1
Admission may be deferred?	Yes
Maximum length of deferment	1 year
Transfer students accepted?	Yes
Nonfall admission available?	No
Admission process need-blind?	Yes

APPLICANTS ALSO LOOK AT

New York University, Columbia University, Hofstra University, Syracuse University, University of Maryland, Boston University, University of California—Los Angeles, Penn State University

EMPLOYMENT PROFILE

Placement rate (%)	70
% of grads employed immediately	70
Average starting salary	$52,036

Grads employed by field (avg. salary):

Accounting	25%	$44,400
Finance	17%	$53,594
General Management	7%	$52,500
Global Management	4%	$40,500
Human Resources	7%	$40,500
Marketing	14%	$44,542
MIS	17%	$53,067
Other	10%	$79,975

DARTMOUTH COLLEGE
The Amos Tuck School of Business Administration

OVERVIEW

Type of school	private
Affiliation	none
Environment	rural
Academic calendar	trimester
Schedule	full-time only

STUDENTS

Enrollment of parent institution	5,618
Enrollment of business school	375
% male/female	71/29
% out-of-state	99
% minorities	18
% international (# of countries represented)	24 (33)
Average age at entry	28
Average years work experience at entry	5

ACADEMICS

Student/faculty ratio	10:1
Hours of study per day	5.90

SPECIALTIES

General management curriculum cited for excellence in Finance, Strategy, Corporate Communications, and Marketing. Graduate Management Education Alliance with Templeton at Oxford (UK) and HEC (France)

JOINT DEGREES

MBA/MALD with Fletcher School at Tufts; MBA/MD with Dartmouth Medical School; MBA/ME with Thayer School of Engineering; MS/MBA with the Center for Evaluative Studies at Dartmouth Medical School

SPECIAL PROGRAMS

Visiting Executive Program, Center for Asia and Emerging Economies, Foster Center for Private Equity

STUDY ABROAD PROGRAMS

London Business School; Instituto de Estudios Superiores de la Empresa, Barcelona, Spain; International University of Japan, WHU, Germany; ISA at HEC, France; IMD in Switzerland

SURVEY SAYS...
HITS
Students are happy
Helping other students

MISSES
Impossible to get into courses

PROMINENT ALUMNI

Paul Raether, General Partner, Kohlberg Kravis Roberts & Co.; Frank Herringer, CEO of TransAmerica; Sherri Carroll Oberg, President of Acusphere

ACADEMICS

There was a time that Dartmouth College's Amos Tuck School of Business Administration was unquestionably the best graduate school of management in the world; founded in 1900, Tuck was the first graduate business school anywhere. And, while it may have necessarily fallen a couple of ticks in the rankings since its inception, Tuck remains one of the best business programs in the East. Offering only the MBA, Tuck focuses all its energies on developing talented general managers with strong quantitative and analytical backgrounds.

First year at Tuck begins with an Outward Bound–style orientation, followed by the Analysis for Managers module, which introduces students to Tuck's in-depth approach to case analysis and problem solving. A thirteen-course integrated core curriculum follows. Writes one student, "The integration of the entire experience is one of Tuck's great strengths. Faculty will co-teach a class if it applies to different areas." Many assignments, such as a three-day simulation exercise and a class consulting project, foster teamwork among first years. Tuck's trimester schedule moves things along pretty quickly. Says one student, "It is a tight schedule, but there is a respect for the limits of the students and their need for a balanced lifestyle." Another disagrees, opining that "the workload is unnecessarily heavy." Second year is less stressful; explains one student, "First year is a heavy load but things ease up second year. The students support each other and help everyone through." The second-year curriculum allows students to choose from more than fifty full-credit electives as well as numerous half-credit "minicourses." Independent study is also available, and students may choose to spend one semester studying overseas. For the extremely ambitious, the Tuck school and Dartmouth College offer several joint-degree options, including study in medicine, engineering, and international affairs (this last option is offered in conjunction with the Fletcher School of Law and Diplomacy at Tufts).

Tuck MBAs are unanimous in their praise of the faculty. Writes one, "The school's faculty is its most impressive aspect. They are tough and expect a lot, but they also care and spend many hours with students one-on-one or in review." Students also appreciate the intimacy their small program provides, telling us that "From the dean down to the professors, everyone knows your name and you can suggest anything. No pretentiousness here."

PLACEMENT AND RECRUITING

Tuck students give their Office of Career Services high marks, saying "the office and its facilities are beyond imagination." Students particularly appreciate the individual attention they receive from career counselors, a fringe benefit of attending such a small program. Like most business schools, Tuck has its strong and weak areas in placement. Writes one student, "If you want I-banking or consulting, you can easily interview with every top company. Also, alumni are incredible and will lobby to get Tuckies hired."

Sally O. Jaeger, Director of Admissions
100 Tuck Hall, Hanover, NH 03755
Admissions: 603-646-3162 Fax: 603-646-1441
Email: tuck.admissions@dartmouth.edu
Internet: www.tuck.dartmouth.edu

Last year more than 180 companies conducted over 5,000 interviews on campus, an average of fourteen interviews per MBA. Another 500 companies posted job listings with the Career Services office. Nearly three-quarters of Tuck grads wind up with jobs in consulting or finance; over half land jobs in either Boston or New York.

STUDENT/CAMPUS LIFE

The Tuck student body is made up "largely [of] people who self-selected Tuck because it fit best with them, not because it was on a *Business Week* list." They describe themselves as an unpretentious group; said one, "They're smart, team-oriented, liking outdoor activities, challenging. They reach out for each other and don't take themselves too seriously." A "broad mix of international students" adds diversity to the largely Northeastern population; complains one student, "We could use more students from outside of NYC and Boston." All told, though, students are happy with their peers. As one explains, "Tuck is a real community. The people here (students, partners, faculty, staff) all work together to make this an amazing learning environment and an enjoyable place to spend two years." Nearly all first-year students live in dorms, an experience that helps build class unity. Although current dorms are functional, students anxiously await new housing units, due in a 2000.

Hometown Hanover is a paradise to those comfortable with frosty, snow-filled winters. Describing the location's merits, one student writes, "I walk through a beautiful town to get to school. I ski ten minutes away and I hike out my backdoor." Another student puts it this way: "Why spend b-school in a city when you'll be there for the rest of your career? Why not ski, mountain bike, play hockey, and have a dog in your free time?" The town itself is quiet, but students find plenty to occupy their time on campus. Says one, "Everyone spends lots of time at school, or in school-related activities. There's not much else in Hanover! Luckily, Tuck students plan tons of social events, including Monthly Tuck Tails and the Fall Social (which was a blast!)." On-campus amenities include an art museum, a performing arts center, and "one of the finest [library] collections in New England." Students are also active in academic/cultural clubs and community service.

ADMISSIONS

The admissions office reports that "although the GMAT, GPA, and work experience are very important, we look for well-roundedness in our candidates; a formula is not used to determine admission. Tuck looks for applicants who exhibit leadership, creativity, and a strong foundation of business skills." Strong letters of recommendation are important.

An interview is also strongly recommended. Tuck admits students by "rounds." It is advisable to apply "within the first three" since the applicant pool is so competitive. Only 12 percent of applications are accepted.

FINANCIAL FACTS

Tuition	$26,100
Fees	$1,000
Cost of books	$2,000
Room & board	$11,600
% of students receiving aid	66
% first-year students receiving aid	72
% of students receiving grants	45
Average award package	$29,700
Average grant	$7,667
Average graduation debt	$49,845

ADMISSIONS

# of applications received	2,916
% applicants accepted	12
% acceptees attending	52
Average GMAT (range)	671 (610–730)
Minimum TOEFL	600
Average GPA (range)	3.40 (3.00–3.80)
Application fee (in-/out-of-state)	$125/$125
Early decision program available	No
Regular application deadline	April 21
Regular notification	May 17
Admission may be deferred?	Yes
Maximum length of deferment	Case-by-case basis
Transfer students accepted?	No
Nonfall admission available?	No
Admission process need-blind?	Yes

APPLICANTS ALSO LOOK AT

Northwestern University, Stanford University, Harvard University, University of Pennsylvania, Duke University, University of Virginia, University of Michigan Business School, MIT

EMPLOYMENT PROFILE

Placement rate (%)	100
# of companies recruiting on campus	180
% of grads employed immediately	98
% grads employed within six months	99
Average starting salary	$82,070

Grads employed by field (avg. salary):

Consulting	40%	$91,329
Finance	35%	$76,576
General Management	5%	$79,900
Marketing	10%	$72,000
Operations	5%	$72,167
Other	5%	$75,222

UNIVERSITY OF DENVER
Daniels College of Business

ACADEMICS

The Daniels College of Business offers a wide array of degree options to incoming students. Although many opt for a traditional MBA, Daniels also offers the internationally minded an MBA-like degree called a Masters in International Management (MIM). In designing this degree, Daniels took advantage of its university setting by incorporating classes at the College of Law and the Graduate School of International Studies to the curriculum. Students widely praise the MIM program, which is chiefly responsible for the school's large international student body. Daniels also offers many subject-specific master's degrees in fields such as accountancy, taxation, finance, real estate, and hotel management. The program encourages MBA and MIM candidates to pursue elective options in these disciplines and even to seek a concurrent master's degree in one.

Students here praise the core curriculum, an integrated and interdisciplinary program. Instead of offering distinct courses in accounting, finance, marketing, and statistics, Daniels offers seven fundamentals courses with names like Foundations of Business Decisions and High Performance Management. These courses require students to take a comprehensive approach to business problem solving by applying diverse analytical skills. Second-year students design their own areas of specialization; writes one student, there are "excellent opportunities for specialization. There is something for everybody." Another praised the "flexible" scheduling that allows him to "concentrate on areas that I feel are most important." According to students, the best specializations here are in finance, management, and accounting. Marketing and operations, on the other hand, earn low grades from our respondents.

"Most professors" at Daniels "are excellent. A couple seem to do just the minimum." Most students agree that "the majority of teachers are well-prepared and always helpful in students' pursuit of academic endeavors," although a few might also add that "some profs are great researchers but lack the ability to teach." Our respondents appreciate Daniels' small class sizes, reporting that "classes have ten to fifteen students, sometimes less." The administration, on the other hand, receives much lower marks for being "way too bureaucratic" and "generally unfriendly." A new b-school building, currently under construction, should remedy current students' dissatisfaction with facilities.

PLACEMENT AND RECRUITING

According to the Daniels Career Placement Center (CPC): "From your first week in orientation, you will interact with the Career Placement Center staff and begin to integrate your academic and career objectives. The creation of the Rocky Mountain MBA Consortium in the fall of 1996 has contributed significantly to the increased number and diversity of companies actively recruiting DCB graduates. The staff of the Career Placement Center aggressively target employers with site visits to promote the Daniels College of Business programs and to identify job and internship opportunities within large- and mid-sized companies as well as within Denver's booming entrepreneurial community. Approximately 85 percent of graduates find employment in the Denver area."

Jan Johnson, Associate Dean
2020 S.Race St. / BA.122, Denver, CO 80208
Admissions: 303, 871-3416 Fax: 303-871-4466
Email: dcb@du.edu
Internet: www.dcb.du.edu

University of Denver

Despite these efforts students in our survey still want more, particularly when it comes to the quality and diversity of companies that recruit on campus. Daniels CPC receives overall average marks from surveyed students. A large portion of our respondents, one-quarter, report that the opportunity to work with mentors is "poor" here.

STUDENT/CAMPUS LIFE

Daniels students describe their program's student body as "very ethnically diverse. There are some language barriers in my work group!" In fact, our survey revealed an unusual amount of tension between Americans and the large international contingent here, with a surprising number of respondents complaining about difficulties communicating with classmates. Still others felt strongly that professors apply a double standard when grading the two groups. These hard feelings are no doubt amplified by the fact that students here are "very competitive. Everyone is out for themselves." Several respondents also complain that "too many students are admitted directly from undergrad." Not surprisingly, our survey shows that students are relatively less happy with their classmates here than are MBAs in other programs. It should also be noted that some of those surveyed characterize their fellow students as "friendly" and "easy to get along with" but that a substantial minority of respondents give their classmates excellent marks for helpfulness and ability to contribute to class discussions.

Students' feelings about the school's location are less ambivalent. In fact, many choose Daniels precisely because it is in Denver. One student sums up: "It's all about location, location, location. Great city, great mountains, great outdoor life." On-campus clubs and activities are not overwhelmingly popular. Students here prefer to use their spare time to explore the city or to take advantage of the great skiing and outdoor activities available in the outlying areas. Explains one: "There are plenty of activities to participate in. Thursday night at the bars, weekend skiing." Most Daniels students are aware of the great temptation that Denver and the mountains offer, and compensate (some would say overcompensate) by burying themselves in their studies. One student explains that his classmates "like to ski and have fun, but still study too much. Most become bookworms on weekends." Academic pressure here is heightened by the quarter system, which many consider "intense. It means students are pressured to perform in the ten-week period." One student simply scribbles: "Too hectic. The quarter system must go!"

ADMISSIONS

Undergraduate academic performance, GMAT results, and work experience are considered most important in the selection process. Writes the school, "Essay responses, letters of recommendation, gender, international background, and ethnic background round out application elements that are converted to a cumulative point system, thereby taking into account the full applicant profile."

FINANCIAL FACTS

Tuition	$18,936
Tuition per credit	$526
Fees	$695
Cost of books	$1,500
Room & board (on-/off-campus)	$8,100/$8,100
% of students receiving aid	27
% first-year students receiving aid	70
Average award package	$25,000
Average grant	$3,500

ADMISSIONS

# of applications received	653
% applicants accepted	78
% acceptees attending	41
Average GMAT (range)	530 (440–640)
Minimum TOEFL	550
Average GPA (range)	3.10 (2.60–3.70)
Application fee (in-/out-of-state)	$50/$50
Early decision program available	Yes
Early decision deadline	Rolling
Early decision notification	Rolling
Regular application deadline	May 1
Regular notification	Rolling
Admission may be deferred?	Yes
Maximum length of deferment	1 year
Transfer students accepted?	Yes
Nonfall admission available?	Yes
Admission process need-blind?	No

APPLICANTS ALSO LOOK AT

University of Colorado at Boulder, Arizona University, University of Washington, Stanford University, University of Texas — Austin, Colorado State University, University of California — Berkeley, Thunderbird

EMPLOYMENT PROFILE

Placement rate (%)	85
# of companies recruiting on campus	86
% of grads employed immediately	85
% grads employed within six months	95
Average starting salary	$45,186

Grads employed by field (avg. salary):

Accounting	10%	$35,700
Consulting	25%	$47,200
Finance	13%	$45,209
General Management	10%	$49,033
Marketing	16%	$44,000
MIS	13%	$44,550
Operations	3%	$44,000
Other	11%	$43,600

DUKE UNIVERSITY
The Fuqua School of Business

ACADEMICS

Teamwork is a key element of most MBA programs, but students at Duke University's Fuqua School of Business feel it's just a little more important at their program. They use the term Team Fuqua to describe the effect; as one student tells us, "The cooperative culture is the school's greatest strength. Team Fuqua really is an important part of the school."

This spirit of togetherness combines with across-the-board departmental strength and curricular innovation to make Fuqua a top-ranked MBA program. Students report that finance, accounting, marketing, and general management are stand-out areas, listing only entrepreneurship and human resources among areas that could use improvement. Respondents are also extremely enthusiastic about the school's Global Academic Travel Experiences (GATE), full-term courses that end in two-week international study tours. Nearly one-third of first-year students participate in GATE courses, traveling to South Africa, Southeast Asia, the Middle East, Russia, and Europe. Also unique to Fuqua are the experiential Integrative Learning Experiences (ILE), four week-long seminars that embrace such fashionable topics as diversity and internationalization. Each ILE precedes a semester of traditional classroom instruction. Throughout the two-year program, students take four ILEs: Team Building and Leadership Development, Competitive Business Strategy, Competitive Advantage Through People and Processes, and Emerging Trends in Management. The last two are the capstone experiences in that they involve business simulation games and team competitions. Raves one student, "Fuqua's updated curriculum is on top of market trends."

Fuqua runs an accelerated schedule of seven-week terms, with each class lasting two-and-a-quarter hours to allow professors to cover complex issues in a single session. Students tell us that "the term system allows us to learn various courses in a short run" and call the system "ingenious," right down to a 'no classes on Wednesday' policy that "breaks up the week well." First-year students must complete fourteen core requirements and two electives. They warn that the curriculum is quant-heavy but also note that "Fuqua requires three terms of communications skills courses. I like that." They also report that "some core professors are weak, but the administration is very responsive to complaints." Concerning the general quality of instruction, one student writes: "As a former liberal arts major, I was prepared to find the classes boring, the professors inarticulate and the administration driven solely by the profit motive. I am happy to say how wrong I was and how much I enjoy each aspect of the academic life here." Second-year students at Fuqua may choose a field of concentration but are not required to do so.

PLACEMENT AND RECRUITING

To make up for the youth of its MBA program (the school was founded in 1970, and has therefore generated a relatively small alumni base), Fuqua's Career Services and Placement Office (CSO) must go the extra mile for its students. According to our respondents, The CSO does just that. An example: five years ago, the CSO asked students to generate a "wish list" of recruiting companies. Students named fifty-eight companies that were not recruiting on campus at the time; today, through the CSO's efforts, all but two of those companies interview at Fuqua. Says one student of Fuqua's "excellent recruiting program," "All the

Liz Riley, Director of Admissions
Box 90104, Durham, NC 27708-0104
Admissions: 919-660-7705 Fax: 919-681-8026
Email: fuqua-admissions@mail.duke.edu
Internet: www.fuqua.duke.edu

Duke University

good companies come to Duke and many Fuqua students get placed well percentage-wise versus other schools."

In response to student complaints, CSO has also more actively sought international placement opportunities for Fuqua grads, as well as more "opportunities with small and mid-sized companies." Among the top recruiters are Chase Manhattan, Coca Cola, Ernst & Young, General Motors, Intel, Mobil, NationsBank, Raymond James and Associates, and the Walt Disney Co.

STUDENT/CAMPUS LIFE

Perhaps the most pressing issue at Fuqua today is the need for more space in its home building, the Keller Center. The growth of the program is currently outpacing construction, but students report that a remedy is at hand. Writes one, "Fuqua has outgrown the size of its facilities, but multiple expansion projects are underway that will rectify this problem. We're getting a new gym, cafeteria, interview rooms, and more class space for 2000." A new building for faculty and PhD students, slated for completion by the fall semester of 1999, will free up space in Keller. Although cramped, Keller is a fine facility packed with state-of-the-art resources.

Duke's campus is one of the nation's most beautiful, complete with neo-Gothic architecture and sweeping lawns. A mile of woodlands divides the campus in two; Fuqua is perched on the edge of Duke Forest on Duke's West Campus. Most students opt to live off campus in small groups in nearby apartment complexes. Housing, both on and off campus, is spacious and quite economical. Most students bring a car, but at peak times parking can be nearly impossible. Students report an active extracurricular scene; there's a FuquaVision show every other month (like a "Saturday Night Live" video), and a Winter Gala Black Tie party. Writes one student, "There are many activities for all types of interests. Life really revolves around school. As a married student, I can attest to the fact that there is an excellent organization for partners of students." Intramural sports are huge, as is golf; Duke has its own "excellent" course. Student clubs play a big part in campus life as well. On the downside, hometown Durham is "not so great." Says one student, "Durham is a fairly small town, and the choices (restaurants, bars, cultural events) are somewhat limited."

Duke's student body boasts a "large number of international students" as well as a wide cross-section of Americans. Students are "great people, most of whom pass the 'airplane to Tokyo' test." Notes one student, "The only knock against them is that the competitive spirit tends to get very intense during interviewing."

ADMISSIONS

The admissions office does not require interviews, but encourages them as "an important part of the application process." Other key components are the GMAT score, college GPA, essays, work experience, letters of recommendation, and extracurricular activities. Decisions are made on a rolling admissions basis. Applicants are notified of a decision six to eight weeks after the admissions office has received a completed application. Accepted applicants may defer admission for up to one year for health issues or special job opportunities. Fuqua may also offer college seniors a two-year deferred admission with the expectation that there will be substantive work experience in the interim.

FINANCIAL FACTS

Tuition	$26,200
Fees	$1,374
Cost of books	$1,050
Room & board	$7,400
% of students receiving aid	70
% first-year students receiving aid	70
% aid that is merit based	30
Average award package	$26,800
Average grant	$10,680
Average graduation debt	$43,000

ADMISSIONS

# of applications received	3,399
% applicants accepted	17
% acceptees attending	56
Average GMAT (range)	664 (580–750)
Average TOEFL	600
Average GPA (range)	3.34 (2.90–3.80)
Application fee (in-/out-of-state)	$135/$135
Early decision program available	No
Regular application deadline	April 26
Admission may be deferred?	Yes
Maximum length of deferment	1 year
Transfer students accepted?	No
Nonfall admission available?	No
Admission process need-blind?	Yes

APPLICANTS ALSO LOOK AT

Northwestern University, University of North Carolina at Chapel Hill, University of Pennsylvania, University of Virginia, Stanford University, University of Michigan Business School, Dartmouth College, Harvard University

EMPLOYMENT PROFILE

Placement rate (%)	99
# of companies recruiting on campus	335
% of grads employed immediately	97
% grads employed within six months	99
Average starting salary	$79,500

Grads employed by field (avg. salary):

Consulting	27%	$89,918
Entrepreneurship	1%	NR
Finance	33%	$74,950
General Management	8%	$76,394
Marketing	19%	$70,250
Operations	2%	$71,500
Other	4%	$80,000
Strategic Planning	5%	$78,179

EMORY UNIVERSITY
Goizueta Business School

OVERVIEW

Type of school	private
Affiliation	methodist
Environment	urban
Academic calendar	semester
Schedule	full-time only

STUDENTS

Enrollment of parent institution	11,000
Enrollment of business school	515
% male/female	69/31
% out-of-state	87
% part-time	37
% minorities	11
% international (# of countries represented)	27 (30)
Average age at entry	27
Average years work experience at entry	4.90

ACADEMICS

Student/faculty ratio	6:1
% female faculty	21
% minority faculty	3
Hours of study per day	4.64

SPECIALTIES

Academic specialties of faculty include Relationship Marketing, Leadership Decision Analysis, Organization/Management, Accounting, and Finance

JOINT DEGREES

JD/MBA, 4 years; MBA/Div, 4 years; MBA/MPH, 2+ years

SPECIAL PROGRAMS

Customer Business Development Track, International Exchange Programs

STUDY ABROAD PROGRAMS

Italy, Spain, France, Finland, Venezuela, Costa Rica, Mexico, Austria, England, Singapore, and Germany

SURVEY SAYS...
HITS
Star faculty
Marketing
Atlanta

MISSES
On-campus housing
Quantitative skills
MIS/operations

PROMINENT ALUMNI

Michael Golden, Vice President, New York Times Company; Ely Callaway, Chairman, Callaway Golf; Jonathan Pond, President, Financial Planning Information, Inc.; Andy Conway, Beverage Analyst, Morgan Stanley

ACADEMICS

Ask students at Goizueta to identify the best aspect of their school and nearly all will mention its rising status in the business world. "There is a sense of excitement at the school that the school is improving immensely," writes one; adds another, "I love the 'up-and-coming' aspect of the school." This excitement is due in no small part to an "exceptional" new facility. The "brand new and state-of-the-art business center" was built with a grant from Roberto Goizueta, CEO of Coca-Cola and namesake of Emory's business school.

International business and marketing are among Goizueta's strong suits (not surprising considering that these are also among the Coca-Cola Company's greatest strengths). Students also speak highly of the management department, but have major complaints about finance. "The finance capacity of the faculty and curriculum [is] severely lacking," is how one typical respondent puts it. On the general availability of second-year electives, students feel that "we need a wider diversity of course offerings." Students are quite voluble about the faculty, to whom they give average marks for teaching ability but high grades for accessibility and willingness to provide extra help when necessary. Several students note that teaching quality consistently improves throughout the program. One says, "Early on in the program, the faculty are less impressive. Those in the later classes are excellent," while another adds, "Core courses in accounting, economics, and especially marketing are weak." Some complain of the "high turnover rate among the faculty. Lots of new faces each semester."

Goizueta allows some choice to first-year students through its Flex/Core program, which helps students develop a specialization they might exploit when searching for summer internships. Still, first-year courses are largely prescribed—as they are at most MBA programs—although Goizueta allows students to place out of core requirements provided they pass a departmental exam. Exploiting one of its greatest assets, Goizueta includes an international business component in its core, a tack not taken by many other leading business schools. Each semester at Goizueta starts with a "lead week" activity; either a game-situation competition or a "focus module" to give students the chance to study a subject in depth. Students with an undergraduate business degree might wish to consider the intensive one-year accelerated MBA. No matter which option they choose, students usually leave Goizueta feeling like this student, who had an "excellent experience, very intellectually stimulating. This has prepared me extensively for real-world complex problems."

PLACEMENT AND RECRUITING

Our survey shows that students have mixed feelings about the Career Services Office at Goizueta; half give the service middling or worse marks. The main concern among our respondents is in the area of recruitment by companies from beyond the Atlanta region. Students feel the school should be doing more to attract farther-flung companies to the campus; several report that the problem is particularly acute "in relation to students who spend a semester abroad." Yet half also express satisfaction with the service, which offers numerous self-assessment, one-on-one counseling, and mock-interview programs for first-year students—all in a new resource center. The office also administers the Goizueta Business

Julie Barefoot, Assistant Dean of Admissions and Student Services
1300 Clifton Road, Atlanta, GA 30322
Admissions: 404-727-6311 Fax: 404-727-4612
Email: Admissions@bus.emory.edu
Internet: www.emory.edu/BUS

School Mentor Program, and a number of off-campus projects and year-long seminars with Atlanta-based companies that continue into the summer as internships, all of which get high marks from students.

Goizueta participates in a "number of off-campus events that expand the number of interviewing opportunities available to students," including MBA consortia, a trip to Wall Street, and a West Coast trip to visit "high-tech firms, consulting firms, and investment banks." The companies hiring the most Goizueta grads recently are IBM, Deloitte & Touche, KPMG Peat Marwick, Ernst & Young, BellSouth, Hewlett-Packard, The Coca-Cola Company, and Intel.

STUDENT/CAMPUS LIFE

The Goizueta student body is "a small community, very close-knit." Students keep to themselves within the university system by necessity, since there is "no time to mingle with students from other schools in the university." Fortunately for them they think highly of each other, regarding classmates as "well-rounded, energetic, insightful, and fun to be around. There is something to learn from each of them." Several remarked that the "exceptional international students" here are "a great asset." Sums up one student: "Although very busy, my life here is great. Not only do we study together, we socialize together on weekends. Emory has made us a very tight and cohesive group."

As if studies didn't keep them busy enough, students here "have high involvement into ALL aspects of running the school." The Graduate Business Association, to which all students belong, either manages or funds many subject-specific and minority clubs, sponsors parties on a regular basis, organizes intramural sports, and holds a weekly "coffee and donuts" breakfast for students and faculty. Furthermore, students form various student advisory groups consult with faculty and administration in such areas as admissions, career services, and marketing the Goizueta MBA program to the rest of the nation. Students love the Emory campus, located in a residential neighborhood just 15 minutes from downtown Atlanta, praising it for its "very collegiate environment" and "Southern feeling." Those so inclined will find "almost a party every weekend," although many prefer to use their sparse spare time to take advantage of all that the South's largest city has to offer: sports, culture, fine dining, and an excellent nightlife.

ADMISSIONS

According to the admissions office, your work experience is considered most important. After that, in descending order, your GMAT scores, interview, essays, college GPA, extracurricular activities, and letters of recommendation are considered. Notes the school, "Interviews are strongly encouraged. Candidates are also encouraged to visit a class with one of our current students." Emory requires that applicants have completed one semester of college calculus and be computer literate. Decisions are made on a rolling admissions basis. The school may allow applicants to defer admission for up to two years; this is decided on a case-by-case basis.

FINANCIAL FACTS

Tuition	$25,400
Fees	$200
Cost of books	$890
Room & board (on-/off-campus)	NR/$10,000
% first-year students receiving aid	50
% aid that is merit based	46
% of students receiving loans	44
Average grant	$7,800
Average graduation debt	$30,000

ADMISSIONS

# of applications received	1,069
% applicants accepted	30
% acceptees attending	46
Average GMAT (range)	640 (570–710)
Minimum TOEFL	600
Average GPA (range)	3.34 (2.78–3.80)
Application fee (in-/out-of-state)	$70/NR
Early decision program available	Yes
Early decision deadline	December 31
Early decision notification	January 31
Regular application deadline	March 31
Regular notification	Rolling
Admission may be deferred?	Yes
Maximum length of deferment	2 years
Transfer students accepted?	Yes
Nonfall admission available?	No
Admission process need-blind?	Yes

APPLICANTS ALSO LOOK AT

Duke University, University of North Carolina at Chapel Hill, University of Virginia, Vanderbilt University, University of Pennsylvania, New York University, Northwestern University, Georgetown University

EMPLOYMENT PROFILE

Placement rate (%)	98
# of companies recruiting on campus	87
% of grads employed immediately	20
% grads employed within six months	98
Average starting salary	$69,187

Grads employed by field (avg. salary):

Consulting	25%	$73,823
Finance	35%	$67,174
General Management	4%	$71,100
Marketing	21%	$67,162
Other	15%	$73,737

UNIVERSITY OF FLORIDA
Florida MBA Programs

ACADEMICS

Diverse offerings in a paradise-like atmosphere are what draw most MBAs to the University of Florida Graduate School of Business. Students here rave about the Entrepreneurship program, the finance department, and the numerous dual- and joint-degree offerings, among which is a popular international business program administered in conjunction with Thunderbird.

In an effort to add flexibility to its list of assets, the Florida MBA recently revamped its schedule, dividing the fall and spring semesters into two seven-and-a-half week modules. The module system is intended to give students greater access to popular courses and allow for more independence in designing their academic programs. Students appreciate the school's efforts, reporting that "the module system gives students the opportunity to be exposed to a greater number of courses, which provides a stronger concentration background and better preparation to meet the needs of corporate America." Several, however, warn, "the module system is yet to be perfected."

Each set of modules is accompanied by a required Professional Development Program (PDP), which—according to the school—is designed "to significantly enhance the MBA experience . . . by providing opportunities for professional growth outside of the classroom through an integrated framework of MBA co-curricular and extracurricular programs." Such activities as a distinguished speaker series, management seminars, technology tutorials, and courses to improve writing and presentation skills are included in the PDP program. One student approves of the entire package, "Our program has really improved student services since I arrived. The electives have been great, giving us lots of opportunity to choose a variety of courses, while the core provides a solid foundation."

Most students agree that "professors are generally very good teachers. They communicate well," although several warn that, "a few are terrible." The administration, which students describe as "reactive and detached in relation to students," gets lower marks.

Finally, Florida offers four unique programs for working professionals seeking an MBA. According to the school's promotional literature, the aptly named Flexible MBA program "combines leading-edge interactive technology, a week-long international trip, and only eight campus visits over twenty months to provide a high caliber MBA degree via the Internet." In addition, the Executive MBA (meets Friday–Sunday, once a month for twenty months); the Manager's MBA (meets Friday–Sunday, once a month for twelve months); and the Weekend MBA (meets Saturday and Sunday, once a month for thirty months) are all creative programs that use work experience as entrance determiners and that target working professionals.

PLACEMENT AND RECRUITING

The Florida MBA Program Career Services Office (CSO) reports that it "has experienced a major improvement in the last two years." Our survey bears out this assertion: student ratings of the CSO have improved with our recent survey. However, our survey also confirms that most students still agree that "the career services office needs improvement."

Laura Parks, Director of Admissions
134 Bryan Hall, P.O. Box 117152 Gainesville, FL 32611-7152
Admissions: 352-392-7992 Fax: 352-392-8791
Email: floridamba@notes.cba.ufl.edu
Internet: www.floridamba.ufl.edu

University of Florida

In its efforts to upgrade services, Florida has added two full-time professional and one administrative staff member and developed a "unique Professional Development Program [to offer] seminars in career search skills including interviewing, presentation, and business communications techniques." The school also notes that "The Class of 1997 was the best ever for placement, setting records for mean average salaries and diversity in placement across the U.S. Approximately 50 percent of the class accepted job offers outside the state of Florida." Top employers for Florida MBAs include CSX, EDS, Ernst & Young, Fannie Mae, GE Capital, Harris Corporation, IBM, and Tech Data.

STUDENT/CAMPUS LIFE

Florida students see their classmates as very practical-minded about their education. "Ends-oriented real learning takes a back seat to grades and a 'where will this get me?' attitude," is how one student puts it. However, students also regard themselves as "very intelligent, motivated, and, most importantly, very cooperative." The word "friendly" pops up frequently in students' descriptions of each other, and many agree with the student who writes that "the strong ties among students make a lot of the work seem almost fun." Diversity is not the strong suit of this student body, however. Several students complain that the population is "not very geographically diverse. They're mainly from Florida and the Southeast." One student does note, however, "A good mix of international students adds to the enjoyment of earning a Florida MBA." Not surprisingly, as one of the best undergrad public business programs in the country, "many students have undergraduate degrees from the University of Florida." The school has recently changed is requirements for work experience; on average, for the fall 1998 entering class, the students have five years' work experience. This should alleviate some student complaints about the diversity and real-world knowledge of their classmates.

As for campus life, one student summarizes it this way: "Quite simply, the Florida MBA program is a bargain financially, has excellent students, and is probably unparalleled socially." Students are active in such clubs as the MBA Association, the Consulting Club, and Graduate Women in Business. Many respondents are quick to point out that "the MBA program is a small part of a large university. There's a lot of diverse activities outside of the MBA program for students to take advantage of." Among those are "a beautiful campus, including a lake, open lawns, and many trees" and "superb athletic programs that provide a feeling of unity and allegiance to the school." One student notes that "most of our activities revolve around drinking beer" but this caused neither him nor anyone else in our survey to complain. Students report that "Gainesville has everything you need but is still a small town. People used to larger cities may find the adjustment difficult." They also note that "the town is geared around the students. If you need a quiet place to study, you can find it. If you need a place to have fun, you can find it."

ADMISSIONS

Florida's admissions office requires an interview, explaining that it "allows applicants to elaborate on strengths and weaknesses that may impact their applications. The admissions committee looks for well-rounded candidates with excellent academic ability, significant work experience, active community involvement, and strong personal character."

FINANCIAL FACTS

Tuition (in-/out-of-state)	$3,582/$12,514
Tuition per credit (in-/out-of-state)	$138/$481
Fees (in-/out-of-state)	$400/$400
Cost of books	$3,600
Room & board (on-/off-campus)	NR/$7,640
% of students receiving aid	70
% first-year students receiving aid	70
% aid that is merit based	43
% of students receiving paid internships	70
Average award package	$11,000

ADMISSIONS

# of applications received	479
% applicants accepted	42
% acceptees attending	58
Average GMAT (range)	610 (520–690)
Minimum TOEFL	600
Average GPA (range)	3.29 (2.74–3.86)
Application fee (in-/out-of-state)	$20/$20
Early decision program available	Yes
Early decision deadline	February 1(Fall), August 15 (Spring), Jan 1(Summer)
Early decision notification	March 15(Fall), October 1 (Spring), Feb 15(Summer)
Regular application deadline	June 1
Regular notification	June 15
Admission may be deferred?	Yes
Maximum length of deferment	1 year
Transfer students accepted?	Yes
Nonfall admission available?	Yes
Admission process need-blind?	Yes

APPLICANTS ALSO LOOK AT

University of North Carolina at Chapel Hill, Duke University, University of Virginia, University of Texas at Austin, Emory University, University of Georgia, Vanderbilt University, University of Pennsylvania

EMPLOYMENT PROFILE

Placement rate (%)	97
# of companies recruiting on campus	200
% of grads employed immediately	80
% grads employed within six months	98
Average starting salary	$54,179

Grads employed by field (avg. salary):

Consulting	24%	$54,843
Finance	36%	$56,300
General Management	10%	$52,901
Marketing	16%	$52,155
MIS	2%	$41,000
Other	9%	$54,750

GEORGETOWN UNIVERSITY
The Robert Emmett McDonough School of Business

OVERVIEW

Type of school	private
Affiliation	Catholic
Environment	urban
Academic calendar	semester
Schedule	full-time only

STUDENTS

Enrollment of parent institution	12,433
Enrollment of business school	519
% male/female	68/32
% minorities	14
% international (# of countries represented)	31 (34)
Average age at entry	28
Average years work experience at entry	4.7

ACADEMICS

Student/faculty ratio	8:1
% female faculty	23
% minority faculty	9
Hours of study per day	5.20

SPECIALTIES
Curriculum is new (as of fall '98) with integrated modules of varying legths. An international experience is required.

JOINT DEGREES
MBA/MSFS, 3 years; MBA/JD, 4 years; MBA/MPP, 3 years; MBA/MD, 5 years; BSBA/MBA, 5 years

SPECIAL PROGRAMS
The International Business Diplomacy Certificate, Area Studies Certificate, Summer Study Abroad Opportunities, International Exchange Opportunities, Summer Pre-Enrollment "Prep" Workshops

STUDY ABROAD PROGRAMS
Spain, France, Australia, Germany, Sweden, Mexico, Belgium, England, Japan, Czech Republic, and Hong Kong

SURVEY SAYS...
HITS
Helping other students
Students are happy

MISSES
Campus is ugly

PROMINENT ALUMNI
Maximo Blandon, Vice President, Morgan Stanley, Investment banking; David Gee, IBM/Java; Daisuke Soejimo, Mitsubishi International

ACADEMICS

"Strong international integration" is the hallmark of McDonough's "totally re-designed curriculum," part of the school's effort to position itself as the premier international business program in the country. The program's international focus dovetails very nicely with McDonough's location in the nation's capital. As one student notes, "The access to the IMF and the World Bank and the SEC is an incredible opportunity for us."

Chief among the distinctive features of a McDonough MBA is the final semester GLOBAL Experience, twelve weeks of intensive coursework followed by one week of "field-based study outside the U.S." Also unique are the one-week Integrative Experience courses that break up the six-week foundation course modules; each of the first-year IEs focuses the previous six weeks' of coursework on an international business issue. Writes one student, "The integrative curriculum brings it all together!" Not all the highlights of McDonough's program center on international trade: a twelve-week requirement in "technology and knowledge management" serves to "connect technology issues to all functional areas." Students tell us that "First year was a killer. The pace is fast and everybody hit the ground running. The good thing is that students are very helpful to each other." Writes another of the grueling core, "The workload is insane, the pace is unreasonable, and the professors are overbearing. I love it. Bring it on. Give me more." Second-year students must complete the required GLOBAL Experience and several IEs but are otherwise free to pursue electives. Some opt for general management ("The school provides a great general management education with an international spin"), while others praise McDonough's marketing and business and public policy departments.

In addition to the new international curriculum, the forward thrust of the program is reflected in a series of changes at the school, including: Robert Emmett McDonough's $30 million endowment gift to the school; the arrival of new dean Christopher Puto last July following an extensive international search; and the opening of an interim MBA facility in Fall 1999.

Students heap high praise on the faculty and administration at McDonough. "Professors are very approachable and helpful in career searches," writes one student. According to another, "The academic experience [here] is as deep as anywhere, without the stress."

PLACEMENT AND RECRUITING

Recent additions to the list of companies recruiting on campus include: Amerada Hess, American Express, Bank Boston, Capital Management, Columbia House, First Union Capital Markets, GE Capital, ICN Pharmaceuticals, IBM Global Services, Lehman Brothers, Merrill Lynch, Oracle Consulting, RCN Corp., SAP Americas, SmithKline Beecham, Texaco, Xerox. In addition, thirty-five employers visit campus in September during McDonough's MBA Careers Extravaganza. The school also touts the MBA Consortium, of which McDonough is a founding member, as a major recruiting event for its students. The Consortium sponsors national recruitment meetings in Atlanta and New York. MBACM works with students throughout the program to develop and update resumes, which the school collects and publicizes, both in print and via the Internet.

Assistant Dean, Admissions
Box 571148, Washington, DC 20057
Admissions: 202-687-4200 Fax: 202-687-7809
Email: MBA@MSB.GEORGETOWN.EDU
Internet: www.msb.georgetown.edu

Georgetown University

Students report that "The placement office needs improvement, but we're a young program so it's not surprising. The service is improving at a very good rate." Of the alumni network, students tell us that "the alumni, although limited in number, are very helpful and resourceful."

STUDENT/CAMPUS LIFE

Thirty-six foreign countries are represented in the class of 2000; writes one student from overseas, "It's nice being an international student at McDonough. I really feel welcome." In addition, "Over 85 percent of the Americans in the program know a second language. Great interaction between American and international students."

The demanding McDonough curriculum means that, for many, "The workload is heavy, but you learn a lot about time management. It can be difficult to find time to socialize." Still, others report that "Extracurricular activities are plentiful. All students are active in at least one club. The student government sponsors happy hours so students can mingle. This allows first- and second-year students to get to know each other better." Adds one student, "We play hard after we've worked hard. It's a huge plus that we all get along so well outside the classroom." MBA students attend classes in the Graduate Center, an interim facility until construction can begin on the new business school building. Within its 32,000 square feet area, it has four case-style classrooms, each with tiered seating for sixty-five, Ethernet connections at every seat, and dual overhead digital projectors. A computer lab accommodates fifty students, and student breakout rooms will also be equipped with networked computers. The student lounge is configured with 100 Ethernet ports to connect laptop computers to the McDonough network. The Career Center features video conferencing capabilities for long-distance interviews, as well as a professional environment for on-campus recruiting. "The facilities need improvement," says one student. "The campus is old and charming but has no room to grow as it is in a historical neighborhood. They need to find more space to build a new dedicated facility." The athletic fields are what you'd expect of a sports powerhouse, and students applaud their first-rate gym. Students say the campus is ultrasafe, and that they love living in the nation's capital, telling us that "This city has the perfect combination of culture and city life."

ADMISSIONS

According to the admissions office, your work experience, college GPA, and GMAT score are considered most important. Then come your essays, interview, (optional) letters of recommendation, and extracurricular activities. Writes the school, "The admissions committee generally numbers twelve individuals, and includes both first- and second-year MBA students, faculty, and administrators. Each applicant's file is reviewed and discussed by the committee. General considerations are professional experience, academic performance and potential, and personal interests, qualities, and skills. International experience and community involvement are of particular interest to the admissions committee, as are positions of leadership held in academic, professional, or community organizations." Decisions are made on a rolling admissions basis. Applicants are notified of a decision four to six weeks after the completed application has been received.

FINANCIAL FACTS

Tuition	$23,880
Tuition per credit	$796
Fees	$3,255
Cost of books	$5,040
Room & board	$8,600
% first-year students receiving aid	26
% aid that is merit based	100
% of students receiving paid internships	30
Average award package	$26,771
Average grant	$10,795
Average graduation debt	$41,941

ADMISSIONS

# of applications received	1,829
% applicants accepted	36
% acceptees attending	39
Average GMAT (range)	637 (570–710)
Minimum TOEFL	600
Average GPA (range)	3.21 (2.75–3.69)
Application fee (in-/out-of-state)	$75/$75
Early decision program available	No
Regular application deadline	April 15
Regular notification	Rolling
Admission may be deferred?	Yes
Maximum length of deferment	1 year
Transfer students accepted?	Yes
Nonfall admission available?	No
Admission process need-blind?	Yes

APPLICANTS ALSO LOOK AT
Duke, Cornell, Wharton, University of Virginia, Columbia, Maryland, New York University

EMPLOYMENT PROFILE

Placement rate (%)	92
# of companies recruiting on campus	109
% of grads employed immediately	75
% grads employed within six months	92
Average starting salary	$75,000

Grads employed by field (avg. salary):

Consulting	28%	$74,348
Finance	36%	$72,442
General Management	4%	$78,834
Marketing	22%	$62,590
Other	6%	$72,875
Strategic Planning	4%	$73,833

UNIVERSITY OF GEORGIA
Terry College of Business

ACADEMICS

Location, a strong, flexible program, and a great return on investment are the reasons most often cited by business graduates as their reasons for selecting the University of Georgia. Students love the "excellent campus and learning environment. Facilities are state-of-the-art and available to everyone," and they appreciate the fact that "the school is very technology oriented, constantly evaluating courses offered to include the newest information in data warehousing, Internet commerce, etc." At the top of students' lists of Georgia's attractions, however, is the cost of tuition; explains one student, "This school is an excellent value. Tuition rates are low and many students—more than 60 percent of the class—have teaching assistantships, which means free tuition. This proves especially helpful for out-of-state students."

Many Georgia MBAs opt for the accelerated one-year program, designed for students with an undergrad degree in business. Most, however, settle in for the traditional two-year MBA, a "well-constructed program in which big blocks [of material] build on each other." Two-year MBAs begin with a year of quant-heavy core courses. Second-year students and one-year MBAs choose two "sequences" from among twenty to develop a specialization. Sequences are unique to UGA—pre-selected courses are packaged to guarantee expertise in an area. They also allow students a surprising degree of flexibility; writes one, "Very flexible curriculum; I have been able to take a specialized international business sequence tailored to my needs." Some of the most popular sequences are international business, corporate finance, MIS, entrepreneurship ("The entrepreneurship program is fantastic. I made a lot of great business contacts"), and real estate. The most interesting component of the program is the year-long professional development series, called the MBA PLUS program, which focuses on teamwork, leadership, and presentation skills. A highlight of the series is Fabulous Friday, in which corporate heavyweights conduct workshops on hot topics.

Students give professors mixed grades for teaching skills; explains one, "I've had some stellar profs, truly masters in their field. It doesn't always translate in the classroom, but overall the profs make learning enjoyable." Others point out that "Many profs are also consultants, so they can add real-world examples to class work." The administration, once considered an obstacle to the program's success, "is moving forward with a new dean and assistant dean and actively solicits students' ideas."

PLACEMENT AND RECRUITING

The UGA Career Services Office offers assistance with resume preparation, interviewing skills, mock interviews, a resume referral program, job search strategies, and a photo and resume profile book, which is distributed to Fortune 500 firms and smaller regional firms in the Southeast. It also conducts the distinctive Executive Breakfast Club, at which students visit with senior management of Fortune 500 companies over breakfast. Off campus UGA markets its MBAs at four Consortium events: the National MBA Consortium at Chicago, the Business Career Expo in Atlanta, and the International Consortium in Orlando.

Some students in our survey express disappointment with the Career Services office, telling us that "it seems like most jobs available through placement are in finance and consulting. We have a strong MIS program that should be more

Donald R. Perry, Jr., Director, MBA Admissions
346 Brooks Hall Athens, GA 30602-6264
Admissions: 706 542-5671 Fax: 706 542-5351
Email: terrymba@terry.uga.edu
Internet: www.terry.uga.edu/mba

exposed." Observes another student, "The placement office facilities are not very impressive, which may not make a good impression on recruiters." UGA MBAs most frequently find work with Intel, Cintas Corporation, Phillip Morris, Federal Express, Coca-Cola Corporation, Delta Airlines, Kimberly Clark, Price Waterhouse Coopers, Andersen Consulting, and Ernst and Young.

STUDENT/CAMPUS LIFE

Georgia MBAs are quick to identify Athens and the university campus among UGA's greatest assets. "Life is extremely easy, comfortable, and fun in Athens," a "wonderful college town to live in." Sums up one student, "Athens epitomizes what a college town should be! There is a broad spectrum of individuals and culture present downtown." As an added bonus, Atlanta—that most cosmopolitan of Southern cities—is just 70 miles away. Students report the campus is safe; still most opt for off-campus living in apartments. For fun, the Graduate Business Association sponsors social, professional, and athletic activities. Especially popular are intramural sports teams of all types. "Almost half the class escapes from the stress of the work week on intramural basketball teams," writes one student. Weekly happy hours provide relief from a diet of regression analysis. Asked to sum up the lifestyle afforded by a Georgia MBA, one student tells us that "the small size of the program allows for real learning in a nonhectic, free-for-all environment. This school, this program, and this town are gems. Overall, it's a solid investment!"

First-year UGA students report a heavy workload and spend an average of from twenty to thirty hours a week studying (in addition to time spent in class). The majority of UGA MBAs use study groups and divvy up the load. By the second year, things lighten up considerably. Students describe their classmates as "team players. They have vision for the future of the Terry MBA and are willing to make personal sacrifices to ensure the continued improvement of the program." This "very diverse and intelligent group . . . [has] many people who do not have a traditional view of business. It helps to keep class discussion fresh and open." Foreign students constitute "a great international student presence" according to some, although others report that "foreign students tend to be isolated from locals," the "majority [of whom] come from the Southeast U.S."

ADMISSIONS

UGA weighs your GMAT score, work experience, and college GPA most heavily. After that, they weigh your letters of recommendation, extracurricular activities, and essays equally. Writes the school, "We are interested in being as service oriented to our applicants as we are to those candidates we admit. We are open to questions and try to respond in a timely manner to requests for information." The school recommends that students complete undergraduate coursework in financial accounting, statistics, and microcomputers (spreadsheet applications) prior to applying. UGA uses a modified rolling admissions process and offers an early decision program. The school permits students to defer admission for up to one year.

FINANCIAL FACTS

Tuition (in-/out-of-state)	$2,670/$10,680
Fees (in-/out-of-state)	$1,020/$1,020
Cost of books	$900
Room & board (on-/off-campus)	$4,880/$6,500
% of students receiving aid	80
% first-year students receiving aid	80
% aid that is merit based	100
% of students receiving grants	25
% of students receiving paid internships	98
Average award package	$5,250
Average grant	$1,750

ADMISSIONS

# of applications received	642
% applicants accepted	27
% acceptees attending	56
Average GMAT (range)	640 (560–720)
Minimum TOEFL	600
Average GPA (range)	3.13 (2.76–3.54)
Application fee (in-/out-of-state)	$30/$30
Early decision program available	Yes
Early decision deadline	November 15; December 15
Early decision notification	January
Regular application deadline	March 1
Regular notification	4–6 weeks after receipt of application
Admission may be deferred?	Yes
Maximum length of deferment	1 year
Transfer students accepted?	No
Nonfall admission available?	Yes
Admission process need-blind?	Yes

APPLICANTS ALSO LOOK AT

University of North Carolina at Chapel Hill, Emory University, University of Texas at Austin, Georgia Institute of Technology, Vanderbilt University, University of Virginia, Duke University, University of Tennessee at Knoxville

EMPLOYMENT PROFILE

Placement rate (%)	95
# of companies recruiting on campus	56
% of grads employed immediately	81
% grads employed within six months	97
Average starting salary	$56,000

Grads employed by field (avg. salary):

Consulting	19%	$51,550
Finance	25%	$59,877
General Management	8%	$60,625
Marketing	22%	$55,790
MIS	10%	$48,400
Operations	8%	$55,500
Other	8%	$51,875

GEORGIA INSTITUTE OF TECHNOLOGY
DuPree School of Management

ACADEMICS

Georgia Tech's DuPree School of Management seeks to distinguish itself from the pack by emphasizing the technological aspects of business education. Even the degree it offers, a Master of Science in Management (MSM), sets the school apart from many other MBA programs (although the school brochure points out that "Georgia Tech's MSM is virtually identical to an MBA offered through a school of business administration"). Students tell us that DuPree's "emphasis on analytic skills and technology as a major driver of management techniques" persuaded them to choose the program; that and Tech's bargain-basement tuition, even for non-Georgians.

First-year students at DuPree must complete a full battery of foundation courses. A quarterly schedule that requires five courses guarantees that first-year is an extremely busy time for students. Students report favorably on the "range of topics covered by the core" and appreciate DuPree's commitment to small classes throughout the foundation sequence. One student notes approvingly that "many core courses consist of students with a background in the subject matter, which sets a fast pace for the rest of the class."

Second-year students give high grades to the finance, management, accounting, and operations departments ("the operations faculty," enthuses one student "is one of the school's great strengths"). They also appreciate the "flexibility" of second year, which stands in sharp contrast to the largely prescribed first-year program. Students give low marks to the marketing department, however. Professors are admired because "almost all do extensive work in their industries," yet remain "always available to students for support and advice." In assessing the administration, students concede to the often frustrating limitations state schools must navigate within, telling us that "the b-school is run well, given the restrictions placed on it," and acknowledging that the "administration has its hands tied by Tech bureaucracy." They are less understanding about such essential facilities as multimedia classrooms, computer labs, and the library, all of which "need a serious upgrade."

PLACEMENT AND RECRUITING

The Graduate Management Career Services (GMCS) office tells us that it "offers students a variety of services: a career seminar series, career planning and advising, mock interviews, and resume books. Additionally, alumni network contacts are available to students, as well as involvement in the New York and Atlanta consortiums. Recruiting companies making the most offers: Allied Signal, Citibank, Delta Airlines, Entergy Corporation, and Ernst and Young."

Students give Career Services merely average grades; detractors complain that the office "needs some help." Although our respondents feel that GMCS attracts high-quality recruiters, they also believe that more could be done to bring a greater quantity and diversity of recruiters to campus. Many students report that their experiences with mentors and alumni have been unhelpful.

Ann Johnston Scott, Director of the MSM Program
755 Ferst Drive, Suite 212, Atlanta, GA 30332-0520
Admissions: 404-894-8722 Fax: 404-894-4199
Email: msm@mgt.gatech.edu
Internet: www.dupree.gatech.edu

Georgia Institute of Technology

STUDENT/CAMPUS LIFE

When 40 percent of a student body holds undergraduate degrees in engineering and computer science, it should come as no surprise that an unusually large proportion of these students have monster quantitative skills. Students report that their classmates buck the stereotype of the nerdy engineer, however, describing them as "surprisingly supportive and congenial, even though most of them are very competitive." One student expresses surprise that his classmates are "helpful, not as many Type A personalities as I expected. Very sharp!" The student body derives "from many different countries and backgrounds," although several students complain that there is "very little interaction between U.S. and international students." In general, "students hang out together during the day, play sports together, and socialize with each other at night."

Our respondents report heavy involvement in DuPree's many clubs, such as the Entrepreneur's Club, Honorary Accounting Organization, and Women in Business. All students are members of the Graduate Students in Management (GSM) organization, which arranges intramural sports, alumni events, and guest lecture series. The GSM also has input on curriculum changes, leading one student to write that there's "lots of student leadership" on campus. Students here also find time for community service. DuPree is conveniently located across the street from the university's Student Athletic Center, and reportedly its facilities are very good. Students also enjoy watching Tech's sixteen intercollegiate teams, especially its "great hockey team." Atlanta, ranked among the "top ten cities in the world for business" by Fortune magazine, is well loved by DuPree students. Writes one, "Atlanta and the surrounding area is a great place to live and provides numerous resources for current research and potential future employment." Other ambitious DuPree students cite the presence of Coca-Cola, CNN, and Bell South in the community as their reason for choosing Tech.

ADMISSIONS

If you're thinking of applying to GT straight out of college, reconsider. The vast majority of DuPree students have at least two years of work experience under their belts. Also of great concern to the admissions committee is your GMAT score: The average GMAT score of accepted applicants over the last four years is a smashing 632—way up in the 87th percentile. Also considered are undergraduate GPA, essays, and letters of recommendation.

FINANCIAL FACTS

Tuition (in-/out-of-state)	$3,627/$12,465
Cost of books	$800
Room & board (on-/off-campus)	$10,200/$10,200
% of students receiving grants	20
% of students receiving paid internships	95

ADMISSIONS

# of applications received	450
% applicants accepted	45
% acceptees attending	46
Average GMAT (range)	632 (590–670)
Minimum TOEFL	250
Average GPA (range)	3.20 (2.80–3.50)
Application fee (in-/out-of-state)	$50/$50
Early decision program available	No
Regular application deadline	April 15
Regular notification	Rolling
Admission may be deferred?	Yes
Maximum length of deferment	1 year
Transfer students accepted?	No
Nonfall admission available?	No
Admission process need-blind?	Yes

APPLICANTS ALSO LOOK AT

Emory University, University of Georgia, University of Texas at Austin, Purdue University, Massachusetts Institute of Technology, Indiana University, Vanderbilt University, Carnegie Mellon University

EMPLOYMENT PROFILE

Placement rate (%)	97
# of companies recruiting on campus	90
% of grads employed immediately	93
% grads employed within six months	98
Average starting salary	$64,000

Grads employed by field (avg. salary):

Accounting	3%	$41,250
Consulting	17%	$67,500
Finance	20%	$61,130
General Management	3%	$80,000
Marketing	28%	$58,700
MIS	25%	$67,200
Operations	21%	$72,150
Other	11%	$61,000

HARVARD UNIVERSITY
Harvard Business School

ACADEMICS

Harvard Business School is indisputably the nation's most famous business school, and it is also one of the most selective. In 1994-95, a class of 900 students was admitted from among over 6,900 applicants. With these numbers and a worldwide reputation as *the* business school, HBS appears to be the envy of almost everybody in graduate business education. Unsurprisingly, the prevalent feeling here is summed up by one student's remarks: "If you're going to do an MBA, don't mess around. Come to the best b-school in the world." Those who are fortunate enough to be accepted usually do. More than 80 percent of last year's "admits" chose to enroll. Indeed, the school's "yield" (percentage of admitted candidates who choose to enroll) is the highest of any b-school in the United States.

How did Harvard come to occupy such an august position? First, as one of the oldest b-schools in the nation (founded in 1908), it got a head start on all the other programs. Second, as the biggest b-school—graduating roughly 800 MBAs per year—it's built a network of more than 60,000 alumni worldwide. And these are uncommonly loyal and generous alumni. Since 1980, the school's endowment has grown from $100 million to approximately $545 million in 1995. HBS also boasts more CEO alums than any other program, a nationally renowned faculty, and authorship of 90 percent of the case materials used worldwide.

HBS is known from coast to coast for its comprehensive coverage of the functional areas of business and how well it integrates them. General management is considered the cornerstone of the program, but all of the departments are strong. In recent years, however Harvard's programs have come under heavy criticism. The complaints: HBS has not been responsive to changes in the marketplace. Its rigid program has featured little of the international perspectives, teamwork, student consulting, or innovative learning experiences now characteristic of b-school education in the United States. Surprisingly, the venerable HBS has done what was considered unthinkable before and decided it's time for change. Recently, HBS has undertaken a stem-to-stern program overhaul called the Leadership Learning Initiative. It offers year-round classes (students can now enroll in September or January), sections of eighty instead of ninety, and greater emphasis on skill building and field-based learning delivered in a much more cross-functional context. The school also has been completely transformed by technology: relying heavily on the Internet and Harvard's own Intranet for everything from course materials to lecture examples.

PLACEMENT AND RECRUITING

HBS students get an average 3.8 job offers each—the most of any b-school. Ninety-nine percent have a job by graduation. On average, Harvard students earn some of the highest starting salaries. The big news: for the last few years, Harvard MBAs have been taking in six-figure-plus starting packages. That makes the tuition investment a little easier to handle now, doesn't it?

James Miller, Acting Director of Admissions
Harvard Business School MBA Admissions Office, Soldiers Field Road
Boston, MA 02163
Admissions: 617-495-6127 Fax: 617-496-9272
Email: admissions@hbs.edu
Internet: www.hbs.edu

Harvard University

STUDENT/CAMPUS LIFE

Harvard boasts one of the most beautiful, well-manicured campuses in the nation. It should. The school has plowed $200 million into its buildings and grounds over the last fifteen years. Over and over, students describe its "country club" ambiance and told us about groundskeepers obsessed with sod and shrubbery. "A plant died here last week," one student told us. "They replaced it within three days. And they use a snowblower to clear leaves." Students rave about the ever-popular Shad Hall, Harvard's gym, which is a veritable temple to sweat: "Shad is worth the tuition alone."

Harvard MBAs enjoy an active social life, although one notes, "There is no such thing as dating at HBS. Local undergrads aren't bad if you hide the fact that you go to Harvard." Fifty-six student clubs keep students fully engaged. Many of the clubs sponsor black-tie affairs such as the well-known Predator's Ball. A favorite spot for section gatherings is the Border Cafe. On warm days, students can be found hanging out on the sun-drenched patios of The Grille at Kresge, an on-campus eatery.

Harvard divides its 800 incoming students into sections of eighty; each section takes an entire year of courses together. Writes one MBA, "Section life is a great experience. You develop great camaraderie with classmates from diverse cultural and professional backgrounds." Most of the first-year social life revolves around the section, which schedules dozens of section events to ensure you get to know those eighty classmates well. The school highly recommends forming study groups. During orientation and the first week of class, students generally seek out classmates with whom to form a group. It's not uncommon for overanxious types to begin doing this in the summer, to lock in someone smart.

Harvard's reputation for intensity and competitiveness is well earned. The first four months are the most difficult. As one student explains, "It ramps up quickly. Students who know zero about accounting and stats get left behind." The pressure to succeed is formidable.

ADMISSIONS

The admissions board at Harvard considers the following criteria (not ranked in order of importance): college GPA/transcripts, essays, letters of recommendation, and extracurricular activities. The essays are considered extremely important. Applicants are interviewed at Harvard's discretion only to further evaluate the student's candidacy. Applications are batched in rounds. A final note: after an eleven-year hiatus, Harvard has decided to add the GMAT as one more criterion in evaluating a candidate's admission to the school. This affects those applying for admission in September 1997 and beyond.

FINANCIAL FACTS

Tuition	$26,260

ADMISSIONS

# of applications received	8,061
% applicants accepted	13
% acceptees attending	87
Average GMAT	689
Average GPA	3.50
Application fee	$160
Early decision program available	No
Regular application deadline	March
Regular notification	Rolling
Admission may be deferred?	No
Transfer students accepted?	No
Nonfall admission available?	Yes
Admission process need-blind?	Yes

EMPLOYMENT PROFILE

Placement rate (%)	99
# of companies recruiting on campus	330
% of grads employed immediately	95
Average starting salary	$86,000

Grads employed by field (avg. salary):

Consulting	30%	$90,000
Entrepreneurship	3%	$75,000
Finance	32%	$85,000
General Management	14%	$85,000
Marketing	11%	$75,500
Operations	2%	$75,000
Other	2%	$75,000
Strategic Planning	7%	$83,500
Venture Capital	10%	$82,625

HOFSTRA UNIVERSITY
Frank G. Zarb School of Business

ACADEMICS

Not too far from the hue and cry of New York City lies Hofstra University, once a commuter school primarily serving Long Islanders but now an institution earning an ever-growing national recognition. One of the jewels of the Hofstra University system is the Frank G. Zarb School of Business, whose reputation has extended far enough beyond New York's borders that nearly half its students arrive from out of state.

Location, of course, is one of Hofstra's chief drawing cards. Located in Hempstead, Long Island, Hofstra is a mere 20-minute train ride from New York City; many of Hofstra's part-timers make the commute daily. But Zarb also offers a quality curriculum to accompany its convenient setting. Zarb revised its MBA program in 1995 to better reflect contemporary business management in a global environment. The new curriculum includes a wide range of introductory courses geared toward students with no previous business education. Residency requirements, for example, cover basics in computer and quantitative skills. Core competency courses, which follow residency requirements in the first-year sequence, cover the basic business concepts that many students learn as undergraduates. Zarb allows those arriving with prior classroom experience in business to place out of this early sequence, and such students can conceivably finish the 66-hour curriculum in as little as 42 hours of class time. Other curricular requirements include the following: an advanced core, which emphasizes the integration of various business principles; a cluster of courses called "the Contemporary Business Environment," which focuses on ethics, the environment, and global aspects of business; a major concentration in one of seven offered areas (marketing, finance, accounting, system management, international business, management, and taxation); and a final project, which may take the form of an internship, a computer-simulated management game, a research project, or a consulting engagement.

One of the most noteworthy aspects of the Zarb School's MBA program is its use of the University's McGraw-Hill Technology Laboratory. MBA students use this software and database laboratory to support virtually every aspect of their studies. Zarb students also participate in consulting projects and engagements for companies ranging from small start-up shops to large, multinational firms. The faculty for this "dynamic and intense" b-school receives slightly above-average grades from students. While respondents feel that "Most professors are interested in students' progress," they also feel that Zarb suffers from "too many foreign teachers, too few women teachers. The administration does not communicate with students." Among other administrative sore points: "The administrative offices are not run by the MBA office. The university registrar's office can be painfully slow."

PLACEMENT AND RECRUITING

The Career Development Office (CDO) offers Zarb students assistance with resume preparation, interviewing skills, and job search strategies. Students may also place their resume in Hofstra's MBA resume book, which is distributed to Fortune 500 firms and small financial institutions in the New York City area. Students describe the CDO's effectiveness as hit-and-miss, telling us that they do well in finance but that "We need better career placement in marketing." On a positive note, students report that "Professors can be very helpful when looking for internships, jobs, or advice."

Susan McTiernan, Senior Assistant Dean
Hofstra University, Hempstead, NY 11550
Admissions: 516-463-5683 Fax: 516-463-5268
Email: HUMBA@HOFSTRA.EDU
Internet: www.hofstra.edu

Hofstra University

In one recent year, forty-five companies interviewed graduating MBAs on campus. Top recruiters in this group included: KPMG Peat Marwick, Chase Manhattan, Citibank, and Andersen Consulting.

STUDENT/CAMPUS LIFE

Zarb caters to large part-time and commuter populations, and as a result the student body here lacks some of the cohesion found at other MBA programs. While students describe their classmates as "motivated, friendly, and helpful," they also report that "It is difficult to form relationships because of the large number of commuters." The result is an atmosphere that is "fairly competitive. Full-time students are friendly with one another, but still strive for a high GPA. Only a very small percentage of the students are interested in social activities outside of the program."

Hofstra's campus is lovely, tree-lined, and dotted with sculpture. It is desperately in need of new parking facilities, however; moaned one commuter, "The parking situation needs to be improved. We spend twenty to thirty minutes a day circling for parking." Campus amenities include an excellent athletic center (good enough for the New York Jets to run their summer training camp on campus), a theater, and a museum. The town of Hempstead itself, like much of Long Island, is densely populated and heavily developed, with plenty of strip malls, fast food establishments, and bars; its greatest distinction is that its residents earn less than do those of neighboring towns. As at most commuter campuses—only a small number of Zarb MBAs live on-campus—social life at Hofstra is subdued but not entirely absent. Students tell us that "There are many clubs for MBA students, such as the MBA club and the Consulting Group, and there are lots of Career Forums to attend. In addition, on Sundays we play sports like volleyball and basketball."

Student-organized social events include tailgate parties before Hofstra football games, a spring picnic, and a graduate cruise around Manhattan.

ADMISSIONS

According to the admissions office, the following are considered most important in your application: Leadership, communication skills, and levels of increasing professional responsibility. After that, in descending order of importance, are your college GPA, GMAT score, work experience, essay, letters of recommendation, and extracurricular activities. "Admission processes," writes the school, "tend to be very similar to the selective to highly selective schools in the United States. All [application] materials are evaluated carefully by a committee comprised of faculty and administrators. We offer perhaps one of the more timely application turnarounds among the group of selective schools; once an application is complete, we generally notify the applicant of a decision within four weeks. Members of American minority groups, for example, African Americans, receive special consideration as do those students whose native language is not English."

Applicants may defer admission up to one year for medical reasons or to accrue additional work experience. There is an admission deferment program for college seniors.

FINANCIAL FACTS

Tuition	$16,000
Fees	$700
Cost of books	$1,500
Room & board (on-/off-campus)	$8,000/$7,500
% of students receiving aid	65
% first-year students receiving aid	60
% aid that is merit based	65
% of students receiving loans	69
% of students receiving paid internships	25
Average award package	$9,000
Average grant	$6,000

ADMISSIONS

% applicants accepted	58
% acceptees attending	36
Average GMAT (range)	570 (480–670)
Minimum TOEFL	600
Average GPA (range)	3.20 (2.80–3.50)
Application fee	$40
Early decision program available	Yes
Early decision deadline	January
Early decision notification	January
Regular application deadline	June 1
Regular notification	Rolling
Admission may be deferred?	Yes
Maximum length of deferment	1 year
Transfer students accepted?	Yes
Nonfall admission available?	Yes
Admission process need-blind?	Yes

APPLICANTS ALSO LOOK AT

New York University, Columbia University, CUNY Baruch College, Boston University, Fordham, Babson College, University of Florida, Northeastern University

EMPLOYMENT PROFILE

# of companies recruiting on campus	47
% of grads employed immediately	91
% grads employed within six months	95
Average starting salary	$64,100

Grads employed by field (avg. salary):

Accounting	13%	NR
Consulting	13%	NR
Finance	40%	NR
Human Resources	4%	NR
Marketing	13%	NR
MIS	7%	NR
Operations	2%	NR
Other	3%	NR
Strategic Planning	5%	NR

UNIVERSITY OF ILLINOIS AT URBANA-CHAMPAIGN
College of Commerce and Business Administration

OVERVIEW

Type of school	public
Affiliation	none
Environment	urban
Academic calendar	semester
Schedule	full-time only

STUDENTS

Enrollment of parent institution	36,000
Enrollment of business school	450
% male/female	70/30
% out-of-state	64
% minorities	17
% international (# of countries represented)	47 (30)
Average age at entry	27
Average years work experience at entry	3.23

ACADEMICS

Student/faculty ratio	9:1
% female faculty	18
% minority faculty	26
Hours of study per day	4.31

SPECIALTIES

Strengths in Accounting and Finance, Marketing and Management, Strong Technology and Management, Alliance with the College of Engineering and the National Center for Supercomputing Applications. The first-year core curriculum is highly integrated and organized around modules instead of separate courses. Focus is on learning the fundamental skills, leadership, and application of business skills to real-world projects. OSBI (Office for the Study of Business Issues) generates numerous real-world projects for students to work on in association with tracks in the College areas of strength. Currently, major projects are under way for Lockheed Martin, Dow AgroSciences, and Lucent Technologies, Cargill, and numerous start-up businesses.

JOINT DEGREES

MBA/MS Agriculture; MBA/MA Architecture; MBA/MS Computer Science; MBA/MS Electrical Engineering; MBA/MS Civil Engineering; MBA/MS General Engineering; MBA/MS Industrial Engineering; MBA/MS Mechanical Engineering; MBA/MS Journalism; MBA/M Education; MBA/JD; MBA/MD; Custom-Designed joint degree. Joint degree programs typically take 5 semesters with the exception of MBA/JD (4.5 years) and the MBA/MD (5 years)

SPECIAL PROGRAMS

Chief Financial Officer Lecture Series, Business Advisory Council, Executive in Residence Program, Internship, Development Program

STUDY ABROAD PROGRAMS

The MBA program has formalized agreements with MBA programs in 11 partnering countries.

ACADEMICS

The University of Illinois at Urbana-Champaign recently retooled its MBA program, integrating the core curriculum and adding more options for "hands-on" learning. Students tell us that it is still "early in the reworking process of the Illinois MBA program. It will take a few years to work out the ticks," but they are pleased with the direction the school is pursuing. Of the integrated core, students tell us, "I like the integrated curriculum, which puts courses in order. During the first seven weeks, we study the foundation of business (strategic, marketing, decision-making). Then in the second seven weeks, we learn the managing process for internal organization (operations, organization, etc.)" The core includes two week-long seminars called Applying Business Perspectives (ABP). Students are "impressed with the ABPs. The student can apply material studies before [putting them] into a real business practice."

Some of the university's innovations take advantage of Urbana's prestigious engineering school. The Office for the Study of Business Issues (OSBI), for example, allows MBAs to work side by side with university engineers, computer researchers, and entrepreneures to evaluate the commercial potential of their innovations and to plan marketing strategies. Other innovations make an Illinois MBA more adaptable to the changing marketplace. Although students may enroll in traditional professional track majors focusing primarily on accounting, finance, marketing, and technology, the school also allows "tremendous flexibility in designing your own MBA if you only ask for it." Nearly one-quarter of the students here pursue joint degrees in such areas as education, computer engineering, law, medicine, and even Slavic languages.

Students give professors high marks, bragging, "The faculty are absolutely wonderful. Profs are always willing to help in and out of class. They make this program worthwhile." Finance and MIS are among students' favorite areas of study; accounting and marketing also earn high ratings among the b-schoolers. Students complain that the administration "needs to be more proactive in improving the program and show a genuine effort to help." They also warn that it can be difficult to get into popular courses. One student sums up the complaints, explaining, "although we are a small program we still deal with the bureaucracy of a big university."

PLACEMENT AND RECRUITING

Our survey shows continued improvement at Illinois' MBA Career Services Office (CSO). After years of very low levels of student satisfaction with the office, this year students give the office a "B-." The number and quality of companies recruiting on campus remains the students' chief bone of contention. Also, nearly a quarter of our respondents report that the alumni they contact are of "no help" in their search for jobs and internships.

The CSO publishes resume books for prospective employers and keeps students informed of "company presentations, workshops, interview schedules, deadlines, and important announcements," through a column in the biweekly student newsletter. The service also conducts mandatory career management classes for first-year students and voluntary forums for students to meet alumni

Andrew Verner, Director of Recruiting, Marketing, and Admission
410 David Kinley Hall, 1407 West Gregory Drive, Urbana, IL 61801
Admissions: 217-244-7602 Fax: 217-333-1156
Email: mba@uiic.edu
Internet: www.mba.uiuc.edu

University of Illinois at Urbana-Champaign

and corporate reps. This fall, a new, comprehensive, web-based recruiting system will streamline placement activities. Illinois participates in two major job fairs for international students. Companies that hire a great number of Illinois MBAs include AlliedSignal, Pillsbury, Hewlett-Packard, Procter & Gamble, Ford, GTE, Arthur Andersen, Andersen Consulting, Citibank, Dow Chemical, Eaton Corp., and Ernst & Young.

STUDENT/CAMPUS LIFE

Illinois boasts a "huge international population," resulting in a program that is "like studying abroad without going abroad. Very cool global business experience." However, as one African American student notes, "we are culturally diverse, but not racially. Out of 286 first-years, only fourteen African Americans." Students describe classmates as "friendly, outgoing, willing to work hard to improve the program for future students," but several told us that "many are young with little experience." As a result, there is a pervasive sense that the "top 25 percent are top-notch versus anybody. Bottom 25 percent are awful. Expected the class overall to be more competitive, disciplined, and professional."

Students give the school's hometown of Champaign mixed reviews. Proponents point out that it provides a "small town atmosphere good for studying" and is an "excellent, safe and quiet place to be with your family (I am married and have one child)." Detractors bemoan the fact that "Champaign is in the middle of nowhere" and that there is "not much entertainment near campus." One minority student came down hardest on Champaign, stating flat-out that "this city is horrible. There isn't much to do besides study and go to class. Socially numbing." Student opinion about campus life is more uniformly positive, owing to a "pretty campus" with "lots of restaurants, shops, and bars on campus." Sums up one student, "life here is great. Campus, intercollegiate sports, and the best libraries." The MBA program has "many clubs where we socialize and mix with classmates beyond the classroom." Our respondents recommend participation, explaining that "the workload here is tough, but it is worthwhile to get involved in MBA clubs and organizations. It will help you out in the long run."

ADMISSIONS

The admissions office considers your work experience to be most important; more than 85 percent of students have more than one year of significant work experience. After that, in descending order, they consider your GMAT scores, college GPA, essays, and letters of recommendation. Applicants are invited to present projects, portfolios, CDs, theses, and the like for review. Because of the quantitative components of the curriculum, applicants are advised to have completed a college-level calculus course. Writes the school, "The admissions program is client-oriented. An applicant can track his or her application through a 1-800-MBA-UIUC number."

Decisions are made on a rolling admissions basis. Applicants are notified of a decision two to three weeks from receipt of the completed application. Wait listed students are notified of a spot by June 15.

FINANCIAL FACTS

Tuition (in-/out-of-state)	$10,525/$17,787
Fees (in-/out-of-state)	$1,666/$1,666
Cost of books	$2,500
Room & board (on-/off-campus)	$6,000/$8,000
% of students receiving aid	46
% first-year students receiving aid	46
% aid that is merit based	26
% of students receiving loans	61
% of students receiving grants	36
% of students receiving paid internships	10
Average award package	$18,833
Average grant	$5,000
Average graduation debt	$17,000

ADMISSIONS

# of applications received	1,084
% applicants accepted	48
% acceptees attending	38
Average GMAT (range)	616 (560–640)
Minimum TOEFL	600
Average GPA (range)	3.27 (3.04–3.60)
Application fee (in-/out-of-state)	$40/$50
Early decision program available	Yes
Regular application deadline	April 1
Regular notification	Rolling
Admission may be deferred?	Yes
Maximum length of deferment	1 year
Transfer students accepted?	No
Nonfall admission available?	No
Admission process need-blind?	Yes

APPLICANTS ALSO LOOK AT

Indiana University, University of Texas at Austin, University of Wisconsin—Madison, Ohio State University, Carnegie Mellon University, Purdue University

EMPLOYMENT PROFILE

Placement rate (%)	94
# of companies recruiting on campus	250
% of grads employed immediately	80
% grads employed within six months	98
Average starting salary	$62,000

Grads employed by field (avg. salary):

Accounting	5%	$42,500
Consulting	18%	$60,319
Finance	25%	$55,641
General Management	9%	$67,379
Human Resources	5%	$56,285
Marketing	19%	$57,570
MIS	12%	$54,478
Operations	5%	$61,188
Other	2%	$50,170

INDIANA UNIVERSITY
Kelley School of Business

OVERVIEW

Type of school	public
Affiliation	none
Environment	suburban
Academic calendar	semester
Schedule	full-time only

STUDENTS

Enrollment of parent institution	35,600
Enrollment of business school	554
% male/female	72/28
% out-of-state	87
% minorities	17
% international (# of countries represented)	20 (36)
Average age at entry	28
Average years work experience at entry	4.5

ACADEMICS

Student/faculty ratio	5:1
% female faculty	15
% minority faculty	13
Hours of study per day	5.17

SPECIALTIES

Finance and Marketing are most popular majors. Intergrated approach gives the curriculum an applied focus. Faculty emphasizes teamwork and skill development. Program taught by full-time experienced faculty who are highly accessible to students.

JOINT DEGREES

MBA/JD, 4 years; MBA/MA in Area Studies, 3 years.

SPECIAL PROGRAMS

Team-based, integrative curriculum, opportunities to specialize in various majors or focus areas such as consulting, investing banking, and emerging technologies. Company support and involvement in the programs is common with case competitions, simulations, and guest lectures.

STUDY ABROAD PROGRAMS

Programs offered in thirteen countries

SURVEY SAYS...
HITS
Teamwork skills

MISSES
Campus is ugly
Impossible to get into classes

PROMINENT ALUMNI

Harold Poling, former Chairperson and CEO, Ford Motor Company; James Lipate, CEO, Penzoil; Frank Popoff, CEO, Dow Chemical John Chambers, CEO, CISCO Systems

ACADEMICS

A recent overhaul of the Graduate School of Business's curriculum has further enhanced the already stellar reputation of IU's MBA program. More thorough integration of core courses, an intensified focus on international business, and an emphasis on teamwork are the chief components of IU's restructured program. Perhaps the most innovative addition here is IU's Focus Academy program, which allows students to dig deeper into a specified area than they would if they pursued a typical major or minor course of study. Focus Academies, which consist of from fifteen to twenty students each, immerse MBAs in such areas as consulting, entrepreneurship, sports and entertainment, investment banking, and the Internet, providing them with opportunities to work on projects with area businesses, internships, and extra coursework. The ultimate goal of the Focus Academies is not just to better prepare students, according to IU, but also to increase students' networking connections.

First year at IU consists of core requirements, divided into two components. The first, taken in the fall, is the Foundation Core, team-taught in four-hour segments, four days a week. As its name implies, the Foundation Core aims to equip students with all the tools they need to maximize their final three semesters at IU. (For incoming students worried that their skills are rusty, IU offers intensive pre-semester, two-day courses in accounting, quantitative methods, and computing). Explains one student, "First semester of first year is extremely challenging from a time-management perspective, but it provides a great foundation for subsequent coursework." Adds another, "The workload is heavy. Having classes four days a week helps." Spring courses focus on teamwork; MBAs are divided into groups of four to attack projects in the Functional Core subjects of accounting, finance, information systems, marketing, and operations. One student tells us, "The first-year core experience is unparalleled. Tremendous integration among courses." First year ends with a four-day Global Business Conference, during which teams must write a report and make a presentation on "a complex international issue."

Second year is given over to major, minor, or Academy study; IU encourages students to either design their own majors, creatively combine a major and a minor, or undertake Academy work. Students speak highly of IU's marketing, finance, and brand management departments. Notes one MBA, "The academic experience is excellent in all respects, but what is best is that professors treat students as their peers, which creates a very powerful and enjoyable learning partnership." IU students appreciate the university's "extremely progressive administration, very innovative and responsive to change." Says one, "Every door at IU is open. If you are a leader, then you have every opportunity to demonstrate your initiative and lead." They are also pleased that "the latest technology is used in many facets of the program."

PLACEMENT AND RECRUITING

In past years, career placement has been the weak link in the IU chain, in large part because the school did not have an MBA-dedicated placement office. That changed with the recent opening of the Graduate Career Services Office. Students happily report that the new office "represents a 180-degree turn toward

James Holmen, Director of Admissions and Financial Aid
1309 East 10th Street, Room 254, Bloomington, IN 47405-1701
Admissions: 812-855-8006 Fax: 812-855-9039
Email: mbaoffice@indiana.edu
Internet: www.kelley.indiana.edu/mba

Indiana University

doing things correctly" but also cautiously note that "The new placement office strictly for MBAs just started. They're still working out the bugs."

In one recent year, more than 200 companies conducted over 3,000 interviews with graduating students; more than 100 interviewed first-years for internship positions. According to one student, "Most recruiters are for marketing. There is a shortage in investment banking and management consulting."

STUDENT/CAMPUS LIFE

IU MBAs describe their classmates as "a diverse group" and "very open to helping others. Not many cut-throats here who would stab you in the back" and they "have a strong work ethic. They make good teammates and are motivated to learn." Some students boast that their peers include "many from both coasts, as well as from other countries. We really get to know each other through the cohort system, as well as through student activities. Previous jobs range from architect to CPA, Peace Corps volunteer to inventory controller for Victoria's Secret!" Others, however, feel that IU needs "more international students. Europe and Latin America are very underrepresented." Another student offered this contumelious opinion: "Most are managers, a few are leaders."

On Thursday nights (there's no class on Friday) MBAs head to the designated bar of the week. Also popular are organized social events, such as picnics, barbecues, and the spring banquet. Many students become involved in the student-run career clubs, such as the Graduate Women of Business or the Finance Club. Students rave about all the career contacts they make through the Marketing Club, which features a "Road Show" that markets MBAs to targeted companies. Writes one student, "The MBA Association has thirty-three clubs and organizations and students are extremely active. Lots of school spirit here—go Hoosiers!" Students love Bloomington, praising its "good restaurants and fantastic arts." Adds one student, "Bloomington is beautiful. The area offers athletics, parks, and the arts. Lots of culture—the music school is one of the best in the country, so we have wonderful operas." The majority opts to live off-campus in Bloomington or surrounding neighborhoods. Public transportation is easily accessible. A car is helpful if you want to go exploring on the weekend, but students say parking is a nightmare.

ADMISSIONS

Indiana looks for students whose academic background, work experience, leadership abilities, and comunication skills meet the demands of the program and promise a successful managerial career. The admissions committee takes a holistic look at each application as they consider the applicant's academic record, GMAT score, work experience, record of leadership, letters of recommendation, and essays. The committee searches for the strengths that balance any deficiency in each candidates's profile. Early application is encouraged, with four domestic deadlines: December 1, January 15, and March 1, and April 15. Interviews, though not required, are strongly encouraged.

FINANCIAL FACTS

Tuition (in-/out-of-state)	$8,232/$16,470
Fees (in-/out-of-state)	$543/$543
Cost of books	$4,360
Room & board (on-/off-campus)	$6,014/$6,014
% of students receiving aid	80
% first-year students receiving aid	86
% aid that is merit based	100
% of students receiving loans	69
Average award package	$18,545
Average graduation debt	$33,646

ADMISSIONS

# of applications received	1,643
% applicants accepted	40
% acceptees attending	45
Average GMAT (range)	631 (600–670)
Minimum TOEFL	580
Average GPA (range)	3.30 (3.00–3.50)
Application fee (in-/out-of-state)	$75/$75
Early decision program available	Yes
Early decision deadline	December 1
Early decision notification	Early February
Regular application deadline	January 15
Regular notification	Mid-March
Admission may be deferred?	Yes
Maximum length of deferment	1 year
Transfer students accepted?	No
Nonfall admission available?	No
Admission process need-blind?	Yes

APPLICANTS ALSO LOOK AT
University of Michigan Business School, University of Texas at Austin

EMPLOYMENT PROFILE

Placement rate (%)	97
# of companies recruiting on campus	214
% of grads employed immediately	82
% grads employed within six months	97
Average starting salary	$71,300

Grads employed by field (avg. salary):	
Accounting	$61,000
Consulting	$85,000
Finance	$71,867
General Management	$71,663
Human Resources	$58,600
Marketing	$69,228
MIS	$70,667
Operations	$74,500

INSEAD

The European Institute of Business Administration

OVERVIEW

Environment   suburban

STUDENTS

Enrollment of business school	601
% male/female	85/15
% international (# of countries represented)	89 (56)
Average age at entry	29
Average years work experience at entry	5

ACADEMICS

% female faculty	13

SPECIALTIES

General Management, intensive, ten-month MBA programs, truly international, and no dominant culture. Teaching and research are given equal weight, so pedagogical material is always revlevent and up to date.

STUDY ABROAD PROGRAMS

For 89 percent of students, France is a foreign country and INSEAD is "study abroad." In addition, INSEAD will open a campus in Singapore in January 2000, and there will be exchange possibilities with the campus in Fontainebleau.

PROMINENT ALUMNI

Lord David Simon of Highbury, Minister for Trade and Competitiveness, Department of Trade and Industry, London; Ms. Helen A. Alexander, Chief Executive, The Economist Group, London; Mr. Lindsay Owen-Jones, CEO, L'Oreal, Paris

ACADEMICS

The fast-track one-year MBA at INSEAD is not for everyone; even the school's promotional literature describes the program as "grueling." But for those looking for a quick turnaround on time invested and a degree from a prestigious international MBA program, INSEAD may just fit the bill.

INSEAD telescopes two years of MBA instruction into a single year, cramming fifteen core courses and seven electives into five eight-week periods. Students have the option of entering in January or September; the programs accompanying the two entry dates are identical, save for the fact that January entrants have the option of pursuing a seven-week summer internship in conjunction with their Insead degrees. INSEAD's curriculum starts with two periods of foundation skills, such as accounting, finance, and economics (a one-week refresher math course and a three-week intensive French language course are available to all entering students). The third and fourth periods cover the "big picture . . . showing how each of the seemingly independent functional areas are really highly interdependent." Students may take two of their seven elective courses during each of the third and fourth periods. The INSEAD curriculum concludes with three electives, taken during the fifth period. Electives may be chosen from a menu of more than sixty courses; students may also undertake a faculty-approved independent study in lieu of one elective. INSEAD supplements its curriculum with Topic Days, covering such areas as ethics, business in Asia, and the Internet, and "a small number of specialized half-credit mini-electives." Entrepreneurial studies are supported by the recently founded 3i Venturelab.

INSEAD will admit students to its second campus, in Singapore, starting with the January 2000 academic session. Initially the Singapore campus will be smaller, housing only forty-five students, but in all other ways it should be quite similar to the school in Fontainebleau.

PLACEMENT AND RECRUITING

INSEAD uses a three-prong approach—based on "well-established links to corporations worldwide," "personal contacts via our extensive alumni network," and "the professional Career Management Service (CMS)"—to provide placement and recruiting services to its MBAs. According to school promotional materials, the CMS "is committed to work with you on all aspects of career planning, from self-assessment and career orientation through to interviewing and decision-making." Toward that end, the CMS provides individual counseling; organizes company presentations; conducts workshops on CV writing, market research, and skills relating to interviewing, presentation, and negotiation; maintains and constantly updates a career database; publishes an annual Recruitment Guide for companies; and arranges on-campus recruitment.

Two hundred and eleven companies visited the INSEAD campus in one recent year, conducting more than 8,000 interviews and proffering over 1,100 firm job offers. In addition, twenty-four companies participated in the school's annual MBA Career Fair. Twenty-five percent of 1997 graduates received placements in the United Kingdom; France accounted for 16 percent of final placements; North

MBA Information Office
Boulevard de Contstance, Fontainebleau, France, 77305
Admissions: 33 (0) 1 60 72 40 05 Fax: 33 (0) 1 60 74 55 30
Email: mbainfo@insead.fr
Internet: www.insead.fr./MBA

INSEAD

America, 12 percent; Germany, 10 percent; and Switzerland, 8 percent. More than half of the companies employing INSEAD graduates are headquartered in he United States.

STUDENT/CAMPUS LIFE

What type of student attends INSEAD? According to the school's viewbook, "The July 1998 graduates . . . included a merchant banker, a software engineer, a vet, a ski instructor . . . a dentist, a former model, a journalist, a lawyer, an accountant, a salesman, a consumer goods brand manager, the First Secretary of an embassy, a retired professional athlete, a Bosnian aid coordinator . . . " Well, you get the picture; INSEAD attracts students from a wide variety of professional, educational, and international backgrounds. Approximately one-third of MBAs here hold undergraduate degrees in engineering; another one-third majored in business or accounting. Students represent 41 countries on all five continents, among them natives of North America (15 percent), France (13 percent), Southern Europe (12 percent), the United Kingdom (11 percent), Asia (7 percent), and Africa (6 percent). Approximately one-third of INSEAD students are accompanied by partners.

INSEAD is located in Fontainebleau, a quaint town approximately 40 miles south of Paris. It is an area so picturesque that it has long been the summer residence of French leaders, from the kings to the current president. Fontainebleau is distinguished by its pleasant summer climate and a huge surrounding forest. The town boasts a number of fine shops, restaurants, movie theaters, and historical landmarks. As an added bonus, rents are reportedly quite reasonable. Accordingly, most students choose to live in Fontainebleau or another town nearby rather than in Paris, which is easily accessible by car or commuter train.

The 19-acre INSEAD campus is located along the periphery of the Fontainebleau Forest. Its modern facilities include amphitheaters, meeting rooms, a library, a subsidized self-service restaurant, a campus bookshop, a travel agency, a dry cleaner, and a "state-of-the-art gym." Students are kept busy with study, clubs, and social events like the Summer Ball, which attracts 3,000 students and alumni. Students also organize regular national weeks, consisting of special events "so that others can learn about a country's culture, music, food, and national pastimes."

ADMISSIONS

According to the admissions office all of the following requirements hold weight in the admissions decisions: GMAT scores, undergraduate GPA, letters of recommendation, essays, work experience, extracurricular activities, and the interview. In addition, "international motivation and languages" are other important criteria in INSEAD's decision to admit students.

FINANCIAL FACTS

Tuition	$25,500
Room & board (on-/off-campus)	$16,600/NR
% first-year students receiving aid	50
Average award package	$25,500
Average grant	$10,000

ADMISSIONS

Average GMAT (range)	677 (550–800)
Minimum TOEFL	620
Application fee (in-/out-of-state)	NR/$110
Admission may be deferred?	Yes
Maximum length of deferment	1
Nonfall admission available?	Yes
Admission process need-blind?	Yes

APPLICANTS ALSO LOOK AT

Harvard Business School, I.M.D, Stanford University, London Business School

EMPLOYMENT PROFILE

Placement rate (%)	96
# of companies recruiting on campus	219
% of grads employed immediately	70
% grads employed within six months	93
Average starting salary	$82,000

Grads employed by field (avg. salary):

Accounting	1%	$89,000
Consulting	46%	$86,000
Finance	21%	$78,000
General Management	7%	$89,000
Human Resources	1%	$74,000
Marketing	6%	$79,000
Management Information Systems	1%	$69,000
Operations	2%	$81,000
Strategic Planning	11%	$81,000
Venture Capitol	3%	$92,000

UNIVERSITY OF IOWA

Iowa School of Management, part of the Henry B. Tippie College of Business

OVERVIEW

Type of school	public
Affiliation	none
Environment	urban
Academic calendar	semester
Schedule	full-time/part-time/evening

STUDENTS

Enrollment of parent institution	28,705
Enrollment of business school	810
% male/female	79/21
% out-of-state	26
% part-time	81
% minorities	7
% international (# of countries represented)	35 (104)
Average age at entry	28
Average years work experience at entry	4.69

ACADEMICS

Student/faculty ratio	7:1
% female faculty	18
% minority faculty	11
Hours of study per day	4.58

SPECIALTIES

Finance/Investments Marketing, Enterpreneurship and Management Information Systems. The curriculum effectively combines lecture, case analyses, and field projects. The curriculum is designed to give students the opportunity during the second semester to begin coursework in their area of concentration.

JOINT DEGREES

Joint-degree MBA programs with Law, 4 years; Hospital and Health Administration, 2.5 years; Library Science, 3 years; Nursing, 3 years; with MIS, 2.5 years

SPECIAL PROGRAMS

Summer internships with entrepreneurs

STUDY ABROAD PROGRAMS

France, Austria, United Kingdom, Germany

SURVEY SAYS...

HITS
Computer skills
Getting into courses a breeze
Quantitative skills

MISSES
Profs not great teachers
General management
School clubs

PROMINENT ALUMNI

Leonard A. Hadley, President and CEO, Maytag Corp.; John Pappajohn, President, Equity Dynamics, Inc.

ACADEMICS

The University of Iowa School of Management is "an MBA program on the rise." Spurred on by a new state-of-the-art facility ("incredibly advanced with the latest multimedia") and an administration that is "fantastic in working to provide a challenging and ever-improving atmosphere," Iowa continues its rise in national prominence as reported in previous editions of this book.

Many students are drawn to Iowa by the opportunity to diversify. "Most students seek dual concentrations," explains one student. Many others note the numerous dual degree offerings as their reason for choosing Iowa. Others come to study under "one of the brightest, most aggressive finance faculties in the nation." Finance remains Iowa's strongest discipline, benefiting from not only a strong faculty but also such innovative programs as "the Applied Securities Management program, which allows students to apply classroom ideas to manage real portfolios" and an online stock market game called the Iowa Electronic Market. Other highly rated departments include management, marketing, and management information systems. Among Iowa's other assets is the relatively small classes for a program of its size. Writes one student, "The dean and 90 percent of his staff knew my name in just six months. The class size here offers the opportunity to develop personal relationships with professors."

First year begins with Impact, a week-long Outward Bound-style orientation, "which fosters a climate of enthusiasm, cooperation, and camaraderie through various professional and recreational activities." Students then proceed to a comprehensive and demanding core that is reinforced at the end of the second year in the program's distinctive "capstone course." Students look favorably on the core, reporting that it builds teamwork skills and "creates good writers. Like it or not, you'll be an excellent report writer by the end of the program. There is a strong push to develop good written presentation skills." Second-year students must choose from among eight concentration areas.

Iowa professors receive high marks for accessibility but get mixed reviews for teaching ability. Although some write that the "faculty is on the cutting edge with their research and are able to express that in their lectures," others tell us that "some professors are excellent while others I question how they got to teach." Students are pleased that the "administration has made an outstanding effort to listen to students' concerns regarding teaching quality and to implement change."

PLACEMENT AND RECRUITING

Iowa's MBA Career Services Office (CSO) reports that its placement operation "has undergone dramatic changes in the recent past in response to requests and suggestions that its staff has solicited from employers, students, and alumni." To entice recruiters to the campus, the CSO has designed single-company "Showcase Days" that allow students to "learn firsthand what that company has to offer them." CSO supplements these efforts with an Internet job-listing service, an alumni network, videoconference interviews, and student efforts: "The student organizations plan multiple trips to disparate job markets to meet with top employers." In addition, "MBA Career Services has an Associate Director dedicated solely to internship placements and the School of Management's

Mary Spreen, Director of MBA Admissions and Financial Aid
108 John Pappajohn Business Administration
Building Suite C140, Iowa City, IA 52242
Admissions: 319-335-1039 Fax: 319-335-3604
Email: IOWAMBA@UIOWA.EDU
Internet: www.biz.uiowa.edu/mba

University of Iowa

International Programs Office coordinates intern assignments for domestic students overseas and international students in the United States."

Student opinion of Iowa's CSO has improved since our last survey. Students are particularly satisfied with the number and quality of opportunities for off-campus projects and internships, and also report vast improvement in the quality of mentoring opportunities. The biggest complaint continues to be the school's difficulty in attracting recruiters from the coasts, particularly the East Coast.

STUDENT/CAMPUS LIFE

Iowa students think highly of their classmates, describing them as "immensely talented and cooperative. The students here have a balance that I have not encountered elsewhere. We are competitive, yet work well together in groups, teams, and organizations. There is a balance between coursework and organizational participation. The students here are very active in creating a better program." A "relaxed atmosphere here allows students to compete and learn from each other rather than just compete against each other." Students also "really enjoy the international perspective" added by the huge overseas segment, reporting that "Iowa's program fosters diversity. Recently a Chinese New Year celebration was held with a successful turnout." But, they add, the American students "mostly come from small cities, thereby limiting their perception of the world." Adds another, "there's only a small group of U.S. minorities, but I think it's typical of the Midwest."

Students report a heavy workload during the first year, but note that "second-years have very light schedules, which leaves plenty of time for fun." For fun, they choose from among "a plethora of activities: academics, social, community service (both formal and informal)." The "very active" MBA Association organizes tailgate parties prior to sporting events, Spring Fling, faculty-student mixers, and lectures. It also manages the many popular student clubs, associations, and community service projects. On campus, the "unofficial hangout is the Dublin Underground," and one student cheerfully notes, "the large graduate population [at the university] means you are not stuck among a bunch of undergrads." Students have no qualms about leaving campus; Iowa City "is an excellent place to live while attending school. The town is beautiful, safe, and small yet can fill all the needs for those looking for big-city conveniences." The town is also "very liberal and supports and embraces cultural diversity."

ADMISSIONS

According to the admissions office, the following components are all weighed equally: essays, college GPA, letters of recommendation, extracurriculars, work experience, and GMAT scores. The school advises, however, "Applicants are encouraged to pay particular attention to the essay component of the application process. In addition to considering quantitative factors such as GMAT scores and the undergraduate transcript, we look at prior work experience (responsibilities, not just titles), career focus and ambition, maturity, and individuality." The school recommends that applicants have some quantitative proficiency (i.e., calculus) before matriculating. Admissions decisions are made on a rolling basis until the final deadline. Students may defer admission for up to one year. Roughly one-third of all applicants are admitted.

FINANCIAL FACTS

Tuition (in-/out-of-state)	$4,316/$11,782
Tuition per credit (in-/out-of-state)	$230/$230
Fees (in-/out-of-state)	$212/$212
Cost of books	$1,362
Room & board (on-/off-campus)	$5,184/$5,184
% of students receiving aid	48
% first-year students receiving aid	53
% aid that is merit based	60
% of students receiving grants	26
% of students receiving paid internships	100
Average award package	$5,535
Average grant	$2,025
Average graduation debt	$15,775

ADMISSIONS

# of applications received	662
% applicants accepted	28
% acceptees attending	40
Average GMAT (range)	613 (570–670)
Minimum TOEFL	600
Average GPA (range)	3.20 (2.97–3.43)
Application fee (in-/out-of-state)	$30/$30
Early decision program available	Yes
Early decision deadline	April 15
Early decision notification	Rolling
Regular application deadline	July 15
Regular notification	Rolling
Admission may be deferred?	Yes
Maximum length of deferment	1 year
Transfer students accepted?	Yes
Nonfall admission available?	Yes
Admission process need-blind?	Yes

APPLICANTS ALSO LOOK AT

University of Wisconsin—Madison, Cornell University, University of Minnesota, Indiana University, Notre Dame University

EMPLOYMENT PROFILE

Placement rate (%)	100
# of companies recruiting on campus	111
% of grads employed immediately	90
% grads employed within six months	100
Average starting salary	$61,847

Grads employed by field (avg. salary):
Consulting	20%	$60,594
Finance	41%	$66,695
Marketing	25%	$59,659

UNIVERSITY OF KANSAS
School of Business

OVERVIEW

Type of school	public
Affiliation	none
Environment	suburban
Academic calendar	semester
Schedule	full-time/evening

STUDENTS

Enrollment of parent institution	27,625
Enrollment of business school	447
% male/female	71/29
% out-of-state	37
% part-time	67
% minorities	5
% international (# of countries represented)	18 (14)
Average age at entry	30
Average years work experience at entry	5

ACADEMICS

Student/faculty ratio	8:1
% female faculty	16
% minority faculty	12
Hours of study per day	4.35

SPECIALTIES
Strengths of faculty include strong research and consulting records and a genuine commitment to teaching.

JOINT DEGREES
JD/MBA, 4 years

STUDY ABROAD PROGRAMS
France, Italy, England, Japan, and Brazil

SURVEY SAYS...
HITS
Star faculty
On-campus housing
Small classes

MISSES
Social life
Quantitative skills
Presentation skills

PROMINENT ALUMNI
Jim Duff, President, U.S. Leasing International; Ed Kangas, National Managing Partner, Deloitte and Touche; Jeannine Strandjord, Vice President and Controller, Sprint Corp.

ACADEMICS

Value and location are the reasons most MBAs give for choosing the University of Kansas School of Business. "The KU MBA program provides a great education for the money," sums up one student. Our survey shows that students are satisfied with the KU experience primarily because it will increase their earning power. Fewer say that the program lives up to their academic expectations, yet most report that they are happy to be earning their MBAs here, where costs are low and their prospects at graduation are high.

The KU MBA program begins with an orientation called "Challenge Week," during which students review basic computer and business research skills. Challenge Week also includes a business simulation contest and an outdoor Challenge Course, both of which are designed to foster "team-building" skills. The emphasis on teamwork carries over into the first-year curriculum, during which each student is assigned to a five-member team for all foundation core projects. Coursework is suspended twice during each of the first-year semesters for students to participate in "immersion weeks" in such subjects as total quality management and entrepreneurship. Students report that "the use of immersion weeks to present business ideas is creative. I think the weeks are excellent."

Second-year students choose from eight concentrations. They must also complete two required courses—one in business law and another in strategic management. All these requirements leave little time for electives, leading one student to write, "Overall I would say KU is conservative and wants us to stick to their laid out plan. However, there are some professors with maverick spirits that add a lot to our learning." Students give the highest marks to KU's management courses but complain that classes in marketing, accounting, information systems, and international business are weak.

KU professors receive mixed reviews. Although some students are "very pleased with the faculty's experience and talent," others complain that "some teachers think you should spend 80+ [hours] a week on school and assign an unreasonable amount of work." Several students write that they are frustrated by the "only moderate communication among administration, faculty, and students."

PLACEMENT AND RECRUITING

University of Kansas's Business Career Services Center, a placement center dedicated to both graduate and undergraduate business students, earns praise from Kansas MBAs. Writes one, "The Business Career Services Center is an excellent resource for students seeking professional employment. The quality, diversity, and number of hiring organizations is outstanding." Adds another happy customer, "The career services center has a very well-connected director and office staff. The past placement statistics are impressive and the possibilities ever-growing. If a company is not recruiting on campus, the center will put you in contact with someone in the home office."

The KU MBA program requires all students to fulfill a professional development requirement, usually by completing an internship or study abroad experience during the summer between their first and second years. The school has

David O. Collins, Associate Director of Masters Programs
206 Summerfield Hall, Lawrence, KS 66045
Admissions: 785-864-4254 Fax: 785-864-5328
Email: grad@bschool.wpo.ukans.edu
Internet: www.bschool.ukans.edu/

University of Kansas

also recently created a new position—the career services coordinator—to develop internship opportunities, provide career counseling and development activities, and market MBA students to recruiting organizations. According to the school, 200 national, regional, and local firms recruited on campus last year seeking undergraduate and/or MBA candidates. Top recruiters at KU include Sprint Corporation, Hallmark Cards, Arthur Andersen, Andersen Consulting, Deloitte & Touche, Ernst & Young, and Koch Industries.

STUDENT/CAMPUS LIFE

The majority of the Kansas student body is young. As one MBA explains, "students here are largely two to three years out of undergrad. They're a little naive." Others describe their classmates as "highly competitive," "ambitious and self-assured." Sums up one student, "There are a few students out for themselves. Overall, it's a good group of friendly, helpful colleagues. We see each other as teammates." According to our survey, KU MBAs perceive themselves as "a diverse group," but the numbers don't back this characterization up: international and minority populations are extremely low, and most students share a similar dearth of real-life work experience.

First-year students warn that "this program is time-consuming, and it is difficult to have an active personal life but that should be expected when entering an MBA program." When students' schedules open up during second year, most find that "student life is excellent. We have a great nightlife, excellent art productions, and a wide variety of activities to choose from." Agrees another, "Activities are varied. Sports events are good and fun. Cultural events are interesting. Louise's Downtown is popular for graduate students." Students enjoy Lawrence (pop. 70,000), which they describe as an "ideal college town," and also praise KU's "beautiful" campus. They warn, however, that housing can be a problem, both on and off campus. When small-town life gets dull, students can head to "Kansas City, which is only thirty minutes away and has a lot to offer."

ADMISSIONS

According to the school, your college GPA, GMAT scores, letters of recommendation, and work experience are all weighed equally. Your extracurricular activities are also considered. Writes the admissions office, "There are no minimum scores for GPA/GMAT when considering candidates. The admissions board will also consider extra submissions, such as resumes and extra letters of recommendation." Decisions are made on a rolling admissions basis. Students are notified of a decision approximately three weeks after all application materials are received. Notes the school, "The application form, supplemental data form, and check for $50 must be received by the deadline. Other materials (GMAT, transcripts, letters of recommendation, TOEFL) can come in after the deadline, but a student will not be admitted without all. We have no auditing of classes for noncredit, no exceptions." Students may defer admission for up to one year with a written request.

FINANCIAL FACTS

Tuition (in-/out-of-state)	$5,304/$11,211
Tuition per credit (in-/out-of-state)	$101/$330
Fees (in-/out-of-state)	$428/$428
Cost of books	$800
Room & board (on-/off-campus)	$4,000/$4,500
% aid that is merit based	80
Average grant	$1,200

ADMISSIONS

# of applications received	248
% applicants accepted	60
% acceptees attending	70
Average GMAT (range)	612 (540–710)
Minimum TOEFL	600
Average GPA (range)	3.21 (2.58–3.74)
Application fee (in-/out-of-state)	$50/$50
Early decision program available	Yes
Regular application deadline	May 1
Regular notification	Rolling
Admission may be deferred?	Yes
Maximum length of deferment	1 year
Transfer students accepted?	Yes
Nonfall admission available?	Yes
Admission process need-blind?	Yes

APPLICANTS ALSO LOOK AT

University of Texas at Austin, Arizona State University, University of Chicago, Indiana University, Harvard University, University of Wisconsin—Madison, University of Pennsylvania, Stanford University

EMPLOYMENT PROFILE

Placement rate (%)	82
# of companies recruiting on campus	188
% of grads employed immediately	82
Average starting salary	$54,500

Grads employed by field (avg. salary):

Accounting	23%	$50,600
Consulting	27%	$57,000
Entrepreneurship	2%	NR
Finance	17%	$52,000
General Management	4%	$52,000
Human Resources	2%	$50,000
Marketing	4%	$55,000
MIS	13%	$61,000
Other	10%	$54,500

UNIVERSITY OF KENTUCKY
Carol Martin Gatton College of Business and Economics

ACADEMICS

Students come to University of Kentucky's Gatton school looking for a high return on their investment. Most leave satisfied, thanks to UK's combination of a solid curriculum and an extremely low tuition. Sums up one student simply, this program is an "excellent buy."

Gatton offers two distinct MBA tracks: a business track for students with undergraduate degrees in business (students with business minors may qualify; contact the school for details); and a nonbusiness track for others. Both tracks can be completed in three semesters; the chief difference between the two tracks is flexibility. Students on the business track may take five electives to supplement the seven required core courses. Nonbusiness trackers, however, must complete four additional required courses that "provide students an understanding of functional problems encountered in business enterprise as related to organizational behavior, production, marketing, and finance." Only business track MBAs, then, can develop an area of specialization. Nonbusiness track students receive a general management degree.

The Gatton faculty receives mixed reviews. One student tells us that "Professors are generally likable and genuinely concerned with the students' learning experience." Others, however, warn that "There is a wide variety of professors as far as competency is concerned. I do not feel that student evaluations are taken seriously." Because the program works to accommodate its many part-time students, many classes are offered only in the evening; complains one full-timer, "We need more day classes!" Students appreciate the fact that "the administration is listening to suggestions to improve the program" but bemoan the "administrative infighting [that] prevents students from getting access to international courses, currently offered only to Diplomacy School students." UK's modern facilities receive high marks; says one MBA, "Every classroom has been networked with a state-of-the-art computing system."

PLACEMENT AND RECRUITING

According to the school's placement office, Kentucky students follow a standard job placement procedure. The school reports: "The job search [process] starts in the first semester, when new students establish email addresses and prepare resumes for submission to the placement director. The placement director notifies all MBA students by email of full- or part-time job opportunities that arise and subsequently submits a file of resumes to recruiters for each advertised position." The Placement Director gives continual supervision to students seeking full-time positions and internships. The school participates in the SEMBA consortium, which holds an annual job fair held in Atlanta. UK also encourages students to seek opportunities abroad through its student exchange program with "top-ranked business schools in England, France, and Austria."

Students tell us that "UK needs to attract more consulting firms to campus. Also, internships are weak." In addition to the placement office, some students utilize MBA Career Central, a free, privately run, Internet-based placement service.

Dr. Susan Jordan, Director MBA Program
1451 Carol Martin Gatton College of Business, Lexington, KY 40506-0034
Admissions: 606-257-1306 Fax: 606-323-9971
Email: mlesteff@pop.uky.edu
Internet: gatton.gws.uky.edu

University of Kentucky

STUDENT/CAMPUS LIFE

UK students describe their classmates as "easy to work with," adding that "students are friendly. Even though the atmosphere is competitive, everyone helps each other with classes and notes and tests." About one-third of the students are part-timers, leading one student to comment that classes include "a lot of part-time students that add a lot to the class sessions." UK works hard to admit students from a variety of foreign countries; Eastern Europe and former Soviet states are well represented here. Approximately 15–20 percent of the 100 students admitted each fall are international students.

At UK the workload is moderate, the pressure light. "It's not cutthroat, thank God," writes one student, "I'll save that for work." The majority of students report that post-class study averages between 15 to 25 hours a week, well below our national average. One student tells us that "life at UK is very focused on learning, but there is still time to socialize and meet new friends. The environment is friendly toward working students." Some students feel that UK would do well to step up the academic pressure: writes one, "Students should spend less time on basketball and more on academics." Fat chance; Kentucky's basketball team is a perennial contender, and most students couldn't be happier about the situation. Beyond basketball—and football—students tell us that extracurricular life is mostly uneventful. The MBA Association sponsors activities such as student orientation, an MBA newsletter, a Thursday night supper club, golf scrambles, and a few intramural sports; students participate in a few professional, religious, and special interest clubs; and that's pretty much it. The situation suits students; since many work and/or have family obligations, few have much time to devote to extracurriculars. Students applaud the facilities, especially the business lab, classrooms, computing facilities, library, and the MBA Center—"a great place to study, socialize, and converse about anything."

Students say one of the main advantages of UK is its location in a region of strong economic growth. Most enjoy Lexington ("Life is 'Midwest safe.' Nothing threatening but nothing very experimental either"); the larger city of Louisville is only a short trip away. "Spring and fall meets at the world-renowned racetrack Keeneland are great!" raves one student. The majority of students opt for off-campus living in nearby apartments. Parking, unfortunately, is a nightmare; students joke that after studying, looking for parking is their most time-consuming activity. Most students drop off their cars at the football stadium and take the shuttle bus to campus.

ADMISSIONS

According to the admissions office, your GMAT score, college GPA/transcript, and the university you attended are considered most important. After that, in descending order, are your work experience, letters of recommendation, essays, and extracurricular activities. Notes the office of admissions: "Undergraduate degrees in engineering or science are considered a plus. The 100 best applications are accepted every year." Deferred admission is now possible.

FINANCIAL FACTS

Tuition (in-/out-of-state)	$3,260/$9,780
Tuition per credit (in-/out-of-state)	$182/$544
Fees (in-/out-of-state)	$336/$336
Cost of books	$600
Room & board (on-/off-campus)	$5,834/$6,234
% of students receiving aid	39
% first-year students receiving aid	33
% aid that is merit based	70
% of students receiving grants	43
Average award package	$5,470
Average grant	$3,556

ADMISSIONS

# of applications received	280
% applicants accepted	42
% acceptees attending	82
Average GMAT (range)	599 (570–650)
Minimum TOEFL	550
Average GPA (range)	3.20 (2.80–3.50)
Application fee (in-/out-of-state)	$30/$35
Early decision program available	Yes
Early decision notification	2 weeks after receipt of all documents
Regular application deadline	July 15
Regular notification	Rolling
Admission may be deferred?	Yes
Maximum length of deferment	3 years
Transfer students accepted?	Yes
Nonfall admission available?	No
Admission process need-blind?	Yes

APPLICANTS ALSO LOOK AT

University of Tennessee at Knoxville, University of Georgia, Vanderbilt University, Indiana University, University of Alabama, Ohio State University, University of Texas at Austin, Arizona State University

EMPLOYMENT PROFILE

# of companies recruiting on campus	128
Average starting salary	$47,365

Grads employed by field (avg. salary):

Accounting	13%	$41,778
Consulting	12%	$42,814
Finance	22%	$55,363
General Management	6%	$47,000
Marketing	12%	$42,971
MIS	12%	$46,185
Operations	10%	$50,083
Other	13%	$50,165

UNIVERSITY OF LONDON
London Business School

OVERVIEW

Environment   urban

STUDENTS

of countries represented: 60

ACADEMICS

Students committed to a career in international business would do well to consider the MBA Program at the London Business School, which offers not only an international curricular focus but also a world-class faculty and an impressive alumni network to the lucky few admitted here. The school also capitalizes on its location in Europe's primary finance center to sustain strong concentrations in finance and entrepreneurship.

The London Business School divides its core curriculum into four categories: Making Decisions and Managing People and Processes, which are stressed during the early stages of the first year; and Strategic Thinking and Theory to Practice, which take place during the second semester of first year and the summer. The core emphasizes group work, placing students in teams of from six to eight for the entire first-year experience. The school reports that "up to 50 percent of first-year assignments can be based on group projects, so it's important to work at making the group gel." Students who are not bilingual must plan to include language studies in their curriculum; the London Business School requires graduates to demonstrate proficiency in a second language. First-year studies also include a week-long "observational exercise" during which students "shadow a senior manager to develop powers of reflection and absorb a great deal of experience in an industry and what it's like to be a manager in that industry."

Second-year students choose twelve electives from among more than seventy-five, and must also complete the Second Year Project, a paid "real-time project for a client organization" culminating in a Management Report. Concentrations are available in finance, international management, strategy, and entrepreneurship. Students may choose to develop an area of expertise but are not required to do so; they may instead opt for a degree in general management. One-third of second-year students decide to spend one term at one of the London Business School's thirty-two exchange school partners, located on all five continents.

In addition to the traditional full-time MBA, the London Business School also offers an Executive MBA Program (part-time study for full-time workers); an accelerated master's program for individuals with ten or more years' business experience; a Master's in Finance; and a PhD Program, in which seventy-five students are currently enrolled.

PLACEMENT AND RECRUITING

Students at the London Business School enjoy the services of the Career Management Centre, a program-dedicated office that provides counseling and recruitment services. The CMC's battery of offerings include workshops (including the compulsory Business Career Interest Inventory, designed at Harvard), a "comprehensive recruiter database and library," London GOLD (a European on-line employment database), and the distribution of biography/resume books. The school also stays in close contact with its 14,000-plus alumni, who are reportedly helpful in students' job searches. In one recent year 131 companies paid recruitment visits to the campus, conducting more than 2,500 individual interviews. Consulting and finance firms claim the lion's share of London Busi-

We apologize for the lack of statistical information for the University of London. This was the first year we included them in the book, and we were unable to obtain the most accurate and current statistics by the time of publication.

Senate House, MBA Information Office
Malet Street, London WCIE 7HU
Phone: 020-7636-8000 Fax: 020-7636-5841
Email: admissions@external.lon.ac.uk
Internet: www.lon.ac.uk

University of London

ness School MBAs. In 1998, two-thirds of the graduating class found work in the United Kingdom; others found placements on the continent (12 percent), North America (9 percent), and Asia (7 percent).

STUDENT/CAMPUS LIFE

London Business School attracts top-flight students from across the globe; in 1998, forty-seven countries were represented among the entering class. North Americans and Asians each make up roughly one-quarter of the student body; British students constitute approximately one-fifth of the population. School promotional materials also tout students' professional diversity, reporting a mix ranging "from engineers, bankers, and consultants to doctors, scientists, lawyers, entrepreneurs, civil servants, and even an opera singer!" Nearly half the graduating class of 2000 hold undergraduate degrees in nonbusiness majors.

Location may not be the main reason students choose the London Business School, but it certainly doesn't dissuade many. The city is a world business center as well as the seat of British government, and so presents numerous opportunities for internships and field study. According to school promotional materials, "executives and government officials regularly attend the School's formal events (the Stockton lectures have recently involved [the late] King Hussein of Jordan, Anita Roddick of Body Shop, and David Potter, Chairman and Chief Executive of Psion Ltd)." In addition, London is one of the world's truly great cities, rich in history, culture, and popular entertainment. Residential rents are expensive, however, and the food, while not as bad as many say it is, will not make you forget American cuisine.

School facilities are excellent, modern, and fully wired. The library includes an "extensive printed collection" and easy computer access to twenty online databases, including Reuters Business Briefing, Dow-Jones News Retrieval, and Bloomburg. Other on-site amenities include restaurants, a wine bar, and a "fully equipped recreation centre."

ADMISSIONS

According to the school the main objective is "to admit tomorrow's leaders" who are "internationally minded, talented, motivated, and experienced professionals with drive, ambition, and commitment from all around the world." To be considered for acceptance, applicants must demonstrate the following through the application, essay, two references, and interview: intellectual capacity (GMAT score), management potential, personal motivation and maturity, team skills, international exposure, and language ability.

FINANCIAL FACTS	
Tuition	£8,000
ADMISSIONS	
Average GMAT	620

LOYOLA UNIVERSITY
Chicago Graduate School of Business

ACADEMICS

Loyola University—Chicago offers an MBA program well-suited to the needs of working Chicagoans. The vast majority of Loyola MBAs are part-timers who are drawn to the school by the availability of evening classes and a quarterly academic schedule that "allows you to complete the program faster." Students report that "Loyola accommodates the part-time student very well with extended office hours, career fairs in the evenings, evening and weekend classes, email announcements, etc."

Loyola is a Jesuit school, and according to the school "is strongly influenced by the Jesuit tradition, which stresses excellence in teaching and research . . . and the role of ethics in business decision making." Students report that Loyola meets these goals, giving professors good grades both for teaching ability and accessibility. Writes one student, "I have found very good teachers, especially in finance . . . they are accessible outside class, too." Adds another, "Professors are very knowledgeable and helpful, and the environment is very good." Ethical perspectives are interwoven in all course material; in addition, all students must complete one course dedicated entirely to ethical issues in business.

To serve the needs of its part-time student body, Loyola allows students a lot of leeway in creating their course schedules. Students are even given options in selecting their core courses, including the option of placing out if they can demonstrate proficiency. One student appreciates the "flexibility of the MBA program, permitting you to make your own schedule and thus concentrate in what you are really interested in." Second-year students may concentrate in a "field of specialization" but need not do so, if they choose instead to pursue a general curriculum. Students speak highly of Loyola's finance, health care administration, and information systems departments. Notes one student, "I chose Loyola because it offers technical MIS classes (e.g. C++). Most other schools do not." Loyola students also praise the school's "great facilities, especially the library and computer labs."

Loyola has recently changed its curriculum in an effort to place greater emphasis on international business studies, adding a required course in international business. The school also encourages students to take advantage of a two-week intensive summer course at its Rome campus, an option students describe as worthwhile. Opportunities to study in Bangkok and Greece are also available.

PLACEMENT AND RECRUITING

Loyola's MBA Career Services office coordinates workshops, job boards, an employer database, internships, and job fairs for its MBAs. In addition, students within six months of graduation can register with Career Services for inclusion in the Loyola resume books, resume referral program, on-campus interviews, and the Midwest MBA Consortium. Furthermore, the office conducts videotaped mock interview sessions twice a year and maintains an alumni database, accessible to students nearing graduation.

Paul Davidovitch, Director
820 North Michigan Avenue, Chicago, IL 60611
Admissions: 312-915-6122 Fax: 312-915-6120
Email: mba-loyola@luc.edu
Internet: www.luc.edu/depts/mba

Loyola University

Students give the service average grades, telling us that "We need to expand career placement. They do a great job, but they could get more employers to recruit on campus." Students also complain that the "fellowship/assistantship program could use a more formal, organized structure." The burden on the service is lessened somewhat by the fact that some Loyola students pursue their MBAs to improve their stature at their current place of employment rather than to find new employers.

STUDENT/CAMPUS LIFE

Loyola's student body is "mainly [made up of] part-time students with a significant amount of work experience." They are a diverse group of people who "differ greatly in age, work experience, and cultural backgrounds," and include "many international students," which means "a lot of students from Thai Loyola University." Writes one student, "In my last four classes—all with group projects—we've had groups with students from the United States, Canada, Thailand, Korea, Ecuador, Venezuela, Colombia, and Brazil . . . we learn a lot." Students describe their classmates as "down-to-earth, intelligent, [and] motivated." African American students warn, however, that their ranks are small; much of the minority population here is made up of Asian Americans.

With so many students attending part-time—often while holding down full-time jobs—it is understandable that campus life at Loyola is subdued. Students report that the "GBA (Graduate Business Association) provides tons of social and professional events, for example a job fair, Cubs games, and wine-tasting." The Distinguished Speaker Series brings national leaders to campus to discuss current events and issues; recent topics have included business ethics, world trade agreements, banking reform, and the future of the American economy. Beyond campus, of course, is Chicago, one of the world's most active financial trading centers. Chicago is also one of the great American cities, offering a cornucopia of culture, entertainment, dining, and nightlife. One student explains, "This school is in the hub of the Chicagoland area and offers many opportunities to relax from the pressures of school." Adds another, "Social life is great. There's plenty to do in Chicago outside school, time permitting."

ADMISSIONS

Despite its generous 46 percent acceptance rate, Loyola places some exacting demands on its applicants. Academic strength, GMAT scores, work experience, recommendations, quality of undergraduate institution and difficulty of major, and extracurricular activities are considered, in that order. These fairly ordinary criteria become somewhat more daunting when you consider that the average Loyola MBA candidate has four years of work experience before enrollment.

FINANCIAL FACTS

Tuition (in-/out-of-state)	$16,542/$18,060
Tuition per credit (in-/out-of-state)	$613
Fees (in-/out-of-state)	$117
Cost of books	$900
Room & board (on-/off-campus)	$6,600/NR
% of students receiving loans	94
Average grant	$17,000

ADMISSIONS

# of applications received	646
% applicants accepted	46
% acceptees attending	72
Average GMAT (range)	530 (400–780)
Average GPA (range)	3.10 (2.50–4.00)
Application fee (in-/out-of-state)	$20/NR
Regular application deadline	July 31
Regular notification	Rolling
Admission may be deferred?	Yes
Maximum length of deferment	1 year
Transfer students accepted?	Yes
Nonfall admission available?	Yes
Admission process need-blind?	Yes

APPLICANTS ALSO LOOK AT

Northwestern University, University of Chicago, University of Illinois at Urbana-Champaign, University of Notre Dame, Georgetown University, University of Michigan Business School, University of California—Los Angeles, New York University

EMPLOYMENT PROFILE

Placement rate (%)	92
% of grads employed immediately	84
% grads employed within six months	80
Average starting salary	$51,578

Grads employed by field (avg. salary):

Accounting	5%	NR
Consulting	13%	NR
Finance	42%	$46,543
General Management	15%	$45,938
Human Resources	8%	NR
Marketing	22%	$41,042
MIS	7%	$55,500
Operations	9%	$58,800
Other	5%	$54,333
Strategic Planning	2%	NR

UNIVERSITY OF MARYLAND
Robert H. Smith School of Business

ACADEMICS

On a campus known to undergraduates as "Party Park," Maryland MBAs seem to be having a party of a very different kind. Cloistered in the southwest quadrant of this huge campus, the Maryland Business School inspires some extremely enthusiastic student responses. And the party is about to get better: a recent $15 million gift from Robert H. Smith, developer of Virginia's mammoth high-rise residential complex, Crystal City, is earmarked for upgrades in faculty, financial assistance to students, and the Graduate Career Management Center. The school was recently renamed in Smith's honor.

Add to this the business school's new, state-of-the-art facility and the full automation of cumbersome administrative tasks, and you can understand why students here are so cheerful. "The school runs like butter since the technology upgrade took effect," writes one student. "Registration, billing, everything is online." No wonder students here view the administration more charitably than do students at other state-run schools. "The school administration," writes one, "is responsive to student demands. If you have a point to make, you'll be heard." Another understanding student adds that the "administration seems understaffed, but they work hard."

Maryland stresses experiential learning, primarily through a series of required courses called, unsurprisingly, Experiential Learning Modules (ELM). Explains one student, "Every term we have two weeks of workshops in different topics (job search, teamwork and diversity, Washington experience). I find these ELMs to be outstanding." Second year requires fewer ELMs, but includes a Group Field Project, in which students are required to "balance theory with practical application." One student explains the difference between the two years this way: "First year carries a heavy workload, numerous team-building activities. Second year entails more career-focused activities, as well as excellent social and academic opportunities." Second-year students also have many more elective options than do first-years, who must complete the core curriculum.

Among the school's departments, students most often praise marketing, finance, and "the best entrepreneurship program locally available." Students also appreciate Maryland's focus on technology, telling us that "one of the reasons I chose MBS was its strong technology emphasis. As an engineer, I feel it's very important to stay current. At MBS, you can." Professors "are good at integrating theory and practice" but "should take a more active role in monitoring GAs/TAs and getting them involved with study groups." Some also complain that "visiting profs and adjunct staff leave a lot to be desired."

PLACEMENT AND RECRUITING

Maryland's Graduate Career Management Center (GCMC) earns high marks from students for its personal service and its ability to attract high-quality recruiters to campus. In addition to their approval of the GCMC's current services, students also note that the "placement office is undergoing substantial improvements."

Sabrina White, Director of MBA/MS Admission
2308 Van Munching Hall., U. of Maryland, College Park, MD 20742-1815
Admissions: 301-405-2278 Fax: 301-314-9862
Email: mba_info@rhsmith.umd.edu
Internet: www.rhsmith.umd.edu

University of Maryland

The GCMC organizes workshops and "networking receptions" for first-year students, assists in the search for summer internships, and runs the Career Management ELM at the beginning of the second year. This program is designed to hone students' interviewing and communications skills by providing "hands-on instruction in everything from business etiquette to salary-offer negotiation." More than 100 companies recruit on campus during a typical year at College Park. The school also participates in the MBA Career Forum in Chicago.

STUDENT/CAMPUS LIFE

As they are about all other aspects of their program, Maryland students are enthusiastic about their classmates. One student sums up the attitude: "The greatest thing about this school has to be the students. My classmates are of exceptional character. They are intelligent, fun, and personable. They bring a wide variety of experiences to the classroom, enriching my educational experience. They are also willing to help their classmates succeed. It is a great environment in which to go to school." Diversity comes in the form of "many foreign students and students from all over the U.S. A very good mix of people and experiences." A substantial portion of the "very competitive but friendly" student body "commute from long distances," and "a large portion are married/engaged." Some students warn that there is a "big rift between the part-time and full-time students."

Because so many students commute to College Park, relatively small portions of Maryland MBAs are active in extracurricular activities. Those who do participate report that there is an "abundance of clubs, social, and career activities." Another student confirms that "campus life offers me lots of options to enjoy my time outside of class. Gym facilities, the Marie Theater, dining halls, etc." Although College Park is a giant campus, students note that "the business school is like a campus in itself: tight-knit, [which makes it] easy to get to know others," and so UM boasts many of the assets of a smaller school. Once off-campus, students find that the "area near College Park sucks. You have to travel about a half-hour to go places that are fun and safe." Nearby Washington, DC, however, "the Mecca for high tech" as well as government, "provides plenty of cultural, political, and night- life activities." Commuters are "pleased with the school's attention to commuter needs" but agree that "parking is a major hassle."

ADMISSIONS

According to the admissions office, your GMAT score, college GPA, and work experience are considered "very important." Your essays, interview, letters of recommendation, and extracurricular activities are considered "important."

Decisions are made on a rolling admissions basis. Typically applicants are notified of a decision eight weeks after the completed application has been received. Accepted applicants may defer admission for up to one year.

FINANCIAL FACTS

Tuition (in-/out-of-state)	$9,558/$14,040
Tuition per credit (in-/out-of-state)	$531/$780
Fees (in-/out-of-state)	$1,220/$1,220
Cost of books	$2,000
Room & board (on-/off-campus)	$2,899/$9,700
% of students receiving aid	175
% first-year students receiving aid	75
% aid that is merit based	35
% of students receiving paid internships	95
Average award package	$14,000
Average grant	$5,000

ADMISSIONS

# of applications received	1,515
% applicants accepted	27
% acceptees attending	55
Average GMAT (range)	653 (600–700)
Minimum TOEFL	600
Average GPA (range)	3.34 (3.10–3.70)
Application fee	$40
Early decision program available	No
Regular application deadline	December 1
Regular notification	Rolling
Admission may be deferred?	Yes
Maximum length of deferment	1 year
Transfer students accepted?	Yes
Nonfall admission available?	No
Admission process need-blind?	Yes

APPLICANTS ALSO LOOK AT

Georgetown University, University of North Carolina at Chapel Hill, University of Virginia, University of Pennsylvania, Duke University, University of Texas at Austin, New York University, Indiana University

EMPLOYMENT PROFILE

Placement rate (%)	96
# of companies recruiting on campus	108
% of grads employed immediately	80
% grads employed within six months	96
Average starting salary	$65,000

Grads employed by field (avg. salary):

Consulting	26%	$62,696
Finance	32%	$64,010
General Management	3%	$68,400
Human Resources	24%	$64,778
Marketing	11%	$65,324
MIS	3%	$52,000
Other	1%	$65,333

UNIVERSITY OF MASSACHUSETTS AT AMHERST
Isenberg School of Management

ACADEMICS

Now may be the time to attend the Isenberg School of Management at the University of Massachusetts. Several years ago, administrators cut class sizes to more effectively conduct a performance review of the program. The program remains downsized today, with each class consisting of fewer than forty students. Benefits to students include tremendous amounts of personal attention from professors and teaching assistantships for nearly all MBAs, practically eliminating the already-low cost of a U Mass MBA. How long this situation will last is uncertain, but it's hard to imagine students being happier than they are right now if and when the program expands.

Current MBA students at Isenberg speak highly of the faculty, telling us that "Professors are excellent and administrators in this program are very supportive." Writes one student, "Most of my professors are excellent teachers, and there are lots of opportunities to interact with professors and administrators." Students are equally sanguine about the "great" assistantships, reporting "one of the great strengths of the program is the financial support provided by the school through assistantships." Because of the small size of the program, only four areas of specialization are available: accounting and auditing information services; general management; marketing; and finance and operations management. Study in the last of these areas is distinguished by student access to the Center for International Security and Derivatives Markets (CISDM), a real-time trading room.

First year at Isenberg consists of eight required, quant-heavy core courses and a single elective. Students appreciate the fact that the core entails "much integration of course materials." Four courses are required during second year, allowing students five electives in which to tailor fields of specialization. Students are encouraged to utilize other areas of the university in tailoring their studies; however, due to the "intensive nature" of the program, students are not permitted to pursue joint degrees. Among their few complaints, students tell us that "There needs to be a stronger mandate to the direction of this program in terms of size, students, and faculty" and also that "We need IT courses for the MBA program." Still, most agree that "the school runs quite smoothly with few hassles" and are satisfied with an academic experience that "has been challenging but still allows for a social life. It's a good balance."

PLACEMENT AND RECRUITING

In response to student complaints, U Mass has recently established a program-dedicated MBA Career Management Office. The new office "provides individual career coaching, resume and cover letter workshops, corporate mock interview sessions, a career seminar at orientation, [and] recruitment and job postings. A strong relationship with other U Mass Amherst career centers allows for additional recruitment opportunities. A central component of the Career Management Office is the establishment of a new MBA Alumni Career Network. The response from alums has been impressive. Additionally, a clear benefit of the small size of the MBA program is the exceptional career networking opportunities that exist with faculty, deans, and fellow students." Students concur that "the alumni base is outstanding" but complain that the CMO "needs help with internships."

Heather Miller, Director of the Office of Graduate Programs
SOM RM209, Amherst, MA 01003
Phone: 413-545-5608 Fax: 413-545-3858
Email: gradprog@som.umass.edu
Internet: www.som.umass.edu

University of Massachusetts at Amherst

STUDENT/CAMPUS LIFE

The size of the UMass academic community is what makes it special. Many cite the sense of community as what they like best about the program. "It's not cutthroat at all," writes one MBA. "There's a good team spirit within the classes," concurs another student. "The class size reduces competition among peers because all students know each other on a personal level." Unusually for a b-school, the students report that the first- and second-year students are quite close.

With such a small student body, MBAs at U Mass get to know each other pretty well. Fortunately, they are a "personable," "very intelligent and friendly" group. The "extremely diverse student body" boasts a large percentage of foreign nationals, leading one student to observe that "You become more globally aware merely by interacting with our diverse student body." While some students report that "Everyone is very easy to get along with and students are very open with each other in terms of sharing information" and that "groups self-organize around studies, sports, and social interests," others note that "not too many people socialize outside of school."

Amherst is a quintessential college town in the Pioneer Valley of Western Massachusetts. Students report that both on- and off-campus housing is more than adequate and affordable. The town itself provides plenty of diversions, including "art and musical events, bar hopping, and intramural sports." The campus offers numerous other diversions; while the U Mass MBA program is tiny, the parent university is a large institution with an enrollment well over 20,000. Students "keep busy with out-of-school projects such as research for professors and working" and "going on company and plant visits with the school."

ADMISSIONS

The admissions office considers your work experience the most important element of your portfolio. After that, in descending order, are your GMAT score, letters of recommendation, college GPA, and essays. Extracurricular activities and interviews are not considered. It is recommended that applicants complete courses in microeconomics and statistics before applying. Writes the school, "We are willing to make a number of academically 'high-risk' admissions decisions if we feel an individual has the potential to make a significant contribution to the business community. The strength of our program lies in its small size. Each student receives a great deal of individual attention from faculty and administrators."

FINANCIAL FACTS

Tuition (in-/out-of-state)	$2,640/$9,018
Tuition per credit (in-/out-of-state)	$378/$378
Fees (in-/out-of-state)	$2,856/$3,204
Cost of books	$1,900
Room & board (on-/off-campus)	$4,520/$4,520
% of students receiving aid	95
% first-year students receiving aid	95
% aid that is merit based	85
% of students receiving loans	40
% of students receiving grants	5
Average award package	$15,000
Average grant	$11,870

ADMISSIONS

# of applications received	230
% applicants accepted	26
% acceptees attending	54
Average GMAT (range)	602 (490–740)
Minimum TOEFL	600
Average GPA (range)	3.30 (2.80–3.80)
Application fee (in-/out-of-state)	$25/$40
Early decision program available	Yes
Regular application deadline	February 1
Regular notification	March 15
Admission may be deferred?	Yes
Maximum length of deferment	1 year
Transfer students accepted?	No
Nonfall admission available?	Yes
Admission process need-blind?	Yes

APPLICANTS ALSO LOOK AT

University of Maryland, Boston University, Dartmouth College, University of California—Los Angeles, University of Connecticut, University of Michigan Business School, University of Texas at Austin, University of Virginia

EMPLOYMENT PROFILE

Placement rate (%)	100
% of grads employed immediately	100
Average starting salary	$60,878

Grads employed by field (avg. salary):

Accounting	8%	$55,000
Consulting	15%	$60,000
General Management	31%	$69,250
Marketing	15%	$63,500
MIS	15%	$44,500
Operations	8%	$50,000
Other	8%	$40,043

MASSACHUSETTS INSTITUTE OF TECHNOLOGY
Sloan School of Management

ACADEMICS

The Sloan School of Management is not just the "top school for high-tech business," as would be expected of a school run under the auspices of MIT. Sloan is also a top performer in finance, management, manufacturing operations, international business, entrepreneurship, and economics (brags one student, "Our economics department has to be the best in the world!"). In fact, students give Sloan top grades in all academic disciplines here except marketing.

Technology, of course, is the bread and butter of parent institution MIT, and students on Sloan's information technology track benefit from the cutting-edge research being done within the university walls. So, too, do finance students, who have access to a $3.5 million trading floor that is virtually identical to the ones in the world's financial capitals. The trading floor not only allows students to gain practical trading experience, but also provides the data for MIT's pioneering research in financial engineering, a new field dedicated primarily to developing the tools with which to analyze the increasingly complex world markets. In manufacturing, the Leaders for Manufacturing program partners the b-school, the school of engineering, and thirteen corporations in a cooperative endeavor to develop new methods of manufacturing and manufacturing education.

Sloan's core requirements take up only a single semester's work, a system that yields mixed results. While students are pleased to get requirements out of the way quickly, they also suggest that the school "make the core courses wider, that is, make it a full year of required courses, not just one semester. The core currently does not require finance theory or marketing, but it should." Furthermore, under the current system "first semester is like boot camp at the Air Force Academy." Students note that the workload lightens appreciably after core courses are completed. They also have the opportunity to choose from more than 100 courses offered each semester.

In all areas at Sloan, "Teamwork is paramount, and group and academic projects reflect this philosophy." Students recognize that they are privileged to study with a "first-rate faculty, second to none." Writes one student, "We have classes with Nobel Prize winners and even get together with them at their places for a beer." They also report that "Administration and professors listen to student comments and complaints, and work to improve courses and overall course load. Professors will make changes mid-semester!"

PLACEMENT AND RECRUITING

Students at Sloan approve of the job done by the school's Career Development Office (CDO), with more than 70 percent expressing a high level of satisfaction with the range and diversity of companies recruiting on campus. Top recruiters here include Hewlett-Packard, McKinsey, A.T. Kearney, Booz-Allen & Hamilton, Motorola, Citibank, Merrill Lynch, and Lehman Brothers. Manufacturers, high-tech, and bio-tech firms are also well represented among those hiring Sloan graduates.

Rod Garcia, Admissions Director
E52-126 50 Memorial Drive, Cambridge, MA 02142
Admissions: 617-253-3730 Fax: 617-253-6405
Email: mbaadmission@sloan.mit.edu
Internet: web.mit.edu/sloan/www

Massachusetts Institute of Technology

Sloan's CDO works hard to stay at the top of the heap, engaging in extensive market development work that has resulted in many new on-campus recruiting companies and an increase in job postings. Marketing is no doubt made easier by Sloan's extremely impressive list of alums. (see "Prominent Alumni on previous page.)

STUDENT/CAMPUS LIFE

It should come as little surprise that most Sloan students find their classmates an impressive bunch: "Sloan's student body makes the school. People here are motivated, interested in a wide variety of subjects, and very willing to help their fellow students. They are collegial both in and out of class." Many describe fellow students as "incredibly intelligent." The student body at this "racially and ethnically diverse," "very international school" is made up of "one-half engineers, one-half from every walk of life." Most students "keep a good balance between private life and school," "working hard but in a friendly team environment. We make time to relax and have fun!"

Students at Sloan describe an active extracurricular scene. "Life at Sloan is a whirlwind of speakers, activities, lectures, and coursework." Another student adds, "You can get involved in as much as you want at Sloan, and can have an impact on the school and community. The variety of activities (speeches, workshops, parties, etc.) offered adds to the quality of life." A "great social life, with mixers and happy hours at least twice a week" is highlighted by Consumption Functions, known as "C-Functions" among students and faculty. "There is a strong sense of community at Sloan. Every Thursday we have a C-Function where almost the entire student community gets together. Most C-Functions have a theme (e.g., Latin America C-Function). Most are sponsored by companies." Students describe the campus as "fairly safe," but complain that "on-campus housing is poor," the "physical plant needs help," and "parking is a big problem." MIT is located in Cambridge, near Harvard and just across the Charles River from downtown Boston. Public transportation makes travel around the student-friendly city easy even for those without cars.

ADMISSIONS

Incoming students are expected to have completed calculus and economic theory before matriculating. If you wind up taking these courses at MIT, as one student put it, expect "math hell!" Gaining admission to MIT is no walk in the park. From an applicant pool of more than 3,400, Sloan fills a class with just over 350 strong. The admissions committee considers GMAT score, undergraduate GPA, quality of undergraduate school and coursework, recommendations, and essays.

FINANCIAL FACTS

Tuition	$25,800
Room & board	$16,000
% of students receiving loans	40
% of students receiving grants	10
% of students receiving paid internships	50

ADMISSIONS

# of applications received	3,394
% applicants accepted	14
% acceptees attending	75
Average GMAT (range)	663 (610–740)
Minimum TOEFL	600
Average GPA (range)	3.50 (3.20–3.90)
Application fee (in-/out-of-state)	$125/$150
Early decision program available	No
Regular application deadline	January 31
Regular notification	March 30
Admission may be deferred?	Yes
Transfer students accepted?	No
Nonfall admission available?	No
Admission process need-blind?	Yes

APPLICANTS ALSO LOOK AT

Harvard University, Stanford University, University of Pennsylvania, University of Chicago, Columbia University, Northwestern University, Dartmouth College, University of California—Berkeley

EMPLOYMENT PROFILE

Placement rate (%)	100
# of companies recruiting on campus	214
% of grads employed immediately	96
% grads employed within six months	98
Average starting salary	$78,200

Grads employed by field (avg. salary):

Communications	3%	$76,200
Consulting	46%	$84,700
Finance	26%	$74,100
Marketing	6%	$74,700
Operations	17%	$74,900
Strategic Planning	3%	$84,700

UNIVERSITY OF MICHIGAN
University of Michigan Business School

OVERVIEW

Type of school	public
Affiliation	none
Environment	suburban
Academic calendar	semester
Schedule	full-time only

STUDENTS

Enrollment of parent institution	37,197
Enrollment of business school	857
% male/female	71/29
% out-of-state	90
% minorities	22
% international (# of countries represented)	24 (40)
Average age at entry	28
Average years work experience at entry	5

ACADEMICS

Student/faculty ratio	17:1
% female faculty	25
% minority faculty	19
Hours of study per day	4.66

SPECIALTIES
Michigan's real strength and value comes from combining across-the-board academic prowess with a set of special programs of management development. These programs develop students' skills and capabilities for standout effectiveness and leadership.

JOINT DEGREES
Manufacturing; Environmental Management; Public & Nonprofit Management; Architecture; Chinese Studies; Construction and Engineering Management; Industrial and Operations Engineering; Public Policy Studies; Japanese Studies; Law; Manufacturing Engineering; Modern Middle Eastern and North African Studies; Music; Natural Resources and Environment; Naval Architecture and Marine Engineering; Nursing; Public Health; Russian and East European Studies; Social Work; South and Southeast Asian Studies

SPECIAL PROGRAMS
Executive Skills Seminars; Leadership Development Program; International in-company learning (Europe, Asia, Africa, S. America); required in-company immersion/development experience; international network of corporate partnerships

STUDY ABROAD PROGRAMS
Programs in 14 countries

SURVEY SAYS...
HITS
Teamwork skills

ACADEMICS

While smaller business programs tend to specialize in a few functional areas, larger programs can marshal the resources necessary for across-the-board excellence. The University of Michigan Business School, according to its students, has achieved this level of proficiency; as a typical MBA explains, "This school has strength across all business disciplines. You cannot say Michigan is just a (fill in the blank: finance, marketing, etc.) school."

But the University of Michigan aims higher than mere meat-and-potatoes functionality. The school has also instituted a progressive curriculum that incorporates interdisciplinary approaches, team-teaching, action-based learning, and 1990s themes like global business and citizenship. A cornerstone of the program is the Multidisciplinary Action Project (MAP), a seven-week business apprenticeship that puts first-year students to work for real-life companies as consultants. The MAP exercise often ends with a presentation to the CEO and other top executives. Confirming the school's commitment to responsive innovation, students report that "the administration is very receptive to the needs of students, pulling unpopular and unsuccessful profs and revamping courses to better meet the needs of students."

Michigan's core curriculum comprises more than half the necessary credits for graduation. Students may waive those required courses in which they can demonstrate proficiency; waived core courses, however, must be replaced by electives. Students have mixed feelings about the core; writes one, "Core course content is taken very seriously, but most often core course professors are only OK. Elective professors are outstanding." Another student, however, counters that "Core curriculum professors are great! Most are highly respected in their fields and all show concern for students' learning." After completing the core, students have a wide range of choices. They may choose to focus on a specific area of management—marketing, finance, and accounting stand out among the many strong departments—or instead pursue a general management degree. Students may engage in ten credit hours of graduate study in other sectors of the university. In addition, Michigan offers seventeen joint-degree options, including the popular Corporate Environmental Management program, which combines an MBA with an MS in Environmental Science.

Students report that the "quality of professors runs the whole spectrum; mostly good, though" and add that "professors are very good at using different methods to explain difficult concepts." Among their few complaints is the widespread feeling that "operations management and technology need improvement," but these deficiencies do little to dampen students' overall enthusiasm for the program.

PLACEMENT AND RECRUITING

Past surveys have revealed some dissatisfaction with Michigan's Office of Career Development, but they have also shown that the office has gradually improved throughout the years we have administered our survey. The trend continues this year, as students gave the OCD high marks for its workshops, one-on-one counseling, and ability to deliver both variety and quality in on-campus recruiters. Approximately 400 organizations visit Michigan's campus each year

Kristina Nebel, Director of Admissions
701 Tappan Street Ann Arbor, MI 48109-1234
Admissions: 734-763-5796 Fax: 734-763-7804
Email: umbusmba@umich.edu
Internet: www.bus.umich.edu

University of Michigan

in their search for interns and full-time employees. Consulting and banking firms claim the lion's share of graduating MBAs here. Consumer goods, manufacturing, and high technology companies account for most of the balance of UMB's employers. The OCD also touts the b-school's alumni network, some 30,000 strong, as one of Michigan's greatest recruiting assets.

STUDENT/CAMPUS LIFE

Describing life at the University of Michigan, one student wrote that "Social life at my school is like social life in a small city. It is what you make of it. Things won't find you, you have to find them, but if you look there are more than enough things going on to enjoy yourself all the time." For most, life is "very, very busy. We are consistently faced with tough trade-off choices: miss class to go to case competition? Take a week off to relax?" Student clubs, ranging from those addressing traditional business topics to the Cigar Club, Open for Business (serving the gay MBA community), and the Ice Hockey Club, are numerous and "keep students very involved." Students appreciate the "huge advantages to attending a Big Ten school with football, hockey, and many other events," recognizing the abundance of social and cultural opportunities generated by the large university population. Students with families report that "The University Family Housing makes this school the place for MBAs with kids. Family housing offers inexpensive units in a vibrant intellectual international family community." Students also enjoy the town of Ann Arbor, referred to by many as 'A2.' Writes one, "It's small enough to be easy to deal with while offering a rich array of cultural events." Downtown Ann Arbor features an unusual variety of ethnic restaurants and boutique shopping. As an added bonus, it is "close enough to a major city (Detroit) to provide a getaway."

Michigan MBAs form a comfortable community of students who "emphasize schoolwork, but most also place social life high among their priorities, so there are plenty of opportunities to blow off steam with friends here." Students have "diverse backgrounds and experiences. There is still a large percentage of Michiganers among the students, though." These "down to earth, humble, smart, risk-takers" are "competitive in all aspects (school, athletics, anything) but also extremely willing to give anyone a hand."

ADMISSIONS

According to the admissions office, the following criteria are considered: essays, college GPA, letters of recommendation, extracurricular activities, work experience, interview, and GMAT score. A college-level calculus course must be completed before enrollment. Applicants are strongly encouraged to interview. The school asks applicants to note alumni ties in their applications, but does not reserve places in the class for those related to alumni. The school notes, "We do not use any 'formulas' or numerical cutoffs in admitting students." Michigan uses a batch admissions system with three deadlines: December 1, January 15, and March 1. There is an advantage to applicants who apply well before the March 1 deadline. Applications past the deadline are considered on a space-available basis. There is not a fixed allocation of space for in-state and out-of-state students.

FINANCIAL FACTS

Tuition (in-/out-of-state)	$20,000/$25,000
Fees (in-/out-of-state)	$185/$185
Cost of books	$1,000
Room & board (on-/off-campus)	$7,800/$7,800
% of students receiving aid	74
% first-year students receiving aid	58
% of students receiving loans	60
% of students receiving grants	34
Average award package	$37,511
Average grant	$12,750
Average graduation debt	$22,000

ADMISSIONS

# of applications received	4,189
% applicants accepted	22
% acceptees attending	47
Average GMAT (range)	672 (610–740)
Minimum TOEFL	600
Average GPA (range)	3.34 (2.90–3.90)
Application fee (in-/out-of-state)	$125/$125
Early decision program available	No
Regular application deadline	November 15
Regular notification	February 15
Admission may be deferred?	No
Transfer students accepted?	No
Nonfall admission available?	No
Admission process need-blind?	Yes

APPLICANTS ALSO LOOK AT

Northwestern University, University of Chicago, Harvard University, University of Virginia, Stanford University, University of Pennsylvania

EMPLOYMENT PROFILE

Placement rate (%)	100
# of companies recruiting on campus	400
% of grads employed immediately	99
% grads employed within six months	100
Average starting salary	$75,000

Grads employed by field (avg. salary):

Accounting	1%	$79,000
Consulting	31%	$121,000
Finance/Banking	32%	$103,000
General Management	8%	$95,000
Human Resources	1%	$95,000
Marketing	19%	$89,000
MIS	2%	$83,000
Operations	3%	$100,000
Other	2%	$74,000
Strategic Planning	1%	$93,000

MICHIGAN STATE UNIVERSITY
Eli Broad Graduate School of Management

ACADEMICS

A strong national reputation, low tuition, and "a program that involves all the important concepts to be an efficient manager" attract applicants from all over the world to the Eli Broad Graduate School of Management at Michigan State University. Broad MBAs report a high degree of satisfaction with their program, telling us that "diversity and the team concept are the greatest strengths of this school. They are ably supported by a very responsive faculty and staff."

The Broad MBA program is a program in transition. It has recently improved many of its facilities, adding high-tech classrooms with a computer interface and power source at every desk, computer labs, and a brand new business library with three times the capacity of its predecessor. Even more importantly, the Broad School has revamped its curriculum to more fully integrate core courses and to increase in-class opportunities for team study and problem solving. The new curriculum notably includes the Leadership Alliance Program: a learning opportunity in which first-year students work with an experienced upper-level executive "from a leading-edge organization" in order to "bring the real-world business environment into the classroom and to demonstrate how academic concepts and theories are implemented in progressive organizations." Of these changes, students tell us, "Coordination of the new curriculum needs work, but there has been considerable improvement already. While there have been problems, the changes have also been very rewarding." Helping to iron out the kinks is an administration that "is extremely receptive to student feedback. The school is very committed to the MBA program."

First-year at Broad begins with two weeks of quantitative review (required of students with poor quant backgrounds and for fast-track students, voluntary for all others) followed by a required orientation, during which students are divided into cohort study teams. The core curriculum is organized by concept, with students focusing on the role of the firm during first semester, and on the value chain during second semester. Second-year students are encouraged to develop dual concentrations. Among Broad's eight areas of concentration, general management, manufacturing, and supply-chain management earn students' highest praises. Broad MBAs give their professors high marks for teaching ability and accessibility, adding that, "teachers are good at directing us to alternative information sources." Writes one student, "Professors really care. Most are approachable. They have the relevant experience." Overall, Broad students appreciate the fact that their school works to foster a "friendly environment. Faculty, staff, and students work together to make this a better program."

PLACEMENT AND RECRUITING

The Broad School's Placement and Career Center (PCC) offers MBAs an assortment of counseling and recruitment services, including seminars and personal consultations covering resume building, interviewing and networking skills, and salary negotiation. The PCC maintains a resume database, which recruiters can access through the school's website. Students and graduates can tap into BroadNet, an exclusive internet site that lists on-campus interview dates, job postings, and alumni contacts. Students may also use the university-wide

Randall Dean, Director, MBA Admissions
215 Eppley Center, East Lansing, MI 48824
Admissions: 517-355-7604 Fax: 517-353-1649
Email: mba@pilot.msu.edu
Internet: www.bus.msu.edu/mba

Michigan State University

Career Services and Placement (CS&P) office. The Broad School claims to be "one of the very few top thirty MBA programs to have a career advisor focus on international students."

Students give the PCC average marks, touting "a solid alumni base around the world" but complain that "more national companies" are needed for on-campus recruitment. According to the school, this year "more than sixty nationally and internationally known firms will recruit MBA students [on campus] for full-time positions."

STUDENT/CAMPUS LIFE

Broad MBAs describe their student body as diverse, citing a population of foreign nationals that constitutes more than one-third of the student body. Others point out, however, that student demographics break down to "a big portion of people from Michigan, a big portion of Asians, then smaller portions of the rest." Among the international students is a large contingent of Korean managers, studying at MSU through a program run in conjunction with Korea's Kyung Hee University. One Asian MBA notes that students here are "very understanding of different cultures," while an American student described his classmates as "generally friendly, although there are some whiners who very much enjoy complaining." Many students arrive at the Broad School with considerable work experience, leading one to report that "because of their experience, they really add to the learning in our program. And, they're a lot of fun to hang out with."

Students describe academics at the Broad School as rigorous, and as a result "life at school is challenging and fun. The constant learning maintains the challenging atmosphere and the camaraderie of the students, staff, and faculty provide the fun." Students are "very involved in activities, especially in community service and making changes and improvements to the program." Student clubs are less popular but are readily available, and those who take advantage of them report that "they are good to be involved with." East Lansing receives high marks from Broad MBAs, who tell us, "There are more things to do in this town than time to do them. The East Lansing area is a great place to live." Included among social activities is "lots of drinking by students," as "bars abound in this very social atmosphere." For those seeking a more urban environment, Detroit is 90 minutes away by car. Students tell us that the campus is very safe, adding that the 5,000-acre campus is "shockingly beautiful." One of the few quality-of-life complaints concerned parking facilities. Gripes one student, "Parking space is the biggest problem here. Something has to be done urgently."

ADMISSIONS

The Broad MBA Program considers applicants on the basis of their academic record, GMAT scores, work experience, personal accomplishments, essays, and interviews. Full-time students need not demonstrate extensive prior business experience either in the workplace or in academia, but must "appear well-suited for management careers based upon academic ability, maturity, motivation, leadership, and communication skills . . . " Applicants for the Fast-Track MBA Program, however, must have at least two years of "quality" work experience. International applicants must score a minimum of 600 on the TOEFL and a minimum of 24 on the verbal section of the GMAT.

FINANCIAL FACTS

Tuition (in-/out-of-state)	$8,344/$12,154
Fees (in-/out-of-state)	$28/$28
Cost of books	$1,300
Room & board (on-/off-campus)	$4,000/$6,364
% of students receiving aid	70
% first-year students receiving aid	70
% aid that is merit based	33
% of students receiving paid internships	85
Average grant	$6,513
Average graduation debt	$62,303

ADMISSIONS

# of applications received	713
% applicants accepted	27
% acceptees attending	50
Average GMAT (range)	628 (580–660)
Minimum TOEFL	600
Average GPA (range)	3.30 (3.00–3.60)
Application fee (in-/out-of-state)	$30/$30
Early decision program available	Yes
Early decision deadline	December 15, February 1
Early decision notification	January 15, March 1
Regular application deadline	June 15
Regular notification	July 15
Admission may be deferred?	Yes
Maximum length of deferment	1 year
Transfer students accepted?	No
Nonfall admission available?	Yes
Admission process need-blind?	Yes

APPLICANTS ALSO LOOK AT

University of Michigan, The Ohio State University, Cornell University, Indiana University, University of Texas—Austin, Thunderbird, Notre Dame, University of Illinois

EMPLOYMENT PROFILE

Placement rate (%)	98
# of companies recruiting on campus	150
% of grads employed immediately	88
% grads employed within six months	98
Average starting salary	$63,862

Grads employed by field (avg. salary):

Consulting	14%	$68,300
Finance	38%	$62,861
Human Resources	7%	NR
Marketing	10%	$59,611
MIS	1%	NR
Operations	26%	$66,285
Other	1%	NR

UNIVERSITY OF MINNESOTA
Curtis L. Carlson School of Management

ACADEMICS

MBAs tend to view a business school's competition for a higher national ranking in terms of a horse race. Applying that metaphor here, one would have to say that the Carlson School of Management is "making its move." Efforts to seriously upgrade the program's national stature are manifest in its new home, a "state-of-the-art building with great facilities (computers, food, study rooms dedicated to groups)." Students agree that the "new building is fantastic. It should really help to develop a sense of community now that the school facilities are very good." Moreover, students "appreciate the administration's efforts to bring this school into the top twenty. Investments in faculty, technology, new buildings, and attracting top students all have played a significant role."

At its heart, Carlson remains the school that first earned national attention as a "small program with accessible professors and helpful students that makes for very cooperative learning environment." First-year students enjoy the program's integrated core, although several warn, "the quarter system is extremely fast-paced. Winter quarter is hell but the best learning experience around. More Harvard Business School case analysis than you can shake a stick at. Be sure to learn how to 'power nap.'" Second-year students must complete a fourteen-week field project and a lab in Managerial Communications but are otherwise free to pursue coursework in their fields of concentration and electives.

Students report favorably on the "excellent technology and strategy programs" and give management courses high marks as well. They give their professors mixed grades, although their rating of professors has improved since our last survey. Explains one student, "all the recently hired professors are 'A++'—as the old guard retires, the teaching gets better and better." Others are even more enthusiastic, asserting that "Professors are excellent! Very responsive—I've gotten answers to email questions after midnight! Exceeded my expectations!" Still, students also complain that the "faculty must improve its 'bench.' The 'starters' are the best round, but beyond that the profs should spend more time teaching than publishing."

PLACEMENT AND RECRUITING

According to the students we surveyed, Minnesota's Career Services Center (CSC) is doing an adequate job. On the up side, the CSC maintains a "strong relationship with an extensive network of corporations in the Twin Cities area." Students report that "the Mentor Program with local CEOs is fantastic." On the downside, students complain that too few out-of-state companies make recruiting trips to their campus. The school reports that "approximately 150 companies come to campus to interview graduating students. Fall and winter interviewing is fairly heavy while spring interviewing is very light."

Sandra Kalzenberg, Director, MBA Marketing and Admissions
CSOM Room 2-210, 321-19th Avenue South, Minneapolis, MN 55455
Admissions: 1-800-926-9431 Fax: 612-626-7785
Email: mbaoffice@csom.umn.edu
Internet: www.csom.umn.edu

University of Minnesota

Carlson offers a standard array of career services: one-on-one counseling, Internet job databases, career nights, and assistance in contacting alumni. Companies hiring Carlson MBAs include Kimberly Clark, Andersen Consulting, Deloitte & Touche, Northwest Airlines, and Pillsbury.

STUDENT/CAMPUS LIFE

Carlson students are "mature, helpful, friendly, and have diverse experiences. They're typical Midwesterners." Although "about one-third of the students are international or minority students," a considerable number of students believe that ethnic and racial minorities are underrepresented. "Even with all the attention given to diversity, the student body is not very diverse ethnically," reports one typical student. Many respondents note a wide disparity between the best and worst students in the program, complaining that "we need stronger students to round out the lower half of the class."

Student life at Carlson is "active! Most students are involved in a broad variety of activities (both school and non-school related)." Studies demand "a rigorous schedule," writes one student. "I'm usually on campus at least twelve hours a day, between classes, group work, study, and work in organizations. Fun days though!" Students agree that "life at school is very community-oriented. Classmates enjoy being in activities with each other outside of class." Those activities include "regular happy hours on Thursday, Friday, or both" and "many clubs and organizations." One such organization is the student government, which works effectively with an "accommodating administration" to improve this program: "Students have driven ninety percent of the changes that will be attributable to this school's success." Although "U of M is a huge campus," students don't mind because "the Carlson School is small and comfortable." Students also appreciated the availability of "inexpensive housing." Their chief complaint: "The winter here is too long and too cold. Except for this, it is a nice place."

ADMISSIONS

The admissions office considers your GMAT score, work experience, and college GPA as the most important elements of your portfolio. Then, in descending order, they consider your letters of recommendation, essays, and extracurricular activities. Applications are processed in semibatches. According to the school, "Applications are reviewed when they become complete. Those not offered admission at the time at which they are received are reviewed again within six weeks of the April 1st deadline." Students may defer admission for one year.

FINANCIAL FACTS

Tuition (in-/out-of-state)	$11,600/$16,622
Tuition per credit (in-/out-of-state)	$474/$692
Fees (in-/out-of-state)	$800/$800
Cost of books	$1,300
Room & board (on-/off-campus)	$4,600/$4,600
Average award package	$14,700
Average grant	$5,300

ADMISSIONS

# of applications received	656
% applicants accepted	46
% acceptees attending	43
Average GMAT (range)	620 (590–650)
Minimum TOEFL	580
Average GPA (range)	3.20 (2.93–3.58)
Application fee (in-/out-of-state)	$60/$90
Early decision program available	Yes
Early decision deadline	March 1
Early decision notification	April 15
Regular application deadline	April 1
Regular notification	May 15
Admission may be deferred?	Yes
Maximum length of deferment	1 year
Transfer students accepted?	No
Nonfall admission available?	No
Admission process need-blind?	Yes

APPLICANTS ALSO LOOK AT

Northwestern University, University of Wisconsin—Madison, University of Michigan Business School, University of Chicago, New York University, University of North Carolina at Chapel Hill, University of Texas at Austin, Georgetown University

EMPLOYMENT PROFILE

Placement rate (%)	99
# of companies recruiting on campus	94
% of grads employed immediately	98
% grads employed within six months	99
Average starting salary	$67,678

Grads employed by field (avg. salary):

Consulting	23%	$70,000
Finance	27%	$64,000
General Management	3%	$70,000
Marketing	28%	$65,500
MIS	14%	$65,500
Operations	5%	$70,000

NEW YORK UNIVERSITY
Leonard N. Stern School of Business

ACADEMICS

The Stern School of Business at New York University is very much a product of its setting. Located just a couple of miles north of Wall Street, Stern boasts the connections and the access to industry heavyweights to sustain a great finance program. Because New York is also America's most international city, Stern has the capacity to focus its curriculum on world business issues. And, because the city is home to so many young execs looking for a leg up, NYU is also home to one of the nation's top-ranked part-time MBA programs.

First year at Stern is devoted almost entirely to core curriculum (this sequence takes two years for most part-timers). Those who cannot demonstrate proficiency in writing, analytical methods, economics, or calculus must begin their tenure at Stern with noncredit courses in those subjects. All students take the Stern Pre-Term, a noncredit "series of exercises, seminars, and other experiences that provide a focused first exposure to the Stern MBA program." They then proceed to a series of required core courses and "menu" core courses (students choose three such courses from a menu of four). Students report that "First year is much more difficult than second year" and happily report that "Stern makes an effort to have core courses taught by senior faculty, which really enhances the first-year learning experience." Second-year students must select a major area requiring twelve hours of course credit; students give glowing reviews to study in finance, marketing, international business, and media studies.

According to our survey, "Most of the professors are good. There are a few great ones and some bad ones. Professors are well tuned to what's going on currently and apply it to the topics of the day. Many are consultants to well-known companies." Students also tell us that "The administration has become much more responsive to student input. Many recent and proposed changes to faculty, facilities, and coursework are very positive" and that "Overall, things run quite smoothly at Stern, including registration, scheduling of events and career resources." On the downside, students complain that the school needs to "maintain a better balance between full-time and part-time student life." Observed one MBA, "There is a lack of participation in team-building and school spirit activities with the part-time students, which leads to a generally lackluster sense of community." Full-time students also complain that "too many classes are given at night to accommodate the schedules of part-timers."

PLACEMENT AND RECRUITING

Stern's Office of Career Development (OCD) receives a natural boost from the school's location in "the heart of New York City's bustling financial, consumer-products, and media industries." More than 175 corporations make the trip to the Stern campus (many are only a short taxicab ride away). Stern's location likewise facilitates alumni networking, since many graduates remain in the city. The school takes advantage of its access to alumni through its Career Advisory Program, which makes more than 1,300 Stern graduates available to students for "informational interviews."

Mary Miller, Assistant Dean, MBA Admissions & Student-Services
44 West 4th Street, Suite 10-160, New York, NY 10012
Admissions: 212 998-0600 Fax: 212-995-4231
Email: sternmba@stern.nyu.edu
Internet: www.stern.nyu.edu

New York University

Stern was a pioneer in publishing student resumes on the Internet, and it administers a state-of-the-art database of available positions and internships. The school reports that, through its efforts, students have online access to more than 2,500 job postings each year. OCD delivers a Career Management Series, which is designed to provide MBA students with the tools necessary to conduct a successful job search: personal skills and values assessment, resume writing, interview training, and networking are just a few examples.

STUDENT/CAMPUS LIFE

Stern MBAs warn that "NYU is a city school. Therefore it's got a different life than a rural/campus school." One major difference: NYU has no campus to speak of; rather, the university consists of a collection of buildings surrounding Washington Square Park in Greenwich Village. In the past the lack of a campus has hurt class unity, but things have improved since Stern moved into its new digs, the Management Education Center, in 1992. Notes one student, "Despite the lack of a traditional campus, the new building fosters a sense of campus/social life." Like most New Yorkers, Stern MBAs carry on a love-hate relationship with the city. They laud its assets, among them the "incredible night life, professional opportunities, and cultural exposure," and point out that "NYC is great for networking and for having outstanding adjunct professors." Then they turn around and bemoan the fact that "New York is a nightmare when it comes to housing" or complain that "New York City is a very expensive place to go to school." The campus social scene centers on student-run clubs such as the Asian Business Society, Entrepreneurs' Exchange, Emerging Markets Association, and Stern Women in Business, which organize conferences, parties, and outings, and "regularly bring in alumni speakers." Students also appreciate the Cole Sports Center, which features an outdoor track, basketball courts, and an Olympic-size swimming pool. Still, for the most part "after class people disperse into the vast city of New York."

The Stern student body consists "mainly of Wall Street–oriented finance types, but there is diversity in terms of backgrounds." The finance-heavy demographic has some students complaining: "The people are largely finance-oriented junior Wall Streeters. Marketing and management students are like second-class citizenry." Students here are highly competitive, leading their classmates to offer some uncharitable characterizations. "They're narrow-minded, self-absorbed, unfriendly," writes one student; says another, "some Columbia/Wharton/Harvard wannabes but very intelligent." The school has "a significant international population, which adds to the dynamic environment at Stern."

ADMISSIONS

According to the admissions office, the following criteria are considered (in order of importance): GPA and GMAT scores, work experience, letters of recommendation, essays, and extracurricular activities. Applicants whose native language is not English are required to submit TOEFL scores. Interviews are conducted by invitation.

FINANCIAL FACTS

Tuition	$27,048
Tuition per credit	$950
Fees	$875
Room & board (on-/off-campus)	$18,768/$18,768
% of students receiving aid	85
% first-year students receiving aid	70
% aid that is merit based	100
% of students receiving loans	85
% of students receiving paid internships	95
Average award package	$45,113
Average grant	$10,000
Average graduation debt	$35,000

ADMISSIONS

# of applications received	4,716
% applicants accepted	18
% acceptees attending	51
Average GMAT (range)	675 (620–730)
Minimum TOEFL	600
Average GPA (range)	3.40 (2.90–3.80)
Application fee (in-/out-of-state)	$75/$75
Early decision program available	Yes
Early decision deadline	January 15
Early decision notification	March 15
Regular application deadline	March 15
Regular notification	Rolling
Admission may be deferred?	No
Transfer students accepted?	No
Nonfall admission available?	Yes
Admission process need-blind?	Yes

APPLICANTS ALSO LOOK AT

Columbia University, University of Pennsylvania, Northwestern University, University of Chicago, Harvard University, University of California—Los Angeles, University of Michigan Business School, Stanford University

EMPLOYMENT PROFILE

Placement rate (%)	97
# of companies recruiting on campus	175
% of grads employed immediately	95
% grads employed within six months	99
Average starting salary	$114,213

Grads employed by field (avg. salary):

Consulting	19%	$119,774
Finance	65%	$107,250
Marketing	11%	$83,725
Other	1%	$86,400
Strategic Planning	4%	$84,150

UNIVERSITY OF NORTH CAROLINA AT CHAPEL HILL

Kenan-Flagler Business School

ACADEMICS

The Kenan-Flagler Business School at the University of North Carolina at Chapel Hill boasts a multitude of charms. One student captured a number of them, telling us: "I don't understand why everyone doesn't want to come here—beautiful town, school, and weather. The faculty is outstanding, jobs are plentiful, students are intelligent, and everyone loves each other." He might also have mentioned KFBS's commitment to curricular innovation and its new home, the $44 million "state-of-the-art" McColl Building, referred to by students as "Taj McColl."

KFBS has always been known as a great general management program. In previous years, the school has avoided organizing its curriculum by functional areas, preferring instead to build courses around business issues and problems. The curriculum is designed around seven-week modules ("mods"), four per year to allow KFBS to offer a variety of topics—such as consulting and environmental issues—not possible under a semester system. While the lockstep first-year core curriculum will continue to take this approach, the school is making alterations to its second-year curriculum starting with the 1999–2000 academic year. Second-year students will soon have the option of pursuing concentrations in one of two areas: career concentrations, which include many of the traditional b-school majors; and enrichment concentrations, which include entrepreneurship, environmentally sustainable business development, and regional studies, eg., Latin America, Southeast Asia. KFBS tells us that students need not choose a single area of concentration, but may instead fashion their own general business curricula by choosing courses from across the various concentrations.

The modular schedule at KFBS means the "pace is very fast and sometimes stressful." Writes one student, "First year is extremely tough. Second year is more manageable." Students appreciate the fact that "classes are small," professors "work together to tie courses together and time course material so you are hitting different aspects of a topic in separate courses," and administrators "work hard to help the students." Several students point out that "the team-oriented, cooperative environment is the school's great strength. Students, faculty, and administration all chip in their support." Others appreciate the "global focus throughout the curriculum," including second-year global immersion options in South Africa, Cuba, and other exotic locales. Still others are most pleased that "the school puts its top professors on the core classes first year, unlike other schools that stick you with the least experienced or least popular professors." And, as if the program needed anything else to recommend it, tuition and fees are at the bargain-basement level for North Carolinians and quite reasonable for everyone else.

PLACEMENT AND RECRUITING

Students at Kenan-Flagler report that the Office of Career Services (OCS) has "improved vastly" in recent years. OCS adds that its 106:1 ratio of students to counselors is "one of the strongest across top business schools" nationwide. Counselors strive to assist each student in achieving their career goals throughout the competitive internship and job search process. They also encourage first-year students to participate in the International Summer Internship program. Of the 99 percent of first-year students who find summer internships, 23 percent are working in an international setting. OCS collaborates with three international programs housed within the school—The Kenan Institute, the North Carolina Global Center, and the MBA Enterprise Corps—to facilitate international placements.

Sherrylyn Ford Wallace, Director, MBA Admissions
CB 3490 McColl Building, Chapel Hill, NC 27599-3490
Admissions: 919-962-3236 Fax: 919-962-0898
Email: mba_info@unc.edu
Internet: www.bschool.unc.edu

University of North Carolina at Chapel Hill

OCS supplements on-campus interviewing with a resume book, Internet job postings, an October job fair, occasional career panels, and a video-conferencing facility. The school also sponsors a unique Student Ambassador program, in which "a group of second-year students [visit] key corporations to share their experiences at Kenan-Flagler. We have found that our students are our best salespeople, and their work increases our exposure with corporations."

STUDENT/CAMPUS LIFE

Chapel Hill MBAs paint an idyllic picture of their classmates and extracurricular life. Explains one student, "The prevailing sentiment is that everyone is smart and everyone is going to succeed, so everyone is more than willing to help one another." Another elaborated on this theme, telling us that students here are "very cooperative, to the point of emailing everyone their review notes before a test and giving away a prospective employer's contact information even when they also want the job." Students are "very international and globally focused. Everyone, it seems, has worked or lived abroad." Over one-third are southerners, and about one-quarter come from the Northeast and Midatlantic states.

Students are equally satisfied with their quality of life. Explains one student, "No beepers, no cell phones. A very relaxed atmosphere." UNC—Chapel Hill boasts a stately, tree-lined campus and buildings listed with the National Historic Register. On campus, intercollegiate sports, particularly the Tar Heels basketball team, are popular. "With tailgate parties, basketball games in the Dean Dome, and the Franklin Street social scene, student life doesn't get much better than Chapel Hill," writes one student. Adds another, "We have plenty of distractions. Great place to raise a family. And, hey, [to you] single guys—the girl-to-guy ratio [university-wide] is excellent on campus." The school is host to a variety of student clubs, and there is a strong tradition of social service among students. The annual mini-biathlon sponsored by the MBA Student Association, for example, raises thousands of dollars for charities, as does a Habitat for Humanity student golf tournament. Because Chapel Hill is a university town with extensive apartment developments, it's a renter's market. Public bus lines make off-campus living especially convenient. And, for a little adventure you can take a short road trip to the coastal beaches to the east, or the Appalachian Mountains to the north and west. The weather is mild and conducive to outdoor activity; as one student noted, "We learn the information quickly, so that we can use our time to get outside and flyfish or mountain bike."

ADMISSIONS

According to the admissions staff, quality of work experience, proven leadership, and demonstrated ability to excel in quantitative material are considered most important. Once the aforementioned are established, essays, college GPA, total GMAT scores, letters of recommendation, interviews (required), and global experience help determine who makes the cut. The admissions office notes that, "because of our large applicant pool, applicants are encouraged to apply as early as possible." Historically, less than 20 percent of those who apply are accepted at Kenan-Flager. Applicants are strongly encouraged to schedule an on-campus interview, sit in on classes, and meet with current MBA students.

FINANCIAL FACTS

Tuition (in-/out-of-state)	$3,950/$16,400
Fees (in-/out-of-state)	$1,947/$1,947
Cost of books	$3,250
Room & board (on-/off-campus)	$4,800/$9,000
% of students receiving aid	56
% first-year students receiving aid	59
% of students receiving paid internships	95
Average award package	$18,859
Average grant	$14,700
Average graduation debt	$29,350

ADMISSIONS

# of applications received	2,123
% applicants accepted	23
% acceptees attending	52
Average GMAT (range)	640 (600–670)
Minimum TOEFL	600
Average GPA (range)	3.20 (2.80–3.40)
Application fee (in-/out-of-state)	$60/$60
Early decision program available	No
Regular application deadline	March 1
Regular notification	May 1
Admission may be deferred?	Yes
Maximum length of deferment	1 year
Transfer students accepted?	No
Nonfall admission available?	No
Admission process need-blind?	Yes

APPLICANTS ALSO LOOK AT

Duke University, University of Virginia, Northwestern University, University of Michigan Business School, University of Pennsylvania, Dartmouth College, Wharton (Pennsylvania), Stanford University

EMPLOYMENT PROFILE

Placement rate (%)	99
# of companies recruiting on campus	105
% of grads employed immediately	97
% grads employed within six months	99
Average starting salary	$71,478

Grads employed by field (avg. salary):

Consulting	25%	$85,250
Finance	31%	$70,477
General Management	10%	$72,263
Human Resources	1%	$77,500
Marketing	23%	$69,351
Operations	1%	$69,000
Other	4%	$70,571
Strategic Planning	2%	$76,667
Venture Capital	3%	$64,000

NORTHEASTERN UNIVERSITY
Graduate School of Business Administration

OVERVIEW

Type of school	private
Affiliation	none
Environment	urban
Academic calendar	quarter
Schedule	full-time/part-time/evening

STUDENTS

Enrollment of parent institution	24,325
Enrollment of business school	1,138
% male/female	55/45
% part-time	72
% minorities	6
% international (# of countries represented)	8 (26)
Average age at entry	26
Average years work experience at entry	3

ACADEMICS

Student/faculty ratio	12:1
Hours of study per day	4.28

SPECIALTIES

Finance, Accounting, Marketing, Logistical and Transportation Management, Information Resources Management, International Business, Enterpreneurship

JOINT DEGREES

JD/MBA; MS/MBA Nursing Administration; MD/MBA; MS/MBA Accounting

SPECIAL PROGRAMS

Executive MBA Program, Cooperative MBA Program, MS in Finance, High Technology MBA

STUDY ABROAD PROGRAMS

France, Eastern Europe, Southeast Asia

SURVEY SAYS...
HITS
Star faculty
Alumni helpful in job search
Study groups

MISSES
School clubs
Unfriendly students
Profs not great teachers

PROMINENT ALUMNI

Dennis J. Picard, Chairman and CEO, Raytheon Co; J. Philip Johnson, President and CEO, CARE; Richard Egan, Chairman of the Board, EMC Corporation

ACADEMICS

A hallmark of Northeastern's business program is that it provides opportunities to combine paid professional work with study. There are five different MBA programs: a part-time program, an Executive MBA, the two-year full-time MBA, the Cooperative Education MBA, and the High Technology MBA. The High Tech MBA is the first of its kind in the nation. In this program, technical professionals take classes one night a week and on alternate Saturdays, and focus on management in the high-tech industry. Observes one student, "High-tech attracts high-caliber, excellent students." Perhaps the most popular and unique of the five programs is the Cooperative Education MBA, which begins in January and June. One MBA's comments typified the feeling among fans: "The Co-op program is excellent! The pace is fast, challenging, and rewarding." This may be because it offers students paid, MBA-level employment for six months during twenty-one months of accelerated study. Raves this happy MBA, "The main reason I chose this business school is because of the Co-op program, which allowed me to gain invaluable work experience while attending school." Especially noteworthy at Northeastern is the MS/MBA in accounting, which enjoys corporate support from major accounting firms. Indeed, it boasts a 100 percent placement rate for its most recent classes. Another academic strength: "The Finance department is strong!"

Northeastern's MBA programs offer generalist perspectives and contain a core of the basic business subjects. Electives are used to broaden or deepen the course of study. Prior to class, a week-long orientation jump-starts the programs with a team-building exercise and a foray into case study. Among the extras: an executive mentoring program that allows students to form personal relationships with CEOs and the like. Also, there are "great options for studying abroad."

The overwhelming majority of MBAs say this program is worth the investment of time and money, with 73 percent saying it's more than meeting their academic expectations. As one student put it: "The MBA program is excellent and very practical—coursework involves lots of 'real life' examples and cases." By all accounts, this allows students to feel proficient in a number of areas. For example, 80 percent of NU MBAs feel well prepared by their studies in finance, accounting, and general management—the school's dominion. Students award themselves even higher marks for their teamwork abilities. There is improvement from last year in students' perception of their marketing and computer acumen—52 percent say they're good or better in these subjects. One repeater weak spot is the efficiency of the school. Unhappily, things have gotten worse. Gripes one MBA, "Unfortunately, the administration has not taken any efforts to ensure quality control." On the upside, 70 percent rated the faculty good or better teachers. Most MBAs agree: "The quality of instruction here is as good as it is at other Boston schools." Reports another, "NU's faculty favor class participation, debates, and adopts a very practical methodology. This is very rewarding." Students gave professors particularly high marks for their after-class availability. But one MBA sounds off: "Some professors use the classroom as a bully pulpit for conservative ... views." Nineteen percent gave the school average or worse marks for equitable treatment of minorities. Foreign students are quite happy: "Being a French student at NU, I really appreciate interacting in class with this ethnically diverse student body." Adds another, "Great program for international students."

Daniel A. Gilbert, Manager, Full-Time MBA Programs
350 Dodge Hall, Boston, MA 02150
Admissions: 617-373-2714 Fax: 617-373-8564
Email: gsba@cba.neu.edu
Internet: w.cba.neu.edu/gsba

Northeastern University

PLACEMENT AND RECRUITING

This go 'round, our survey shows that more students feel the MBA Career Center has improved. Thirty-seven percent of NU students say the range of companies recruiting on campus is now good to excellent. For some extra help, the remainder might suggest you head over to the university's main career office in Stearn's Hall. The majority of students go into finance and consulting. The average starting salary is $54,457. The major recruiters: State Street Bank, Texas Instruments, Lucent Technologies, M&M Mars, Digital, and Staples.

STUDENT/CAMPUS LIFE

Northeastern relies on the case-study method, which tends to produce late-night, intensive study sessions. Students here study an average of twenty-five to thirty-five hours a week. The vast majority report there are few corners to cut; it's important to do all or most of the assigned reading. Depending on the program you're in, the pressure ranges from manageable to formidable. Fortunately, study groups play an integral part in case preparation. Class participation counts for 20 to 40 percent of the grade. Classes are generally kept to twenty-five to fifty students. Students here are fairly competitive, in fact, 73 percent say very competitive, but this does not necessarily translate into one-upmanship. Cooperation and teamwork are the accepted mode of behavior. Northeastern MBAs say the student body is both professionally and racially diverse, a claim that most b-schools can't make. Seventy-seven percent also say fellow students are very bright. However, 27 percent report that classmates aren't the type of people they like to hang with a whole lot. In all likelihood, this has to do with the influx of part- and semi-full-time attendees who tend to be focused on their own thing. Still, the majority report an active social life. Observes this student, "The campus is exciting, and it's easy to make friends." B-school classes are held in Dodge Hall, a recently unveiled, gleaming new facility, which features state-of-the-art classrooms, high-tech computer facilities, a student lounge, case rooms, and a modern Career Center office. As for Boston, everyone loves this preppy East Coast city, which one student describes as an "intellectually exciting place to be." (But finding affordable housing is difficult, and almost no one lives on campus.) For extracurriculars, the MBA Association sponsors corporate speaker events, as well as barbecues. Students advise: "Participation is important."

ADMISSIONS

The admissions office considers the following criteria (in no particular order): essays, college GPA, letters of recommendation, work experience, and GMAT scores. The office of admissions notes, "Decisions are made by small committees after an application has been read by at least three professionals who independently assess several factors: academic preparation (GMAT scores and transcripts), maturity, motivation, and direction (essays, recommendations, and work experience). These factors are considered equally important."

FINANCIAL FACTS

Tuition	$21,000
Tuition per credit	$500
Fees	$250
Cost of books	$850
Room & board (on-/off-campus)	$10,380/$10,380
% aid that is merit based	1
% of students receiving loans	19
% of students receiving grants	22
% of students receiving paid internships	16
Average award package	$18,500

ADMISSIONS

% applicants accepted	60
Average GMAT	550
Minimum TOEFL	600
Average GPA	3.22
Application fee (in-/out-of-state)	$50/$50
Early decision program available	Yes
Early decision deadline	February 15
Early decision notification	March 1
Regular application deadline	Rolling
Regular notification	Rolling
Admission may be deferred?	Yes
Maximum length of deferment	1 year
Transfer students accepted?	Yes
Nonfall admission available?	Yes
Admission process need-blind?	Yes

APPLICANTS ALSO LOOK AT

Boston University, Babson College, Harvard University, New York University, University of Connecticut, Loyola University, University of Massachusetts, Northwestern University

EMPLOYMENT PROFILE

# of companies recruiting on campus	117
% of grads employed immediately	86
% grads employed within six months	95
Average starting salary	$54,457

Grads employed by field (avg. salary):

Consulting	25%	NR
Finance	37%	NR
General Management	2%	NR
Marketing	16%	NR
MIS	12%	NR
Operations	4%	NR
Other	2%	NR
Strategic Planning	2%	NR

NORTHWESTERN UNIVERSITY
Kellogg Graduate School of Management

OVERVIEW

Type of school	private
Affiliation	none
Environment	suburban
Academic calendar	quarter
Schedule	full-time only

STUDENTS

Enrollment of parent institution	16,018
Enrollment of business school	2,504
% male/female	68/32
% out-of-state	61
% part-time	51
% minorities	21
% international (# of countries represented)	24 (61)
Average age at entry	27
Average years work experience at entry	4.40

ACADEMICS

Student/faculty ratio	12:1
% female faculty	19
% minority faculty	15
Hours of study per day	4.16

SPECIALTIES

All areas of business and entrepreneurship. Special strengths—General Management, Finance, Marketing, Technology, and E-commerce.

JOINT DEGREES

MM/RN (nursing school, 4 years); MM/MD (medical school, 4 years); MM/JD (law school, 4 years); and MM/M (engineering school, 4 years)

SPECIAL PROGRAMS

Pre-enrollment math "Prep"; Foreign study in sixteen countries

STUDY ABROAD PROGRAMS

Austrailia, Austria, Belgium, Chile, Denmark, France, Germany, Hong Kong, Israel, Italy, Japan, Mexico, Norway, Spain, Thailand, United Kingdom

SURVEY SAYS...

HITS
Students are happy
Social life
Cozy student community

MISSES
Campus is ugly

PROMINENT ALUMNI

Chris Galvin, CEO, Motorola; Scott Smith, CEO, Publisher, *Chicago Tribune*

ACADEMICS

The Kellogg Graduate School of Management offers an "innovative generalist's approach" to business education. It is an approach that appeals to the 1,200+ full-timers at Northwestern's b-school. "Kellogg is great in every respect—it's the balance that makes it special," explained one satisfied student. Kellogg offers students a Master's of Management (MM) rather than an MBA, explaining that the MM degree serves as a better umbrella for its many areas of professional specialization, which include health services, public and nonprofit, transportation and real estate as well as traditional management disciplines.

Kellogg students have several scheduling options. A traditional two-year program is available, but so are two accelerated options (one takes one year to complete, the other takes one-and-a-half years). Kellogg's quarterly academic schedule affords students increased flexibility but also eliminates any hope of slack time; the quarters just fly by too quickly for that. First year at Kellogg consists of nine required courses and three electives. Students may place out of some core requirements—in fact, about one-half of the students in the accelerated programs do—but must replace each with an advanced course in the same field. Once students have completed core requirements, their options are numerous (one of the fringe benefits of attending a large school). Electives are available in six academic departments: Accounting and Information Systems; Finance; Management and Strategy; Managerial Economics and Decision Sciences; Marketing; and Organization Behavior. International Business and Entrepreneurship are also options, available through interdisciplinary study. Writes one student, "Kellogg really offers a program 'a la carte.' This, combined with the availability of the faculty allows the school to meet all kinds of expectations." Our survey shows that "overall, professors are very good. Teaching quality ranges from excellent to good, and teachers are surprisingly engaged in your learning process. It's very personal." However, the survey also confirms that "it is sometimes very tough to get the best professors."

Kellogg has a strong reputation as a marketing school, although more students enroll for classes in finance (another power subject) than in any other department. The program has many other strong suits, notably: transportation management, real estate management, public and nonprofit management, and manufacturing. Tons of international business courses, a global focus in the core, and nine foreign study programs in Europe and Thailand make Kellogg a player in international business study as well. Students speak highly of the Master in Manufacturing Program (MMM), designed primarily for engineers who are in manufacturing/operations. Reports one, "The MMM program is positioning itself as a leading national operations/manufacturing program and is recognized among leading companies as a feeder to management training programs. Professors teaching the core courses are excellent."

PLACEMENT AND RECRUITING

Students report a high satisfaction rate with Kellogg's Career Management Center. More than 300 firms conduct 13,500 on-campus interviews, with another 200 firms visiting the campus to interview for summer internships. The CMC boasts that it coordinates more interviews annually than does any other graduate busi-

Michele Rogers, Assistant Dean, Director of Admissions, and Financial Aid
2001 Sheridan Road, Leverone Hall, 2nd Floor, Evanston, IL 60208
Admissions: 847-491-3308 Fax: 847-491-4960
Email: kellogg-admissions@nwu.edu
Internet: www.kellogg.nwu.edu

Northwestern University

ness program. The office also reports that its resources include "an extensive career resource library, counseling seminars, mock interviews with corporate recruiters, and videos of corporate presentations."

STUDENT/CAMPUS LIFE

Kellogg MMs are "generally laid-back about life, but somewhat serious about school. They are very friendly and helpful, the type of people you want to know and spend time with." Students here enjoy an atmosphere that is "very friendly, no backstabbing. Students are eager to help each other, in classes and during job search." Although Kellogg attracts a fair number of minority and international students, many students still feel that diversity here often breaks down to, "Which consulting firm did you work for before coming to Kellogg?"

Much of the social scene at Kellogg revolves around activities successfully sponsored by the Graduate Management Association (GMA). The GMA coordinates Kellogg's two largest social events, the Charity Ball in February and the Black Tie Spring Fling, as well as weekly Friday afternoon keggers. The GMA also participates in the administration of the school, coordinating quarterly teacher evaluations, co-designing curriculum with the faculty and administration, and advising on alumni affairs and career placement issues. Students are also active in clubs and activities and describe the overall school environment as "very social—there are more activities, events, and opportunities than I can do." Students warn that, a reputation for 'soft academics' notwithstanding, Kellogg imposes a "heavier workload than I expected. This is not a party school!" Agrees another student, "There's not a lot of time for personal stuff."

The Northwestern campus itself is beautiful, located along a half-mile stretch of Lake Michigan, twelve miles from downtown Chicago in the suburb of Evanston. Students describe Evanston as "very safe, clean, and pretty." With Chicago so close by, students have the best of both worlds: a peaceful environment in which to study, and one of the world's great cities in which to dine, shop, and network. On-campus housing is fair, with space available to 250 single students and fifty apartments for married students. The school itself is housed in a modern facility built in 1995; further additions to the complex are scheduled for completion by 2000.

ADMISSIONS

According to the Kellogg admissions office, your GPA, GMAT score, essays, work experience, extracurricular activities, recommendations, and interviews (which are required) are all "equally important." GMAT scores of applicants are typically high, undergrad grades are strong, and applicants have several years of impressive work experience. Applications are reviewed in rounds. As for when to apply, applicants are advised, "The earlier the better." Admission deferrals are considered on a case-by-case basis, but professional circumstances may be considered.

FINANCIAL FACTS

Tuition	$25,872
Room & board (on-/off-campus)	$18,984/$18,984
% of students receiving aid	60
% of students receiving loans	60
Average award package	$8,500

ADMISSIONS

# of applications received	6,128
% applicants accepted	17
% acceptees attending	11
Average GMAT (range)	695 (610–740)
Average GPA (range)	3.45 (3.00–3.80)
Application fee (in-/out-of-state)	$125/$125
Early decision program available	No
Regular application deadline	March 16
Regular notification	Rolling
Admission may be deferred?	Yes
Maximum length of deferment	Case by case
Transfer students accepted?	No
Nonfall admission available?	No
Admission process need-blind?	Yes

APPLICANTS ALSO LOOK AT

Harvard University, Stanford University, University of Pennsylvania

EMPLOYMENT PROFILE

Placement rate (%)	100
# of companies recruiting on campus	315
% of grads employed immediately	97
% grads employed within six months	99
Average starting salary	$90,000

Grads employed by field (avg. salary):

Consulting	40%	$100,000
Finance	27%	$95,000
General Management	6%	$80,000
Marketing	18%	$80,000
Operations	1%	$79,000
Other	8%	$80,000

UNIVERSITY OF NOTRE DAME
College of Business

ACADEMICS

Notre Dame takes a traditional approach to the MBA. The first year of its two-year program is crammed with intensive review courses in management, operations, and quantitative skills. Notre Dame then allows students a great deal of freedom in their second year, requiring study in two disciplines (ethics and international business) and a course in corporate strategy, but otherwise giving students free rein of the course catalogue. Even though the program doesn't include some of the bells and whistles that other schools add so they stand out in the MBA crowd, that doesn't seem to bother students here, most of whom prefer conservative, traditional approaches. Says one student, "The school itself has a lot of history and lore. The tradition inspires you to contribute and do well."

One unique feature of the Notre Dame MBA is the optional three-semester program, which is available only to students with an undergraduate degree in business. It takes one full year to complete the three-semester program. Participants cover the material taught in the traditional first-year MBA curriculum during an intensive nine-week summer semester, then join the second-year students in the fall. According to one student in the program, "three-semester students are extremely motivated, friendly, fun, and helpful. Traditional MBA students are nice, too, but I wouldn't trade my three-semester friends for the world."

Among the academic departments, finance gets the highest marks. Typical among our respondents is the one who writes "In finance and investment, I believe that our faculty is second to none." Management also scores high, while entrepreneurship is given low grades, although one student notes that "while the entrepreneurship program is very weak, it's expected to improve with the new dean." Students describe the administration as "extremely approachable. If you need any problem addressed, there is someone available to listen and help." Professors and facilities also get the students' thumbs up. About the only complaint students register is that the program "could use more and better course selection. [The] school's small size prohibits some electives that would have been nice."

PLACEMENT AND RECRUITING

Notre Dame students are satisfied with their prospects upon graduation; this is due more to "one of the strongest alumni networks in the world" and "name recognition" than to the Career Development Office (CDO), to which students give an average grade. Alumni return to campus to participate in career panels, serve as mock interviewers, volunteer as mentors, provide career advice, and support the recruitment of Notre Dame MBAs.

The CDO manages popular off-campus projects and internships, which the majority of our respondents find both plentiful and useful. Students wishing to use the services of the CDO must attend career management seminars, essentially making these seminars mandatory.

Notre Dame participates in several MBA recruiting consortia, including two aimed specifically at placement in the international market. Among the compa-

Michele Rogers, Assistant Dean, Director of Admissions, and Financial Aid
276 College of Business, P.O. Box 399, Notre Dame, IN 46556-0399
Admissions: 219-631-8488 Fax: 219-631-8800
Email: mba.1@nd.edu
Internet: www.nd.edu/~mba

University of Notre Dame

nies that have recently recruited on campus are: Andersen Consulting, Citibank NA, Fidelity Investments, GE, Kimberly-Clark, Nissan Motor Company, Price Waterhouse, and Whirlpool.

STUDENT/CAMPUS LIFE

Notre Dame students report a high degree of satisfaction with their classmates and social lives. "The people are, without question, the greatest strength of this school," writes a typical student, adding, "this place is a community. People care about each other and all learning takes place in that context. The community has heart, spirit, and soul. We emphasize a well-rounded, balanced life." The "vast majority" has "excellent professional credentials, which provides for very challenging class and teamwork discussions." Students are friendly ("spontaneous review sessions form in the team rooms before exams, and you can drop in on any group and be welcome"). One student describes her peers thusly: "Blue-collar type people. They have all worked very hard to achieve their successes. They are the most personable people I've met." A detractor complains that "there is zero diversity in this program. My classmates are the poster children for the Young Republicans."

MBAs form a "very close-knit group" at Notre Dame: "Students work hard during the week and stick together over the weekend." Our survey confirms one student's opinion that "the workload is challenging yet not overwhelming. There is a good balance between academics and quality of life." Athletic events figure prominently into students' spare time, in the form of intramurals ("Everyone is really athletic. The athletic facilities are awesome, and the intramural leagues are really competitive, but you should know that we consistently beat the law school in intramurals") and intercollegiate sports ("Football season is killer at Notre Dame"). The campus even has its own golf course. The school and student organizations maintain a full slate of "outstanding on-campus social activities including a talent show, holiday dance, weekly TGIT (Thank Goodness it's Thursday!), and spring formal." Students also praise the "weekly happy hour with profs." All these events help mitigate the fact that the closest town, South Bend, is "boring" and "not very attractive."

ADMISSIONS

The admissions committee considers the following criteria (not necessarily in order of importance): work experience, GMAT scores, college GPA, extracurricular activities, letters of recommendation, and the required essays. According to the admissions office, "We require a minimum of two years of work experience, but prefer three or more, particularly for our three-semester program. An undergraduate business degree is required for our three-semester program. There are no specific curricular requirements for our two-year MBA, although the school does advise applicants to have academic preparation in statistics. We highly recommend interviewing; we conduct off-campus interviews with MBA alumni as well as schedule on-campus interviews. Applicants should have a demonstrated history of leadership through professional or community activities. Students are advised to apply as early as possible, especially if requesting fellowship consideration.

FINANCIAL FACTS

Tuition	$22,600
Cost of books	$925
Room & board (on-/off-campus)	$4,800/$4,800
% of students receiving aid	80
% first-year students receiving aid	53
% aid that is merit based	100
% of students receiving loans	50
Average award package	$13,061
Average grant	$14,064
Average graduation debt	$36,500

ADMISSIONS

# of applications received	379
% applicants accepted	64
% acceptees attending	50
Average GMAT (range)	613 (570–660)
Minimum TOEFL	600
Average GPA (range)	3.20 (2.80–3.50)
Application fee (in-/out-of-state)	$75/$75
Early decision program available	Yes
Early decision deadline	December 1
Early decision notification	4–6 weeks after completed application is received
Regular application deadline	April 16
Admission may be deferred?	Yes
Maximum length of deferment	1 year
Transfer students accepted?	No
Nonfall admission available?	Yes
Admission process need-blind?	Yes

APPLICANTS ALSO LOOK AT

Northwestern University, Georgetown University, University of Texas at Austin, University of Michigan, University of Chicago, New York University, Indiana University, Purdue University

EMPLOYMENT PROFILE

Placement rate (%)	93
# of companies recruiting on campus	90
% of grads employed immediately	75
% grads employed within six months	93
Average starting salary	$60,079

Grads employed by field (avg. salary):

Consulting	27%	$62,128
Finance	44%	$59,560
General Management	4%	$58,600
Human Resources	1%	$55,000
Marketing	14%	$59,111
Operations	9%	$59,456
Other	1%	$42,500

OHIO STATE UNIVERSITY
Fisher College of Business

ACADEMICS

Ohio State has rightly earned a reputation for the quantitative emphasis of its curriculum. In all areas, students at the Fisher College of Business "really develop a knack for quantifying criteria and evaluating situations and alternatives effectively." To ensure that entering students are prepared for this aspect of the program, Fisher requires a pre-enrollment review of accounting, economics, statistics, and computer literacy. It's a rigorous start to a program that remains extremely challenging throughout the first-year core curriculum; an exhaustive, tightly integrated overview of essential business skills and concepts. In the final quarter of their first year, students must select a major in one of four areas or craft their own "interdisciplinary studies" major from among eleven areas of minor concentration. The latter option requires faculty approval.

Students give the highest marks to the finance department, describing its faculty as "top-notch." They also praise accounting, marketing, supply management, consulting, operations and logistics, and real estate studies. Professors are "very knowledgeable" and are "great in one-on-one interaction with students," but our respondents also warned that "teaching ability is very wide! Some are great, others are terrible." Explains one student, "professors are brilliant and accessible, yet a little too research-oriented." An administration that "is always helpful and supportive" and an awareness that the education they receive is "very cost-effective for such high quality" contribute to a high level of student satisfaction with the Fisher MBA program.

Fisher's physical components get mixed reviews. Students explain that "the computer labs are great; the classroom facilities are not" and also complain that "the library needs improvement." Hopes are up, however: "A state-of-the-art, new business complex is expected to be ready by June 1999, and then we will have the best of the best facilities in the world." Students would like to see OSU add programs in entrepreneurship and international business. Also on the student wish-list are smaller core classes and abandoning the frantic quarterly academic schedule.

PLACEMENT AND RECRUITING

Ohio State students give their Career Services office average grades, complaining that "The office is overworked and has trouble helping all students adequately. The school needs to devote more resources to this office." Another student offers a slightly more positive spin, noting that the "Career office seems confused and inactive, but opportunities are available in spite of them." That's probably because of "very strong corporate involvement. A lot of companies are coming to campus."

Almost 200 companies conduct on-campus interviews with OSU MBAs, according to Career Services statistics. Other employment opportunities are made available through the school's participation in the National MBA Consortium in Chicago, the International MBA Consortium Employment Conference, Ohio State Career Day, and the Ohio State Minority Job Fair.

Cindy Holodnak, Director, Graduate Programs Office
100 Gerlach Hall, 2108 Neil Ave, Columbus, OH 43210-1144
Admissions: 614-292-8511 Fax: 614-292-9006
Email: cobgrd@cob.ohio-state.edu
Internet: www.cob.ohio-state.edu

Ohio State University

STUDENT/CAMPUS LIFE

Fisher MBAs describe their classmates as a "homogenous, Midwestern, married" group. Students enjoy the fact that their peers are friendly and not overly competitive, but some worry about an overall lack of work experience. "Many students don't really have 'real work' experience," laments one student. "Many are right out of four-year college, and they act like it." Another agrees, "The maturity level varies considerably. The people with no work experience, or out only a year or two, tend to be less mature."

OSU's quarterly academic schedule results in increased but manageable pressure. Students report that "this is a rigorous program, yet diligent work allows for a good balance between work and social affairs. You make time and integrate the two: study groups over dinner, for example." Adds another, "First year has a heavy workload. Second year is less time consuming, allowing time for a job search." Participation in student organizations and school activities is relatively low. Still, numerous clubs based on academic major, minority standing, and extracurricular interests are available for those who are interested. Campus life is "fun, especially during football season. Football, in fact, is the greatest unifying factor here. Also, the campus is beautiful during spring and summer." Another student is especially pleased to note that the "golf facilities are fantastic!" Unmarried students agree that "social life is good. MBAs often go out in packs of five to ten for fun activities." Hometown Columbus offers "all the luxuries of a metropolitan urban economic center with the feeling of a small town in the Midwest. Great place for families, education, and employment," although it's "a little depressing in the winter." Incoming students, be forewarned: the parking situation on campus is "horrifying."

ADMISSIONS

The admissions office at Ohio State considers your work experience to be the most important element of your application. The school then considers, in descending order of importance, your GMAT scores, college GPA, work experience, letters of recommendation, essays, and extracurricular activities. Decisions are made in five blocks. The school adds, "Our self-completing application allows applicants to manage their files. Once they submit a completed application, an admission decision will be sent to them within four weeks. Early application completion and a campus visit are strongly recommended."

FINANCIAL FACTS

Tuition (in-/out-of-state)	$5,898/$14,598
Fees (in-/out-of-state)	$360/$360
Cost of books	$1,000
Room & board (on-/off-campus)	$6,032/$7,200
% of students receiving aid	56
% first-year students receiving aid	31
% aid that is merit based	100
% of students receiving grants	20
% of students receiving paid internships	97
Average award package	$9,262
Average grant	$3,636

ADMISSIONS

# of applications received	1,244
% applicants accepted	27
% acceptees attending	43
Average GMAT (range)	641 (570–710)
Minimum TOEFL	600
Average GPA (range)	3.20 (2.73–3.70)
Application fee (in-/out-of-state)	$30/$40
Early decision program available	Yes
Early decision deadline	January 15
Early decision notification	February 28
Regular application deadline	April 30
Regular notification	May 30
Admission may be deferred?	Yes
Maximum length of deferment	1 year
Transfer students accepted?	No
Nonfall admission available?	No
Admission process need-blind?	Yes

APPLICANTS ALSO LOOK AT

University of Texas at Austin, University of Michigan Business School, Case Western Reserve, Penn State University, Indiana University, Northwestern University, Purdue University, University of Illinois

EMPLOYMENT PROFILE

Placement rate (%)	98
# of companies recruiting on campus	194
% of grads employed immediately	90
% grads employed within six months	98
Average starting salary	$74,276

Grads employed by field (avg. salary):

Accounting	4%	$62,500
Consulting	29%	$82,654
Finance	21%	$68,450
General Management	2%	$65,000
Marketing	18%	$66,713
MIS	10%	NR
Operations	14%	$57,375
Other	9%	$79,250

THE PENNSYLVANIA STATE UNIVERSITY
Mary Jean and Frank P. Smeal College of Business Administration

ACADEMICS

Great value could be the mantra of all Smeal MBAs, whose high level of satisfaction with their program stems from the combined effects of low tuition and a small but effective program. The tiny student body guarantees that students can't fall through the cracks, while state support keeps tuition low, especially for Pennsylvania State residents.

Team teaching and the substitution of seven-week course "blocks" for traditional semesters keeps things fast-paced and dynamic. Smeal loads the first year of its MBA program with thirteen core courses in quantitative analysis, accounting, management, finance, and communications, and then opens up the second year to a surprisingly wide choice of electives and concentrations. Students give the highest grades to "the communications department. The three components—speech, visual, and writing—get you ready for just about anything that could happen to you in your job." They are also pleased with the marketing, logistics, and finance departments. One student writes, "One of the best kept secrets is our finance department. We have a strong Wall Street alumni network. If you are interested in investment banking but don't want to pay $35,000 a year to get there, then Penn State is the place to go." Students give their lowest marks to the accounting department, although somewhat contradictorily they report that they believe themselves "very well prepared" in quantitative skills. Regardless of the department, students here feel that "the practical nature of the majority of classes is a strength . . . the professors use practical and useful course materials." Professors, according to almost everyone, are "great," providing "one-on-one interaction when needed. Very accessible and willing to offer help." The administration is similarly "nice, helpful, and friendly." The school's multimedia classrooms and facilities are universally considered "excellent."

Smeal offers a number of options to particularly ambitious students. Because Penn State offers study in practically every academic discipline under the sun, Smeal can provide many opportunities for dual degrees. Most popular among these is a combined MBA/MHA (Masters in Health Administration), offered in conjunction with the College of Health and Human Development. Students are also encouraged to study abroad during the fall semester of their second year; Smeal currently sponsors study in Australia, Europe, and East Asia.

PLACEMENT AND RECRUITING

Smeal students report that "Student/alumni relations are one of Penn State's strengths. There is a strong sense of pride in PSU. Everyone helps each other so that we all succeed together." It should come as no surprise, then, that alumni contacts are a primary resource for Penn State MBAs as they enter the job market. The network is huge: as the school often boasts, "one in every 700 Americans holds a Penn State degree."

Antoinette (Toni) Irvin, Marketing, Recruitment & Admissions Director &
Instructor in Business Administration
106 Business Administration Building, University Park, PA 16802-3000
Admissions: 814-863-0474 Fax: 814-863-8072
Email: smealmba@psu.edu
Internet: www.smeal.psu.edu/mba

The Pennsylvania State University

Companies that regularly hire Smeal graduates include AMP, Andersen Consulting, AT&T, Citibank/Citicorp, Ford Motor Company, Hewlett-Packard, IBM, Intel, and Pfizer. The MBA Professional Development staff emphasize intensive, personal attention and work closely with alumni, faculty, and corporate partners to mentor students. Students participate in MBA consortia and job fairs to supplement the active on-campus recruiting. Smeal students often find job opportunities most plentiful in the automotive, consulting, electronics and computer technology, and pharmaceutical and health care industries.

STUDENT/CAMPUS LIFE

The tiny student body at Smeal means that "everybody knows everybody well. Profs know every student by first name. Being in a small program helps us all." One student reports, "There is a concerted attempt to include spouses and significant others in activities," which not only helps married students adjust to graduate life but also helps to flesh out the crowds a little. Students describe each other as "conservative" and "down-to-earth." Most agree that the student body represents an "excellent mix of various countries, ages, [and] races."

Although Smeal is a small program, the university system it occupies is anything but. Penn State is enormous; as one student explains, "The small college has the personal benefits of a small cutting-edge program with the resources of one of the largest universities in the nation." Adds another, "The large campus, which is one of the most beautiful in the country, allows each student to pursue hobbies and interests in numerous ways. Large events, such as school-sponsored tailgates, add to an enjoyable experience outside the classroom." Social life "is very available in this college town . . . the problem is finding time for it" since "academics is the primary focus of most students, and it needs to be. Plan on working." When it's time to blow off steam, students can find plenty going on. "Sports teams and concerts provide entertainment . . . the restaurant and bar scene is great, and cheap!" Penn State's perennially successful football team "adds an esprit de corps like I have never felt before. That enthusiasm gets carried over into our academic and social lives." Many students report participation in sports as their primary diversion. On the downside, off-campus housing "is too expensive" and parking "is a major problem throughout Penn State. Oh, and the weather can be rough, too." Students also warn that University Park is "inconvenient to major cities and airports."

ADMISSIONS

According to the admissions office, your GMAT score, work experience, and college GPA are considered most important, and then, in descending order, your interview, essays, and letters of recommendation. They note, "Interviews are strongly encouraged and considered on a par with work experience." Applications are handled on a rolling admissions basis. It generally takes two to six weeks "depending on the backlog" for a student to be notified of a decision after receiving the completed application. Students may defer admissions for up to one year for personal reasons.

FINANCIAL FACTS

Tuition (in-/out-of-state)	$7,216/$14,140
Fees (in-/out-of-state)	$616/$616
Cost of books	$1,500
Room & board (on-/off-campus)	$4,700/NR
% aid that is merit based	100
Average award package	$10,000
Average grant	$10,000

ADMISSIONS

# of applications received	1,208
% applicants accepted	27
% acceptees attending	11
Average GMAT (range)	618 (560–680)
Minimum TOEFL	580
Average GPA (range)	3.28 (2.74–3.71)
Application fee (in-/out-of-state)	$40/$40
Early decision program available	Yes
Early decision deadline	February 1
Early decision notification	March 1
Regular application deadline	April 1
Regular notification	June 1
Admission may be deferred?	Yes
Maximum length of deferment	2 years
Transfer students accepted?	No
Nonfall admission available?	No
Admission process need-blind?	Yes

APPLICANTS ALSO LOOK AT

University of Virginia, University of Maryland, University of Pittsburgh, University of North Carolina at Chapel Hill, New York University, University of Texas at Austin, Duke University, University of Pennsylvania

EMPLOYMENT PROFILE

Placement rate (%)	92
# of companies recruiting on campus	121
% of grads employed immediately	82
% grads employed within six months	96
Average starting salary	$62,900

Grads employed by field (avg. salary):

Consulting	16%	$66,200
Finance	42%	$60,800
General Management	1%	NR
Human Resources	1%	NR
Marketing	22%	$62,600
Operations	18%	$64,200

UNIVERSITY OF PENNSYLVANIA
The Wharton School

OVERVIEW

Type of school	private
Affiliation	none
Environment	urban
Academic calendar	quarter/semester

STUDENTS

Enrollment of parent institution	20,000
Enrollment of business school	1,542
% male/female	71/29
% minorities	18
% international (# of countries represented)	32 (51)
Average age at entry	28
Average years work experience at entry	5

ACADEMICS

Student/faculty ratio	8:1
% female faculty	13
Hours of study per day	4.55

SPECIALTIES

Wharton has always been a leader in extending the frontiers of management education. The MBA curriculum takes builds upon Wharton's substantial strengths — expertise across the widest range of areas, extensive global initiatives, and long-standing commitment to innovation and entrepreneurship.

JOINT DEGREES

MBA/JD; MBA/MD; MBA/DMD-Dental; MBA/MSE Engineering; Communication; MBA/MA; MBA/MSW; MBA/PhD; MBA/Animal Health Economics Training Program; MBA/VMD (Veterinary); MBA/MSN (nursing)

SPECIAL PROGRAMS

Wharton's Sol C. Snider Entrepreneurial Research Center; the Goergen Entrepreneurial Management Program, the Lauder Institute's Program in International Studies: paid consulting available; summer pre-enrollment; "pre-term" foreign study

STUDY ABROAD PROGRAMS

Eleven countries

SURVEY SAYS...
HITS
Quality of recruiting
Small classes
School clubs

MISSES
Study groups
On-campus housing

PROMINENT ALUMNI

Lewis E. Platt, Chairman, President & CEO, Hewlett-Packard; Peter Lynch, Vice Chairman, Fidelity Management & Research Co.; Yotaro Kabayashi, Chairman & CEO, Fuji Xerox Ltd.

ACADEMICS

In many ways, the Wharton School Graduate Division at the University of Pennsylvania is the Lexus of business programs. It's big, it's expensive, its name impresses people, and it offers many, many options. With across-the-board departmental strength, several top-flight nontraditional business disciplines, and the university resources to support a hand-crafted curriculum, a Wharton MBA can be tailored to suit the needs of just about any business student.

Wharton built its reputation as a premier finance program, and finance continues to hold a prominent place here, so much so that students complain: "The reputation in finance is so strong that people forget that Wharton is also very good at marketing and operations." Accounting, general management, and business law are also reportedly strong, as are health care, real estate, and nonprofit. Several students single out entrepreneurial studies; writes one, "The Entrepreneurial Center is fantastic, a real standout. Wharton's greatest strength, though, is its excellence in so many departments." Global perspectives are emphasized throughout the program by an international student body, international courses, two international joint-degree programs, and a global immersion program in China, the ASEAN countries, and Latin America.

First year at Wharton flies by due to a quarterly Academic calendar (second year reverts to the more traditional semester system). The schedule, while intense, allows students to cover a great deal of material in a relatively short period, a necessity given that the curriculum here is "very thorough." First-year students are divided into five-member teams to tackle foundation projects during the first two quarters and a Field Application Project during the second half of the year. Notes one student, "The first year is very demanding and stressful. As a result, life becomes less enjoyable for a while. Second year, fortunately, is more relaxed." Another points out that "Teamwork is key. If you have a team that works well together, your life is about 1,000 times easier." All second-year students must complete at least one major in one of more than two dozen fields; students may also design their own majors. In a change from previous surveys, students give professors high praise for teaching ability, reporting that "professors take teaching very seriously," although several warn that "you've got to watch out for the new hires." Writes one student, "The professors rock! When I was ill last term, my profs offered me extra help, on their own time, to help me catch up." Students are similarly pleased with the administration, describing it as "very receptive to student concerns."

PLACEMENT AND RECRUITING

Students are extremely happy with the quality, range, and number of companies recruiting on campus at Wharton, not surprising given the school's stellar reputation. Writes one student, "All the best companies come here. The job opportunities are unbelievable." Students also give high marks to the Career Management Office itself and speak highly of the alumni network. The CMO offers more than thirty-five programs to students, including seminars, alumni panels, and individual counseling.

Robert J. Alig, Director of Admissions and Financial Aid
102 Vance Hall, 3733 Spruce Street, Philadelphia, PA 19104-6361
Admissions: 215-898-6183 Fax: 215-898-0120
Email: mba.admission@wharton.upenn.edu
Internet: www.wharton.upenn.edu/mba

University of Pennsylvania

In one recent year, "nearly 600 firms" representing 49 industries in 40 countries made offers to Wharton graduates and summer interns. About 20 percent of MBAs are placed overseas, with the largest groups heading for Asia and Europe. More than 25 percent of first-year students find internships overseas, primarily in the areas of investment and consulting.

STUDENT/CAMPUS LIFE

Each fall 765 students enter Wharton, making it the second-largest MBA program in the nation. Classes are held in amphitheater-style rooms, where students are identified with name plates. To counter this impersonal environment, the entering class is divided into lettered cohorts, each made up of 65 students who remain together throughout the core courses. The cohort system is meant to foster teamwork skills, and students report that the system works; reports one MBA, "Students here are very team oriented and very willing to help each other out. The opposite of the b-school shark stereotype." Wharton's MBA program is presently housed in the outdated Vance Hall. It will soon be replaced with the Jon M. Huntsman Hall with more than 100 classrooms, case study rooms, teaching labs, and social lounges. It is scheduled for completion in 2002. The rest of University of Pennsylvania's 260-acre campus is lovely, especially by urban standards, with many historic buildings and spacious lawns.

The neighborhood surrounding U Penn, however, is considerably less hospitable. West Philadelphia suffers the ills of urban poverty; students hasten to note, however, that the campus is safe. They also point out that "While the MBA campus is located in the undesirable West Philly section of town, almost all of us live in Center City (downtown Philadelphia), which is a beautiful area with abundant cultural and social entertainments." Adds one student, "Philadelphia gets a bad rap. It has great bars and restaurants." Students describe an active extracurricular scene, telling us that "There is so much to do outside of class! Clubs, social events, career forums, etc. Wharton is definitely more than just classes." As for housing, married or single students can live in the Graduate Towers, where twelve floors are set aside for MBA students.

Wharton MBAs describe their classmates as "intelligent beyond booksmarts, able to balance many responsibilities and complex ideas at once." Notes one student, "I was scared by how intelligent people were when the term started, but I have learned that if you are good enough to get in, you'll be fine." The majority of incoming students have accumulated five or more years of work experience before arriving at Wharton.

ADMISSIONS

The admissions office considers the following criteria (in no particular order): essays, GMAT score, undergraduate or graduate transcripts, letters of recommendation, extracurricular activities, and work experience. The interview is strongly encouraged. Writes the school, "The admissions committee evaluates applicants individually. Selection of students is not driven by categories or quotas. Applicants should represent themselves as they truly are versus what they may feel Wharton wants to hear. Applicants should also help the committee fully understand any unusual or nontraditional aspects of their candidacy." It is advisable to apply early in the rolling admissions cycle.

FINANCIAL FACTS

Tuition	$28,116
Cost of books	$1,682
Room & board (on-/off-campus)	$11,100/$11,100
% of students receiving aid	87
% first-year students receiving aid	60
% aid that is merit based	10
% of students receiving loans	60
% of students receiving grants	40
Average award package	$22,000
Average grant	$3,500
Average graduation debt	$40,000

ADMISSIONS

# of applications received	8,313
% applicants accepted	13
% acceptees attending	70
Average GMAT (range)	684.5 (580–750)
Average GPA	3.50
Application fee (online/other)	$140/$160
Early decision program available	No
Regular application deadline	April 10
Regular notification	Rolling
Admission may be deferred?	Yes
Maximum length of deferment	Case by case
Transfer students accepted?	No
Nonfall admission available?	No
Admission process need-blind?	Yes

APPLICANTS ALSO LOOK AT

Stanford University, Harvard University, University of Chicago, Columbia University

EMPLOYMENT PROFILE

Placement rate (%)		97
# of companies recruiting on campus		420
% of grads employed immediately		97
% grads employed within six months		98
Average starting salary		$95,000

Grads employed by field (avg. salary):

Accounting	4%	$70,000
Communications	2%	NR
Consulting	35%	$92,000
Entrepreneurship	2%	NR
Finance	40%	$75,000
General Management	4%	$75,000
Marketing	9%	$71,500
MIS	6%	$75,000
Other	1%	$70,000
Strategic Planning	3%	$80,000
Venture Capital	1%	$80,000

PEPPERDINE UNIVERSITY
The George L. Graziadio School of Business and Management

ACADEMICS

Pepperdine's Graziadio School of Management and Business provides "practical approaches to the business world" alongside an emphasis on the "rapidly expanding global marketplace." According to students we surveyed, these attributes combine with a powerful job networking system—both local and abroad—to make Pepperdine an appealing choice for business students.

Students appreciate the fact that in both its traditional MBA program and its Masters in International Business (MIB) program, Pepperdine integrates international issues into the curriculum. Students in both programs are encouraged to pursue summer internships abroad. MIB students, who complete their second-year studies overseas, describe the "intensive language program" here as "very effective," preparing them well to spend their second year at schools in France, Germany, or Mexico. One MIB tells us, "One great strength is the quality of schools with which Pepperdine is affiliated abroad. They're the best schools in Europe and Mexico." The second year of the MIB track culminates in a four-month internship in the European Union, Switzerland, or Mexico.

Students also praise Pepperdine's "conservative curriculum" that "prioritizes practical knowledge ahead of theory." (Pepperdine's conservatism should come as no surprise, given its affiliation with the Churches of Christ and the fact that the university once offered Whitewater special prosecutor Kenneth Starr the deanship of its law school.) Explains one student approvingly, "My professors are able to apply real-life situations to most of my assignments and readings." Teachers are "very knowledgeable and always accessible through home phone or email." However, students give professors merely average grades for teaching ability. In fact, their assessment of academics here are generally lukewarm, with most departments earning only middling marks. Students are much more enthusiastic about Pepperdine's ability to place them in the job market (see Placement and Recruiting below), with many citing this knack for placement as their main reason for choosing the school. They also appreciate the school's personal touch, noting that "the faculty and staff are extremely supportive to all students. Almost all staff members know your name, and they are always ready and willing to help." Among the complaints most frequently voiced: "We need a new building with a library." Pepperdine offers a one-year MBA program to students with undergraduate business experience. Respondents in the program describe it as "very fast paced. It has involved a lot of hard work." Pepperdine also offers a joint JD/MBA.

PLACEMENT AND RECRUITING

Students at Pepperdine are pleased with the school's "excellent career development program." In fact, a considerable number of survey respondents list the school's placement services among their top reasons for choosing Pepperdine. They are particularly happy with the quality and selection of opportunities for off-campus projects and internships, both in the L.A. area and abroad. Furthermore, they tout a "wonderful alumni network" and applaud the fact that "the school has strong relationships with businesses in the L.A. area." These factors mitigate students' relative dissatisfaction with the number of companies that recruit on campus.

Darrell Eriksen, Director of Admissions
400 Corporate Pointe, Culver City, CA 90230
Admissions: 310-568-5525 Fax: 310-568-5779
Email: gsbmadm@pepperdine.edu
Internet: http://bschool.pepperdine.edu

Pepperdine University

Pepperdine's Career Development Center (CDC) offers the standard assortment of career counseling services, including skills development seminars and an extensive resource library. The CDC hosts numerous industry forums and "career exploration events" throughout the year and also coordinates Pepperdine's participation in the West Coast MBA Consortium. The school's automated resume service matches incoming job offers with student resumes, which students may update via the Internet.

STUDENT/CAMPUS LIFE

Pepperdine's student body consists of two groups: students in the MBA program, and a smaller contingent pursuing the MIB. Minority and international enrollment is greater among MBAs, of whom Asian students constitute the greatest part of the minority population. Nearly half the MBA students are foreign nationals; in contrast, only 13 percent of MIB students arrive from overseas. Hispanic students make up the largest minority among Pepperdine MIBs. Students in both programs "come from all different backgrounds ranging from accounting and finance to hospital employees." One student describes his classmates as "the most eclectic group of people I've ever been surrounded by. Brilliant people, eccentric, successful, children of interesting parents and others contribute to the mix." Pepperdine's emphasis on team learning results in a student body that is "very collaborative, taking a team approach to problem solving." Notes one student, "Our entering class was small. The communications workshop united us very quickly. As classes began, we were very comfortable with each other." Students also happily report that their classmates are "leaders, entrepreneurs, people with excellent international connections and excellent local networking connections."

Pepperdine's Malibu paradise offers a pleasant mix of quiet surroundings and beautiful weather complemented by its proximity to Los Angeles. Although a few (insane?) students complain that Malibu is "boring and a far distance from any real nightlife activities," the majority love the town. Writes one student, "Life in Malibu is like a dream for an East Coaster like myself. Sun, ocean, campus—I'm very happy here." A Michigan native praises the "outstanding opportunities for me to be exposed to many new experiences, such as surfing," others point out that because L.A. is only about 30 miles from campus, it's an easy drive and "there is so much to do in the L.A. area." "Most students live in the Valley and commute to Malibu. The cost of living is cheaper in the Valley." On campus, students tell us about "copious amounts of social activities," community service opportunities, and student organizations. They describe the 830-acre campus as "one of the most beautiful settings in the world."

ADMISSIONS

The admissions office at Pepperdine considers an applicant's GMAT scores, completed application including three personal essays, transcripts, letters of recommendation, and current resume. A personal interview, although not required, is recommended. In addition, international students must score a minimum of 550 on the TOEFL and submit an Evidence of Financial Support Form. MIB applicants are strongly encouraged to enter with intermediate level proficiency in a foreign language. Applicants to the one-year MBA program must demonstrate at least two years of professional work experience and hold a business-related undergraduate degree.

FINANCIAL FACTS

Tuition	$23,000
Tuition per credit	$748
Cost of books	$1,500
Room & board (on-/off-campus)	$7,450/$7,450
% of students receiving aid	70
Average award package	$36,000
Average grant	$6,100

ADMISSIONS

# of applications received	366
% applicants accepted	54
% acceptees attending	42
Average GMAT (range)	600 (555–630)
Minimum TOEFL	550
Average GPA (range)	3.15 (2.90–3.40)
Application fee (in-/out-of-state)	$45/$45
Early decision program available	Yes
Early decision deadline	December 15
Early decision notification	January 31
Regular application deadline	May 1
Regular notification	Rolling
Admission may be deferred?	Yes
Maximum length of deferment	1 year
Transfer students accepted?	Yes
Nonfall admission available?	Yes

APPLICANTS ALSO LOOK AT

Univeristy of California—Los Angeles, Thunderbird, University of Texas at Austin, University of California—Berkeley, Univeristy of California—Irvine, Loyola Marymount, Stanford, New York University

EMPLOYMENT PROFILE

Placement rate (%)	89
# of companies recruiting on campus	80
% of grads employed immediately	43
% grads employed within six months	89
Average starting salary	$57,500

Grads employed by field (avg. salary):

Accounting	2%	$40,000
Consulting	9%	$56,000
Entrepreneurship	9%	NR
Finance	26%	$52,500
General Management	15%	$65,000
Marketing	22%	$47,000
Operations	3%	$50,000
Other	8%	$45,000
Strategic Planning	3%	$75,000
Venture Capital	3%	$56,000

UNIVERSITY OF PITTSBURGH
Katz Graduate School of Business

ACADEMICS

The Katz School at the University of Pittsburgh constantly lands on best buys in MBA programs lists. The reason is simple: the Katz program lasts only a single year, cutting tuition costs, and lost income, in half. Many students use the one-year program to jump start their business careers. Others stay for two years, committing the extra time so they can graduate with a dual degree.

Students explain that the condensed program makes for a grueling academic experience, especially in the early phase. Writes one student, "The first four months are an academic boot camp" with an "intense workload." Finals are every seven weeks. The program is best suited to those arriving with solid back-grounds. As one student puts it, "For a liberal arts undergrad major like myself, Katz is definitely a challenge and may be too quick. If I could do it again I would probably go to a two-year program. I think I'd learn more and not have to cram so much into so short a period of time." To prepare for the July through June sprint, students can take optional pre-program workshops to improve their skills in areas in which they are weak. While some students warn that "it is possible in such a condensed program for the substance of the classes to lose out to attempts to manage time," most students feel that "the program produces a high-quality learning environment and educational experience in half the traditional time."

A Katz MBA centers on twelve integrated, globally oriented core courses in such areas as accounting, decision technologies, information systems, business ethics, and financial management. Beyond the core lies "a good selection of elective courses" in seven areas of concentration. Students enjoy the "flexibility of the program" and applaud the emphasis on teamwork, telling us that "team structure teaches valuable interpersonal skills." Teamwork skills are particularly important in the student-run Management Learning Organizations, an internship-like as-signment in which teams consult on a real-world project, combining skills they learn in economics and strategic performance classes. Students feel that "MLO is a great learning tool" that "prepares us for the team-based environment of the real world." Students praise the school for its departments in MIS, operations, and finance and are particularly excited about the dual-degree program in MBA/MOIS, which "provides an excellent mix of management and technical skills."

Students say the faculty at Katz is extremely accessible, but the teaching quality gets mixed reviews. "The majority of faculty is excellent—they use real-world situations to apply theories, one MBA tells us." "The tenured profs are behind the times," says another. The administration doesn't score too well either. "The dual-degree program administration needs better continuity," advises one student. Some also complain that "The school is too tailored to developing middle management talent. We need to develop more leaders."

PLACEMENT AND RECRUITING

Katz's Career Services Center (CSC) describes itself as "one of the most ambitious MBA placement offices in the nation," an assessment with which most students concur. The CSC "goes the extra mile," reports one satisfied student. Because a Katz MBA is completed in a brief eleven months, the CSC hits the ground running, meeting with all students during the first week of classes. "It's

Kathleen Riehle Valentine, Director of Admissions
276 Mervis Hall, Pittsburgh, PA 15260
Admissions: 412 648-1700 Fax: 412-648-1659
Email: mba-admissions@katz.pitt.edu
Internet: www.katz.pitt.edu

University of Pittsburgh

important that our students get up to speed quickly," says Joan Craig, director of the Career Services Center. "We put a premium on getting to know every student who wants to compete in the job market, and helping them to develop an effective job search strategy." Agrees one MBA, "Katz is best for people who are fairly sure about what they want to do. Interviewing starts quickly, before a lot of classroom knowledge."

The CSC program includes abundant one-on-one counseling, mandatory interview workshops, an on-campus career fair featuring the school's top twenty-five recruiters, and national MBA consortia. More than 100 companies recruit on campus. Placements are strongest in the region immediately surrounding Pittsburgh, but the CSC reports that the number of placements in the Southwest and on the West Coast is increasing. Students are also pleased that both the curriculum and school-sponsored events "present tremendous opportunities for networking with executive-level business professionals."

STUDENT/CAMPUS LIFE

Because most students here are in the one-year program (there are also some part-timers and evening students in the mix), life at Katz is extremely fast-paced. Notes one student, "Because of the nature of the program, there is very little time available for social pursuits." Asked to describe a typical week, one student says, "Come in the morning, leave at 11 p.m., on and on. On weekends I have time to exercise, but on weekdays it's hard." Many extracurriculars focus on business education, such as the Executive Briefings series, hour-long presentations held several times a month at which chief executives from major corporations come to Katz to speak on career and industry issues. Equally exciting is the American Assembly Dialogue, which brings business leaders to campus to discuss major economic and social issues of the day. Community service is popular among many students.

Katz MBAs describe their classmates as "ethnically diverse, highly intelligent, and motivated," although several note that "too many have little or no work experience and so offer very little to the overall education of others." This "very energetic" crowd "manages time very well, a necessary skill in a one-year program" and also know how to let down their hair; reports one student, "They're fun as hell—good partiers, good teammates."

ADMISSIONS

Katz first considers your work experience and then, in descending order, GMAT score (TOEFL for international students), college GPA, essays, interview, letters of recommendation, and extracurricular activities. According to the school, "Quantitative information is important, but a student's work background and experiences through their college years can be as important as actual performance numbers on the GMAT or academic record." Minorities, international, and handicapped students are given special consideration. Each application is individually considered, then evaluated in groups of 100 or more.

FINANCIAL FACTS

Tuition (in-/out-of-state)	$15,990/$27,237
Tuition per credit (in-/out-of-state)	$446/$834
Fees (in-/out-of-state)	$4,911/$4,911
Cost of books	$1,000
Room & board	$14,000
% of students receiving aid	27
% first-year students receiving aid	26
% aid that is merit based	80
% of students receiving loans	40
Average award package	$8,000
Average grant	$10,000

ADMISSIONS

# of applications received	903
% applicants accepted	49
% acceptees attending	48
Average GMAT (range)	(550–700)
Minimum TOEFL	600
Average GPA (range)	3.20 (2.70–3.80)
Application fee (in-/out-of-state)	$50/$50
Early decision program available	Yes
Early decision deadline	January 15
Early decision notification	Rolling
Regular application deadline	April 15
Regular notification	Rolling
Admission may be deferred?	Yes
Maximum length of deferment	1 year
Transfer students accepted?	Yes
Nonfall admission available?	Yes
Admission process need-blind?	Yes

APPLICANTS ALSO LOOK AT
Penn State University, New York University, University of Pennsylvania, University of Maryland, Carnegie Mellon University, University of Chicago, Ohio State University, Babson College (Indiana)

EMPLOYMENT PROFILE

Placement rate (%)	98
# of companies recruiting on campus	100
% of grads employed immediately	94
% grads employed within six months	97
Average starting salary	$60,000

Grads employed by field (avg. salary):

Accounting	5%	$43,000
Communications	4%	$57,000
Consulting	29%	$64,000
Finance	28%	$59,000
General Management	3%	$65,000
Human Resources	2%	$47,000
Marketing	11%	$63,000
MIS	10%	$56,000
Operations	8%	$63,000
Other	4%	$58,000
Strategic Planning	4%	$61,000

PURDUE UNIVERSITY
Krannert Graduate School of Management

ACADEMICS

The Krannert Graduate School of Management serves its small student body with four degree offerings. Most popular among them is the Master of Science in Management (MSM), a two-year program characterized by its heavy emphasis on information technology. Krannert also offers a Master of Science in Human Resources Management (MSHRM) and a one-year Master of Science in Industrial Administration (MSIA), and has recently added a 30-hour Master of Science in Accounting, available to students with bachelor's degrees in accounting or master's degree students with a concentration in accounting or finance. Of the four degree programs, only the MSM currently enrolls more than thirty students per year.

Students describe theirs as "an intense program leading to a great technology MBA" housed in a facility in which computers and classrooms are "state of the art." They approve of recent changes to the curriculum, which now features two eight-week modules instead of the traditional sixteen-week semester. The shorter modules lighten up the core requirement load, provide students greater exposure to a variety of courses, and permit them to take more electives during the first year. According to several students, the core remains burdensome, but they are confident that further changes are forthcoming. Writes one student, "The administration is making an effort to improve in many lacking areas. The core curriculum, for example, needs to be reduced, and the administration is at work on the problem." Students also report that "Krannert offers excellent international exposure. I am involved in a challenging steel-consulting project with a company in Austria."

First-year students in all Krannert degree programs take many of their core requirements together. Second-year students must fulfill several requirements but are also free to take numerous electives and develop areas of concentration, called option areas at Krannert. Of these areas, students are most enthusiastic about manufacturing and technology management, organization behavior and human resources management, finance, and operations. Of the last, students write: "We are the strongest in the country when it comes to using computers for quantitative analysis." As in the past, students are ambivalent about the quality of teaching here. Writes one student, "Some teachers could improve their coordination with each other, equalizing the materials received by the students."

PLACEMENT AND RECRUITING

Students give high marks to the "excellent career placement services" provided by the Krannert Management Placement Office (MPO), and no wonder. Small class size works to students' advantage here, resulting in a great deal of personal attention from career counselors. Also to students' advantage is the fact that many employers find Krannert's emphasis on engineering and quantitative skills attractive.

Like many other placement offices, MPO has developed an Internet-based approach to marketing its graduates, posting student resumes and submitting them electronically to any (and all) of the 1,600 companies in its database that students choose. Writes one student, "The new on-line application and informa-

Dr. Ward D. Snearly, Director of Admissions
1310 Krannert Center West Lafayette, IN 47907-1310
Admissions: 317 494-0773 Fax: 317 494-9481
Email: krannert_ms@mgmt.prudue.edu
Internet: www.mgmt.purdue.edu

Purdue University

tion system is excellent." Top recruiters at Krannert include Andersen Consulting, Booz-Allen, Ford, Deloitte & Touche, Ernst & Young, General Motors, Hewlett-Packard, IBM, Intel, Procter & Gamble, SAP, Tektronix, and United Technologies.

STUDENT/CAMPUS LIFE

Kranner MBAs are a "technically oriented, hardworking, and focused" group. Writes one student, "I was surprised by how many excellent team players I met here at Krannert. Teamwork becomes a really enriching experience here." Students also report, however, that the sizable group of internationals here "tend to remain isolated from the U.S. students." Some feel that "admissions standards need to become tighter with regard to the amount of work experience that incoming students have." Finally, students report that diversity is not one of the student body's strong suits. Says one student, "my classmates are all white, male engineers from the Midwest. There is no diversity of thought."

The Krannert School is small, which fosters a cooperative team atmosphere. "I know everyone in my class," writes one MBA, "We're like a family." Adds another student, "The class is relatively small, so we have great opportunities to socialize and get to know each other." Students report that the workload here is heavy, especially during first year. Writes one student, "Life here is busy. I am up at 6 a.m. and in bed by midnight and sometimes I still can't get all the work done." However, a social life can be found here if one looks hard enough. As one student puts it: "A school full of engineers does not create *Animal House*, but evenings are fun." Another agrees, "Social life is what you make of it. There are plenty of activities: football-tailgates, movies with student discounts, parties. You can always find a group of friends at Harry's (the campus bar)." Students work out at the "Co-Rec," an impressive gym featuring amusement-park-like facilities—from bowling to golf courses to archery. Planned events include school picnics in the fall, the annual alumni/student banquet, tailgate parties, a talent show, and a charity ball. If all else fails, big city entertainment can be found in Indianapolis (one hour away by car) and Chicago (about a two hours' drive).

ADMISSIONS

The admissions office reports, "Although applicants come from diverse backgrounds in terms of education, experience, and cultures, they tend to have in common a strong analytical and problem-solving background." Krannert first considers an applicant's GPA, then in descending order of importance: GMAT scores, work experience, interview, letters of recommendation, essays, and extracurriculars. Applications are handled on a rolling admissions basis; students are notified of a decision three to six weeks after their file is completed. Students can defer admission up to two years, and fewer than 3 percent of applicants are accepted with no work experience. Krannert uses a self-managed application (you accumulate documents and submit them all together), so applicants know the application is complete at the time of submission.

FINANCIAL FACTS

Tuition (in-/out-of-state)	$7,176/$15,424
Fees (in-/out-of-state)	$307/$307
Cost of books	$900
Room & board (on-/off-campus)	$4,500/$4,000
% of students receiving aid	50
% first-year students receiving aid	51
% aid that is merit based	50
% of students receiving loans	38
% of students receiving grants	21
% of students receiving paid internships	95
Average award package	$12,112
Average grant	$17,010

ADMISSIONS

# of applications received	1,202
% applicants accepted	25
% acceptees attending	41
Average GMAT (range)	624 (600–660)
Minimum TOEFL	575
Average GPA (range)	3.26 (2.75–3.50)
Application fee (in-/out-of-state)	$30/$30
Early decision program available	Yes
Early decision deadline	November 1
Early decision notification	December 15
Regular application deadline	April 15
Admission may be deferred?	Yes
Maximum length of deferment	2 years
Transfer students accepted?	No
Nonfall admission available?	No
Admission process need-blind?	Yes

APPLICANTS ALSO LOOK AT

University of Texas at Austin, University of Michigan Business School, Michigan State University, Indiana University, University of Chicago, Univeirsity of North Carolina, Carnegie Melon University, Washington University

EMPLOYMENT PROFILE

Placement rate (%)	100
# of companies recruiting on campus	101
% of grads employed immediately	97
% grads employed within six months	100
Average starting salary	$67,818

Grads employed by field (avg. salary):

Consulting	22%	$75,225
Finance	28%	$66,100
General Management	8%	$64,945
Marketing	10%	$63,680
MIS	8%	$63,136
Operations	24%	$67,400

RENSSELAER POLYTECHNIC INSTITUTE
Lally School of Management and Technology

OVERVIEW

Type of school	private
Affiliation	none
Environment	suburban
Academic calendar	semester
Schedule	full-time/part-time/evening

STUDENTS

Enrollment of parent institution	1,577
Enrollment of business school	296
% male/female	77/23
% out-of-state	75
% part-time	49
% minorities	13
% international (# of countries represented)	45 (30)
Average age at entry	26
Average years work experience at entry	3

ACADEMICS

Student/faculty ratio	12:1
% female faculty	13
% minority faculty	2
Hours of study per day	4.52

SPECIALTIES

Management and Technology Emphasis, with strengths in value creation (New Product Development & Management, Technological Entrepreneurship, R&D Management, Production & Operations Research), Systems (MIS, Manufacturing Systems) and Financial Technology

JOINT DEGREES

BS/MBA, 5 years; MBA/MS, 2.5–3 years; MBA/ Masters in Engineering, 2.5–3 years; MBA/JD, 3–4 years

SPECIAL PROGRAMS

International Exchange in seven countries, Sino-U.S. MBA, Executive MBA

STUDY ABROAD PROGRAMS

Denmark, Finland, Hong Kong, Australia, France, Italy, Spain

SURVEY SAYS...
HITS
Helping other students
Students are happy
Quantitative skills

MISSES
Social life
Gym

PROMINENT ALUMNI

Sal Alfiero, CEO, Mark IV Industries; Robert Bozzone, Vice Chairman of the Board, Allegheny Ludlum Corp.; John Broadbent, Vice President-Finance, Treasurer, and Director, Arrow International Corp.

ACADEMICS

Technology is the name of the game at Rensselaer's Lally School of Management and Technology. In fact, a Lally MBA is distinguished as a Management and Technology (M&T) MBA, to emphasize its dual focus on traditional management training and technological proficiency. This school is not for the technophobic: if you attend Lally, nearly all of your classmates will have extensive backgrounds in computers, science, and engineering. About one-fifth of them will be pursuing dual graduate degrees, with second degrees primarily in engineering or science.

The Lally curriculum is, unsurprisingly, skewed toward quantitative study. The first-year curriculum is composed entirely of core competencies of "variable-length modules" and organized thematically in "streams." One stream, for example, takes product development as its theme and incorporates modules covering design, manufacturing, marketing, pricing, distribution, and performance measurement. Writes one student who recently completed one such stream, "Case study is very important at this school. Professors combine the practical, real-life cases with the theory in the textbooks. A course I recently took required us to through-design a product, all the way through to manufacturing and marketing." First-year students remain in a single cohort, breaking down into smaller teams for projects.

Lally's second year is somewhat less structured, although students still must take two strategy courses, an international elective, and an ethics course. They must complete a practicum—a field project with a local business—as well. The rest of the year is given over to study in a field of concentration. Lally offers concentrations in seven areas, among them MIS, operations, manufacturing, and technological entrepreneurship, the last of which boasts "the best entrepreneurship faculty you will find anywhere," according to students.

Students give their professors surprisingly high grades, considering that tech professors are often below-average teachers. According to our respondents, "Professors have a wealth of both academic and professional experience to draw from" and "the good ones are truly top-notch, although there are a few duds." However, "Some of the non-American professors are very hard to understand." Given the parent institute's focus on research, we were pleasantly surprised to learn that the "faculty is very accessible and assists students outside of class."

Those interested in Lally's approach but squeamish about the rigors of its MBA program should consider the school's MS in Business Management and Technology. This less prestigious degree requires only 30 hours of class credit (as opposed to the 60 hours mandated by the MBA).

PLACEMENT AND RECRUITING

The Career Resources Office (CRO) at Lally has the capacity to provide students with a great deal of personal attention because of the small size of the MBA program. According to the CRO, counselors "seek out" those students who don't visit their offices, especially as graduation approaches. The placement office works as hard on summer internships, participating in the Kauffman Summer Intern Program, which places ten students with start-up companies.

Zamiul Haque, Director of MBA/MS Admissions
Pittsburgh Building, Suite 3200, Troy, NY 12180-3590
Admissions: 518-276-6586 Fax: 518-276-2665
Email: management@rpi.edu
Internet: http://lallyschool.rpi.edu

Rensselaer Polytechnic Institute

According to the CRO, the program provides "a real entrepreneurial summer experience, followed by a fall term independent study when students write a business plan for the company." The CRO brings about 100 companies to campus for interviews each year. Students may also take advantage of Rensselaer's Career Development Center, which attracts an additional 300 firms interviewing on campus. Top recruiters include Andersen, American Management Systems, IBM, and GE. Further business opportunities for students arise through Venture Affiliates of RPI (VARPI), the Center for Technological Entrepreneurship, and New Business Incubator, all of which focus on entrepreneurial ventures.

STUDENT/CAMPUS LIFE

A small school, RPI boasts small classes, great computing facilities, and a lot of student/faculty interaction. The workload, however, is not for the feint of heart: students' self-reported hours studying per week is among the highest in our survey. Accordingly, Lally MBAs are "focused and serious," "friendly but busy." Although many nations are represented among Lally's large international population, one nation dominates the field: writes one student, "About half of the class is from China." Students also tell us their classmates "almost all have abundant working experience. They know a lot about management in real organizations." As should be expected, there is "a high concentration of engineering backgrounds" among the student body.

Students disagree about the quality of extracurricular life (what little of it there is, given the demands of the curriculum) at Lally. Some tell us that "There are many opportunities to get involved with faculty, extracurricular activities, and alumni." Others note that "every Thursday, MBA Associates organizes happy hours for MBA students" and that the group also sponsors barbecues, golf outings, and guest speaker series. Others, however, are adamant that "extracurricular activities are horrible!" Several point out that "There is no night life in the general vicinity of the school" and also remind prospective students to bring long johns and a heavy overcoat: Troy winters can be brutal. Albany is not too far away, and the occasional longer road trip to New York or Boston is certainly doable. About 30 percent of students live on campus in graduate housing, which they grade favorably.

ADMISSIONS

The admissions office considers candidates with strong technical, quantitative, leadership, and teamwork skills. All components of the application—college GPA, GMAT score, work experience, extracurricular activities, interview, letters of recommendation, and essays—are equally weighed. A TOEFL of 570 or greater is required of those who speak English as a second language. The school favors applicants with a technically oriented undergraduate background: "Our focus is the intersection of management and technology. Everything we do begins with the conviction that for all firms in all future markets, sustainable competitive advantage is built upon a technological foundation."

FINANCIAL FACTS

Tuition	$19,950
Tuition per credit	$665
Fees	$1,065
Cost of books	$1,684
Room & board (on-/off-campus)	$7,361/$7,361
% of students receiving aid	70
% first-year students receiving aid	50
% aid that is merit based	100
% of students receiving loans	75
% of students receiving grants	45
% of students receiving paid internships	25
Average grant	$15,120

ADMISSIONS

# of applications received	180
% applicants accepted	61
% acceptees attending	56
Average GMAT	604
Minimum TOEFL	600
Average GPA	3.30
Application fee	$35
Early decision program available	Yes
Early decision deadline	February 1
Early decision notification	March 1
Regular application deadline	April 1
Regular notification	Rolling
Admission may be deferred?	Yes
Maximum length of deferment	1 year
Transfer students accepted?	Yes
Nonfall admission available?	Yes
Admission process need-blind?	Yes

APPLICANTS ALSO LOOK AT

Cornell University, Massachusetts Institute of Technology, Carnegie Mellon University, Columbia, University of Maryland, New York University, George Washington University, Purdue

EMPLOYMENT PROFILE

Placement rate (%)	96
# of companies recruiting on campus	115
% of grads employed immediately	85
% grads employed within six months	92
Average starting salary	$58,477

Grads employed by field (avg. salary):

Consulting	11%	$53,600
Finance	19%	$67,429
General Management	2%	$42,000
Marketing	11%	$50,500
MIS	35%	$55,033
Operations	13%	$56,571
Other	9%	$77,250

RICE UNIVERSITY
Jesse H. Jones Graduate School of Management

ACADEMICS

Rice University's Jones School of Administration may be on the threshold of some major changes. In March of 1997 a blue-ribbon steering committee of senior business executives and prominent academicians published its suggestions for the school's future. Among those recommendations: increase the size of the student body and faculty, establish an Executive MBA program, pursue more joint ventures with area hospitals, businesses, and other departments at Rice, and secure national accreditation from the American Assembly of Collegiate Schools of Business. The following July, the school appointed Gilbert Whitaker Jr. as dean of the program. Whitaker, a Rice graduate, previously piloted the University of Michigan School of Business's rise to national prominence.

All of these changes are intended to address the only perceived shortcoming in this highly regarded program, namely that its size and lack of American Assembly of Collegiate Schools of Business accreditation (all top-fifty ranked schools have this accreditation) have prevented the Jones School from entering the top echelon of national MBA programs. Even so, the Jones School currently enjoys a well-deserved reputation as an excellent program, albeit one that draws students primarily from its immediate region. Students attribute the school's standing to an "excellent faculty, challenging curriculum, and beneficial utilization of the case-study method." Students here also benefit from the fact that "the new dean and administration are very focused on student concerns and improving the program" and a "very low student-faculty ratio," where "students and professors spend time outside of class discussing business and topical matters." Students give professors high marks for teaching ability as well as accessibility.

Jones MBAs praise the school's finance department and entrepreneurship program. They also approve of the marketing and accounting departments. In all departments, students report that professors rely heavily on quantitative analysis and the case method. Writes one, "Almost all classes use the case method. Classes that use it most extensively—marketing and economics—are more difficult, but immensely more rewarding. It is hard work but it pays off." The result is a "major work load with many group projects," especially during the first-year core curriculum.

Several features distinguish the Jones program. Among them are required courses in entrepreneurship and global strategy/operations. Another is its unusual focus on legal, ethical, and governmental issues in business administration. Rice offers a joint MBA/Masters in Engineering through the Jones School and the George R. Brown School of Engineering. Rice's location in Houston, national headquarters of the energy industry, greatly enhances the value of this degree.

PLACEMENT AND RECRUITING

Students at Rice University give their Career Planning Center above average marks, although a sizable minority feels that the service needs substantial improvement. In the plus column are Rice's "great connection to oil and gas industry, as well as to [the] Houston business community" and a "strong alumni network." In the debit column, students complain that the school does not do enough to attract on-campus recruiters from outside the Texas region. Writes

Jill L. Deutser, Director of Admissions and Marketing
Herring Hall, Suite 245 MS531, Houston, TX 77005-1892
Admissions: 713-527-4918 Fax: 713-737-6147
Email: enterjgs@rice.edu
Internet: www.rice.edu/jgs

Rice University

one typical respondent, "There is a need for more national recognition and an increase in the number of companies recruiting at Rice University."

In addition to on-campus recruiting, Rice creates recruitment opportunities through participation in the Atlanta MBA Consortium and the Foreign National MBA Career Forums in Miami and Orlando.

STUDENT/CAMPUS LIFE

As would be expected at so highly regarded an academic institution, students at Rice are "highly intelligent." Many are "competitive in nature, sometimes overly concerned with grades, but mostly very friendly, sociable, and fun." The student demographic is "very mixed—all ages, all backgrounds" with "lots of married students." Furthermore, "Rice has a great mix of quantitative students (former engineers) and qualitative students that makes for great class discussions." The minority population, however, is small. Although "extremely hardworking," Rice students are also "involved in nonschool activities."

A large married contingent and a demanding academic schedule result in low participation levels in school activities and clubs, although those with the available time note that the Rice community provides "a lot of clubs and organizations. A real sense of community among students, faculty, and staff." Although a few students complain that they "have no life other than school," most agree that "life at Rice is good. Plenty of learning, lots of networking, tons of opportunity, and an active social scene." During a typical week, "Monday to Wednesday is serious and then the weekend kicks off Thursday afternoon with a party on the back patio [called a partio]—fun!" Furthermore, "social activities happen often and in big groups. It is very common for a group of twenty plus students to meet for drinks on Friday night." Located in a residential section of Houston, Rice offers a surprisingly tranquil and beautiful 300-acre campus encircled by a tree-lined jogging path.

ADMISSIONS

The Jones admissions department considers the following criteria the most important part of an application: essays, college GPA, letters of recommendation, and work experience. Extracurricular activities and leadership skills are also considered. An interview is strongly encouraged; the school plans to make interviews mandatory for all applicants and schedule them in conjunction with weekly information sessions. According to the school, "Each applicant receives a comprehensive evaluation due to the composition of our admissions committee, which includes two graduating MBA students, a recent alumnus or alumna, a tenured faculty member, and the admissions directors. We do not select or reject an applicant based solely on his or her academic record or GMAT score; instead we evaluate each applicant in the context of the entire application." Decisions are made on a rolling basis with four major deadlines: December 1, January 15, March 1, and April 15.

FINANCIAL FACTS

Tuition	$17,000
Fees	$550
Cost of books	$5,625
Room & board (on-/off-campus)	$8,136/$11,100
% of students receiving aid	70
% first-year students receiving aid	70
% aid that is merit based	50
% of students receiving loans	70
% of students receiving grants	45
% of students receiving paid internships	100
Average grant	$5,100

ADMISSIONS

# of applications received	511
% applicants accepted	48
% acceptees attending	53
Average GMAT (range)	630 (590–660)
Minimum TOEFL	600
Average GPA (range)	3.20 (2.90–3.50)
Application fee (in-/out-of-state)	$75/$75
Early decision program available	Yes
Early decision deadline	December 1, January 15, March 1
Early decision notification	January 15, March 1, April 30
Regular application deadline	April 15
Regular notification	May 14
Admission may be deferred?	Yes
Maximum length of deferment	1 year
Transfer students accepted?	No
Nonfall admission available?	No
Admission process need-blind?	Yes

APPLICANTS ALSO LOOK AT

University of Texas at Austin, University of Pennsylvania, University of Virginia, Harvard University, Northwestern University, University of North Carolina at Chapel Hill, Stanford University, University of California — Los Angeles

EMPLOYMENT PROFILE

Placement rate (%)		100
# of companies recruiting on campus		113
% of grads employed immediately		90
% grads employed within six months		100
Average starting salary		$67,000
Grads employed by field (avg. salary):		
Consulting	10%	$78,000
Finance	46%	$78,000
Marketing	21%	$59,000
Operations	23%	$69,000

UNIVERSITY OF ROCHESTER
William E. Simon Graduate School of Business Administration

OVERVIEW

Type of school	private
Affiliation	none
Environment	suburban
Academic calendar	quarter
Schedule	full-time/part-time/evening

STUDENTS

Enrollment of parent institution	8,246
Enrollment of business school	756
% male/female	67/33
% out-of-state	22
% part-time	29
% minorities	9
% international (# of countries represented)	31 (48)
Average age at entry	28
Average years work experience at entry	5

ACADEMICS

Student/faculty ratio	15:1
% female faculty	15
Hours of study per day	4.80

SPECIALTIES
The Simon School offers thirteen concentrations, ranging from the more broad-based, i.e. Finance, to the more specialized, i.e. Health Care Management. The hallmarks of a Simon School education are its integration around economic principles and its long-term applicability.

JOINT DEGREES
MBA/MS in Microbiology and Immunology, 2.5 years for Microbiology and Immunology; MBA/MS in Nursing, 2.5 years; MBA/Master of Public Health, 3 years, MD/MBA, 5 years

SPECIAL PROGRAMS
VISION, Broaden Your Horizons Intercultural Seminar Series, the Executive Seminar Series, International Exchange Programs, Coach-Mentor Program

STUDY ABROAD PROGRAMS
Seven foreign exchange programs are available.

SURVEY SAYS...
HITS
Finance
Ethnic and racial diversity
Quantitative skills

MISSES
Social life
Gym
General management

PROMINENT ALUMNI
Paul A. Brands, CEO, American Mgmt Systems; Charles R Hughes, CEO and President, Land Rover North America; Charles A. Dowd, President, MASCO Corporation

ACADEMICS

"Finance" is the magic word at the Simon Graduate School of Business Administration, where a staggering 82 percent of all students give the finance department our highest rating. The department is the most-often cited reason students give for choosing the Rochester MBA program. Explains one student, "The finance teachers are great and present current research that can be used in real-world situations." Another articulates the belief commonly held here, that "in finance and data analysis we are unequaled, with the possible exception of Chicago."

The Simon School's strength lies in its world-class, research-oriented faculty who, unlike many researchers, also happen to be excellent teachers. At Simon, "the big name professors actually teach, and they do it well." One student noted that these "world-famous professors devote incredible energy to teaching, and you can walk into their offices and have a chat any time!" The vaunted finance faculty features Gregg A. Jarrell, one-time chief economist of the U.S. Securities and Exchange Commission, and Clifford W. Smith Jr., author of numerous books and winner of even more teaching awards. Accounting is the other standout department here. Students also give good marks to courses in management and operations.

School brochures boast "the most integrated MBA curriculum" of all business schools, and students apparently agree. Explains one, "The other day I was reading a case for econometrics. One of the case questions was from my finance professor who thought it would be interesting for us to explore a couple of finance issues. That's integration! The profs are always on top of who's doing what in each class." First-year studies emphasize teamwork through five-member cohorts and student management teams. Students remain in their assigned cohort throughout the three-quarter-long core sequence and collectively tackle numerous case studies and group projects. Our respondents appreciated the "strong grounding in economic theory" they received through the core but warn that the sequence is "very quantitative—challenging, especially for nonquant folks." Students agree that "the experience is worth it!" Second-year students choose from among thirteen areas of concentration, and many pursue a double concentration. Grade-conscious students, beware. "The Simon School's relative grading system (curve) is very competitive," complains a student.

PLACEMENT AND RECRUITING

Simon's Career Services Office (CSO) writes that the program's small size allows it to offer "uniquely personal and individualized assistance to all Simon students during the recruiting and placement process." Among the "full range of services" offered are individual counseling, mock interviews, career workshops, resume books, and alumni programs. In addition to scheduling on-campus recruiting, the CSO organizes the New York Recruiting Program, "which gives students an opportunity to interview in Manhattan with New York City–area firms," and participation in MBA consortia and international student recruiting events.

Pamela Black-Colton, Assistant Dean for M.B.A. Admissions
and Administration
304B Schlegel Hall, Rochester, NY 14627
Admissions: 716-275-3533 Fax: 716-271-3907
Email: mbaadm@ssb.rochester.edu
Internet: www.ssb.rochester.edu

Our survey revealed dissatisfaction with the CSO, "especially for nonfinance students." Students complain that the school needs to "bring more recruiters on campus. We don't advertise our product—the student—enough. We need to show corporations that the trip to Rochester is worthwhile, because we are!" Other students agree that "the school is making an effort to improve its placement office," and "its reputation . . . it is paying off—literally."

STUDENT/CAMPUS LIFE

The student body at the Simon School is "a true embodiment of positive diversity. They draw from almost all countries, all educational and professional backgrounds." The nearly 50 percent from overseas meet with the approval of all the students, who feel that "the diversity of the student body really prepares us to work in global environments." Students are "surprisingly helpful despite the relative grading system." The first-year emphasis on teamwork helps, fashioning a group that is "very teamwork oriented, and willing to learn about the cultural backgrounds of all students." According to one student, another reason that "students are generally helpful" is the "sense that the school is underrated, and by helping each other we will have greater collective success that will eventually reflect on the school." Finally, students grow close during this program because "it's a small group; we all know each other."

Students write that "it is a challenge to find a balance between school, social life, and sports" because "the workload can be intense." This is especially true during the first year, when "you practically live with your study team." A second-year student reflects, "social life is a sore subject the first year. The second-year students seem to have a lot more fun because the workload eases up dramatically." In their spare time, students become "highly involved in a diverse range of academic/club activities. Simon has everything big schools offer in a small package with top facilities." The "administration and student government have worked to improve social life by arranging school-funded ski trips, sporting events, and parties." Snowy during winter, but located in a beautiful part of upstate New York, the weather does not hurt an active social life. One student commented, "There is always something going on in Rochester to take a break from the challenging and rewarding Simon Program."

ADMISSIONS

Three-fourths of the full-time graduating class start in September; the remaining one-fourth start in January and complete the program in an accelerated eighteen-month schedule.

The admissions committee considers the following criteria (not listed in order of importance): Quality of undergraduate school; academic accomplishments and ability; essays, college GPA, letters of recommendation, and GMAT. Interviews are suggested for all students. Decisions are made on a rolling admissions basis. Applicants are notified of a decision within three weeks of applying.

Accepted students may defer admission for up to one year.

FINANCIAL FACTS

Tuition	$23,760
Tuition per credit	$792
Fees	$546
Cost of books	$1,300
Room & board (on-/off-campus)	$7,289/$7,289
% aid that is merit based	100
% of students receiving grants	69
% of students receiving paid internships	99
Average grant	$10,248

ADMISSIONS

# of applications received	1,661
% applicants accepted	28
% acceptees attending	38
Average GMAT (range)	639 (580–680)
Minimum TOEFL	600
Average GPA (range)	3.20 (2.90–3.60)
Application fee (in-/out-of-state)	$75/$75
Early decision program available	No
Regular application deadline	June 1
Regular notification	Rolling
Admission may be deferred?	Yes
Maximum length of deferment	1 year
Transfer students accepted?	Yes
Nonfall admission available?	Yes
Admission process need-blind?	Yes

APPLICANTS ALSO LOOK AT

New York University, Cornell University, Columbia University, University of Pennsylvania, University of Chicago, University of Michigan—Ann Arbor, Dartmouth College, Duke University

EMPLOYMENT PROFILE

Placement rate (%)	90
# of companies recruiting on campus	125
% of grads employed immediately	90
% grads employed within six months	99
Average starting salary	$70,746

Grads employed by field (avg. salary):

Accounting	2%	NR
Consulting	30%	$77,569
Finance	45%	$69,108
General Management	5%	$67,500
Marketing	12%	$67,400
Operations	4%	$60,800
Strategic Planning	2%	NR

UNIVERSITY OF SOUTH CAROLINA
Darla Moore School of Business

OVERVIEW

Type of school	public
Affiliation	none
Environment	suburban
Academic calendar	semester

STUDENTS

Enrollment of parent institution	25,250
Enrollment of business school	906
% male/female	65/35
% out-of-state	48
% part-time	39
% minorities	6
% international (# of countries represented)	26 (33)
Average age at entry	27
Average years work experience at entry	4

ACADEMICS

Student/faculty ratio	30:1
% female faculty	17
% minority faculty	2

SPECIALTIES

The Darla Moore School of Business is noted for its programs in International Business. Teamwork is stressed throughout MBA programs.

JOINT DEGREES

JD/MBA, 3 years; JD/MACC, 3 years; JD/MIBS, 3–4 years; JD/MHR, 3 years; JD/MSBA, 3 years; JD/MA Econ, 3 years

SPECIAL PROGRAMS

The MBA Enterprise Corps, international internships, foreign language studies (eight languages), plus English for foreign nationalist, six joint degree programs, specialized degree programs in Accounting, Taxation, Human Resources, Economics, and MIS, MBA Accord (Consulting Service for non-profits), field study program

STUDY ABROAD PROGRAMS

Denmark, Germany, France, Finland, Holland, United Kingdom, Austrailia, Norway, and Belgium

SURVEY SAYS...
HITS
Students are happy
Teamwork skills

MISSES
MIS/Operations

PROMINENT ALUMNI

Ms. Darla Moore, President-Rainwater, Inc.; Keith Elliott, Chairman and CEO, Hercules, Inc.; William W. Johnson, Chairman of the Executive Committee, Bank of America Corporation

ACADEMICS

International business is the focal point of University of South Carolina's Darla Moore School of Business. The school offers two innovative international business degrees, the Master of International Business Studies (MIBS) and the accelerated International Master of Business Administration (IMBA). USC also offers a traditional MBA, but nearly all the students we spoke with concede that international business is USC's star attraction. "Everyone is dedicated to making the school the best international business school in the country," explains one student.

Of the three degree programs at Darla Moore, the MIBS is most popular, enrolling more than 300 students. Intensive language training, a fully integrated core international business curriculum, and a six-month overseas internship are the centerpieces of the MIBS program. The curriculum is presented in segments of varying length, allowing professors to focus on a subject for exactly as long as it takes to learn it and then move on. One student tells us that "The modular approach (up to nine courses a semester during first year) is not for everybody, but the stress is worth the reward: a nine-month overseas internship/education."

Moore's IMBA runs for fifteen months, the first seven of which are spent at the Vienna University of Economics and Business Administration in Austria, and the last eight on the USC campus; courses on both campuses are taught entirely in English. The IMBA program begins in Vienna with a summer course in business foundations, then proceeds to classes in global management and cross-cultural communications. The USC segment of the IMBA program consists of 12 hours of elective courses, a course in international strategy and policy, and a final field-consulting project. Explains one student, "The IMBA program is fifteen months long, requiring time from both students and faculty. Faculty are easy to reach, willing to help even when they are on a different continent than the one you're on!"

A Moore MBA requires 60 hours of course credit. First-year students take a combination of core courses, which cover business fundamentals, and electives. During the summer following first year, students may work at an approved internship. Second-year studies are given over to electives and major studies, and MBA students can study abroad for one semester at one of thirteen schools.

USC professors receive high marks from students. Writes one, "Lots of talent among the professors. I wish I could take more electives. There were too many great classes I just couldn't fit into my schedule!" A somewhat less sanguine student adds, "Overall, 70 percent of professors are good at their fields and do great jobs teaching. Twenty percent are OK. Ten percent are not very qualified." Students complain that "required courses have the weakest, most inexperienced professors." Generally, students complained of disorganization in the administration of the school.

Ms. Reena Lichtenfeld, Managing Director—Graduate Admissions
Graduate Admissions, Room 520, Columbia, SC 29208
Admissions: 803-777-4346 Fax: 803-777-0414
Email: gradadmit@darla.badm.sc.edu
Internet: www.business.sc.edu

University of South Carolina

PLACEMENT AND RECRUITING

Moore's Office of Career Management serves USC business master's students with a series of seminars, discussion groups, and publications. The office also offers one-on-one counseling and advising and compiles resume books for graduating students, organized by degree. Placement services are handled by the university's Graduate Placement Office (for MBAs) or the International Placement Office (for MIBS and IMBA students). More than 100 companies visit the USC campus to recruit business graduates each year. Top recruiters in 1998 included Citicorp, Andersen Consulting, NationsBank, General Motors, Texaco, Intel, BMW, and Texas Instruments.

STUDENT/CAMPUS LIFE

As one might expect, Moore students have an atypical interest in all things international. Writes one student, "Most North American students speak a second language and have collected significant experience in a foreign country. Well-educated foreigners round out the body." The IMBA program in particular "is split almost 50/50 between Americans and foreign nationals." When only the American population is considered, however, the USC student body looks somewhat less diverse. Writes one student from San Jose, "Students are varied, but most come from the South. This school is virtually unknown on the West Coast; I only found it by chance." A black student tells us, "I'm one of only three African Americans. We need to diversify racially!"

Students have mixed feelings about Columbia, South Carolina. Writes one, "Columbia is both a capital and a university town. This adds to its dynamic." Others, however, find Columbia an insufficiently stimulating environment. Campus life is alive with "many student organizations and activities. School pride is prevalent." As an added bonus, USC is "a major university with SEC sports. This is a great school if you love college football and hoops." Students enjoy the "great Southern lifestyle with awesome weather" and also appreciate the fact that "housing is convenient to campus." Of course, many students here spend a good portion of their time overseas in study and/or internships. Notes one IMBA student, "Studying in Vienna, Austria, and Columbia, South Carolina, we get living experiences in two places. This is special because it pulls students together as Americans to adjust to life overseas. The non-Americans come here and do the same."

ADMISSIONS

According to the admissions office your GMAT scores, undergraduate GPA, work experience, and essays are considered the most important elements of your portfolio; then, in descending order of importance, letters of recommendation, interview, extracurricular activities, and state residency. The TOEFL is required for nonnative English speakers.

FINANCIAL FACTS

Tuition (in-/out-of-state)	$3,844/$8,114
Tuition per credit (in-/out-of-state)	$193/$710
Fees (in-/out-of-state)	$4,000/$6,600
Cost of books	$2,000
Room & board (on-/off-campus)	$13,000/$13,000
% of students receiving aid	50
% first-year students receiving aid	50
% aid that is merit based	100
% of students receiving paid internships	90
Average award package	$4,000
Average grant	$2,000

ADMISSIONS

# of applications received	1,101
% applicants accepted	68
% acceptees attending	38
Average GMAT (range)	583 (540–680)
Minimum TOEFL	600
Average GPA (range)	3.26 (2.60–3.75)
Application fee (in-/out-of-state)	$35/$35
Early decision program available	Yes
Early decision deadline	IMBA—Dec 1
Early decision notification	IMBA—Jan 1
Regular application deadline	February 1
Regular notification	March 15
Admission may be deferred?	Yes
Maximum length of deferment	1 year
Transfer students accepted?	Yes
Nonfall admission available?	Yes
Admission process need-blind?	Yes

APPLICANTS ALSO LOOK AT

Thunderbird, Wharton (Pennsylvania), Wake Forest University, University of Georgia, University of Virginia, Georgetown University, University of North Carolina—Chapel Hill, University of Florida

EMPLOYMENT PROFILE

Placement rate (%)	93
# of companies recruiting on campus	116
% of grads employed immediately	61
% grads employed within six months	92
Average starting salary	$59,600

Grads employed by field (avg. salary):

Accounting	7%	$59,600
Consulting	27%	$59,900
Entrepreneurship	3%	$53,000
Finance	17%	$60,200
General Management	11%	$65,300
Global Management	7%	$60,000
Human Resources	2%	$52,000
Marketing	14%	$56,500
Management Information Systems	4%	$60,900
Operations	3%	$57,900
Quantitative	3%	$59,800
Strategic Planning	2%	$59,000
Other	2%	$58,900

UNIVERSITY OF SOUTHERN CALIFORNIA
Marshall School of Business

ACADEMICS

The Marshall School of Business boasts strength in an impressive array of areas for a program of its size. Students praise the "strong academic programs in finance, accounting, and marketing," an "excellent information systems program," and the school's entrepreneurship program, which is consistently among the top-ranked in the nation. In addition, Marshall's Los Angeles location is a huge boon for those seeking opportunity in the entertainment business.

Many students tell us that they chose USC primarily because of its Pacific Rim Education (PRIME) program, a recent addition to the Marshall curriculum. PRIME consists of a four-week course covering business practices and management styles on the Pacific Rim. Team-taught by Marshall professors and faculty from "Pacific Rim partner institutions," PRIME exemplifies Marshall's emphasis on a "global perspective" in business. PRIME concludes with a trip to China, Japan, or Mexico, where students visit and study overseas businesses and financial institutions.

First-year courses at Marshall are organized sequentially so that concepts and skills build on each other. Courses are staggered to maximize the integration of the curriculum and may begin or end in the middle of a semester. Marshall's core curriculum emphasizes case studies, student presentations, and team projects, while trying to minimize the amount of class time spent in conventional lectures. Students are assigned to six-member teams during the orientation "team-building retreat" and remain with their team throughout first-year, completing core assignments and studying together. The result is a close-knit and happy student body.

Marshall professors earn high marks from their students, who tell us that their professors are "clearly experts, yet extremely approachable and personable." The prominence of the faculty has other benefits as well. As one student puts it, "I love talking about my professors' research while in my job interviews." Students caution that "professors expect you to work very hard, and they reward for hard work." According to our survey, students are also happy with their administration. "The administration is very responsive to student input and is working very hard to attract more recruiters and better-qualified students," writes one. Another explains, "When I applied, I inquired about a joint MBA/MA in Asian Studies. In response, the school created the dual degree. This is an example of how responsive they are!" No wonder students tell us "the program is student service–oriented, with lots of personal attention."

PLACEMENT AND RECRUITING

Our previous surveys indicated increased student satisfaction with Marshall's Career Resource Center, a trend that continues this year. Student opinion of on-campus recruiting, internship opportunities, and mentoring opportunities all reached new peaks this year. Our respondents save their highest praise for the "tremendous" alumni network "that is active and eager to help students."

Keith Vaughn, Director of MBA Admissions
Popovich Hall 308, Los Angeles, CA 90089-1421
Admissions: 213-740-7846 Fax: 213-740-8520
Email: uscmba@bus.usc.edu
Internet: www.marshall.usc.edu

The top full-time employers of recent graduates include Ernst & Young, Deloitte & Touche, AlliedSignal, Price Waterhouse, Intel, Hunt-Wesson, Arthur Andersen, Bank of America, Hewlett-Packard, HPM-Stadco, and IBM. Top employers of recent summer interns included Avery Dennison, Walt Disney Co., Wells Fargo Bank, and Intel.

STUDENT/CAMPUS LIFE

Marshall students think highly of their classmates, whom they describe as "intelligent, congenial, and teamwork oriented." Students come from a variety of business backgrounds. As a result, "everyone brings something different to the table, which is essential because so much of the work is team based." Students of Asian descent make up a large portion of the student body: nearly one-quarter are Asian American, and a substantial portion of the international contingent arrives from the Far East. Our respondents agree that "international students add significantly to the quality of education," reinforcing the feeling that the "students are one of the great strengths of the school." Although the workload here is heavy, students "seem to be able to balance their academic and social lives very well."

USC began construction on Popovich Hall, a new facility to house the MBA program, in the fall of 1997. Students believe that the facility, when completed, will remedy current concerns about classroom space and access to computer labs (which MBAs currently share with undergraduates). Campus life at USC is active, with students reporting strong participation in school activities and organizations such as the Graduate Marketing Association and the Graduate Latin Business Leaders. MBA candidates enjoy "great mixers every week, sponsored by companies that provide excellent opportunities for networking with potential employers and second years. The same applies to the scheduled 'brown bag' lunches every week." Sums up one student, "There are more resources available to me than I could possibly take advantage of. Life at school is all about time management." USC's park-like 150-acre campus is another of the program's many assets. Beyond the classroom, students agree that "social life is excellent," abetted by easy access to all that Los Angeles has to offer. Students give on-campus housing low marks, and most students here live off-campus in the beach communities of Manhattan, Hermosa, and Redondo Beach.

ADMISSIONS

According to the school, USC considers essays, college GPA, letters of recommendation, extracurricular activities, work experience, GMAT scores, leadership, and interviews. USC recommends that applicants be proficient in mathematics through calculus. Students are notified of a decision approximately three weeks after receipt of the completed application, including test scores. The final deadline for applicants is April 1. Students who are placed on a waitlist decision are notified of a post by June 30. On a case-by-case basis, students may defer admission for one year. According to the school, "We are a member of the Consortium for Graduate Study in Management, offering fellowships for talented minorities."

FINANCIAL FACTS

Tuition	$23,958
Tuition per credit	$726
Fees	$894
Cost of books	$2,200
Room & board (on-/off-campus)	$11,000/$11,000
% of students receiving aid	95
% first-year students receiving aid	95
% aid that is merit based	21
% of students receiving loans	95
% of students receiving grants	17
Average award package	$39,000
Average grant	$19,000

ADMISSIONS

# of applications received	2,150
% applicants accepted	25
% acceptees attending	45
Average GMAT (range)	650 (600–710)
Minimum TOEFL	600
Average GPA (range)	3.30 (2.91–3.65)
Application fee (in-/out-of-state)	$90/$90
Early decision program available	Yes
Early decision deadline	November 1
Early decision notification	December 15
Regular application deadline	April 1
Regular notification	April 15
Admission may be deferred?	Yes
Maximum length of deferment	1 year
Transfer students accepted?	No
Nonfall admission available?	No
Admission process need-blind?	Yes

APPLICANTS ALSO LOOK AT

University of California—Los Angeles, University of California—Berkeley, Stanford University, Northwestern University, University of Texas at Austin, Georgetown University, New York University, University of Michigan Business School

EMPLOYMENT PROFILE

# of companies recruiting on campus	254
% of grads employed immediately	76
% grads employed within six months	99
Average starting salary	$71,000

Grads employed by field (avg. salary):

Consulting	27%	$70,000
Finance	33%	$75,000
General Management	8%	$70,000
Marketing	26%	$70,000
Operations	4%	$61,307
Other	2%	NR

SOUTHERN METHODIST UNIVERSITY
Edwin L. Cox School of Business

OVERVIEW

Type of school	private
Affiliation	Methodist
Environment	urban
Academic calendar	semester
Schedule	full-time/part-time

STUDENTS

Enrollment of parent institution	9,513
Enrollment of business school	855
% male/female	72/28
% out-of-state	52
% part-time	68
% minorities	9
% international (# of countries represented)	23(36)
Average age at entry	28
Average years work experience at entry	4.30

ACADEMICS

Student/faculty ratio	7:1
% female faculty	29
% minority faculty	10
Hours of study per day	4.61

SPECIALTIES

Finance, Real Estate, Insurance, Marketing, Accounting, Entrepreneurial Studies, Organizational Behavior and Business Policy, and Information Sciences & Operations Management

JOINT DEGREES

JD/MBA, 4 years and 1 semester; MA/MBA Arts Administration, 2 years

SPECIAL PROGRAMS

Executive Mentor Program, Business Leadership Center, International Exchange Opportunities, Business Information Center, Global Leadership Program, Career Management Training Program, Caruth Institute, Maguire Institute, The FINA Foundation Business Leaders Spotlight Series, and The PriceWaterhouseCoopers Management Briefing Series

STUDY ABROAD PROGRAMS

Programs offered in ten countries

SURVEY SAYS...
HITS
Students are happy
Diversity of work experience

MISSES
Campus is ugly
Impossible to get into courses

PROMINENT ALUMNI

Eckard Pfeiffer, CEO, COMPAQ Computers; Lodwrick M Cook, Chairman Retired, Atlantic Richfield; Robert J. Paluck, CEO, Convex Computers

ACADEMICS

The Cox School of Business at Southern Methodist University offers a solid curriculum enhanced by plenty of personal attention from professors and administrators. But according to students, what really distinguishes a Cox MBA are three unique program features: the Business Leadership Center; Executive Mentor Program; and the newly instated Global Leadership Program, a three-week experimental module designed to give all first-year MBAs exposure to the complexities of international business. Both take advantage of the heavy concentration of business movers and shakers in the Dallas area.

The Business Leadership Center offers courses "organized by business leaders" and "taught by outside consultants," thus providing students not only with valuable insights but also important networking opportunities. Perhaps that explains why more than 90 percent of Cox MBAs attend the BLC's nonrequired seminars and workshops. BLC courses focus on "four major areas of effective leadership": Preparing for Academic and Career Success; Communication and Interpersonal Skills; Team Work and Team Building; and Coaching, Developing, Motivating and Influencing. Praising the program, one student tells us that "Noncurricular training is a real strength at Cox. Public speaking skills and other training seminars are provided, free, by the Business Learning Center." The Executive Mentor Program matches MBA students with a professional mentor from the Dallas business community; each mentor takes on up to five protégés. The mentor-student relationship begins from the very start of the MBA program. Students appreciate this structured networking program and say, "It's of incredible personal and professional value." Reports one student, "The rigorous academic work, coupled with our mentor program and the Business Leadership Center, allows us to excel not only in academics but also in presentation and real-life management skills."

The Cox curriculum is comprised of demanding and qualitatively rigorous courses that provide students with a broad graduate management education with opportunities to concentrate in specific areas. Classes are taught in both lecture and case-study style. Students complain of "too many core courses, but the electives are excellent and well taught." They also rue the fact that "there is a complete absence of information technology in the program." Most, however, agree that the top-quality instruction and attention they receive more than makes up for program deficiencies. Writes one student, "Open-door policy doesn't even describe it. We can meet with our professors at any time. We have their home phone numbers and often have happy hours together." Notes another, "I went to a large public university. When I came to Cox, I was seeking personal attention from professors, administrators, and classmates, and that's exactly what I've found."

PLACEMENT AND RECRUITING

A central component of the placement and recruiting process at Cox is the two-year Career Management Training Program, a combination of required and optional workshops. The first year of the CMTP includes resume workshops, career opportunity panels, and mock interviews. The second year focuses on defining individuals' career paths.

Students give the Cox CMO only fair grades. A typical student response says, "Recruitment is much sparser than I anticipated. I expected the job search to be

Deonna Lau Smith, Director, MBA Admissions
P.O. Box 750333, Dallas, TX 75275-0333
Admissions: 214-768-2630 Fax: 214-768-3956
Email: mbainfo@mail.cox.smu.edu
Internet: www.cox.smu.edu

less of a burden." A "strong alumni network within Dallas" helps, making the CMO "good on a regional basis, but it needs to expand its borders outside of Texas a bit better." Several students commented that on-campus recruiting in marketing is particularly weak. Last year more than 130 corporations recruited on campus. Cox also participates in the MBA Consortium, which organizes annual national interviewing events in New York and Atlanta. Cox grads most frequently move on to work at Ernst & Young, American Airlines, SABRE Group, and Chase Bank.

STUDENT/CAMPUS LIFE

Cox students regard their classmates as "dedicated and helpful, whether it be for class work or contacts in your career search." Agrees another MBA, "We're amiable and competitive. As a group of Type As we still look out for one another. We're very competitive, but we compete with ourselves, not to the detriment of our classmates." A "large concentration of Texans" makes up the lion's share of the student body, as it does at Cox's parent institution, but students adamantly point out that "Cox MBA students are completely unlike the SMU undergraduate students. The MBA students are of the same caliber as Rice, Emory, Vanderbilt, etc.—no comparison to the undergraduate division." MBAs say the student body is internationally diverse, which provides "an interesting mix of cultures," though a few wish there were "more women!" "I couldn't ask for better classmates!" enthuses a happy student.

The small size of Cox's MBA program promotes an intimate learning environment. "At a school of this size, you really get to meet everyone," remarks one MBA. "I learn as much from the other students as I do from my classes." Although students say it's critical to do all the assigned reading, the workload is manageable and the pressure is moderate, so that plenty of time remains for "students [to be] extensively involved in extracurricular and club activities." Intramural sports are also popular, especially tennis and volleyball. Students also look forward to an annual golf tournament, held in the spring. Every Thursday night is highlighted by a 'drink-and-be-happy' hour. On weekends, groups of students venture off campus to enjoy the city delights of Dallas, one advantage of SMU's "beautiful campus right in the middle of it all." According to students, "Dallas is an incredible resource for jobs and a great lifestyle."

The Cox school is housed in a three-building complex, which students describe as a "state-of-the-art facility." The electronic resources of the Business Information Center are considered outstanding. "A bigger snack bar would be nice," muses one MBA, "but I think the many benefits of being a Cox student outweigh having to go next door for lunch." Both off-campus and on-campus housing are reportedly attractive and readily available.

ADMISSIONS

The Cox admissions office told us, "We look for students who will take advantage of the variety of professional growth opportunities offered by the school for it is these individuals who can most clearly contribute to and benefit from our MBA Program." They enroll such students by searching out individuals who are well rounded, have clearly demonstrated academic achievement, and have a commitment and a capacity for leadership in business. Cox school admissions committee also emphasizes a strong GPA and GMAT score and prior work experience as important factors in their decision.

FINANCIAL FACTS

Tuition	$22,400
Fees	$2,200
Cost of books	$6,900
Room & board	$10,000
% of students receiving aid	75
% first-year students receiving aid	75
% of students receiving loans	56
% of students receiving grants	54
% of students receiving paid internships	100
Average award package	$14,000
Average grant	$19,306

ADMISSIONS

# of applications received	598
% applicants accepted	32
% acceptees attending	57
Average GMAT (range)	636 (520–790)
Minimum TOEFL	600
Average GPA (range)	3.20 (2.30–4.00)
Application fee (in-/out-of-state)	$50/$50
Early decision program available	Yes
Early decision deadline	November 30
Early decision notification	January 15
Regular application deadline	January 15
Regular notification	February 15
Admission may be deferred?	Yes
Maximum length of deferment	1 year
Transfer students accepted?	Yes
Nonfall admission available?	No
Admission process need-blind?	Yes

APPLICANTS ALSO LOOK AT

University of Texas at Austin, Vanderbilt University, Rice University, Emory, Georgetown

EMPLOYMENT PROFILE

Placement rate (%)	99
# of companies recruiting on campus	142
% of grads employed immediately	84
% grads employed within six months	99
Average starting salary	$63,408

Grads employed by field (avg. salary):

Consulting	17%	$64,066
Finance	51%	$65,160
General Management	6%	$67,844
Marketing	21%	$58,942
Other	5%	$58,200

STANFORD UNIVERSITY
Stanford Graduate School of Business

ACADEMICS

The Stanford Graduate School of Business is indisputably one of America's great b-schools. If you study here, you will study among the nation's best and brightest, learn from Nobel Prize–winning faculty, and gain access to power employers. The first-year curriculum features a quantitative orientation and is extremely demanding. It's common for first-years to experience anxiety about whether they'll make it or not. Despite their fears, almost no one flunks out. An extensive first-year mentoring and support system eases the way.

Stanford breaks its year into three quarters: fall, winter, and spring. The core curriculm has been designed to develop understanding and competence in four broad areas: internal environment of the organization (organizational behavior and human resource management); external environment (economics, political economy); functional areas (accounting, finance, marketing, production); and quantitative techniques (computer methods, decision analysis, statistics). The first-year core includes fourteen classes covering these topics. Students can take exemption exams to place out of cores. During the second year, students may choose from more than 100 electives. Favorites are: Strategic Management in the Nonprofit Environment, Personal Creativity in Business, Strategy and Action in the Information Processing Industry, and Power and Politics in Organizations. The interest in nonprofit topics is related to the popularity of the school's Public Management Program (PMP), which students describe as excellent. PMP is a certificate that is earned by taking three public management electives in addition to the required courses. Stanford also offers a Global Management Program within the MBA.

One of the hottest courses of study at Stanford is entrepreneurship. In fact, MBAs who take Entrepreneurship: Formation of New Ventures, have been known to come out with original and successful start-ups. Unique to Stanford is a de-emphasis on grades: Notes this MBA: "No-disclosure grading allows you to focus on what's most important/interesting to you." As for the faculty, while our prior survey revealed that students found less-than-exciting teaching in the core, much has been done to remedy this. A significant majority now rate professors good or better teachers. Some of the best learning experiences are found in the visiting speakers program, which features a greater number of speakers than most schools have in faculty. In a span of just nine days, Stanford was host to the following celebrities of the cyberworld: Apple Founder Steve Jobs, Jim Barksdale of Netscape, Ed McCracken, CEO of Silicon Graphics, Michael Nevens, leader of Mckinsey's worldwide electronics practice, and Andrew Grove, CEO of Intel. If that's not enough, in a creative pairing of expertise, Stanford Professor Robert A. Burgelman and Andrew Grove, CEO of Intel, team-teach Strategy and Action in the Information Processing Industry.

PLACEMENT AND RECRUITING

In 1997, more than 270 companies interviewed on campus. A large number of graduates go to work for smaller, high-growth ventures and computer businesses in both Silicon Valley and elsewhere. Ninety-nine percent of the class had a job within three months of graduation. Average starting salaries were among the three highest of schools profiled in this book—$80,000 (which does not include lucrative sign-on bonuses)—a solid return on one's investment.

Marie Mookini, Director of Admissions
518 Memorial Way, Stanford University Stanford, CA 94305-5015
Admissions: 415-723-2766 Fax: 415-725-7831
Email: mbainquiries@gsb.stanford.edu
Internet: www.gsb.stanford.edu

Stanford University

STUDENT/CAMPUS LIFE

As one former student put it, several factors make Stanford stand out: "The absolute irrelevance of grades, the entrepreneurial spirit of the class, the supportive and comfortable atmosphere, the emphasis on social life, and the access to Silicon Valley." Much of student life revolves around the student clubs, of which there are over 100, including one for spouses and partners, The High Tech Club, and the I Have a Dream Program, unique to the Stanford Business School. Indeed, there is "a lot of emphasis on social and community responsibility." To judge by the responses to our survey, students are "the crown jewel of this program." Compliments one MBA: "The people are what makes the place. Friendly, happy, intelligent, fun classmates." Raves another, "The most impressive group of people I've ever been with!" But they eye Harvard warily for which school deserves to be King of the Hill. According to these students, Stanford has a certain edge on Harvard: "All the benefits of Harvard (i.e., great jobs) but nicer people, and almost no academic pressure." Indeed, what students find at Stanford is an informal, noncompetitive, intimate type of environment. All that, and a world-class education. In suburban Palo Alto, Stanford MBAs are treated to an amazing atmosphere: sunny days, breathtaking views, hot tubs, year-round swimming in the school's outdoor pool, and, just a few hours' drive away, skiing in Lake Tahoe. A sprawling golf course on campus makes golf clubs de rigueur. Friday afternoons are reserved for Liquidity Preference Functions (LPF). Tuesday nights it's the "Friends of Arjay Miller," a.k.a. FOAM (which includes everyone). As for the campus, it's beautiful. The Spanish-style, red-tiled roofs are "a Stanford trademark." Facilities—including the research center and the library—are considered top-notch. On-campus housing for MBAs is available in a new facility, which opened in the summer of 1997. Most second-year students opt to rent shared houses in the hilly communities nearby. Many of these belong on the cover of Architectural Digest and verge on expensive (a four bedroom runs $1,800-$2,400 per month). However, all this atmosphere doesn't go to Stanford MBAs' heads: according to our survey, students spend twenty to thirty hours per week studying. There is a major emphasis on teamwork and group projects. Students say classmates are ethnically and socially diverse. Recent classes boasted two Jesuit priests, an Olympic Medalist from New Zealand, a stand-up comic, a Washington lobbyist, and a shrimp farmer from Ecuador. All in all, students are in agreement with this very happy classmate: "I wouldn't want to be anywhere else!"

ADMISSIONS

Notes the admissions office, "We do not interview individual applicants. We ask that you treat your essay as an interview on paper. We have tried to design our essays to elicit the same type of information that you would share in a face-to-face meeting. Focus on the essays. We want to get to know you, so don't simply reiterate information we find elsewhere in your application. We use the nation's most selective admissions process to admit students who represent a broad range of professional and personal achievement." Affirmative action is considered for Native Americans, Mexican Americans, African Americans, and Puerto Ricans. Applications are batched in one of three rounds. According to the school, "The earlier you apply, the better." College seniors are admitted with a mandatory two-year deferral.

FINANCIAL FACTS

Tuition	$24,990
Fees	$0
Cost of books	$1,851
Room & board (on-/off-campus)	$14,130/$16,240
% of students receiving aid	70
Average graduation debt	$46,416

ADMISSIONS

# of applications received	7,061
Average GMAT	722
Average GPA	3.60
Application fee (in-/out-of-state)	$150/$150
Early decision program available	Yes
Regular application deadline	November 4
Regular notification	January 20, March 31, May 26
Admission may be deferred?	Yes
Maximum length of deferment	Case by case
Transfer students accepted?	No
Nonfall admission available?	No
Admission process need-blind?	Yes

APPLICANTS ALSO LOOK AT

Harvard University, Northwestern University, University of Pennsylvania, University of California— Los Angeles, University of Chicago, University of California— Berkeley, Massachusetts Institute of Technology, University of Michigan Business School

EMPLOYMENT PROFILE

Placement rate (%)	99
# of companies recruiting on campus	288
% of grads employed immediately	80
% grads employed within six months	99
Average starting salary	$85,685

Grads employed by field (avg. salary):

Communications	4%	NR
Consulting	29%	$91,042
Entrepreneurship	5%	NR
Finance	20%	$77,137
General Management	3%	$102,889
Marketing	10%	$81,248
Other	24%	$86,903
Venture Capital	8%	NR

Syracuse University
School of Management

OVERVIEW

Type of school	private
Affiliation	none
Environment	urban
Academic calendar	semester
Schedule	full-time/part-time/evening

STUDENTS

Enrollment of parent institution	15,000
Enrollment of business school	599
% male/female	63/37
% part-time	67
% minorities	12
% international (# of countries represented)	43 (28)
Average age at entry	26
Average years work experience at entry	5

ACADEMICS

Student/faculty ratio	9:1
% female faculty	18
% minority faculty	21
Hours of study per day	4.59

SPECIALTIES

Entrepreneurship & Emerging Enterprises; Management of Technology; International Business; Supply Chain Management; Innovation Management; Finance

JOINT DEGREES

JD/MBA, 4 years; MS in Media Management, 1 year

SPECIAL PROGRAMS

Innovation Management Program, MS in Accounting, MS in Finance, Accelerated MBA, Executive MBA, Distance Learning MBA (ISD Program), International Study and Internships (DIPA Programs), Individualized Concentrations, Several part-time programs

STUDY ABROAD PROGRAMS

China (Shanghai Univ. of Science and Technology), Hong Kong, Singapore, United Kingdom/London, South Africa, Spain

SURVEY SAYS...
HITS
Computer skills
Students are happy
Ethnic and racial diversity
Teamwork skills

PROMINENT ALUMNI

Craig Benson, CEO, Cabletron; Arthur Rock, Venture Capitalist; Alfonse D'Amato, U.S. Senator

ACADEMICS

In an effort to keep up with the rapidly changing times, Syracuse University completely revamped its curriculum in 1992. The school has been revising the program ever since, soliciting feedback from students, faculty, and the business community to sculpt a thoroughly modern program. This year's model stresses technical proficiency and global perspectives, both areas cited as program strengths by the students we surveyed.

Syracuse begins its program with a "broad first-year foundation." The program is divided into several categories. Most important are the Pervasive Theme courses, which Syracuse calls "the signatures of the program"; these classes take an integrative approach toward such areas as globalization, quality, ethics, diversity, the environment, critical thinking, and management paradigms. The lion's share of the core consists of Professional Core courses, which cover traditional b-school skills areas such as accounting, management, operations, and data analysis. Personal Skills courses—more like workshops, actually—round out the core curriculum. Students are generally pleased with the core, although one student complains that "there should be more focus on accounting and finance in the core courses."

Core requirements bleed into the second year, but students are still afforded enough leeway to craft one or two areas of concentration (although concentrations are not required). Students speak most highly of the school's marketing and entrepreneurship programs; writes one student, "The entrepreneurship professors are exceptional. Beyond this area, there are very few good professors here." Students also appreciate the opportunity to pursue a concentration in supply chain management, acknowledging that few schools offer study in this field. Still others take advantage of the university's famous S. I. Newhouse School of Public Administration, which offers an MS in Media Administration in conjunction with the School of Management.

Students give professors here mediocre grades for teaching ability. Complains one student, "Some professors have other agendas and don't really care about teaching." Another agrees, "Teaching is spotty, especially in the core courses. It's disappointing." Students are similarly disappointed in the administration, telling us that "The administration is not very receptive to student needs and suggestions" and "the whole program is not student-friendly."

PLACEMENT AND RECRUITING

The Syracuse Career Center points out that its strength is in the numbers: that is, the low ratio of students to staffers, which allows the school to "focus on the needs and skills of each of our students." On-campus recruiting is supplemented by two off-campus events, an MBA consortium in Washington, DC, and a recruitment meeting held in New York City exclusively for Syracuse students. The school also maintains offices in Shanghai, South Africa, Hong Kong, London, and Singapore, through which it provides students with opportunities for internships abroad. According to Career Center reports, the average starting salary of Syracuse graduates (see sidebar) is especially impressive because "a number of our graduates prefer to work with regional or entrepreneurial com-

Paula Charland, Assistant Dean, Master's Enrollment
Suite 100, School of Management, Syracuse, NY 13244-2130
Admissions: 315-443-9214 Fax: 315-443-9517
Email: mbainfo@som.syr.edu
Internet: sominfo.syr.edu

panies where the starting salaries are generally lower on a gross basis than those obtained in the larger metropolitan areas or with larger firms." Still, some students report being "disappointed in the companies recruiting at the university." Top hiring companies include Andersen, Ford Motor Co., Goldman Sachs, IBM, and Price Waterhouse.

STUDENT/CAMPUS LIFE

Life at Syracuse University is tempered by the university's hometown, a small city susceptible to brutal winters. Although there is a decent downtown bar and restaurant scene (including the Dinosaur, a blues club that serves the only great barbecue north of the Mason-Dixon line), students complain that "the city is boring, the weather is terrible, and there is no real life outside the program." Weather permitting, students enjoy a beautiful, 200-acre campus replete with grassy lawns and historic buildings. Of extracurricular activities, students note that "There are student groups, such as the MBASA, that provide opportunities for students to mix outside of the classroom." Mainstays of life at the School of Management include the "Friday Experience"; instead of holding classes, Syracuse opens Fridays to "informal meetings with managers, panel discussions, job fairs, site visits, and the like." Among recent Friday visitors: Alan Greenspan, Jack Kemp, and Carmen Policy. Also earning students' praise is the Orange Consulting Group, a student-run organization that arranges for MBAs to consult with area corporations. The OCG charges for students' consultations, with the earnings placed in a scholarship fund for other students.

Students describe themselves as "overall very friendly. I think this is due to the extensive teamwork within the program and the relatively small size of the class. Everybody knows everybody else." There does seem to be tension between Americans and the "many internationals," however. Writes one American student, "International students get exceptional treatment by faculty. There's a double standard here!" Providing a counterpoint, one student from East Asia described his American classmates this way: "Some of them are friendly and have global vision but others are narrow-minded and self-centered."

ADMISSIONS

The admissions office considers (not listed in order of importance) your essays, college GPA, letters of recommendation, extracurricular activities, work experience, and GMAT score. An interview is encouraged. Writes the school, "Each candidate is evaluated individually. Acceptance is based on the ability to excel in the classroom and eventually the career in business. We evaluate intellectual compatibility and academic potential through an in-depth review of the applicant's educational record, references, and performance on the GMAT exam. Program selection, major, and undergraduate institution are also considered. Full-time work experience is highly recommended. Evidence of leadership potential, perseverance, and teamwork ability is also a plus." Decisions are made on a rolling admissions basis. Candidates may defer admission for up to one year.

FINANCIAL FACTS

Tuition	$17,490
Tuition per credit	$583
Fees	$583
Cost of books	$1,155
Room & board (on-/off-campus)	NR/$8,956
% aid that is merit based	80
% of students receiving loans	30
% of students receiving paid internships	13
Average award package	$15,000
Average grant	$8,000
Average graduation debt	$9,633

ADMISSIONS

# of applications received	719
% applicants accepted	28
% acceptees attending	54
Average GMAT (range)	605 (570–640)
Minimum TOEFL	580
Average GPA (range)	3.20 (2.95–3.50)
Application fee (in-/out-of-state)	$40/$40
Early decision program available	Yes
Regular application deadline	May 1
Regular notification	Rolling
Admission may be deferred?	Yes
Maximum length of deferment	1 year
Transfer students accepted?	No
Nonfall admission available?	Yes
Admission process need-blind?	Yes

APPLICANTS ALSO LOOK AT

Boston University, New York University, Cornell University, George Washington University, University of Buffalo/SUNY, University of Rochester

EMPLOYMENT PROFILE

Placement rate (%)	97
# of companies recruiting on campus	157
% of grads employed immediately	94
% grads employed within six months	99
Average starting salary	$69,000

Grads employed by field (avg. salary):

Accounting	4%	$67,000
Consulting	17%	$62,175
Finance	30%	$67,000
General Management	8%	$72,000
Human Resources	7%	$54,500
Marketing	20%	$76,450
MIS	7%	$69,000
Operations	7%	$79,500
Strategic Planning	1%	NR

UNIVERSITY OF TENNESSEE AT KNOXVILLE
College of Business Administration

OVERVIEW

Type of school	public
Affiliation	none
Environment	urban
Academic calendar	semester
Schedule	full-time only

STUDENTS

Enrollment of parent institution	26,000
Enrollment of business school	180
% male/female	69/31
% out-of-state	70
% minorities	7
% international (# of countries represented)	12 (7)
Average age at entry	25
Average years work experience at entry	4

ACADEMICS

Student/faculty ratio	15:1
% female faculty	10
% minority faculty	5
Hours of study per day	5.38

SPECIALTIES

Technology, Entrepreneurship, Logistics/
Transportation, Marketing, Health Care, MIS

JOINT DEGREES

JD/MBA, 4–4.4 years; BA/MBA, 5 years; MBA/
Masters in Industrial Engineering, 2 years and 1/2
summer session

SPECIAL PROGRAMS

The MBA Symposia, TOMBA, The Oak Ridge National
Laboratory, Summer Internships, Corporate
Connections, Community Connections, also Case
Competition Teams

SURVEY SAYS...

HITS
Presentation skills
Interpersonal skills prep
Marketing

MISSES
Quantitative skills
On-campus housing
Gym

ACADEMICS

The University of Tennessee at Knoxville b-school has overhauled its program to introduce a new paradigm for learning: Cross-functional courses, team-teaching, team-building, global study, and experiential exercises. This roll-up-your-shirtsleeves, activity-based program offers students more real-world experience than they could hope to find at most other b-schools. Distinct to UTK is the Oak Ridge National Laboratory (ORNL), which offers students access to pioneering technology. According to the school, "Students develop marketing strategies for commercializing technologies developed by ORNL. Selected students from any concentration may serve as consultants and market analysts who work with scientists from ORNL to identify, research and, when possible, market technologies with commercial potential."

UTK has the most innovative program in its regional area, and students rave about the academics. "Beyond expectations—the best learning experience I ever enjoyed," enthused one student. "Very strong academic program," advised another, "It's great value for the money." The core curriculum centers on a yearlong case experience in which students run their own businesses. Working in teams, students make the management decisions necessary to keep the business in operation. At the end of the year they give presentations about their experience to companies who have faced similar problems. Students report that "taking a company from its birth through the entire business cycle" is one of their favorite aspects of the first-year experience.

The second year is less structured. Students take eight specialized electives to build an area of concentration. UTK MBAs give themselves strong ratings in marketing, management, finance, operations, and teamwork skills. In fact, ratings went up from last year's survey in all academic areas, including professorial quality and accessibility. "Faculty is 100 percent behind student success," asserted one MBA. The only items on student wish lists were a stronger international business curriculum and better facilities. "The business building should either be renovated or demolished." wrote one student. Complaints in prior surveys focus on computer facilities, now that each MBA student is required to own a computer, there is little or no need to visit a computer lab and hang out with the undergrads. Overall, students are satisfied at UTK and want to get the word out about what a good time they're having.

PLACEMENT AND RECRUITING

The small number of Tennessee MBAs ensures that students receive plenty of individual attention from career counselors. The downside of a small program, of course, is that many companies pass it over during their recruitment drives, but the Career Services (CS) office claims to have countered this problem through its cooperative efforts with the campus-wide placement office (the university as a whole is huge), and 95 percent of 1998 MBAs were placed at graduation. CS also maintains a video-conferencing center to facilitate interviews with businesses that do not visit the campus, as well as a web-based resume book for employers to peruse. In 1998 the employers most aggressively recruiting UTK MBAs were Andersen Consulting, Coopers & Lybrand SysteCon, Cummins Engin, FedEx, Fleetguard, IBM, Lexmark International, and Lowe's.

Donna Potts, Director of Admissions, MBA Program
527 Stokely Management Center, Knoxville, TN 37996-0552
Admissions: 423-974-5033 Fax: 423-974-3826
Email: gchapma1@uth.edu
Internet: mba.bus.utk.edu

University of Tennessee at Knoxville

STUDENT/CAMPUS LIFE

UTK sports a very small program. All entering students participate in the same year long first-year program. The small size promotes an "intimate" atmosphere and a cooperative learning environment. Remarked one student, "There is a strong all-for-one attitude here." A unique grading system also encourages co-operation in which "grading is based on team and individual performance and comprehensive written evaluations, NOT exams." Students have a heavy workload and hit the books an average of thirty to forty hours a week. This results in a fair amount of pressure, though not enough to cause a heart attack. To lighten the load, the majority of students work in study groups. MBAs agree that minorities are easily accepted, though they don't make up a high percentage of the student body.

Students report a high quality of life. This is due in part to the terrific social scene. "There's plenty to do here," wrote one MBA, "concerts, intramurals. Clubs and bars are also hot spots. We have a great time." The campus also boasts state-of-the-art facilities. TOMBA, the Tennessee Organization of MBAs, is the professional and social association for full- and part-time MBA students. The heart and soul of student life, TOMBA not only organizes the social events for students, but also organizes the network of UTK MBA alums, runs a professional speaker series, and orchestrates a major community service project. All MBA students are expected to join. As for Knoxville, one student wrote, "It's a great little city. Excellent restaurants—and the Smoky Mountains within one hour, a huge plus!" UT is known for its great basketball and football teams. One student told us, "Sports are huge. Football has a big impact on daily life."

ADMISSIONS

According to the admissions office, your work experience is considered to be the most important criteria for admission followed by GPA, GMAT score, interview, essays, extracurricular activities, and letters of recommendation. "Since the UTK program is relatively small," writes the office of admissions, "we can give a good deal of individual attention to our applicants in order to determine whether ours is the right program for them and whether they are right for our program. As often as possible, we invite students to visit the campus, sit in on classes, and talk with current MBA students. In addition, we involve the faculty and administration in the admissions process."

FINANCIAL FACTS

Tuition (in-/out-of-state)	$3,154/$8,210
Tuition per credit (in-/out-of-state)	$150/$408
Fees (in-/out-of-state)	$244/$244
Cost of books	$1,622
Room & board (on-/off-campus)	$3,000/$6,000
% of students receiving aid	50
% first-year students receiving aid	50
% aid that is merit based	27
% of students receiving loans	80
% of students receiving paid internships	100
Average grant	$4,000
Average graduation debt	$6,000

ADMISSIONS

# of applications received	550
% applicants accepted	33
% acceptees attending	52
Average GMAT (range)	615 (510–690)
Minimum TOEFL	550
Average GPA (range)	3.33 (2.90–3.80)
Application fee (in-/out-of-state)	$35/$35
Early decision program available	Yes
Early decision deadline	Rolling
Early decision notification	Rolling
Regular application deadline	March 1
Regular notification	Rolling
Admission may be deferred?	No
Transfer students accepted?	No
Nonfall admission available?	No
Admission process need-blind?	No

APPLICANTS ALSO LOOK AT

Vanderbilt University, University of Georgia, University of North Carolina at Chapel Hill, University of Virginia, Duke University, University of Alabama, University of Texas at Austin, Wake Forest University

EMPLOYMENT PROFILE

Placement rate (%)		100
% of grads employed immediately		87
% grads employed within six months		100
Average starting salary		$59,092

Grads employed by field (avg. salary):

Consulting	19%	$70,380
Finance	11%	$55,387
General Management	5%	$48,175
Human Resources	8%	$57,550
Marketing	14%	$70,753
MIS	1%	$67,200
Operations	32%	$65,979
Other	2%	$118,750
Strategic Planning	5%	$57,500

TEXAS A&M UNIVERSITY
Mays Graduate School of Business

OVERVIEW

Type of school	public
Affiliation	none
Environment	suburban
Academic calendar	semester
Schedule	full-time only

STUDENTS

Enrollment of parent institution	43,000
Enrollment of business school	180
% male/female	76/24
% out-of-state	20
% minorities	5
% international (# of countries represented)	25 (19)
Average age at entry	28
Average years work experience at entry	4.40

ACADEMICS

Student/faculty ratio	10:1
% female faculty	35
% minority faculty	10
Hours of study per day	3.93

SPECIALTIES

Strengths of faculty and curriculum in Accounting, Taxation, Finance, Marketing, Management, Information Systems, Human Resources Management, Real Estate, Organizational Behavior, Business/Public Policy, International Business, Management Science. Outstanding training in teamwork.

JOINT DEGREES

MBA/MA in International Management with Johannes Kepler University; MBA with Ecole Superieur de Commerce; MS in five business fields

SPECIAL PROGRAMS

TechnoMBA track for MIS careers; Dual-degree with one year abroad; semester exchange programs, Graduate Certificate in International Business; four-week international immersion; short-term study abroad during semester breaks; Washington Campus; Aggies on Wall Street.

STUDY ABROAD PROGRAMS

Austria, France, Germany, Mexico, Southeast Asia, England, Netherlands, Japan, Spain, Switzerland, CIBER School—Center for International Business and Educational Research

SURVEY SAYS...
HITS
Cozy student community
Teamwork skills

MISSES
Quantitative skills
On-campus housing
Computer skills

ACADEMICS

One might suspect that a program of just over 200 students could easily be overwhelmed within a university of more than 40,000. Students of the Mays MBA Program at Texas A&M University, however, tell us that nothing could be further from the truth. Mays MBAs enjoy a "program that is very well rounded and material that is presented in an extremely well-tuned lockstep method," an administration that "is constantly working to improve the program," and state-of-the-art facilities. Brags one student, "The Mays MBA offers a unique mix of qualities of both small and very large universities, supported in the vibrant College Station environment." As an added bonus, a Mays MBA is "a bargain."

First-year studies at Mays offer an "integrated, multifunctional approach" through a combination of core competencies (teamwork, communication, strategic decision analysis, global awareness) and business courses (accounting, economics, IT, marketing, operations). Students applaud the core but also note that "We could use more flexibility in core classes. CPAs shouldn't have to take the first accounting course!" They are quick to add, however, "the core faculty is very open to working with the students to change the program." Teamwork is heavily stressed through several mandatory team projects: a financial forecasting project, two large-scale consulting projects, and the International Business Case Competition. In the summer following first year, students may choose to continue to study by taking electives (either on campus or abroad) or pursue an internship.

Second-year students at Mays must complete two further core requirements (one in business strategy, another in international business) but are otherwise free to pursue elective study in any of twelve areas of concentration. Students are also encouraged to make use of Texas A&M's many other academic departments in order to design their own fields of study. The school suggests, for example, that students interested in public policy create a curriculum consisting of courses offered at Mays and at the George Bush School of Government and Public Service. Students report that "A&M is a great MBA for those considering a career in information systems and technology" and also praise the focus on international studies across the curriculum. Students also appreciate both the faculty and administration, reporting that "Professors and administration offer an egalitarian, positive, and developmental environment." A few select finance students participate each year in "Aggies On Wall Street," a three-week immersion program that sends students to New York to tour the major exchanges and commercial banks and hobnob with industry leaders.

PLACEMENT AND RECRUITING

In response to prior complaints, Mays now maintains a placement office dedicated solely to the needs of MBA students. Because the Graduate Business Career Services Office serves a small student body, placement officers have the opportunity to get to know students personally. The office takes an aggressive approach in securing relationships with corporations, which results in high placement for grads, as do services such as resume books, recruiting events, and job search seminars. Students speak highly of A&M's alumni network, which includes more than 200,000 university graduates and more than 33,000 graduates of the Mays College and Graduate School of Business. Top on-campus re-

Wendy Blake, Assistant Director
212 Wehner Building College Station, TX 77843-4117
Admissions: 409 845-4714 Fax: 409 862-2393
Email: maysMBA@tamu.edu
Internet: mba.tamu.edu

Texas A&M University

cruiters include Exxon, Andersen Consulting, Koch Industries, and Houston Industries. Suggests one student, "We need to bring more high-tech companies to campus."

STUDENT/CAMPUS LIFE

The Mays curriculum is designed to foster an atmosphere that is "extremely team oriented. While there is friendly competition in the program, the very cooperative atmosphere here is very noticeable." Explains one student, "We attend classes in cohorts; after class we have team meetings. Every Thursday we have happy hour, and before every exam the study rooms are filled with MBA study groups. We spend a lot of time together." The program's international focus attracts many students from beyond U.S. borders, resulting in "complete global diversity. Every day is a blast—the people are not only bright but also fun!" Adds another student, "The international students provide a vast array of different discussion opportunities. We all bonded pretty quickly in the first semester." Previous work experiences "range from a student who was a tenured faculty member at a university in India to someone who was working as an engineer at NASA for the MIR space station."

During a typical week at Mays, students "work hard Sunday through Thursday, then take a break on Thursday when we all still get together. It's great to be able to stick together even after you've rumbled over issues with your team." Extracurricular events are often sponsored by the MBA Association, which holds a case competition, executive lecture series, and a recruiter/faculty/student golf tournament. Athletics are very popular among students and are nicely facilitated by A&M's new recreation center, which features an Olympic-size pool, a weight and fitness room, an aerobics room, an indoor track, and an indoor climbing wall. Students study hard but also find time to support the school's intercollegiate sports teams, especially in football, basketball, and baseball. In many ways, A&M extends college-style social life into the graduate years; school spirit and "tradition [are] strong at this school," reports one student. Among the few negatives here: "There is no on-campus housing for graduate students and it is difficult to find a parking space at times." Students consider College Station the "perfect-size city. Plenty to do, but very safe and clean" and point out Texas's enviable climate: writes one, "Let's see Harvard beat 70 degrees in January."

ADMISSIONS

While Texas A&M has no cut-and-dried formula for selecting MBA applicants, they do hold them to fairly rigorous standards. Above all, your GPA and GMAT score ought to be well above average. Beyond those, your work experience (they like to see a resume and require two years' post-baccalaureate work), personal essay, recommendations, and the quality and rigor of your undergraduate program are all taken into consideration. Leadership in any pursuit makes a good impression. There are no set math requirements, but A&M appreciates a strong quantitative background in its applicants. The Mays MBA program requires all candidates under consideration for admission to interview. Decisions are made on a rolling admissions basis.

FINANCIAL FACTS

Tuition (in-/out-of-state)	$1,325/$3,988
Tuition per credit (in-/out-of-state)	$75/$288
Fees (in-/out-of-state)	$447/$452
Cost of books	$1,000
Room & board (on-/off-campus)	$7,516/$7,516
% of students receiving paid internships	40
Average grant	$2,800
Average graduation debt	$2,000

ADMISSIONS

# of applications received	530
% applicants accepted	33
% acceptees attending	51
Average GMAT (range)	619 (550–700)
Minimum TOEFL	600
Average GPA (range)	3.30 (2.60–3.86)
Application fee (in-/out-of-state)	$35/$35
Early decision program available	Yes
Early decision deadline	February 1
Early decision notification	Rolling
Regular application deadline	May 1
Regular notification	Rolling
Admission may be deferred?	Yes
Maximum length of deferment	1 year
Transfer students accepted?	No
Nonfall admission available?	No
Admission process need-blind?	Yes

APPLICANTS ALSO LOOK AT

University of Texas at Austin, Rice University, Southern Methodist University, Arizona State University, Texas Christian University, Duke University, University of North Carolina at Chapel Hill, Purdue University

EMPLOYMENT PROFILE

Placement rate (%)	98
# of companies recruiting on campus	184
% of grads employed immediately	95
% grads employed within six months	99
Average starting salary	$63,100

Grads employed by field (avg. salary):		
Consulting	22%	$62,500
Finance	24%	$61,900
General Management	7%	$67,300
Marketing	14%	$59,900
MIS	5%	$62,000
Operations	7%	$67,300
Other	7%	$72,200

UNIVERSITY OF TEXAS AT ARLINGTON
College of Business Administration

OVERVIEW

Type of school	public
Affiliation	none
Environment	urban
Academic calendar	semester
Schedule	full-time/part-time/evening

STUDENTS

Enrollment of parent institution	18,662
Enrollment of business school	448
% male/female	84/16
% out-of-state	1
% part-time	6
% minorities	4
% international (# of countries represented)	22 (41)
Average age at entry	30
Average years work experience at entry	5

ACADEMICS

Student/faculty ratio	7:1
% female faculty	20
% minority faculty	15
Hours of study per day	3.02

SPECIALTIES

Finance, Accounting, Information Systems, International Business

JOINT DEGREES

Accounting, Economics, Information Systems, Marketing Research, Human Resource Management, Real Estate, and Taxation. Other graduate degrees including Engineering, Architecture, Science, and Nursing

SPECIAL PROGRAMS

Careers Program that includes comprehensive assessment, industry analysis, career exploration and interviews, managing in a diverse environment, career-focused academic advising, and internships

STUDY ABROAD PROGRAMS

Norway, England, France, Australia, Mexico, Germany, and Korea

SURVEY SAYS...
HITS
Star faculty
Small classes
Ethnic and racial diversity

MISSES
Unfriendly students
Social life
General management

ACADEMICS

The University of Texas at Arlington (UTA) has tailored its MBA program to create a "good fit" for a particular niche of prospective business grads. Chief among UTA's assets is its location in the Metroplex region, which, along with Houston, is the center of the active, high-stakes Texas business world. This location allows UTA not only to feed area businesses but also to draw students from them, and accordingly the school has created a program that suits the needs of both full and part-timers well. Writes one student, "I like how UTA offers flexibility to MBA students, with most classes held in the evening." UTA is also extremely accessible to students with limited business experience, although the school prefers applicants with prior work experience. Finally, UTA provides all this without a heavy price tag, allowing graduates, unlike many MBAs, to enter the business world unencumbered by debt.

For incoming students with little or no academic business background, UTA provides "deficiency courses" in mathematics, computer information systems, and statistics. More experienced students may begin with "core" courses in accounting, finance, marketing, management, and computers and information systems. Students who have completed courses similar to the foundation courses may place out of them and proceed directly to advanced study, which includes several required courses, concentration in one academic field, and a number of electives that must be spread across several academic disciplines. Students report that, within these parameters, UTA is quite flexible. Writes one student, "The administration has supported me through numerous curriculum changes that have enabled me to enhance my market value."

The UTA faculty consists of "a good mix of 'academic' professors and part-time instructors with 'real-world' experience." Our survey shows a widespread perception that "Some professors are very good, others are awful. Lots of variation in quality." At one end of the spectrum are those who are "excellent and seem very concerned about the students"; at the other are professors who "don't really care if students learn. They're just interested in putting out the information." Students are most complimentary of the marketing and accounting departments. They also approve of UTA's "excellent resources: library, health facilities, student center, etc.," and report happily that "UTA is upgrading b-school facilities, computer labs, and adding a much-needed, MBA-only placement center."

PLACEMENT AND RECRUITING

UTA tells us, "The Dallas/Fort Worth Metroplex, with more than 115,000 businesses, provides a fertile lab for the exploration and pursuit of hundreds of career alternatives. The University annually hosts one of the largest 'career day events' in Texas and also serves as a cosponsor of the Metroplex Area Consortium of Career Centers' (MAC3) semiannual career day programs that attract top employers throughout the region. These events help maintain one of the nation's largest student employment services, which offers daily 8,000–10,000 part-time jobs, co-ops, and internships. These opportunities are available year-round to students. A core of career professionals participate in a comprehensive MBA careers program and present an array of seminars designed to enhance the

Alisa Johnson, Director of Graduate Business Services
Box 19376, Arlington, TX 76019
Admissions: 817-272-3005 Fax: 817-272-5799
Email: admit@uta.edu
Internet: www.uta.edu/gradbiz/

University of Texas at Arlington

student's mobility skills and improve their circle of opportunities. Traditional on-campus interviews are complemented by cooperative career fairs, extended electronic job listings, and an interactive resume data bank."

Our survey reveals that UTA students are only mildly satisfied with the school's placement office, approving of internship opportunities but expressing disappointment with on-campus recruiting. One student complains about the "lack of business jobs [listed at the career center]. Most of the job postings I saw were for engineers or were computer related." Students also remark that UTA alumni are rarely helpful when contacted for assistance with job searches.

STUDENT/CAMPUS LIFE

While half of the classroom consists of full-time students, many of UTA's MBAs are part time and "commuter students. Most work; some have families. The part-time students bring a wide range of experiences to the classroom." These "hard-working, hard-earning, future-focused professionals" include a large international contingent that is "open and receptive." The result of this combination is that students receive "a lot of exposure to international perspectives and [input] from professionals [who are] working and taking courses at the same time." Because many students come to campus only to attend class and study, students find "very little opportunity to get to know each other." Notes one student, "I was not expecting such a commuter school. Also, I just graduated with my BA from Texas. I was not expecting to be the only one in my early twenties in most of my classes." Those who make the effort, however, do make contacts among the student body: "The best aspect of this program is the networking relationship I have formed with my classmates."

Typically, UTA students feel that "due to doing the MBA part time, overall life is a bit stressed. It would be better doing this full time." Part-time students warn that " because the MBA program runs in the evenings and Saturdays, campus life is nonexistent," although full-time students tell us, "There are lots of activities going on on campus. One usually gets involved in extracurricular activities." For those who have the time to appreciate it, UTA's "lovely campus" is also an asset. Students can access a wide range of extracurricular options in the Metroplex area. Arlington is a city of nearly 300,000, and is home to the American League's Texas Rangers as well as two huge amusement parks, numerous theaters, and several museums and art galleries. Fifteen miles to the east is Dallas, one of the cultural and retail centers of Texas. Forth Worth, twenty minutes to the west by car, boasts a world-renowned art museum as well as many historical remnants of the region's pioneering and cattle-herding heritage.

ADMISSIONS

While it accepts more applicants than it rejects, Arlington does expect its entering class to have a great deal of work experience to draw from. GMAT scores followed by undergraduate GPA and letters of recommendation rank highest in importance for admissions.

FINANCIAL FACTS

Tuition (in-/out-of-state)	$2,160/$8,550
Tuition per credit (in-/out-of-state)	$72/$285
Fees (in-/out-of-state)	$1,957/$2,257
Cost of books	$1,000
Room & board (on-/off-campus)	$9,000/$9,000

ADMISSIONS

# of applications received	452
% applicants accepted	42
% acceptees attending	56
Average GMAT (range)	55ADMISSIONS
# of applications received	280
% applicants accepted	42
% acceptees attending	82
Average GMAT (range)	550 (490–610)
Minimum TOEFL	550
Average GPA (range)	3.20 (2.80–3.60)
Application fee	$25
Early decision program available	Yes
Regular notification	Rolling
Admission may be deferred?	Yes
Maximum length of deferment	1 year
Transfer students accepted?	Yes
Nonfall admission available?	Yes
Admission process need-blind?	Yes

APPLICANTS ALSO LOOK AT

University of Texas at Austin, Texas Christian University, Southern Methodist University, Texas A&M University, Arizona State University, Rice University, Ohio State University, University of Texas at Dallas

EMPLOYMENT PROFILE

# of companies recruiting on campus	851
% grads employed within six months	84
Average starting salary	$48,000

UNIVERSITY OF TEXAS AT AUSTIN
Graduate School of Business

OVERVIEW

Type of school	public
Affiliation	none
Environment	urban
Academic calendar	semester
Schedule	full-time only

STUDENTS

Enrollment of parent institution	50,000
Enrollment of business school	726
% male/female	75/25
% out-of-state	57
% minorities	7
% international (# of countries represented)	20 (28)
Average age at entry	29
Average years work experience at entry	5

ACADEMICS

Student/faculty ratio	10:1
% female faculty	20
% minority faculty	6
Hours of study per day	4.39

SPECIALTIES
Accounting, Finance, Information Systems, Marketing, Entrepreneurship

JOINT DEGREES
MBA/Master of Public Accounting; MBA/MA Asian Studies; MBA/MA Latin American Studies; MBA/MA Middle Eastern Studies; MBA/MA Public Affairs; MBA/MA Post-Soviet Studies; MBA/MA Communications; MBA/MS Manufacturing Systems Engineering; MBA/MS Nursing; MBA/JD. Most are 72–75 credit hours, MBA/JD is 134 credit hours

SPECIAL PROGRAMS
Spanish Language Track, Foreign Study, Masters in Professional Accounting Program, Investment Fund, Energy Finance, Quality Management Consortium, MOOT Corp.

STUDY ABROAD PROGRAMS
Germany, France, Mexico, Brazil, Chile, Australia, Hong Kong, Denmark, Peru, Spain, Finland, Venezuela, Japan, England, Canada, Singapore, Netherlands, Sweden, Switzerland

SURVEY SAYS...
HITS
Austin
School clubs
Accounting

MISSES
On-campus housing
Quantitative skills
Computer skills

PROMINENT ALUMNI
Kenneth M. Jastrow II, CFO, Temple-Inland; William R. Johnson, President and CEO, HJ Heinz

ACADEMICS

Over the past several years, the University of Texas at Austin (UT) MBA program has made a major commitment to upgrading its information resources, an effort appreciated by students. Writes one, "UT is dedicated to continuous improvement and it shows. You can't beat the bang for the buck you get at UT." Among these improvements is the EDS Financial Trading and Technology Center, a state-of-the-art research facility that, according to UT, uses technology that is "more advanced than what you would find in the leading investment houses." UT Austin is also home to the IC2 (Innovation, Creativity, Capital) Institute, a "virtual organization" that links research institutes to businesses in an effort to develop and test modern business practices. IC2 includes the "Austin Technology Incubator," which assists start-up technology entrepreneurs and in so doing provides more than 150 students with hands-on entrepreneurial experience.

UT Austin boasts a number of other notable features. Students manage the TEXASMBA Investment Fund, which has managed more than $3 million in investments (the fund brought in an annualized return of 21 percent during its first two years of operation). Other students serve as paid consultants to area businesses through the Quality Management Consortia (also student-managed). A unique feature of QMC is that its internships run for an entire year, rather than three months (as is typical of many internship programs). The extended period allows interns to "accumulate in-depth, practical experience," according to the university.

UT Austin places its first-year students in cohorts of sixty students, who as a group complete the year-long core curriculum. Students approve, noting that "the cohort system fosters cooperation and networking and sharing of knowledge" and that "professors in the core are very good: great lecturers and terrific preparers." Second-year students may pursue any of a number of traditional majors and fields of concentration, or they may design their own courses of study. Students praise UT's "practical approach to business" in the marketing, entrepreneurship, finance, and IT programs, also asserting that UT is a "strong quantitative school." Professors, who earn very good marks from our respondents, are described as "excellent, experienced, and accessible," and "very supportive.... They motivate you to investigate, analyze, and to carry through your own ideas and projects." Although "there are a few lemons [on the faculty], there are a lot more stars." Students warn that "the administration is somewhat bureaucratic, but it still gets the job done."

PLACEMENT AND RECRUITING

Students give the UT Austin Business Career Services office better-than-average grades, noting that the office does a good job of organizing "lots of recruiting receptions, career panels, and career workshops." According to the school, "The Career Services Office at UT Austin begins working with students before they enroll on resume and job search issues to help them get a jump start on the internship search."

UT Austin also reports that in recent years as many as 575 companies conducted on-campus interviews for MBAs at UT Austin. Past top recruiters have in-

Dr. Carl H. Harris, Director of Admissions, MBA Programs
CBA 2.316, Austin, TX 78712
Admissions: 512-471-7612 Fax: 512-471-4243
Email: TEXASMBA@BUS.UTEXAS.EDU
Internet: texasinfo.bus.utexas.edu

University of Texas at Austin

cluded: Ernst & Young Consulting, Intel, Procter & Gamble, Deloitte & Touche, Exxon, Ford, IBM Consulting, AT Kearney, Citibank, NationsBank, SAP America, and Morgan Stanley. Students expressed great satisfaction with both the quantity and quality of companies performing on-campus searches. Our survey results indicate that UT Austin alumni were very helpful to those MBAs who contacted them for help in their job searches.

STUDENT/CAMPUS LIFE

Austin MBAs describe a friendly atmosphere: "People are genuinely helpful. We have great networking opportunities, and we foster a cooperative, not competitive, spirit." Incoming students appreciate a "great support system set up by second-years for first-years," and African American students report that "African Americans form a great support network" for each other. An entrepreneurial spirit pervades the student body; as one student explains, "While the big dream at Wharton may be to make millions working for a prestigious firm, the big dream at UT is to make millions working for yourself." More than three-fifths of the students arrive with four or more years of work experience under their belts, bringing with them "diverse backgrounds that contribute to excellent classroom discussions."

The student-friendly town of Austin contributes heavily to the high level of overall happiness reported by the respondents in our survey; the majority of students rate the town "excellent." "The city of Austin has a wonderful culture of live music and arts in a beautiful setting," explains one student. Others comment on the city's vibrant bar scene, and others still praise a climate that "allows us to participate in outdoor sports all year." On campus, there's "tons going on," because "there are so many interesting courses to take, companies to do projects with, clubs to join, [and] activities to do, that you have to learn to set priorities and optimize your use of time." Many students meet every Thursday at an event called "Think and Drink," and clubs and organizations are "always organizing a get-together ranging from UT athletics events to a charitable fund raiser." Students also appreciate the "newly renovated campus recreation facilities," including an excellent gym "right across the street from the school." Although "everyone here is very focused . . . and puts school/job search first," they're also "always up for a good time."

ADMISSIONS

The admissions office uses the following criteria to evaluate applicants (not listed in order of importance): GMAT scores, essays, academic record and college GPA, work experience, and letters of recommendation. Interviews are not required, but a visit to the campus is encouraged if at all possible. Writes the school: "Although grades and GMAT scores are important, other areas receive substantial consideration. Personal and professional goals, achievements, extracurriculars, community involvement, and evidence of leadership and management abilities are considered in the admissions decision." The school places a high priority on increasing the representation of qualified women and minorities in the program. Decisions are made on a rolling admissions basis. Advises the school, "Apply as early as possible." After their files have been referred to the admissions committee, applicants are notified of the decision within six to eight weeks. On a case-by-case basis, admission may be deferred for one year.

FINANCIAL FACTS

Tuition (in-/out-of-state)	$3,420/$14,700
Tuition per credit (in-/out-of-state)	$114/$490
Fees (in-/out-of-state)	$3,154/$3,154
Cost of books	$850
Room & board (on-/off-campus)	$9,932/$9,932
% of students receiving aid	82
% first-year students receiving aid	82
% aid that is merit based	10
% of students receiving loans	72
% of students receiving grants	10
% of students receiving paid internships	85
Average award package	$16,000
Average grant	$1,000
Average graduation debt	$22,191

ADMISSIONS

# of applications received	2,684
% applicants accepted	23
% acceptees attending	56
Average GMAT (range)	660 (500–790)
Minimum TOEFL	550
Average GPA (range)	3.37 (2.15–4.00)
Application fee (in-/out-of-state)	$80/$100
Early decision program available	No
Regular application deadline	April 15
Regular notification	May 1
Admission may be deferred?	Yes
Maximum length of deferment	1 year
Transfer students accepted?	No
Nonfall admission available?	No
Admission process need-blind?	Yes

APPLICANTS ALSO LOOK AT

University of North Carolina at Chapel Hill, University of Michigan Business School, University of California—Los Angeles, University of California—Berkeley, Stanford University, Texas A&M, Northwestern University, University of Pennsylvania

EMPLOYMENT PROFILE

Placement rate (%)	95
# of companies recruiting on campus	437
% of grads employed immediately	90
% grads employed within six months	100
Average starting salary	$78,840

Grads employed by field (avg. salary):

Accounting	1%	$61,250
Consulting	22%	$84,636
Entrepreneurship	2%	$77,700
Finance	15%	$66,782
General Management	13%	$65,460
Human Resources	1%	$50,000
Marketing	20%	$65,788
MIS	9%	$70,346
Operations	4%	$76,500

TCU

M. J. Neeley School of Business

ACADEMICS

The M.J. Neeley School of Business at TCU offers a solid general management MBA at an extremely affordable price. Students gave TCU strong marks in all areas of basic functionality: finance, accounting, general management, and teamwork and communication skills.

In addition to solid academics, Neeley also boasts several unique assets. Students appreciate the presence of the Center for Productive Communication, which offers one-on-one counseling and intensive personal coaching. Writes one MBA, "The Center for Production Communication offers great opportunities and assistance to develop your presentation and communication skills." Also of interest is the Student Enterprise Program, through which affiliated businesses hire TCU MBAs as consultants. Because the Student Enterprise Program, which "gives us a lot of hands-on experience," is not keyed to a specific class, these consultancies encompass many different business areas. Students also speak highly of the finance elective that allows students to manage the $1.7 million William C. Connor Educational Investment Fund. The EIF is the highlight of TCU's finance concentration, considered by many to be the school's strongest. Neeley also offers opportunities to study overseas through its Global Initiatives Network, which includes partnerships with schools in Europe and Mexico.

More than half of the students surveyed rate their teachers as "good," and one-quarter call them "outstanding!" Students report that "faculty brings real-world experience to the classroom" and are "energetic and available outside of class. Very willing to get to know you." The administration, however, "is relatively out of touch with the students." Respondents also warn that "the workload is very challenging, a big adjustment from undergraduate work, but it gets easier to handle with time." As one student puts it, "The first-year workload is like drinking water out of a fire hose, but it slows down during the second year." Students appreciate the opportunity to "get practical experience" and think the location in the Dallas/Fort Worth Metroplex gives the school strong corporate ties and provides good opportunities to network. "Business leaders from the area speak to us regularly," says one MBA.

PLACEMENT AND RECRUITING

The Career Services office at Neeley provides all the standard services to students, including career counseling, mock interviews, and a video-conferencing center. It also features some unique programs, such as Student Enterprises, in which students "compete for 'real' consulting projects for 'real' corporate clients." The Career Services office points out that students manage the school's $1.7 million William C. Connor Educational Investment Fund, through which they can establish contacts among Fund alumni and investment professionals.

According to students, TCU is the best school to go to for "GREAT connections to businesses in the Dallas/Fort Worth area." Beyond the immediate region, however, TCU's influence wanes considerably; complains one student, "very few quality companies come to campus." Perhaps things will soon improve, since "Career Services just changed directors. I think the change will be very

Peggy Conway, Director of MBA Admissions
P.O. Box 298540, Fort Worth, TX 76129
Admissions: 817-257-7531 Fax: 817-257-6431
Email: mbainfo@tcu.edu
Internet: www.neeley.tcu.edu/mba

TCU

positive in the long run." Recent big employers of Neeley grads are GTE, Harris Methodist Health Systems, American Airlines, the SABRE Group, Andersen Consulting, Burlington Northern-Santa Fe, Frito-Lay, EDS, and Sprinx Health Systems.

STUDENT/CAMPUS LIFE

TCU's small student body—its enrollment of 300 is about half the national average for top b-schools—means that students here get to know all their classmates pretty well. Students happily report that "The community is friendly and accessible. It's easy to meet people." Many are "very competitive," "very ambitious and motivated overachievers," but the curricular emphasis on teamwork mollifies students' cutthroat tendencies somewhat. As at many small schools, students can be somewhat cliquish; writes one "Some groups form that are hard to break into, but everyone at least speaks to everyone else." Our respondents also pointed out that "there isn't a lot of work experience among students," but also that "international diversity promotes great work and personal experiences."

The university supports more than 140 student clubs, of which sixteen are geared specifically toward MBAs. Some clubs are major-related, while others are community service, student government, or religious life oriented. Chief among them is the MBA Association, which organizes parties at a designated eatery or bar of the week for Thursday night get-togethers. Reports one student, "There's plenty to do and most students take time out from their work to socialize." Otherwise, students report that the TCU campus is relatively quiet except on game days, when TCU students turn out to support their Horned Frogs. Football is a particular favorite among MBAs and undergraduates alike.

Students are favorably disposed to TCU's hometown of Fort Worth, although they report that it is an expensive town in which to entertain yourself. They particularly appreciate the "great job market in [the] Dallas/Fort Worth area," reporting that "networking opportunities are abundant" both on campus and in town. Only one apartment complex is within walking distance of school, so most MBAs live off campus in apartment complexes in the Hulen area of Fort Worth, a ten-minute commute by car from campus.

ADMISSIONS

According to the school, no single criterion is most important. The admissions committee considers the composite application of each student. Prerequisites include: quantitative proficiency and a foundation in macroeconomics and microeconomics. Writes the school, "Consistent with TCU's emphasis on the individual, our admissions staff looks closely at the specific merits of each application. No single admissions formula is used. Our goal is to select applicants from a variety of backgrounds who possess a balanced set of credentials: strong academic aptitude, demonstrated leadership skills, and meaningful work and lifetime experiences."

FINANCIAL FACTS

Tuition	$8,760
Tuition per credit	$365
Fees	$1,340
Cost of books	$750
Room & board (on-/off-campus)	NR/$8,500
% of students receiving aid	80
% first-year students receiving aid	80
% aid that is merit based	48
% of students receiving loans	46
% of students receiving grants	48
% of students receiving paid internships	95
Average award package	$10,623
Average grant	$5,650

ADMISSIONS

# of applications received	322
% applicants accepted	51
% acceptees attending	56
Average GMAT (range)	560 (520–620)
Minimum TOEFL	550
Average GPA (range)	3.10 (2.80–3.50)
Application fee (in-/out-of-state)	$50/$50
Early decision program available	Yes
Early decision notification	Rolling
Regular application deadline	April 30
Regular notification	Rolling
Admission may be deferred?	Yes
Maximum length of deferment	1 year
Transfer students accepted?	Yes
Nonfall admission available?	No
Admission process need-blind?	Yes

APPLICANTS ALSO LOOK AT

University of Texas at Austin, Southern Methodist University, Texas A&M University, University of Texas at Arlington, Rice University, Vanderbilt University, Wake Forest University, Baylor University

EMPLOYMENT PROFILE

Placement rate (%)	95
# of companies recruiting on campus	80
% of grads employed immediately	28
% grads employed within six months	89
Average starting salary	$50,350

Grads employed by field (avg. salary):

Accounting	7%	$43,700
Consulting	12%	$57,400
Finance	35%	$51,500
General Management	12%	$45,400
Marketing	25%	$49,700
MIS	9%	$50,300

THUNDERBIRD

The Thunderbird American Graduate School of International Management

ACADEMICS

Like a great steak house that serves only one dish but does so exceedingly well, Thunderbird—officially, Thunderbird, The American Graduate School of International Management—focuses on doing one thing right: international business. Students at Thunderbird can study all the traditional b-school disciplines of management, finance, marketing, consulting, and information systems, but they do so in the context of the international market. Students who choose Thunderbird know what they're coming for. Writes one, "It is exactly the type of curriculum I was looking for, and you can finish the program in one year!"

One year at Thunderbird is the exception rather than the norm, since the program requires forty-two course hours. However, students qualified to place out of some foundation courses can finish their MIMs (Masters in International Management; Thunderbird does not offer a traditional MBA) in twelve months by attending the summer session. The Thunderbird curriculum consists of three components: international studies, which is actually a series of foundation courses covering the international economy and the characteristics of regional markets overseas; modern languages, which requires proficiency in a foreign language; and world business, which makes up the bulk of MIM's coursework at Thunderbird and covers a wide range of business studies. Students write that the curriculum's "strength lies in tailored classes on global business, recommended by the Board of Trustees and the Thunderbird Global Council—real-world execs with Fortune 500 companies." Among the few complaints about the curriculum is that it "should put greater emphasis on quantitative skills."

Thunderbird offers students many opportunities for study overseas, with centers in Tokyo and Geneva. The school also sponsors summer programs in Mexico, the People's Republic of China, the Czech Republic, and Russia. Cooperative education programs take Thunderbird students to b-schools on four continents.

Students tell us, "Some teachers here are outstanding, truly leaders in their fields, and some aren't. If you get into the best teachers' classes, you're going to learn a lot." Another student notes that "profs' doors are always open." The administration, "like many, is bureaucratic. Some organizational skills are lacking." On the positive side, "the administration is constantly changing the curriculum to remain competitive."

PLACEMENT AND RECRUITING

Thunderbird's Career Services Center (CSC) faces a singular challenge in that "everyone [in the program] wants to work internationally." The explosive growth of nearby Phoenix, now the nation's sixth largest city, has provided new opportunities, and Thunderbirds are increasingly finding positions in Arizona at major firms such as Motorola, Intel, Amex, and Honeywell. Somehow, though, Thunderbird attracts nearly 300 companies to recruit on campus. The school uses extensive video-teleconferencing, telephone, email, and an Internet-based resume book to market its students to more than 400 off-campus recruiters. The school also boasts an alumni list of more than 30,000; students in our survey who contacted alums for help in their job search found them to be helpful.

Judy Johnson, Associate Vice President
Thunderbird Campus, 15249 N. 59th Avenue, Glendale, AZ 85306
Admissions: 602-978-7210 Fax: 602-439-5432
Email: admissions@t-bird.dom
Internet: www.t-bird.edu

Students give the CSC average grades, even though they are highly satisfied with the quality and quantity of recruiters and with their opportunities for off-campus projects and internships. Furthermore, the perception on campus is that the CSC has gotten better in recent years. Writes one student, "Thunderbird has improved dramatically in internship placement, but they could still probably do better."

STUDENT/CAMPUS LIFE

Thunderbird students, who refer to themselves as T-Birds, are a "very diverse group . . . we come from all walks of life and experiences." Notes one student, "Ethnic diversity is our strength. Half the students here are foreign nationals." According to another T-Bird, students here are "very teamwork oriented. We're all in this together! They are very talented and intelligent, and they're willing to share knowledge." Adds still another, "Overall, people are very interesting here—not your usual 'serious accountant' type of MBA."

Thunderbird students participate in more than sixty campus clubs and organizations, a number of which serve students of common national or ethnic origin. International theme events are common, and students report that there are "so many activities on campus, you're always missing one to attend another." Students also lead active social lives, which "take place primarily in clubs. We also have a pub that many T-birds find themselves at on Thursdays." Many of respondents mention the on-campus pub, noting with approval that it serves an unusually wide variety of imported beers. Students agree that there are "more than enough choices of what to do on any given night between Thursday and Sunday," but also tell us that "Some people work. Some people work and play. Some people play. You do with it what you want. But if you come to work, it will definitely pay off." Students are less pleased with Glendale, which they describe as "a little behind the times," and "in need of a charm transfusion." When they leave campus, T-Birds head for nearby Phoenix or take "bonding trips to California and Vegas."

ADMISSIONS

Thunderbird considers GMAT scores, TOEFL test scores for non-native English speakers, undergrad and graduate education, a personal essay, and references in evaluating a prospective students candidacy. The minimum TOEFL score for consideration is 550.

FINANCIAL FACTS

Tuition	$21,000
Fees	$200
Cost of books	$1,360
Room & board (on-/off-campus)	$7,350/$6,000
% of students receiving aid	67
% first-year students receiving aid	65
% aid that is merit based	20
% of students receiving loans	68
% of students receiving grants	25
% of students receiving paid internships	32
Average award package	$20,000
Average grant	$6,194
Average graduation debt	$35,000

ADMISSIONS

# of applications received	1,317
% applicants accepted	68
% acceptees attending	34
Average GMAT (range)	601 (550–650)
Minimum TOEFL	550
Average GPA (range)	3.44 (3.10–3.70)
Application fee (in-/out-of-state)	$100/$100
Early decision program available	Yes
Regular application deadline	January 31
Admission may be deferred?	Yes
Maximum length of deferment	1 year
Transfer students accepted?	Yes
Nonfall admission available?	Yes
Admission process need-blind?	Yes

APPLICANTS ALSO LOOK AT

Columbia University, Harvard University, University of Texas at Austin, Georgetown University, University of California—Berkeley, Stanford University, University of California—Los Angeles, New York University

EMPLOYMENT PROFILE

Placement rate (%)	92
# of companies recruiting on campus	271
% of grads employed immediately	72
% grads employed within six months	91
Average starting salary	$62,648

Grads employed by field (avg. salary):

Accounting	1%	NR
Communications	1%	NR
Finance	32%	$62,440
General Management	1%	NR
Marketing	34%	$57,383
MIS	2%	NR
Operations	3%	NR
Other	19%	$58,691

TULANE UNIVERSITY
A. B. Freeman School of Business

OVERVIEW

Type of school	private
Affiliation	nonsectarian
Environment	urban
Academic calendar	semester
Schedule	full-time/part-time/evening

STUDENTS

Enrollment of parent institution	11,604
Enrollment of business school	394
% male/female	73/27
% part-time	46
% minorities	5
% international (# of countries represented)	38 (21)
Average age at entry	26
Average years work experience at entry	4

ACADEMICS

Student/faculty ratio	20:1
% female faculty	13
% minority faculty	15
Hours of study per day	4.37

SPECIALTIES

The Freeman School's academic strengths are focused on international business and finance and Latin American studies. The Goldring Institute of International Business coordinates the school's international business courses, study abroad programs, and the research efforts of the Center for Research on Latin American Financial Markets.

JOINT DEGREES

MBA/JD, 4 years; MBA/Master of Arts in Latin American Studies, 2 1/2 years; MBA/Master of Public Health, 3 years

STUDY ABROAD PROGRAMS

Argentina, Austria, Brazil, Chile, China, Colombia, Czech Republic, Ecuador, England, France, Germany, Hong Kong, Hungary, Mexico, Spain, Taiwan and Venezuela

SURVEY SAYS...
HITS
City
Interpersonal skills prep
Students are happy

PROMINENT ALUMNI

Lawrence A. Gordon, president, Lawrence Gordon Entertainment, motion picture industry; Frank B. Stewart, Jr., chairman, Stewart Enterprises, nation's 3rd-largest deathcare corp; Francis Fraenkel, President, Delta Capital Corp.

ACADEMICS

Like many up-and-coming MBA programs determined to elevate their national reputations, the A. B. Freeman School of Business at Tulane University is a program in transition. A new curriculum was introduced in fall 1999 based on the input of current students, faculty, administrators, corporate recruiters, and alumni. Reports one student, "The school is going through some growing pains in redefining its curriculum. The administration has been very proactive in setting a new curriculum and is extremely receptive to student collaboration."

One thing is certain: Freeman knows well enough not to tinker with its strongest departments, which are currently accounting and finance. Students tell us that "The finance department is filled with superstars" who share a "tremendous ability to articulate complex financial ideas and generate stimulating managerial discussions." According to our respondents, "the school is currently recruiting young, bright professors" to plug holes in other departments. As the school makes changes, students are pleased to report that "The administration is very eager to adapt the program to our needs." Writes one student, "The assistant dean often has lunch with us and he constantly surveys us about how things are going and what could be better."

The new curriculum offers most core courses as well as many elective courses in seven-week sessions, rather than the traditional semester format. New courses are required in leadership, internal reporting, and negotiations. Students may choose nine hours of electives in the first year, which allows for greater depth in a career-specific area prior to summer internships or abroad programs. In the second year, students may select up to 27 hours of electives. Concentrations exist in finance, marketing, management, and organizational behavior/human resources. Within each area, specific career tracks assist students in the selection of electives to meet their professional goals. With the introduction of the new curriculum, a notebook computer is required of all full-time students.

Students describe professors as "astute" and "approachable." One student writes, "The faculty here is interested in students learning skills as opposed to raking us over the coals of a grade curve distribution." Overall, MBAs agree that their academic experience is "blissfully challenging." But there were a few weak spots: entrepreneurial studies and marketing could use improvement, and students want more offerings in the MIS area and more female faculty.

PLACEMENT AND RECRUITING

When it comes to placement, Tulane students benefit from their school's location: what recruiter, after all, is going to pass up a visit to New Orleans? The Career Development Center (CDC) exploits this advantage by holding a Mardi Gras Job Fair. The CDC adds that "in addition to inviting companies to visit us with our active on-campus recruiting program and the popular Mardi Gras Job Fair, we bring our students directly to them, as well. Events such as the New York MBA Internship Consortium, the Atlanta MBA Consortium, Freeman Days in New York, and the International Job Fairs in Miami and Orlando showcase our students . . ." Freeman MBAs also have the advantage of the school's "superior experiential learning opportunities," such as the hands-on research they conduct to produce reports on select publicly traded companies in the area.

John C. Silbernagel, Assistant Dean for Admissions and Financial Aid
7 McAlister Drive, New Orleans, LA 70118-5669
Admissions: 504-865-5410 Fax: 504-865-6770
Email: Freeman.Admissions@Tulane.edu
Internet: freeman.tulane.edu

Tulane University

Networking with alumni is "a major resource" for Freeman grads. Nearly one-third of Tulane students find work in banking; manufacturing claims nearly half of Tulane MBAs.

STUDENT/CAMPUS LIFE

Tulane MBAs describe their classmates as a "a good group of people, a lot like the friends I made as an undergrad, but a little more career focused." Students point out that "since we are a small program, we get to know each other very well." Occasionally this means that they see each others' shortcomings, leading some to comment that this is a "great group, but too many engineers" or to complain that "most of them have never worked in a professional setting." Tulane attracts a "high percentage of international students," some of who feel welcome—"Our students come from all over the world and are open to new experiences," writes one Ukrainian student—and some of who don't feel the same warm fuzzies, such as one MBA from East Asia who complains about "very poor relations between United States and foreign students."

Freeman is housed in Goldring/Woldenberg hall, a completely wired building with available connectivity in all private and group study areas for notebook computers. Network connectivity throughout this "virtual computer lab" allows access to internal and external computing facilities for the effective dissemination of instructional material, both on-site and at remote locations. The building also houses a state-of-the-art technology/computer center with 50 networked multimedia workstations, auditorium, three-story atrium, library, audiovisual studio complete with television studio and editing and viewing room, and a computer classroom with 42 networked multimedia workstations. Writes one student, "The physical facilities—building, classrooms, services—are superb." Beyond campus is New Orleans, one of the great Southern cities and perhaps America's preeminent party town. According to the school, Tulane's location in New Orleans plays a critical role in the success of the program. Students strongly agree. Writes one, "Hanging out on Bourbon Street is a great break from the rigors of Tulane." Adds another, "New Orleans is the place for food, festivities, fun!" Unless you are among the few who can block out this city's enticements, prepare to gain weight and lose sleep during your two years here. Jocks, beware: Tulane offers "lots of varied activities (but limited outdoor recreational activities)."

ADMISSIONS

The admissions committee considers work experience, GMAT scores, and college GPA as the most important elements in an application, and then, in descending order of importance, the interview (required for all domestic applicants), letters of recommendation, essays, and extracurricular activities. Quantitative coursework is highly recommended, but not mandatory. Tulane uses a rolling admissions process. All applicants are automatically considered for merit-based fellowships at the time of admission. College seniors who are admitted may defer for up to two years. Tulane features a combined five-year baccalaureate/MBA program. Wrote one student, "The five-year program is excellent and extremely competitive. Students in this program were among Tulane's best undergraduates."

FINANCIAL FACTS

Tuition	$22,590
Tuition per credit	$753
Fees	$1,624
Cost of books	$800
Room & board (on-/off-campus)	$7,070/$7,070
% of students receiving aid	68
% first-year students receiving aid	76
% aid that is merit based	42
% of students receiving loans	43
% of students receiving grants	42
Average grant	$16,000

ADMISSIONS

# of applications received	500
% applicants accepted	45
% acceptees attending	46
Average GMAT (range)	632 (580–660)
Average GPA (range)	3.40 (3.05–3.60)
Application fee (in-/out-of-state)	$40/$40
Early decision program available	Yes
Regular application deadline	May 1
Regular notification	Rolling
Admission may be deferred?	Yes
Maximum length of deferment	2 years
Transfer students accepted?	No
Nonfall admission available?	Yes
Admission process need-blind?	Yes

APPLICANTS ALSO LOOK AT

University of Texas at Austin, Vanderbilt University, Duke University, New York University, Georgetown University, Emory University, Columbia University

EMPLOYMENT PROFILE

Placement rate (%)	77
# of companies recruiting on campus	259
% of grads employed immediately	77
% grads employed within six months	92
Average starting salary	$59,880

Grads employed by field (avg. salary):

Consulting	12%	$63,333
Finance	54%	$60,083
General Management	13%	$57,625
Marketing	14%	$59,071
MIS	1%	$65,000
Operations	6%	$57,975

VANDERBILT UNIVERSITY
Owen Graduate School of Management

ACADEMICS

An intimate setting, innovative programs, and a top-flight faculty are the distinguishing characteristics of the Owen Graduate School of Management at Vanderbilt University. As an added bonus, the package is wrapped in a genial, laid-back southern setting. Explains one happy student, "Owen has succeeded at providing top-notch students, professors, and surroundings while avoiding the cutthroat traits of other top programs."

Students here are particularly excited about Owen's "extremely unique" electronic commerce program. Writes one student, "What I love about this school is the foresight it shows to take risks on developing innovative curriculums. We had the first Telecommunications and Electronic Commerce program in the nation." Owen MBAs also praise the school's offerings in health care, human resources, marketing, and especially finance. Writes one student, "We have some fantastic finance professors. Nearly all of them are highly recognized in their field."

First year begins with core courses taught in "modules," two of which make up each semester. Lecture classes make up roughly 50 percent of class time, with 30 percent dedicated to case studies and the remainder of class time devoted to student presentations. The "well-rounded" core curriculum takes up most but not all of the first year; explains one student, "The module system allows for more first-year electives and provides flexibility in tailoring the curriculum to students' needs." Classes are generally limited to thirty-five students or fewer, leading one student to report that "Class size combined with faculty size plays a major role in my development. We can interact a lot with professors. The fact that Vanderbilt has no undergraduate business program is an advantage!" Toward the end of the first year and throughout the second, students focus on one or more areas of concentration, the most popular of which are finance, human resource management, marketing, and operations. Students may also pursue "emphases" in such areas as international business, entrepreneurship, service, and e-commerce. The school encourages students to design their own concentrations and emphases by using the many courses and resources available throughout the university.

Owen professors "are outstanding, friendly, and eager to teach. They are very accessible in and out of class." The administration "is highly responsive to students' requests" but sometimes "tends to micromanage." Despite the current availability of interdisciplinary study, some students still feel that "Owen should become more integrated with the university and draw from the strengths of its other programs. We could, for example, have a law school professor teach business law rather than an adjunct."

PLACEMENT AND RECRUITING

The Career Planning and Placement Office at Vanderbilt was cited as a strength in our student surveys. "They pay close, individual attention to students," writes one MBA. The CPPO supplements traditional counseling and job-search assistance with weekly workshops. Each year approximately 100 companies make recruiting trips to the Vanderbilt campus; another 200 meet with Vandy MBAs in Atlanta, Miami, Orlando, and New York. Major recruiters include AT&T, American Airlines, Andersen Consulting, MCI, GE, PepsiCo, Northern

Todd Reale, Director of Admissions and Marketing
401 21st Avenue, South Nashville, TN 37203
Admissions: 615-322-6469 Fax: 615-343-1175
Email: admissions@owen.vanderbilt.edu
Internet: mba.vanderbilt.edu

Vanderbilt University

Telecom, Deloitte & Touche, Eli Lilly, Taco Bell, Federal Express, Sara Lee, and Procter & Gamble. About the only student complaint is that "CPPO is heavily focused toward finance. More marketing and general management jobs would be nice."

Students also find career opportunities through the student-run Owen Consulting Service, which provides both short-term and long-term placement assistance with small- and medium-sized companies in the region. They are also happy to report that "alumni are very willing to help with your job search."

STUDENT/CAMPUS LIFE

Owen MBAs describe their surroundings in near-idyllic terms. Noting that "southern charm is evident in the school's friendly and easygoing atmosphere," students tell us that they "make a point of balancing school with social, community service, and time with their families and spouses." Student clubs "are very active and strive to allow many students to be involved in active roles within the club and the school." Furthermore, students are "very social. We have events every week, such as our keg parties every Thursday, and we involve other graduate schools. Plenty of social activities help us become better acquainted with faculty, alumni, and fellow students." There are also "a lot of activities and social gatherings geared specifically toward married couples." Amenities of the Vanderbilt experience include a "great gym" and a "perfect location. Seventy-five percent of the class lives one to two blocks from school. The cost of living here is low, and the campus is very attractive." And, of course, there's Nashville, one of the nation's music capitals and a growing southern city. Students can enjoy the same watering holes once frequented by Hank Williams, Sr., or shop for records and Western gear down on Lower Broadway. "Downtown Nashville is a blast," reports a typical student.

The Owen student body describes itself as "intelligent, talented, supportive, like a big family" but "a tad shy on the hard-core work experience and diversity." Writes one student, "I would prefer to see more geographic diversity, with fewer students from Nashville and the Southeast." Adds another, "We need more minorities and women applicants." Among the many assets of this group is that "students support each other in many ways, especially in sharing the benefits of their past experiences, in job searches, and helping each other with interviewing skills." The small program "lends to getting to know everyone" and means that students are "always able to find someone to grab a beer or a round of golf with."

ADMISSIONS

The admissions office considers your work experience to be the most important element in your application, then, in descending order, your college GPA, interview, GMAT scores, essays, letters of recommendation, and extracurricular activities. The school adds, however, this order "differs according to the background of each candidate."

FINANCIAL FACTS

Tuition	$24,000
Fees	$240
Cost of books	$1,100
Room & board	$7,850
% of students receiving aid	60
% first-year students receiving aid	66
% aid that is merit based	100
% of students receiving loans	50
Average award package	$37,900
Average grant	$15,000

ADMISSIONS

# of applications received	1,140
% applicants accepted	45
% acceptees attending	45
Average GMAT (range)	630 (580–670)
Minimum TOEFL	600
Average GPA (range)	3.10 (2.62–3.63)
Application fee	$50
Early decision program available	Yes
Early decision deadline	November 19
Early decision notification	December 17
Regular application deadline	March 17
Regular notification	April 14
Admission may be deferred?	Yes
Maximum length of deferment	2 years
Transfer students accepted?	Yes
Nonfall admission available?	Yes
Admission process need-blind?	Yes

APPLICANTS ALSO LOOK AT

Duke University, University of Virginia, Northwestern University, Emory University, University of Texas at Austin, University of North Carolina at Chapel Hill, Washington University, Indiana University

EMPLOYMENT PROFILE

Placement rate (%)	95
# of companies recruiting on campus	120
% of grads employed immediately	90
% grads employed within six months	95
Average starting salary	$69,000

Grads employed by field (avg. salary):

Accounting	1%	NR
Consulting	26%	$73,750
Finance	16%	$64,209
General Management	6%	$69,428
Human Resources	4%	$61,667
Marketing	16%	$65,993
MIS	2%	$76,625
Operations	3%	$69,800
Other	4%	$76,500
Venture Capital	22%	$68,000

UNIVERSITY OF VIRGINIA
Darden Graduate School of Business Administration

OVERVIEW

Type of school	public
Affiliation	none
Environment	suburban
Academic calendar	semester
Schedule	full-time only

STUDENTS

Enrollment of parent institution	18,500
Enrollment of business school	491
% male/female	70/30
% out-of-state	73
% minorities	15
% international (# of countries represented)	20 (37)
Average age at entry	27
Average years work experience at entry	4.5

ACADEMICS

Student/faculty ratio	8:1
% female faculty	28
% minority faculty	4
Hours of study per day	5.86

SPECIALTIES
Excellent teachers; most have business experience; over one-half have taught overseas; 14% international. Curriculum strengths: general mgmt.; case method; integrated, holistic curriculum; required ethics course; teamwork; student-centered learning.

JOINT DEGREES
MBA/JD, 4 years; MBA/MA in Asian Studies 3 years; MBA/MA in Government, Foreign Affairs or Public Administration, 3 years; MBA/ME, 3 years; MBA/MSN, 3 years; MBA/Ph.D., 4 years

STUDY ABROAD PROGRAMS
Hong Kong U. of Science and Technology; Solvay Business School; China Europe International Business School; Universite Libre de Bruxelles; International U. of Japan; Sweden, Finland, Mexico, Australia, Canada

SURVEY SAYS...

HITS
Campus is attractive
Teamwork skills
Safety

MISSES
On-campus housing

PROMINENT ALUMNI
George David, chairman, CEO, United Technologies; Steven S. Reinemund, Chairman and CEO, Frito-Lay; Henri A. M. Termeer, Pres. Ceo, and Chairman, Genzyme Corporation

ACADEMICS

The University of Virginia's Darden Graduate School of Business Administration demands a lot from its MBAs. Writes one student, "Our dean refers to Darden as a 'stretch' experience, where a student is challenged almost to the breaking point. This is a strength of Darden because much learning and growth occurs near the breaking point. We are proud to be at Darden for the same reasons a Marine is proud to be a Marine, or a Navy SEAL is proud to be a SEAL." Another agreed in principle, although offering this slight modification: "Darden is certainly rigorous, but the boot-camp mantra is oversold. This is not a boot camp. It is an intense but enjoyable and rewarding atmosphere." According to nearly everyone we surveyed, the Darden system works. Writes one typical respondent, "Darden has stretched me in ways I never imagined. It has made me a master at time management, which is key to a future in business. This school believes in developing whole people, which I greatly appreciate."

First-year MBAs must complete an integrated curriculum of ten required courses, interlocked so as to create the net effect of one massive course in the fundamentals of business. Darden relies heavily on the case-study method, integrating it into the curriculum in such a way that students often study the same case in several courses simultaneously. This method requires students to consider and integrate a variety of perspectives on a given situation. The case-study method is popular with students even though it places great demands on their time: "There is little life during first year, especially if you come from a nonbusiness background. Three cases per day to read and prepare takes 16 hours a day." Second-year courses revisit first-year case studies in one required course (in leadership) and a selection of more than eighty electives, which range from one-week seminars to full-semester classes. Second-year students must also complete a Business Project, usually a consulting assignment that requires extensive extracurricular work with a local company.

Darden officials point out that a curriculum this tightly integrated requires an outstanding faculty. According to students, Darden's teaching staff is more than up to the challenge. This "outstanding teaching faculty is great—very supportive, easy to get time with, and on the whole excellent teachers. A lot of work, but I feel very prepared for my next job." The administration also earns its share of kudos; MBAs told us that "the administration makes a great effort to promote a 'Darden community' with events from morning coffee to awards presentations." A low tuition and a new, state-of-the-art facility round out "an experience beyond [all] expectations," in the words of one student. All in all students feel "there is an unusually strong loyalty to Darden and a view that 'this is the best place for me to earn an MBA.'"

PLACEMENT AND RECRUITING

The Darden Career Services Center provides students a wide range of services, including not only career and internship search assistance but also counseling for self-assessment, development of networking skills, and long-term career planning. As do many schools, Darden uses the Internet to market its MBAs, maintaining a password-protected job bulletin board to extend opportunities beyond those offered by companies visiting the campus. Approximately 200 companies visit Darden each year, conducting more than 2,800 interviews with graduating MBAs.

A. Jon Megibow, Director of Admissions
P.O. Box 6550, Charlottesville, VA 22906-6550
Admissions: 800-UVA-MBA1 Fax: 804-243-5033
Email: darden@virginia.edu
Internet: www.darden.virginia.edu

University of Virginia

Students are most enthusiastic about Darden's "incredibly loyal and tight alumni base." Their wish list includes "more West Coast recruiters" and "more medium and small companies available on campus or through correspondence opportunities." Major recruiters include McKinsey, Microsoft, Merrill Lynch, Procter & Gamble, and Lucent Technologies.

STUDENT/CAMPUS LIFE

Darden students tell us that they enjoy a nurturing environment fostered by "an awesome group of fellow students. All are very ambitious and intelligent, but at the same time very friendly, supportive, and fun to work with. Great team players." This elite crowd—most arrive with extensive work experience and GMAT scores approaching 700—forms a "very close group. People here care about each other. Students tutor, hold review sessions, and make sure their peers do not get left behind." More than one-quarter hold degrees in engineering and science; groups of roughly the same size majored in the humanities/ social sciences and business administration during their undergraduate studies. Boasts one Darden MBA, "Everyone has a passion to learn. They're not just here to get the degree and get a job."

As for day-to-day life on the Darden campus, students say that "In a word, life at Darden is intense. Balancing the academic workload, job search, family time, and club activities is tough, but these are also the same types of pressures we will face in the real world. It also makes the accomplishment of graduating that much sweeter." Explains another student, "Life here revolves around three things: 1) learning; 2) recruiting; 3) community work. All parts, to different degrees, contribute to our education. Outside of school, it's pretty much typical student life." First year is toughest, while "second year is a bit more relaxing than first. We spend more time socializing and getting to know one another." Darden "supports frequent social events that allow students to interact outside the class. It also supports events specifically for Darden Partners." Hometown Charlottesville "is relatively isolated, which makes the Darden community that much stronger." Students quickly point out the dual benefits of Charlottesville: "You're within striking distance of DC, yet outdoor activities are plentiful. You can mountain bike, hike, rock climb, or camp." This sublime mix led one student to offer: "I can't imagine being anywhere else. The quality of life is outstanding."

ADMISSIONS

Each of the following components count for roughly one-third in the admissions decision: Academics (GPA, GMAT); work/professional experience; personal attributes (essays, interview, extracurriculars). The interview is strongly encouraged but not required. The committee explains, "We look for evidence of competitive academic performance, intellectual ability, significant work and life experiences, as well as other qualities of character that cannot be quantitatively measured. Factors such as breadth of perspective, international exposure, and diversity are also taken into consideration." Applications are processed in one of three rounds. Students are rarely granted a deferral; possible reasons for one are military obligation or visa restrictions.

FINANCIAL FACTS

Tuition (in-/out-of-state)	$16,851/$22,577
Cost of books	$2,000
Room & board	$10,400
% of students receiving aid	75
% first-year students receiving aid	60
% aid that is merit based	50
% of students receiving loans	75
Average award package	$26,900
Average grant	$9,050

ADMISSIONS

# of applications received	3,277
% applicants accepted	15
% acceptees attending	50
Average GMAT (range)	685
Average GPA (range)	3.36
Application fee (in-/out-of-state)	$100/$100
Early decision program available	No
Regular application deadline	March 15
Regular notification	May 1
Admission may be deferred?	No
Transfer students accepted?	No
Nonfall admission available?	No
Admission process need-blind?	Yes

APPLICANTS ALSO LOOK AT

Northwestern University, Duke University, Stanford University, Harvard University, Dartmouth College, University of Pennsylvania, University of North Carolina at Chapel Hill, University of Michigan

EMPLOYMENT PROFILE

Placement rate (%)	100
# of companies recruiting on campus	188
% of grads employed immediately	94
% grads employed within six months	100
Average starting salary	$78,000

Grads employed by field (avg. salary):

Consulting	31%	$90,000
Entrepreneurship	4%	$65,000
Finance	32%	$75,000
General Management	16%	NR
Marketing	10%	$70,000
Strategic Planning	7%	$77,500

WAKE FOREST UNIVERSITY
Babcock Graduate School of Management

OVERVIEW

Type of school	private
Affiliation	none
Environment	urban
Academic calendar	semester
Schedule	full-time/part-time/evening

STUDENTS

Enrollment of parent institution	6,015
Enrollment of business school	673
% male/female	76/24
% out-of-state	69
% part-time	63
% minorities	8
% international (# of countries represented)	19 (22)
Average age at entry	26
Average years work experience at entry	3.5

ACADEMICS

Student/faculty ratio	7:1
% female faculty	15
% minority faculty	10
Hours of study per day	5.41

SPECIALTIES

Integrated curriculum with functional area tracks offered in the second year. First year: Integrated curriculum taught in three modules. Second year twelve tracks offered within the following disciplines: finance, marketing, operations, management consulting, and enterpreneurship/family business.

JOINT DEGREES

JD/MBA Law and Business, 4 years; MD/MBA Medicine and Business, 5 years

SPECIAL PROGRAMS

Babcock Leadership Series; Mentor Program; Field Study Program

STUDY ABROAD PROGRAMS

England, Latin America, Japan, China, Continental Europe

SURVEY SAYS...

HITS
Administration
Computer skills
Teamwork skills

MISSES
On-campus housing
Gym
School clubs

PROMINENT ALUMNI

Ann Morrison, author *Breaking the Glass Ceiling*; Charles Ergen, founder & CEO, Echo Start Communication; Peter Daks, President, GTE Florida; Steve Lineberger-President, Sara Lee Casualwear

ACADEMICS

Babcock students agree that of their program's many assets, the greatest is "its size. It is small enough to have good relationships with the professors. The team-oriented environment encourages students to help one another." It is an asset that just got even better: in 1998, the school introduced its "3/38 Plan," which divides incoming students into three sections of thirty-eight. The goal is to create "the smallest section sizes of any major MBA program" in the country.

The first year at Babcock entails a mandatory integrated core curriculum with courses that are frequently team taught and require student teams to complete assignments collectively. Students speak approvingly of the core, reporting that "the combination of lecture and case analysis is ideal, and contributions from the students add great value to the classroom experience." The core includes two courses in international business and another in law and ethics, perhaps explaining why one student describes Babcock as "a business school with ethics."

Second-year students must complete two required courses: one in management control and yet another in international business. Those with fewer than three years of relevant work experience must also complete a field study project in which student teams undertake a consulting project with a local or national company. Otherwise, however, second-year students are free to focus on their concentration of choice. Students speak highly of the finance, management consulting, and operations departments. They also rave about the program's international focus.

Most students like the faculty, whom they describe as "real people . . . not at all bookish. They are brilliant in the classroom but fun to go to lunch with, too." Adds another: "Professors are very willing to help and will put all else aside for students. They truly take an interest in each individual." Students are particularly impressed with how accessible professors—many of whom remain active in the business world—make themselves to students. Says one: "Professors do not post office hours because they are available all the time and are willing to talk about subjects ranging from classes to careers to personal issues." Academic facilities here are top-notch, and students appreciate the fact that the school "provides laptops for everybody. Tech system is first rate."

PLACEMENT AND RECRUITING

The Babcock Career Services Office (CSO) provides a combination of personal counseling and computer support to students searching for internships and post-graduate employment. Counselors use workshops, mock interviews, and one-on-one meetings to prepare students for their job search. They also maintain an Internet site of student resumes and an intranet system, accessible to Babcock students only, to post potential career opportunities. CSO staff meet with more than 350 companies a year in their efforts to market the Babcock program.

Our survey shows a high level of student satisfaction with the CSO. Says one student, "Career services didn't hand me my job. But, they did give me the tools I needed to land a great job. They taught me how to network, interview, follow up, and negotiate compensation. Outstanding preparation!" More than sixty

Mary Goss, Assistant Dean
P.O. Box 7659, Winston-Salem, NC 27109
Admissions: 336-758-5422 Fax: 336-758-5830
Email: admissions@mba.wfu.edu
Internet: www.mba.wfu.edu

Wake Forest University

companies visited the campus to interview prospective Babcock graduates last year. However, the survey also reveals a vocal minority who feel strongly that Babcock must attract more recruiters from beyond the immediate region. Wake Forest helps conduct MBA Consortia in Atlanta and New York and participates in several smaller international consortia held by private vendors. Companies hiring Babcock grads last year included KPMG Peat Marwick, Pepsico Foods, Bear Sterns, Merck, and NationsBank.

STUDENT/CAMPUS LIFE

Because of the size of the program, Babcock students form a tight-knit group. Writes one, "Due to our small class size, students get to know each other pretty well. This creates an environment of free interaction where we can learn from other students' backgrounds and experiences." The intimacy of the program means that students also get a close-up look at each others' flaws, leading one to describe classmates as "young, yuppie, financially stable, not the most aggressive." Several respondents mentioned the relative inexperience of Babcock MBAs, noting that they "wish they had a few more years of experience. Sometimes the youth of the class shows in classroom discussion." The student who writes this is quick to add, however, this his classmates are "overall a great group of supportive, intelligent people." Many students note that they "really enjoy" the "large number of international students. There is much to gain from other cultures."

MBAs here spend a lot of time together outside the classroom. Clubs and student government–run activities are very popular, and students here frequently socialize with each other off campus. Basketball games are particularly popular, since Wake Forest competes in one of the most talent-rich conferences in the country. Married students happily find that their spouses are invited to "become active in all school functions. It has been the best two years of our lives!" All this explains why students say, "there is a genuine sense of community here that extends to faculty, staff, students, and their families, and even their pets! Everyone helps each other however they can. We really like each other here!" Because there is only limited on-campus housing available to graduate students, most MBAs live off campus, where housing is reportedly comfortable and affordable. The campus itself ranks among the safest and prettiest in the country. Of their adopted hometown, Babcock students write that "there is not much night life in Winston-Salem, but we make the best of it with road trips to Greensboro and Charlotte."

ADMISSIONS

GMAT scores tops the list of admissions criteria at Babcock, followed by work experience, undergrad GPA, interview, recommendations, and leadership abilities. Writes the school, "The admissions committee evaluates the applicant's scholastic ability for graduate study, character qualities, motivation, and managerial potential. Interviews are strongly recommended and required for applicants who lack full-time work experience. Applicants who schedule interviews are matched with a student host who takes them to class, gives them a tour of the facility, and takes them to lunch."

FINANCIAL FACTS

Tuition	$21,200
Tuition per credit	$666
Fees	$100
Cost of books	$1,500
Room & board (on-/off-campus)	NR/$5,600
% of students receiving aid	77
% first-year students receiving aid	77
% aid that is merit based	100
% of students receiving loans	55
% of students receiving paid internships	100
Average award package	$35,667
Average grant	$9,384
Average graduation debt	$37,785

ADMISSIONS

# of applications received	583
% applicants accepted	42
% acceptees attending	45
Average GMAT (range)	633 (600–670)
Minimum TOEFL	600
Average GPA (range)	3.20 (2.90–3.50)
Application fee (in-/out-of-state)	$75/$75
Early decision program available	Yes
Early decision deadline	December 1
Early decision notification	December 25
Regular application deadline	April 1
Regular notification	Rolling
Admission may be deferred?	Yes
Maximum length of deferment	1 year
Transfer students accepted?	No
Nonfall admission available?	Yes
Admission process need-blind?	Yes

APPLICANTS ALSO LOOK AT

University of North Carolina at Chapel Hill, Duke University, Vanderbilt University, Emory University, University of Virginia, College of William and Mary, Georgetown University, University of Maryland

EMPLOYMENT PROFILE

Placement rate (%)		89
# of companies recruiting on campus		85
% of grads employed immediately		89
% grads employed within six months		99
Average starting salary		$59,000
Grads employed by field (avg. salary):		
Communications	NR	$61,829
Consulting	18%	$61,362
Finance	42%	$57,105
General Management	NR	$66,800
Marketing	27%	$57,920
Operations	6%	$59,250
Other	7%	$56,071

UNIVERSITY OF WASHINGTON
Graduate School of Business Administration

OVERVIEW

Type of school	public
Affiliation	none
Environment	urban
Academic calendar	quarter

STUDENTS

Enrollment of parent institution	35,108
Enrollment of business school	458
% male/female	63/37
% out-of-state	48
% part-time	3
% minorities	11
% international (# of countries represented)	20 (14)
Average age at entry	29
Average years work experience at entry	5.5

ACADEMICS

Student/faculty ratio	35:1
% female faculty	13
% minority faculty	9
Hours of study per day	4.68

SPECIALTIES

Marketing, Finance, Entrepreneurship, International Business

JOINT DEGREES

MP Accounting; JD/MBA; MBA/MAIS; MBA/MHA Health Administration; MBA/MS Engineering; (PEMM) Program in Engineering and Manufacturing Management

SPECIAL PROGRAMS

Overseas Study, Global Business Program, Program in Entrepreneurship and Innovation

STUDY ABROAD PROGRAMS

Chile, Mexico, China, Denmark, England, Finland, France, Germany, India, Japan, Spain, Switzerland, Singapore

SURVEY SAYS...

HITS
Seattle
Campus is attractive
Star faculty

MISSES
Finance
General management
MIS/operations

PROMINENT ALUMNI

Bill Ayer, President and CEO, Alaska Airlines; James McTaggart, Chairman, Marakon Assoc.; H. Stewart Parker, CEO, Targeted Genetics

ACADEMICS

There is little mystery to the popularity of the University of Washington's MBA Program. As one student succinctly puts it, "It has a great reputation and the tuition is cheap." UW adds a third asset to the mix: "proximity to a high-tech and rapidly growing economy" in a fun, growing city. The substantial Japanese presence in the Seattle business community means greater "ties to Asian markets" for this MBA program and outstanding opportunities for students interested in international business studies.

UW MBAs praise the "coordinated first-year core curriculum," described in the catalogue as a "year-long sequence of three courses taught by an interdisciplinary team of professors." Students describe the "excellent, rounded first core year with all of the best instructors" as "academically challenging but still friendly" and particularly like the "emphasis on group work." One student writes, "the work is intense and challenging, and the amount we're learning is amazing. Even so, the pressure is manageable because everyone's so motivated. The administration is full of great, innovative ideas."

Second-year students have numerous choices. They may take electives in any of the program's eleven disciplines, or they may pursue the more structured "special-study options," which award certificates in International Management; Management of Technology; Environmental Management; Global Trade, Transportation, and Logistics Studies; and Entrepreneurship and Innovation. Furthermore, students also have the option of pursuing concurrent degrees in Law; International Studies; Engineering; and Public Health and Community Medicine. Students praise professors in all departments for their teaching ability and accessibility, although some warn that students "need to do some selective hunting for second year profs."

About the only consistent bone of contention at UW are the facilities. The new Seafirst Executive Center is "great, but some of the classrooms could be improved," as could computer labs. One student complains, "Although rooms are equipped with multimedia resources, they are often not functioning and most people are not capable of using them because the system is convoluted." The School of Business is currently undergoing renovations—it already has "a great new library, remodeled lounge, and a new restaurant"—that may remedy this situation. Among those who complain, many concede that the "University is well on its way" toward necessary improvements.

PLACEMENT AND RECRUITING

The University of Washington Business Career Center writes, "University of Washington students gravitate toward high tech companies and get experience in the industry through internships. In return, high tech companies seek out students interested and experienced in the field . . . The Business Career Center staff works closely with students to help them assess and identify their interests. The program staff also organizes a number of networking events geared to put students in touch with hard-to-locate constituencies such as entrepreneurs." Among those events is on-campus recruiting visits from sixty-one companies and MBA consortia in Chicago; Irvine, CA; and Michigan. Top employers include Andersen Consulting, ATL Ultrasound, Deloitte & Touche, Ernst &

David Williams, Director of MBA Program
110 Mackenzie Hall, Box 353200 Seattle, WA 98195
Admissions: 206-543-4660 Fax: 206-616-7351
Email: mba@u.washington.edu
Internet: www.weber.u.washington.edu/~bschool/mba

University of Washington

Young, Fluke Corporation, Hewlett-Packard Company, Intel Corporation, and Price Waterhouse.

Washington students give their career center average grades, telling us that the school does a good job of attracting high-quality area companies, but that it "needs to diversify recruiting beyond the Pacific Northwest." Students also give low marks to the school's mentoring system.

STUDENT/CAMPUS LIFE

University of Washington draws heavily from the Pacific Rim, a situation agreeable to students from both sides of the Pacific. One American student notes that "international students add a much needed layer of depth and insight to our education." A Japanese student observes that "many students are open to foreign students. They [invite] us to their parties often. In group academic projects, basically they are helpful." Regardless of their national origin, students praise their classmates as "smart," "friendly," and "awesome! Bright, energetic, hardworking, diverse in interests and backgrounds." One MBA with an unusual facility for class demographics writes, "I like the fact that there are 'older' people (average age: 29) with work experience (average 5.5 years)." Not surprisingly for a predominantly West Coast group, UW students are both "high-tech oriented" and "outdoorsy, more environmentally concerned than motivated by money."

Life on the UW campus is "very busy. Too much to do, too little time to enjoy the experience." The amount of time students devote to study here is above the national average, especially during the first year, which is "stressful but with a congenial atmosphere and many group projects." Adds one student, "You feel the camaraderie the moment you arrive. My class is a tight group—you know they care about your academic and professional success." Our survey shows that "most students socialize and work together in clubs and other activities," of which there are "lots." They love their beautiful 700-acre campus and they also love Seattle, which they describe as "safe," "fun-filled," and "growing economically." They especially love their proximity to "hundreds of little software firms in the area, including mother Microsoft." On the downside, campus housing "needs improvement" and off-campus housing is "very expensive."

ADMISSIONS

The admissions office considers the following criteria (in no particular order): essays, college GPA, extracurricular activities, work experience, the interview, GMAT scores, and letters of recommendation. Notes the school, "We look closely at GPA and GMAT scores, but high quantitative measures do not ensure admissions—strong work experience or extensive extracurricular or community activities can significantly improve an applicant's chances of admission." The admissions office has implemented a round-based admission cycle, with an early deadline of December 1, and early notification by January 15. Decisions are made on a rolling basis. Notes the office, "We strongly encourage early application." The final deadline is March 15, but students are encouraged to apply by the January 8 or February 1 dates. Notification is generally received in six to eight weeks. Students must complete a college-level calculus course before enrollment.

FINANCIAL FACTS

Tuition (in-/out-of-state)	$5,640/$14,007
Cost of books	$1,200
Room & board (on-/off-campus)	$8,319/$8,319
% of students receiving aid	153
% first-year students receiving aid	65
% aid that is merit based	5
% of students receiving grants	15
Average award package	$13,772
Average grant	$2,962

ADMISSIONS

# of applications received	1,159
% applicants accepted	32
% acceptees attending	42
Average GMAT (range)	647 (530–760)
Minimum TOEFL	600
Average GPA (range)	3.26 (2.36–3.98)
Application fee (in-/out-of-state)	$49/$49
Early decision program available	Yes
Early decision deadline	December 1
Early decision notification	January 15
Regular application deadline	Rolling
Admission may be deferred?	No
Transfer students accepted?	No
Nonfall admission available?	No
Admission process need-blind?	Yes

APPLICANTS ALSO LOOK AT

University of California—Berkeley, Cornell University, University of California—Santa Barbara, University of Oregon, University of Wisconsin—Madison, University of Colorado, Boulder

EMPLOYMENT PROFILE

Placement rate (%)	89
# of companies recruiting on campus	61
% of grads employed immediately	89
Average starting salary	$58,777

Grads employed by field (avg. salary):

Consulting	24%	$64,875
Finance	37%	$58,915
General Management	7%	$45,200
Human Resources	4%	NR
Marketing	20%	$57,973
MIS	5%	$51,500
Operations	2%	NR
Other	1%	$52,000

WASHINGTON UNIVERSITY
John M. Olin School of Business

ACADEMICS

MBAs at Washington University tell us that a flexible curriculum and opportunities for experiential learning are the distinguishing characteristics of a degree from the Olin School of Business. In addition, students laud Olin's intimate size, high-quality instructors, and the program's "potential for dynamic growth."

Praising Olin's curricular approach, one student told us that "70 percent of our courses are electives. It's one of the great strengths of the program." Students at Olin are aggressively encouraged to design their own curricula, although the school hastens to point out that it requires core studies in management, economics, accounting, statistics, business strategy, finance, marketing, and operations. The core, writes one student, benefits from "a good balance of quants and management." Most core courses can be completed during the first semester, leaving students three semesters to pursue their own interests. Sums up one student, "We take forty courses. There is a wide selection, and we get the best education, period."

Experiential learning is another major focal point of the Olin approach. Practicum, for example, allows students to consult for area companies on matters ranging from marketing to strategy. Practicum concludes with a formal presentation to the client company; thus far, fifty-seven organizations, including Enterprise Rent-A-Car, Ford Motor Company, PriceWaterhouse, Ralston Purina, Apple Computer, and Monsanto, have asked Olin students to advise them on select issues. For students interested in nonprofit and community issues, the Taylor Community Consulting Program provides free services to local nonprofits. The Hatchery, an experiential program for entrepreneurs, pairs students with fledgling companies to develop business plans to present to potential investors. Finance students manage a school investment fund through the Investments Praxis program. Writes one student, "I can experience the business world through the Hatchery, Practicum, Taylor, etc. They are called 'experiential learning' programs."

Students praise their professors, telling us "There are some heavy hitters among the professors. We need more senior faculty, though." Adds another, "I was very surprised to find so many professors with PhDs from Michigan, University of Chicago, Stanford, Western Ontario, etc. My professors have all been excellent." Students single out finance, accounting, and entrepreneurial studies as Olin's top areas.

PLACEMENT AND RECRUITING

Olin's approach to career placement is more "touchy-feely" than the hard-nosed approach of many of the top b-schools. The school takes steps to ensure that their MBAs realize their interests and values and in turn place them—often through nontraditional means—in a job that will "make [their dreams] come true." To achieve this aim, Olin offers some unique career placement services, including a mandatory half-credit course in Professional Development Planning during students' first weeks and a later noncredit Career Management Series.

Students admire Olin's approach, but many are not pleased with the results. Discussing the shortcomings of the placement office, students tell us: "We need a lot of help with recruitment office. It is seriously understaffed." But another

Pamela Wiese, Director of MBA Admissions
One Brookings Drive, Campus Box 1133, St. Louis, MO 63130-4899
Admissions: 314-935-7301 Fax: 314-935-6309
Email: mba@mail.olin.wush.edu
Internet: www.olin.wustl.edu

Washington University

counters, "Although the placement office is in the Dark Ages, firms come to campus and most importantly students get great, high-paying jobs."

STUDENT/CAMPUS LIFE

Olin students appreciate the quality of life afforded by their school's suburban location. St. Louis's largest park, Forest Park, is within walking distance of the school; its grounds include a golf course, zoo, skating rinks, and other recreation facilities. The city's recently renovated and expanded downtown is only a short car ride away. Writes one student, "I like to take advantage of St. Louis by going to Cardinals games, Blues games, and the symphony." Housing near campus is plentiful, attractive, and reasonably priced; most students live off campus in nearby apartments. The campus itself is beautiful and spacious, although the b-school facilities are reportedly growing a little crowded. The social scene at WU ranges from weekly Friday afternoon keg parties to student fund-raisers. Major student clubs include the Entrepreneurs Club, the Business Minority Council, the International Business Council, the Operations and Manufacturing Club, the Voluntary Action Committee, and Women in Management. Students also "have a very active role in the management of the school. We're treated as equals." No wonder many students find that "Olin is a comfortable place, not at all pretentious."

Olin MBAs report a steady, heavy dose of work, especially during the first year. Students prepare for class roughly 25 hours a week and describe the academic pressure as intense, forcing the efficient use of study groups, which are considered integral to student life. The small size of the school (approximately 150 students in each full-time class) offers many advantages: small classes, personal attention, and a supportive environment. Students say this school is competitive but, not surprisingly, teamwork is the overriding theme here. The student body includes "Many smart people, with great strengths in mathematics and finance. First-year students have a much stronger social bond than do second-years." Roughly one-third of the students are foreign. "I was surprised how much the international population influences this environment," remarks an MBA. While some students described their class as diverse, others disagree; writes one Latino MBA, "The students are mostly Midwest Caucasians. Little real diversity here."

ADMISSIONS

According to the admissions office, a candidate's setting and achieving challenging goals in all aspects of their lives is the most important criterion. After that, the school considers, in descending order, your college GPA, GMAT scores, interview, letters of recommendation, and essay. Writes the school, "The interview is not required, but strongly recommended, and can be a determining factor." The school also requires students to submit a very detailed work history. Olin's Consortium for Graduate Study in Management is dedicated to funding fellowships for talented minorities. Admissions are handled on a rolling basis; students are notified of a decision three to five weeks after their applications are received. Students may defer admission for up to one year for work- or cost-related reasons. Students who defer must pay a deposit to hold a spot in the class.

FINANCIAL FACTS

Tuition	$25,750
Tuition per credit	$715
Fees	$0
Cost of books	$2,500
Room & board (on-/off-campus)	NR/$11,000
% of students receiving aid	73
% first-year students receiving aid	69
% aid that is merit based	47
% of students receiving loans	49
% of students receiving grants	55
Average award package	$22,450
Average grant	$7,250
Average graduation debt	$38,880

ADMISSIONS

# of applications received	1,091
% applicants accepted	33
% acceptees attending	42
Average GMAT (range)	624 (590–660)
Minimum TOEFL	590
Average GPA (range)	3.13 (2.90–3.33)
Application fee (in-/out-of-state)	$80/$80
Early decision program available	No
Regular application deadline	April 30
Regular notification	Rolling
Admission may be deferred?	No
Transfer students accepted?	No
Nonfall admission available?	No
Admission process need-blind?	Yes

APPLICANTS ALSO LOOK AT

Northwestern University, University of Michigan, University of Chicago, Duke University, New York University, Vanderbilt University, Indiana University, University of Virginia

EMPLOYMENT PROFILE

Placement rate (%)	98
# of companies recruiting on campus	138
% of grads employed immediately	79
% grads employed within six months	98
Average starting salary	$65,000

Grads employed by field (avg. salary):

Consulting	27%	$76,000
Finance	36%	$64,500
Marketing	19%	$62,500
Other	13%	$63,000
Strategic Planning	4%	$64,000

UNIVERSITY OF WESTERN ONTARIO
Ivey Business School

ACADEMICS

Students cite the Richard Ivey School of Business's "strong focus on general management," the school's reputation as "the best MBA program in Canada," and its heavy reliance on the case method as the University of Western Ontario MBA program's greatest assets. In this last category, Ivey claims the distinction of being among the largest producers of case studies in the world. Notes the school's promotional material: "Over the duration of the Ivey MBA Program, [students] tackle more than 600 real-world business cases." According to students, "The case-study method is one of the school's great strengths. The program uses its own cases for teaching purposes. Very realistic and challenging method."

Entering MBAs are divided into sections of seventy and then into smaller learning teams of from six to eight, within which they tackle many of the program's case studies. Ivey's "highly integrated core" incorporates international and local business issues as well as aspects of the many fields of business study: marketing, operations, communications, finance, information technology, statistics, and accounting. Writes one student, "First year involves a very challenging workload. Great profs, great experiences." Second-year students are given wide berth to design their own programs. Elective choices include traditional, single-subject courses as well as a number of interdisciplinary courses. Students are less enthusiastic about the second-year program, telling us that "second year needs more presentations. There are some weak classes and not enough selection" and also that "popular second-year courses need to be made more accessible." Students applaud their instructors, telling us that "most profs are quite good. Being a case-study teacher is tougher than lecturing, so I have to give them credit." They also report, however, that "there are concerns regarding the school's ability to retain world-class professors." The Ivey administration wins points for keeping the program current ("the program seems to be changing with the times, i.e., technology, etc. and up-to-date cases"). Wrote one student, "We have an extremely professional administration. They have a very fast response time." Students wish, however, that the school would increase the quantitative and technical content of the curriculum; writes one, "We often study and discuss IT, but we do not learn 'how to.' The SAP module, for example, had no hands-on activity. I didn't know what it looked like."

Ivey offers exchange programs with schools in Asia, Latin America, Scandinavia, Europe, and Australia. Other interesting international opportunities include the Leader Project and the China Project, which send fifty MBA candidates to Eastern Europe and China to teach basic management skills to "selected officials and entrepreneurs."

PLACEMENT AND RECRUITING

The Ivey School's Career Services Office (CSO) offers the standard battery of career counseling and placement services, including an orientation-period job-skills seminar, resume books, and individual counseling. The school hosts an autumn job fair for all second-year students.

The Ivey School attracts more than 400 recruiting companies to its campus each year; visits occur year-round for full-time job offerings and in the spring for summer internships. Discussing the variety of recruiters, students tell us that

Larysa Gamula, Director, MBA Program Services
1151 Richmond St., North London, ON Canada
Admissions: 519-661-3212 Fax: 519-661-3431
Email: mba@ivey.uwo.ca
Internet: www.ivey.uwo.ca

"[The CSO] should decrease the focus on I-banking and consulting" and place "more emphasis on attracting high-tech companies." Ivey boasts a strong alumni network of more than 26,000, of whom "one in six . . . has the title Chair, President, CEO, Vice-President, Vice-Chair, or Managing Director/Partner in his or her company."

STUDENT/CAMPUS LIFE

Two-thirds of Ivey MBAs are native to Canada; the rest are drawn from more than twenty countries, including the United States, Switzerland, Germany, France, Taiwan, Singapore, China, Hong Kong, Mexico, Colombia, Venezuela, Russia, Ukraine, United Kingdom, and Ireland; notes one student, "the international students in particular are very supportive." The average incoming student is 29 and has five years of work experience, leading students to describe their classmates as "diverse in perspectives, experiences, age, and career goals." Ivey MBAs are "very helpful, interesting, and sophisticated. I've yet to come across a student who wouldn't offer assistance when asked" and are "much less status oriented and materialistic than I expected." That's probably why one student sums up life here as "like being a member of a family of seventy-one. The clubs and activities allow excellent opportunities to branch out to other sections."

Students report that "the workload is heavy and fast-paced," especially during first year. Writes one first-year student, "It is a lot of work, but it has been an intellectual boot camp—it has changed my way of thinking and raised my goals." Second year is somewhat easier; says one student, "A typical day is balanced among class time, prep time, and social activities. In year two the workload is much more manageable and allows for other activities."

The Ivey School is located in London, Ontario, a town with a population of 350,000. London is a quaint, picturesque town with many parks and tree-lined streets, thus earning it the nickname The Forest City. The university, construction, and light manufacturing drive the London economy; the city is host to manufacturing plants owned by GM, Serco, Siemens Automotive, and 3M, among others. London offers little in the way of big-city entertainment, but is large enough to support a pleasant variety of restaurants, bars, and nightclubs. The university is large (25,000 students) and accordingly provides many of the social opportunities available at big schools in the United States. MBAs constitute their own subpopulation within the university, forming clubs that sponsor various professional and social events, as well as guest lectures and recruiting trips. One student tells us that "there is no excuse to be alone. There are plenty of clubs for every taste. The wine tasting club is always entertaining!" Toronto and Detroit are within 130 miles of London; Great Lakes resorts are within an hour's drive.

ADMISSIONS

According to the program's promotional materials, Ivey's "admissions committee takes into account as many factors as possible. Considerable weight is placed on [applicants'] intellectual performance and potential, full-time work experience and accomplishments, leadership, and interpersonal skills." All applicants must take the GMAT; in addition, ESL applicants must score at least a 600 on the TOEFL.

FINANCIAL FACTS

Tuition	$16,000
Cost of books	$2,000
Room & board (on-/off-campus)	$6,000/$6,000
% aid that is merit based	100

ADMISSIONS

# of applications received	925
% applicants accepted	46
% acceptees attending	50
Average GMAT (range)	660 (560–770)
Minimum TOEFL	600
Average GPA (range)	3.30 (2.70–3.90)
Application fee (in-/out-of-state)	$100/$100
Early decision program available	Yes
Early decision deadline	Rolling
Regular application deadline	April 1
Admission may be deferred?	Yes
Maximum length of deferment	1 year
Transfer students accepted?	No
Nonfall admission available?	No
Admission process need-blind?	Yes

EMPLOYMENT PROFILE

Placement rate (%)	91
# of companies recruiting on campus	485
Average starting salary	$88,736

Grads employed by field (avg. salary):

Accounting	NR%	$61,462
Consulting	28%	$118,307
Finance	38%	$82,600
General Management	7%	$60,000
Global Management	40%	$60,000
Human Resources	2%	$61,250
Marketing	17%	$64,919
MIS	3%	$73,400
Operations	1%	$76,000
Other	4%	$57,000

COLLEGE OF WILLIAM AND MARY
Graduate School of Business

OVERVIEW

Type of school	public
Affiliation	none
Environment	suburban
Academic calendar	semester

STUDENTS

Enrollment of parent institution	5,326
Enrollment of business school	361
% male/female	65/35
% out-of-state	40
% part-time	4
% minorities	17
% international (# of countries represented)	12 (12)
Average age at entry	28
Average years work experience at entry	5.5

ACADEMICS

Student/faculty ratio	4:1
% female faculty	20
% minority faculty	5
Hours of study per day	5.48

SPECIALTIES

Special strengths in finance; operations management and info. technology; marketing; and leadership

JOINT DEGREES

MBA/JD, 4 years; MBA/MPP, 3 years

SPECIAL PROGRAMS

Field Studies

STUDY ABROAD PROGRAMS

Norway, Costa Rica, France

SURVEY SAYS...

HITS
Marketing
MIS/operations
Cozy student community

MISSES
Social life
School clubs
Computer skills

PROMINENT ALUMNI

William P. Fricks, Chairman, President and CEO, Newport News Shipbuilding; Daniel J. Ludman, Chairman and CEO, Moentor Investment Group; Robert J. Murphy, senior vice president, Hard News, ABC News

ACADEMICS

An intense, intimate program at state-school prices is what attracts MBAs to the College of William and Mary Graduate School of Business. A little more than 100 students are admitted each year, making this program ideal for those who want a "smaller program with personal attention and non-competitive attitude" at an "excellent value for in-state students."

William and Mary emphasizes building teamwork even before the first day of classes. Incoming students participate in an Outward Bound–style Orientation Week, during which they divide into teams of six and meet the challenges of a high ropes course, zip-line water crossing, and a raft-building competition. The six-member teams remain in place throughout first year to serve as study groups; the college takes care to build teams of students whose diverse areas of expertise supplement others'. First-year students must complete a twelve-course core, sequenced "to provide the greatest crossover benefits among courses and disciplines." Case studies, computer simulations, and lectures (by both faculty and visiting speakers) are integrated throughout the year. Writes one student, "The case/lecture method is very effective."

Second-year students may choose from a variety of electives in accounting, finance and economics, marketing, and operations and information technology. Respondents give these departments high grades across the board, citing a uniformly excellent faculty as the school's distinguishing trait. Professors "are very enthusiastic, very capable," and offer each student "a great deal of personal attention. Teachers are very responsive to performances of students." They're hardly pushovers, however; as one student explains, "The professors are great. They really want you to learn the material. They are very tough though, and they will push you very hard." Students hold the administration and staff in similarly high regard. Major complaints concern facilities—the library is considered "weak" and the computer labs "need more computers and more frequent upgrades"—and a grading system that "is too severe and puts us at a disadvantage with grads from other schools."

PLACEMENT AND RECRUITING

Students at William and Mary agree that the "placement office is the weak link here," although some feel that "perhaps as the stature of the school grows, the placement office will become more effective." Most common among student complaints is the feeling that "we need increased on-campus recruiting opportunities." Among the companies that visit Williamsburg are Andersen Consulting, Bristol-Myers Squibb, Champion, Delta Airlines, GE, Merrill Lynch, and Whirlpool.

The placement office tries to supplement on-campus recruiting through participation in MBA consortia in Atlanta and New York City. The Office of Career and Employer Development also manages two programs designed to interweave "real life experience" into the MBA experience: the Mentor Program, "which enables students to form professional relationships with business leaders chosen from a nationwide list"; and the Internship Program, "which provides hands-on experience in the students' field of choice."

Susan Rivera, Director of MBA Admissions/and Director, MBA Program
PO Box 8795, Williamsburg, VA 23187
Admissions: 757-221-2900 Fax: 757-221-2958
Email: sgrive@business.wm.edu
Internet: www.business.tyler.wm.edu

College of William and Mary

STUDENT/CAMPUS LIFE

The rigorous academics required for a William and Mary MBA demand that students be "bright," "very serious about their careers," and ready to "study, study, study." They're a driven group, but "not competitive to the point [that] they aren't friendly. Everyone here wants their fellow students to succeed." Students spend a lot of time working together in groups, so it's a good thing that they're "very team oriented. For example, if information is received individually from a professor, students will email all relevant facts to classmates on a given assignment." Our survey shows their work experiences to be "very diverse, ranging from banking and consulting to the Peace Corps," but also shows little ethnic/racial diversity in the program. Although students are "sometimes pretty stressed out," they are generally "tremendously professional, helpful, and cooperative." Most would agree with the student who tells us that "my fellow students have become my extended family. They help me when I need it, I help them when they need it, and everyone is supportive of each other!"

The school is located in historic Williamsburg, a re-creation of a colonial town that is more tourist trap than thriving metropolis. "The town is a graveyard," is how one MBA bluntly puts it. Another warns that "night life is scarce." It should be noted, however, that at least one student thinks that "the historic setting is a big plus," and that others point out that the town is "very safe and friendly, if a little boring at times." For most, the school's setting is irrelevant, since "life is school. We work so much there is little time to spend doing other activities." In fact, the most frequent complaint about the program is that it is too time-consuming. "We need a better balance between academic work and social events," is typical of responses. "Only half of the phrase work hard, play hard applies to the W & M b-school environment." Students occasionally find time to participate in a "great intramural sports program that allows us to interact with students from other programs." They also take advantage of "tremendous opportunities for personal growth in the many clubs available on campus." Occasionally students slip out of Williamsburg. Their destinations? "Virginia Beach is only 45 minutes away. The Blue Ridge Mountains are only 1 hour away. D.C. is not far."

ADMISSIONS

According to the admissions office, work experience is considered most important. Then the following in descending order: GMAT scores, required interview (phone interviews are arranged for those unable to travel to Williamsburg), letters of recommendation and essays, and college GPA. William and Mary features a rolling admissions process beginning early October and running through May 1. The school advises prospective students to submit applications prior to December 1.

FINANCIAL FACTS

Tuition (in-/out-of-state)	$6,500/$16,200
Tuition per credit (in-/out-of-state)	$510/NR
Fees (in-/out-of-state)	$80/$80
Cost of books	$1,600
Room & board (on-/off-campus)	$7,500/$7,500
% of students receiving aid	90
% first-year students receiving aid	60
% aid that is merit based	75
% of students receiving loans	90
% of students receiving grants	85
% of students receiving paid internships	100
Average award package	$30,000
Average grant	$5,000
Average graduation debt	$30,000

ADMISSIONS

# of applications received	450
% applicants accepted	33
% acceptees attending	70
Average GMAT (range)	620 (580–680)
Minimum TOEFL	600
Average GPA (range)	3.20 (2.70–3.80)
Application fee (in-/out-of-state)	$50/$50
Early decision program available	Yes
Early decision deadline	December 1
Early decision notification	December 15
Regular application deadline	May 1
Regular notification	Rolling
Admission may be deferred?	Yes
Maximum length of deferment	1 year
Transfer students accepted?	No
Nonfall admission available?	No
Admission process need-blind?	Yes

APPLICANTS ALSO LOOK AT

University of Virginia, Wake Forest University, Duke University, University of North Carolina at Chapel Hill, Georgetown University, University of Texas at Austin

EMPLOYMENT PROFILE

Placement rate (%)		90
# of companies recruiting on campus		72
% of grads employed immediately		90
% grads employed within six months		95
Average starting salary		$59,000

Grads employed by field (avg. salary):
Accounting	1%	$60,860
Consulting	37%	$54,610
Entrepreneurship	1%	NR
Finance	39%	$60,860
General Management	4%	$64,200
Global Management	1%	NR
Human Resources	NR%	$64,000
Marketing	9%	$58,500
MIS	2%	$56,600
Operations	4%	$64,500
Strategic Planning	2%	$64,000

UNIVERSITY OF WISCONSIN — MADISON
Business School

OVERVIEW

Type of school	public
Affiliation	none
Environment	urban
Academic calendar	semester

STUDENTS

Enrollment of parent institution	40,000
Enrollment of business school	570
% male/female	68/32
% out-of-state	50
% part-time	7
% minorities	13
% international (# of countries represented)	31 (28)
Average age at entry	28
Average years work experience at entry	4

ACADEMICS

Student/faculty ratio	6:1
% female faculty	15
% minority faculty	5
Hours of study per day	4.35

SPECIALTIES

Seven-week modules combined with semester courses. The shorter segments allow material to be more current and tailored to individual needs. Schedule also allows greater opportunity for students to take electives in their majors, both inside and outside of the Business School.

JOINT DEGREES

JD/MBA, 4 years; Agribusiness MBA, 2 years

SPECIAL PROGRAMS

UW—Madison is known for its "niche" programs: Marketing Research, Arts Administration, Applied Security Analysis, Real Estate, Enterprise, Supply-chain Management, Manufacturing & Technology Management, and Agribusiness. These areas of concentration are available to students who want in-depth course work within the MBA or master's curriculum. Noted for strong faculty, staff, alumni support systems and excellent placement success.

STUDY ABROAD PROGRAMS

Germany, France, Chile, Mexico, Denmark, Austria, Thailand, China, and England

SURVEY SAYS...
HITS
Campus is attractive
Madison

MISSES
On-campus housing

PROMINENT ALUMNI

John Morgridge, chairman of the Board, Cisco Systems

ACADEMICS

University of Wisconsin at Madison's School of Business is fast gaining a national reputation for a number of "high-quality specialty/niche programs," such as the real estate specialization. Students agree that these programs are among the reasons they chose Madison, singling out real estate ("Among the best in the nation . . . the program has over 1,200 alumni who are extremely helpful"), the Applied Security Analysis Program ("unlike any other experience on campus. We manage millions of dollars, interact with alumni, and receive excellent interviews. The program has given me the opportunity to compete with students from any school"), and the AC Nielsen Center for Market Research ("which provides top-notch training . . . great connections to the industry"). Other students in our survey single out specializations in insurance and risk management, agribusiness, supply-chain management, and entrepreneurship for praise.

Students express satisfaction with UWM's recently revamped curriculum, taught in seven-week modules in order to make the program "more streamlined and flexible than ever before." As an added benefit, the new curriculum makes it easier for students to place out of core courses, providing them extra opportunities to pursue more interesting studies in elective areas. One student happily reports that "the flexibility in the program requirements has allowed me to custom design my studies."

A warning to the mathematically challenged: UWM's heavy quantitative focus sends many students running for help. (The school strongly advises students to bolster their number-crunching skills before applying.) Fortunately, students can brush up during the week-long math camp offered before orientation or take tutorial sessions at the Learning Center during the school year. A similarly strong emphasis is placed on international business, with many international course offerings, summer and semester abroad programs, yearly student/faculty trips to destinations like the Pacific Rim, Latin America, and Europe, and foreign language classes in other UW departments to prep for it all.

PLACEMENT AND RECRUITING

Students report that the Business Career Center (BCC) is among U. Wisconsin's greatest assets. "The placement office bends over backwards for us," writes one student. The BCC provides many of the services that are standard at the best b-schools: continual counseling, mock interviews, job fairs, MBA consortia, and video-conferencing all fit into the mix. Small classes and an effective BCC staff allow counselors to give students that extra bit of attention that almost always results in a high level of student satisfaction.

More than 300 companies visited the Madison campus to recruit MBAs for full-time positions and internships during 1998–1999. Companies recruiting on campus include Ameritech, Andersen Consulting, Chrysler, Ernst & Young, General Electric, General Mills, Oscar Mayer, and Procter & Gamble. MBAs here place primarily in the Midwest: nearly 30 percent stay in Wisconsin, while another 36 percent head for either Chicago or Minneapolis.

Lisa Urban, Director of Marketing and Recruiting
975 University Avenue, Madison, WI 53706
Admissions: 608-262-1556 Fax: 608-265-4192
Email: uwmadmba@bus.wisc.edu
Internet: www.wisc.edu/bschool

University of Wisconsin—Madison

STUDENT/CAMPUS LIFE

Wisconsin MBAs speak highly of their classmates, telling us that "students have had excellent work experience and come from diverse backgrounds, which makes class interesting." These "very globally oriented" students also report that "there is a great international group of students. It's a wonderful opportunity to learn about other cultures." The American students hail mostly from the region and share "very conservative Midwestern values." Minority representation within the program is high—around 20 percent—but not all groups are well represented. Notes one, "The African American population is small. There's a huge Asian population in the program, many from East Asia."

Students tell us that life at Madison's School of Business consists of a "comfortable mix of school and leisure activities." Writes one first-year student, "An average day consists of team meetings with focused and committed colleagues, classes with engaging professors, and a club activity." Roughly forty student clubs offer ample opportunity for group involvement, such as Women in Business, Graduate Marketing Network, and Toastmasters. Social opportunities also abound. During the long winters, parties in dorms and nearby apartments are frequent events. When the weather warms up, everyone hangs out at Memorial Union on the Terrace facing Lake Mendota. On Thursday nights "there is a social activity to keep things light," usually accompanied by live music and kegs of beer. Intramural sports are popular—especially basketball, volleyball, and six-man football—as are UWM's intercollegiate sports teams (football, men's basketball, and hockey in particular). Students also enjoy half-price green's fees at the University Ridge Golf Course, one of the top courses in the state, and report that "the gym, pool, and weight room are also great."

UWM's hometown of Madison, the capital of Wisconsin, also receives high marks from MBAs. Students write that "Madison is a wonderful place to be a student. There is a plethora of restaurants, bars, and arts activities that can't be sampled in just two years." Another remarks, "The city is great for outdoor enthusiasts. There are bike paths, parks, and lakes for all kinds of activities." Others add snowboarding and skating to the list of available activities. But students savetheir highest praise for their "awesome new $40 million school building" which is specially equipped with multimedia applications in the classroom. They particularly appreciate the "beautiful, clean facilities with modern equipment and many conveniences, such as lockers, computer lab, refreshments, the Blue Chip Deli, etc." Adds one MBA, "Having all your classes in one building is a real bonus during a Wisconsin winter."

ADMISSIONS

UW considers a prospective student's work experience an important factor in the selection process. Wisconsin is also looking for students with strong GMAT scores, good grade point averages, good references, and a dynamite essay. Wisconsin admits by major, so essays should address the student's interest in a specific field of study. Interviews are not required, but a campus visit is encouraged. The deadline for fall admission is May 1, for spring October 1. The deadline for merit-based financial aid is February 15. However, students with exceptional academic qualifications should apply by January 1 to be considered for All-University Fellowships. Wisconsin is a founding member of the Consortium for Graduate Study in Management, which offers full-tuition scholarships for talented minority students.

FINANCIAL FACTS

Tuition (in-/out-of-state)	$5,950/$16,230
Cost of books	$665
Room & board (on-/off-campus)	NR/$10,600
% of students receiving aid	46
% first-year students receiving aid	43
% aid that is merit based	100
% of students receiving paid internships	54
Average award package	$5,636
Average grant	$500
Average graduation debt	$0

ADMISSIONS

# of applications received	799
% applicants accepted	45
% acceptees attending	42
Average GMAT (range)	613 (570–660)
Minimum TOEFL	600
Average GPA (range)	3.30 (3.00–3.50)
Application fee (in-/out-of-state)	$45/$45
Early decision program available	Yes
Early decision deadline	Rolling
Regular application deadline	May 1
Regular notification	Rolling
Admission may be deferred?	No
Transfer students accepted?	Yes
Nonfall admission available?	Yes
Admission process need-blind?	Yes

APPLICANTS ALSO LOOK AT

Northwestern University, University of Texas at Austin, University of Michigan Business School, Indiana University, University of Illinois—Urbana, University of Minnesota, Purdue University, Ohio State University

EMPLOYMENT PROFILE

Placement rate (%)	98
# of companies recruiting on campus	310
% of grads employed immediately	84
% grads employed within six months	97
Average starting salary	$57,047

Grads employed by field (avg. salary):

Accounting	4%	$44,500
Consulting	12%	$54,113
Entrepreneurship	2%	$61,285
Finance	30%	$60,513
General Management	4%	$62,860
Human Resources	2%	$53,150
Marketing	22%	$56,446
MIS	8%	$48,462
Operations	4%	$56,666
Other	12%	$62,566
Strategic Planning	1%	$47,000
Quantitative	1%	$60,000
Venture Capital	2%	$61,000

YALE UNIVERSITY
Yale School of Management

ACADEMICS

The Yale School of Management has been a pioneer of graduate management education since its founding in 1974, training Yale MBA candidates to work in teams and teaching management skills applicable to business, government, and nonprofit enterprises. According to students, this unusual approach yields an additional bonus: it attracts a more intellectually curious student body. Writes one, "The public/nonprofit/private embrace draws the best, brightest, and most diverse management students."

During their first year, Yale students complete a fairly standard battery of core courses covering general management topics. First-years also attend the year-long Perspectives on Leadership lectures, which bring "distinguished senior managers" to campus; visitors during one recent academic year included John Browne (British Petroleum); Mort Meyerson (2M); and Rajat Gupta (McKinsey & Company). Students report that the first-year curriculum is "strong in both analytical and the softer skills." Second-year students focus on a specialization and take up to seven electives. By nearly all accounts, finance is the star department here, with an "outstanding faculty" boasting "well-published, innovative thinkers." One student cautions that "new hires in finance lack classroom experience. Overall, however, the entire faculty of Yale is very strong; brilliant, accomplished, and 100 percent accessible." This fall, Yale SOM will open the doors of a new International Center for Finance. Others praise the nonprofit management program; conversely, several reported that "accounting and marketing are weak."

Students are most pleased that Yale offers a "very flexible program that allows students to pursue areas of personal importance." They report that "students have tremendous say in the curriculum" and are "encouraged to create work groups, even with students from other schools." Concludes one student, "The course load is as heavy or as light as you want to make it. The people are very friendly. I can't imagine a better business school experience."

PLACEMENT AND RECRUITING

The Career Development Office (CDO) at Yale offers a personal and customized approach, actively linking diverse carreer interests to select, top-tier employment opportunities. To address the challenge, this fall the CDO will offer a virtual Career Information Center. This web-based program will enable students to do interview bidding and scheduling at their convenience from any computer. A Professional Strategies Program pairs students and CDO staff to help students "plan and implement their career objectives." SOM has also added a new interviewing center.

Finance is a strong suit; writes one student, "Yale has had tremendous success in placing banking and finance people, due to the reputation of its faculty." Thirty percent of the recruiting companies to visit campus are finance-related. In addition, The Wall Street Journal recently identified Yale SOM as a favorite hunting ground for top consulting firms, with Booz Allen & Hamilton, McKinsey & Co., and Mitchell Madison Groupall vying for little more than 200 Yale MBA's per year..

James Stevens, Director
Box 208200, New Haven, CT 06520-8200
Admissions: 203-432-5932 Fax: 203-432-7004
Email: som.admissions@yale.edu
Internet: www.yale.edu/som

Yale University

STUDENT/CAMPUS LIFE

Eli MBAs hold their classmates in exceptionally high regard. All were complimentary of their fellow students; writes a typical respondent, "I've never seen a more stimulating, diverse, smart, intensely driven yet community-oriented and supportive group of people. Between classmates and excellent courses and professors, learning is exponentially fast and rewarding and, of course, fun." Another describes classmates as "very cooperative, very smart, very diverse—especially internationally. The quality of students here is extremely high; they are talented, dedicated, and good people." One student points out that "fellow students all have strong areas of expertise or particular strengths that complement the abilities and experiences of other students." Yale students come from across the country and around the globe; only about one-quarter originate from the surrounding New England/New York area.

Students report a demanding workload and spend an average of from 35 to 40 hours a week preparing for class. SOM's grading system (distinction, proficient, pass, and fail) de-emphasizes student-against-student competition. Some believe it is key to the whole SOM experience: "The forging of great community spirit begins with the noncompetitive grading system." Notes another, the "nontraditional grading system encourages students to take risks with difficult coursework." Still, like many MBAs, Yale students report a fair amount of academic pressure, although one student says this "varies because it's self-imposed."

Yale's hometown of New Haven has long been derided as both uninteresting and unsafe, but things may be changing. Writes one student, "New Haven gets a bad rap. The off-campus housing is cheap and has great value. There is an abundance of parks, beaches, and playing fields nearby. It is close to NYC and Boston, which is good for the job search." Another was a bit more cautious, telling us that "New Haven is much better than it used to be. It takes some getting used to. There are evident disparities between locals and students." The heavy workload means that life is "very busy, with a premium on time management." Students tell us that "life is focused around SOM activities, of which there are many." Students "are very involved, especially during International Month. Lots of student organizations and social opportunities." Yale is "extremely gay-friendly; with an active gay and lesbian student group and alumni network." Students know how to "get zany when it's time to blow off steam, like at the weekly keg on Thursdays (where they always serve good beer!)." The keg party kicks off Yale's three-day weekend; no classes are held on Fridays here.

ADMISSIONS

Applicants to Yale must have remarkable academic and professional profiles if they hope to attract the attention of the admissions committee, which accepts less than a quarter of those who apply to the MBA program. One student writes, "Nearly everyone here is a genius! No one that I've compared backgrounds with has a GMAT below 700." Solid work experience, strong letters of recommendation, winning personal qualities, and clear focus and goals complete the list of admissions criteria. In fact, in recent years there has been a trend toward increasing numbers of applications from candidates with engineering or physical science backgrounds. Yale reports that this group made up 30 percent of applicants in this year's pool.

FINANCIAL FACTS

Tuition	$26,380
Fees	$14,280
Cost of books	$940
Room & board (on-/off-campus)	NR/$8,815
% of students receiving aid	66
% first-year students receiving aid	64
% of students receiving loans	55
% of students receiving grants	51
Average award package	$26,100
Average grant	$7,680
Average graduation debt	$35,000

ADMISSIONS

# of applications received	1,896
% applicants accepted	23
% acceptees attending	51
Average GMAT (range)	691(640–740)
Minimum TOEFL	600
Average GPA (range)	3.4(3.1/3.8)
Application fee (in-/out-of-state)	$125/$125
Early decision program available	Yes
Regular application deadline	March 15
Regular notification	May 20
Admission may be deferred?	Yes
Maximum length of deferment	1 year
Transfer students accepted?	No
Nonfall admission available?	No
Admission process need-blind?	Yes

APPLICANTS ALSO LOOK AT

University of Pennsylvania, Columbia University, Harvard University, Stanford University, New York University, Dartmouth College, University of Chicago, Duke University

EMPLOYMENT PROFILE

Placement rate (%)	99
# of companies recruiting on campus	109
% of grads employed immediately	90
% grads employed within six months	99
Average starting salary	$75,996

Grads employed by field (avg. salary):

Accounting	1%	$55,000
Communications	1%	$50,333
Consulting	33%	$81,984
Entrepreneurship	1%	$55,000
Finance	41%	$72,230
General Management	5%	$74,444
Human Resources	1%	$66,333
Marketing	5%	$69,778
MIS	7%	$74,643
Operations	NR	$68,000
Strategic Planning	5%	$87,600
Venture Capital	NR	$73,000

ALPHABETICAL INDEX

LOCATION INDEX

ABOUT THE AUTHOR

Nedda Gilbert is a graduate of the University of Pennsylvania and holds a master's degree from Columbia University. She has worked for The Princeton Review since 1985. In 1987, she created The Princeton Review corporate test preparation service, which provides Wall Street firms and premier companies tailored educational programs for their employees. She currently resides in New Jersey.

NOTES

NOTES

NOTES

NOTES

NOTES

NOTES

NOTES

Looking for a Tutor?

--Don't have time to scrounge around the coffee houses searching for these flyers?

--Wondering where you will find someone to help you with your conversational Urdu?

--Tired of worrying that your tutor is a known Serial Killer?

Looking for People to Teach?

--Don't have the patience to pre-cut the tabs at the bottom of these flyers?

--Wondering if majoring in Hindu Studies was the best business decision?

--Tired of explaining that you only look like number 3 on the FBI's most wanted list?

Call US Visit Our Website Now.

| tutor.com www.tutor.com | tutor.com www.tutor.com | tutor.com www.tutor.com | tutor.com www.tutor.com | tutor.com www.tutor.com | tutor.com www.tutor.com | tutor.com www.tutor.com |

www.review.com

Expert Advice

Talk About It

www.review.com

Pop Surveys

Paying for it

www.review.com

THE
PRINCETON
REVIEW

Getting in

Word du Jour

www.review.com

Find-O-Rama School & Career Search

www.review.com

Best Schools

Finding it

www.review.com

FIND US...

International

Hong Kong
4/F Sun Hung Kai Centre
30 Harbour Road, Wan Chai,
Hong Kong
Tel: (011)85-2-517-3016

Japan
Fuji Building 40, 15-14
Sakuragaokacho, Shibuya Ku,
Tokyo 150, Japan
Tel: (011)81-3-3463-1343

Korea
Tae Young Bldg, 944-24,
Daechi- Dong, Kangnam-Ku
The Princeton Review- ANC
Seoul, Korea 135-280,
South Korea
Tel: (011)82-2-554-7763

Mexico City
PR Mex S De RL De Cv
Guanajuato 228 Col. Roma
06700 Mexico D.F., Mexico
Tel: 525-564-9468

Montreal
666 Sherbrooke St.
West, Suite 202
Montreal, QC H3A 1E7 Canada
Tel: (514) 499-0870

Pakistan
1 Bawa Park - 90 Upper Mall
Lahore, Pakistan
Tel: (011)92-42-571-2315

Spain
Pza. Castilla, 3 - 5° A, 28046
Madrid, Spain
Tel: (011)341-323-4212

Taiwan
155 Chung Hsiao East Road
Section 4 - 4th Floor,
Taipei R.O.C., Taiwan
Tel: (011)886-2-751-1243

Thailand
Building One, 99 Wireless Road
Bangkok, Thailand 10330
Tel: (662) 256-7080

Toronto
1240 Bay Street, Suite 300
Toronto M5R 2A7 Canada
Tel: (800) 495-7737
Tel: (716) 839-4391

Vancouver
4212 University Way NE,
Suite 204
Seattle, WA 98105
Tel: (206) 548-1100

National (U.S.)

We have over 60 offices around the U.S. and
run courses in over 400 sites. For courses and locations
within the U.S. call 1 (800) 2/Review and you will be
routed to the nearest office.